GIORDANO BRUNO

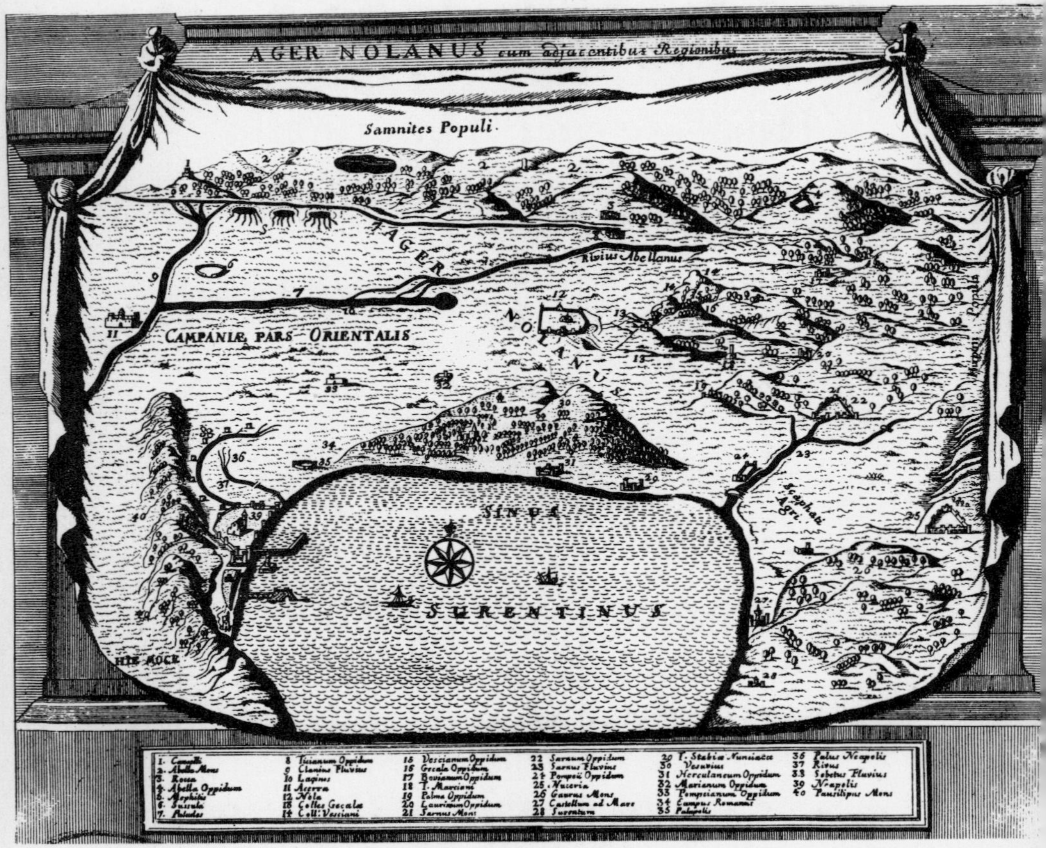

A sixteenth century sketch-map of the environs of Nola. From Graevius, after Ambrosio Leo of Nola.

Giordano

BRUNO

His Life and Thought

With Annotated Translation of His Work

On the Infinite Universe and Worlds

by Dorothea Waley Singer

Henry Schuman New York

Printed in the United States of America
by H. Wolff Book Manufacturing Co.

PREFACE

BRUNO died, despised and suffering, after eight years of agony. From that moment, his works have attracted interest, and he has long been recognized as an important figure in the development of modern thought. Nevertheless, few are familiar with the many and often bewildering pages of his writings. His Italian works have their place in the history of Italian literature. The Latin works in prose and verse are much more bulky and diffuse, but the few who grapple with them are rewarded by passages of great beauty and eloquence.

Though he came in time between Copernicus (1473-1543), whom he constantly cites, and Galileo (1564-1642), who had considered his views, it would nevertheless be altogether misleading to regard Bruno as developing the tradition of the one or as leading to the work of the other. Rather his place is in the line of philosophic thought which has taken its somewhat surprising course from the mystic Pseudo-Dionysius (fifth century) to modern exponents of dialectic materialism. But though in no sense a man of science, he betrays certain remarkable premonitions of modern physical thought. Again, he has a place in the long series of writers on the plurality of worlds, following Nicolaus of Cusa (1401-1464) and leading on to Wilkins (1614-1672), Huygens (1629-1695) and Fontenelle (1657-1757).

In the sixteen years of his freedom, Bruno wandered over half of Europe. At first welcomed by groups anxious to hear his teaching, his presence always led to embarrassment, and he was passed on to fresh patrons. It is remarkable that such a wanderer should have become so well read. Paradoxically, the two writers who most influenced his cosmological views were Lucretius and Nicolaus of Cusa who occupy opposite philosophical poles, Lucretius denying the validity of theological or metaphysical thinking while Nicolaus sought in his cosmology and even in his physical experiments a reinforcement of his theology. Bruno was neither astronomer nor theologian; but contemporary astronomical writings contributed to the cosmology which was the passionate faith of his life, and he was led by his cosmology to a new ethic and a new philosophy.

In presenting an account of the life and thought of Bruno, it might seem more logical to give a narrative of the facts of his life, followed by a study of his cosmology and philosophy. But Bruno's life and especially his wanderings are inextricably involved in the development of his thought, and the main interest of the years after he left England is in the works that he produced in the places where he sojourned. It has seemed best therefore first to describe his early life and then to build up an account of his environment during the crucial and fruitful period in London. The main lines of his cosmology and philosophy were determined before he left London, so that is the point chosen for a general survey of Bruno's thought, and a somewhat detailed analysis is given of the six Italian works that were the immediate product of the London period. We then follow the wanderer after he left London. During these years the most important events were the completion and publication of his Latin works. The MSS so far discovered, not published by Bruno himself, do not add to his serious contribution. (Cf. Appendices I and III.)

We have chosen for translation the slender Italian volume, *On the Infinite Universe and Worlds,* because it was Bruno's ecstatic vision of a single infinite universe that was most fatal to him in the judgement of the Papal Tribunal, that sustained him "in enchantment" during the years of agony, and that has contributed most to the thought of his successors. In preparing the translation, the first question to determine was the desirability of pruning Bruno's exuberant repetitions. On the whole it has seemed best to give the work as it was published. Abbreviated editions are apt to be flat, and the reader will probably prefer to choose his own cuts. This decision having been made, it seemed that the English of Bruno's own day would fit his redundant style better than more modern language. It was the more tempting to choose this medium since it has led to the employment of the very phrases given by Florio, who used this work of Bruno in preparing the second edition of his *Worlde of Wordes.*

I should like to express my warm thanks to Professor Foligno who most generously went through with me the whole translation of *On the Infinite Universe and Worlds.* To Professor Farrington I am indebted for help with some of the more obscure of Bruno's Latin passages. It is to be hoped that he will find leisure to give an English version of some of the greater Latin writings of Bruno. In common with all who are interested in the group of brilliant foreigners who form part of the picture of Elizabethan London, I am indebted to the scholarly works of Miss Frances Yates. Professor Linetta Richardson was kind enough to read the typescript and to make helpful suggestions. From Professor P. O. Kristeller I have received valuable criticism. To all these I tender grateful thanks, and to my husband whose study of William Gilbert first suggested to us both more than ten years ago that a study of Bruno's influence on cosmological thought would be of interest. He has contributed to the final revision of the work; but he must not be held responsible for its errors.

I am indebted to Doctor Cyril Bailey and to the Clarendon Press for permission to quote from his fine translation of Lucretius (Oxford, 1910); and to the late Lord Willoughby de Broke for a photograph of his beautiful portrait of Sir Fulke Greville, with permission to reproduce it.

The first sketch of the present work was written in the Library of the University of California at Berkeley. I cannot sufficiently express my admiration and gratitude for the hospitality of this institution and for the splendid organization for the reader's convenience. The bulk of the material for the study of Bruno's thought I have found in the treasury collected at the Warburg Institute, now incorporated in the University of London. To its late Director, its Deputy Director and Staff I tender cordial thanks. I have once more to express my thanks also to the never-failing kindness received from the Staff of the British Museum.

The events of the last years have delayed the completion of this work, and it probably bears marks of the interruption in its progress. The important place given to Giordano Bruno by modern thinkers bears a message of encouragement to many in our own day whose life work has also been broken by violence and injustice. To them we say with him, "*Veritas filia temporis.*"

D. W. S.

CONTENTS

ILLUSTRATIONS

GIORDANO BRUNO

His Life and Thought

CHAPTER ONE

YOUTH

a. Introduction: Early Years (1548–76)

THE author of the work here translated was despised and miserable during almost the whole of his tempestuous life course. Unsuccessful in human relations, devoid of social tact or worldly wisdom, unpractical to an almost insane degree, he yet played a crucial part in the reshaping of European thought that began in the sixteenth and took form in the subsequent century. It was particularly in England that his thought developed, and perhaps it was through the Englishman, William Gilbert, that news of him reached his countryman Galileo.

We will endeavour to enter the thought of this fearless and exasperating personality as he rises to heights of mystic exaltation in the apprehension of an infinite universe, a Unity informed by immanent Mind, embracing every individual soul and manifested throughout Nature, animate and inanimate. With him we shall recognize that, in the search for an interpretation of existence, the senses, fallible though they be, are indispensable instruments, and that their evidence, always subjected to the interpretation of reason, is itself a revelation. He follows unflinchingly the implications of his vision of infinity, as he bids us mark that in an infinite universe we can have but a relative grasp of time or place, insisting that all events, including human acts, are not solely the result of external force, but rather the expression of the interaction of the natures inherent in each part—partial impressions of the Mind informing the whole. Our own limitations will always deflect our own view of the particular, yet will yield an apprehension of beauty, of symmetry, of

Mind without end. For him, man (like all natural objects) is not merely a part of Nature but a part which, like all the other parts, is essential for the integration of the whole.

Bruno sets forth the essential element in the faith of the new age, the attitude that will accept no preconceived idea concerning any part of the infinite universe. Thereby he opened up a new approach to the interpretation of Nature and with it a new ethic and a new philosophy. Yet to regard him as a forerunner of the scientific age would be to misconceive his contribution, both by reading into it something that is not there and by omitting something that is there. His real philosophic contribution was his realization and pursuit of universal relativity deriving from an infinite single universe.

Bruno, the fallible, foolish, blundering mortal, stumbles along his course, oblivious to much that would have been obvious to a mind less set on a vision that is afar, credulous of diverse forms of "natural magic" that we now reject, and that cooler minds even then rejected, throwing out with feverish activity devices to assist man to compass and to marshal knowledge and to retain it in memory. Capable of hero worship, he sometimes chooses heroes who would have been strangely out of touch with him, as for example that saintly and mystical, muddled and truculent Franciscan, Raymond Lull, on whose worst works he wasted many years. Bruno was compact of contradictions and we have to consider rather his achievement than his weakness.

Filippo Bruno was the son of Juano Bruno,[1] "man of arms" of Nola in the Campania (Frontispiece) and of his wife Fraulissa Savolino. "Born in 1548, so my people tell me,"[2] he informed the Holy Office at

---

[1] Or Bruni. Cf. E. Mariani, *Filippo Bruni* (Naples, 1928).

[2] For the facts of Bruno's life we are mainly indebted to the record of his evidence before the Venetian Inquisition. His monastic career can be traced in the archives in Italy of the Order of Friar Preachers. Further light is thrown by passages in his works and by the archives of the universities that he visited. There are interesting notes of a few conversations with Bruno in 1585-86 in the diary of one Guillaume Cotin (pp. 136-8), librarian of the Abbey of St. Victor in Paris whom Bruno met in 1586, while entries in the official registers of the universities where he sojourned help to fix the dates of his wanderings. The archives of the Inquisition in Rome have yielded sparse but significant records concerning his seven years in their prison; and there is contemporary evidence, both in the news-sheets

Venice. Nola is a town of great antiquity (Fig. 1). Its foundation has been ascribed to the eighth pre-Christian century[3] and it is mentioned by many ancient writers. There are Greek coins from Nola and a vague traditional Nolan friendship for the Greeks. The Emperor Augustus died at Nola and it was several times unsuccessfully besieged by Hannibal. Nola was one of the earliest bishoprics, and tradition alleges that St. Peter himself preached there. There still survive in Nola some ruins from early times, and much more was extant in Bruno's childhood. The town spreads over the Campania by the river Agno, within full view of Vesuvius. It has still some 10,000 inhabitants.

Bruno gives in his greatest Latin work, the *De immenso*,[4] a description

---

and by an onlooker, of the final tragedy in 1600. The various documents have been printed repeatedly, but there has not yet appeared a complete edition of the documents together with an account of their discovery. Vincenzo Spampanato, *Vita di Giordano Bruno con documenti editi e inediti* (Messina, 1921), Vol. II, gives a detailed account of the discovery and successive publication of many of the documents. This information is omitted in the more complete collection of documents published by him as *Documenti della vita di Giordano Bruno* (Florence, 1933). Our references will be to this latter volume which, however, lacks also the two German documents discovered by Sigwart. See below, pp. 150-1, 158 *seqq.*, 168, and p. 171 for a further document published from the Papal Archives in 1940; cf. also the manuscripts noted in Appendix III.

[3] Archaeologists believe Nola to have been populated in turn by pre-Etruscans, Etruscans, Oscans and Samnites before its conquest by Rome, when it became an Allied City. An Oscan inscription gives the name as NUVLA. Nola retained its importance in the mediaeval period and has been the subject of monographs up to modern times. Cf. especially Ambrosius Leo, *Lib. III antiquitatum et historiarum urbi et agri Nolani* (Venice, 1514 and 1594), reprinted in J. G. Graevius, *Thesaurus antiquitatum hist. ital.*, Vol. IX, Part iv; and G. S. Remondini, *Della Nolana ecclesiastica storia* (Naples, 1747 and 1781), and references in later works on the Campania. Cf. also T. Trede, *Das Heidentum in der römischen Kirche* (Gotha, 1889), especially I, 33-48. In a subsequent chapter Trede recounts the story of Bruno and of the Vatican's attempt to deny the fact of his immolation. Trede's German patriotism leads him to great indignation at the fame acquired by Bruno: "Was such apotheosis granted in Germany to the mystic Nature-philosophers Agrippa von Nettesheim of Salzburg and Jakob Boehme the shoemaker of Goerlitz?"

[4] Lib. III, Cap. 1. Cf. I, i, 313 of the National Edition, *Jordani Bruni Nolani opera latine conscripta.* Vol. I, Parts i and ii are edited by F. Fiorentino (Naples, 1879 and 1884); Vol I, Parts iii and iv by Tocco and Vitelli (Florence, 1889); Vol. II, Part i by Imbriano and Tallarigo (Naples, 1886); Vol. II, Part ii by Tocco

of an episode in childhood, which made a deep impression on him. His home was in a hamlet just outside Nola, on the lower slopes of Cicada, a foot-hill of the Appenines some twenty miles east of Naples.[5] He tells with affectionate detail of the beauty and fertility of the land around, overlooked from afar by the seemingly stern bare steeps of Vesuvius. One day a suspicion of the deceptiveness of appearances dawned on the boy. Mount Cicada, he tells us, assured him that "brother Vesuvius" was no less beautiful and fertile. So, girding his loins, he climbed the opposite mountain. "Look now," said Brother Vesuvius, "look at Brother Cicada, dark and drear against the sky." The boy assured Vesuvius that such also was his appearance viewed from Cicada. "Thus did his parents [the two mountains] first teach the lad to doubt, and revealed to him how distance changes the face of things." So in after-life he interprets the experience and continues: "In whatever region of the globe I may be, I shall realize that both time and place are similarly distant from me." The incident gives the impression of an adventurous and happy child with a vivid imagination and a mind already active. We see too the germ of creative power and of philosophic insight as well as the element of whimsy.[6]

But Bruno's birthplace must have yielded another and yet stronger impression which helps to explain a certain strain in his character—the passion for elaborate and unrestrained symbolism. We refer to the annual celebration at Nola to which is attached the name of Bishop

and Vitelli (Florence, 1890); Vol. II, Part iii by Tocco and Vitelli (Florence, 1889); and Vol. III by Tocco and Vitelli (Florence, 1891). This National Edition will be cited as *Op. lat.*

[5] Bruno calls the mountain Cicada though modern writers name it Cicala. Both are names of insects common in that part of the world. Cicadas and cicalas are often confused, for both are famous for the shrill note of the male. Ambrosio Leo, however, calls the hill *Cicala* and, praising it for its beauty and fertility, notes that on it the notes of the cicada never offend the ear! He derives the name from Greek γῆ καλλά (beautiful country), and mentions that his contemporaries name it Cicala or Cecala (Lib. III, Cap. 5). Part of the slope belonged to Nola and part to the town named Cicala.

[6] Since Vesuvius is some ten miles from Nola, we must admit a certain degree of reconstruction of the incident in Bruno's mind. But the passage must be based on a vivid childhood experience.

Paulinus (*circ.* 353-431) who is alleged[7] not only to have sold all his possessions to redeem Nolans from slavery to the Vandals in North Africa, but also himself to have gone into slavery in place of the son of a Nolan widow. The story relates that at length, moved by the generosity of Paulinus, the Vandals gave their freedom both to him and to all the Nolans in captivity with him. They are said to have arrived home on 26th June, now the day sacred to Paulinus.[8] On this day, which recalls at once the midsummer season, there were held at Nola until quite recent times, in the name of Paulinus, the strangest celebrations.[9] Perhaps the festival survives today. Every year, the nine Guilds of Nola brought forth in procession the nine pagodas, five stories high, taller than the tallest houses, whose construction had occupied six months. None might peep behind the canvas-covered scaffolding that enveloped the three outer

---

[7] The historical record of Paulinus is as follows. Born about the year 353, he was the son of a Roman Prefect of Gaul, a patrician and a pagan. Paulinus came to Rome where he gained fame both in affairs and as a poet and scholar. He attained the position of Consul. Soon after, he embarked on a period of western travel that lasted more than fifteen years. He was baptized in Bordeaux in the year 391 and presently travelled to Barcelona where his wife Thebasia (or Theresa) owned estates. They now sold all their possessions and presently Paulinus was received into the priesthood. He and Thebasia travelled to Milan where he studied with St. Ambrose. They proceeded to Rome, and thence to Nola where husband and wife led the lives of solitary recluses until, on the death of their bishop, the Nolans elected Paulinus to take his place.

[8] Sabine Baring-Gould (*Lives of the Saints* [Edinburgh, 1914], VI, 304-6) places the date of the Feast as 22nd June. He also states that the pious deed thus celebrated was enacted by Paulinus III, Bishop of Nola from 513 to 535. Without attempting to establish the claim of either bishop, we would point out that Genseric landed in Africa in 428, and was engaged in war against Rome at least from 429.

[9] A vivid account of his own experience of the celebrations at Nola was published by F. Gregorovius in 1861 in the volume *Siciliana; Wanderungen in Neapel und Sicilien,* and was translated by Mrs. M. Hamilton (London, 1914). Those who read the exquisite sketch of the celebrations by Mr. Sacheverell Sitwell in *Primitive Scenes and Festivals* (London, 1942) will be well rewarded. This is not the celebration chosen by Ambrosio Leo for detailed description. But the last chapters of Leo's work on Nola relate annual frolics and mummeries led by the priests and bishop in which Leo truly discerns "as it were the shadows of ancient institutions."

sides of the slowly rising towers, nor behind the greenery that admitted the workers on the fourth side. At length, on the morning of the Feast, each edifice of cardboard and lathes with its innumerable figures and paintings was revealed to the delighted populace. Young folk took their place on the lowest floor of each tower, and behind them the musicians. Above were the serried rows of strange figures, paladins, cherubs, genii, saints and warriors, painted in brilliant colours, while the whole was surmounted by the figure of a saint on either a gold cupola or a carved lotus blossom.[10] Those who have stood by these towers have seen in them reminiscences of Indian art. But even stranger than the towers themselves was the ceremony which was next enacted. Each tower was hoisted on the shoulders of thirty stalwart young citizens and was carried in procession to the Cathedral square, where a dance took place in which the towers approached and receded, were made to bow to one another and to carry out elaborate figures of the dance. Meanwhile, before each tower in turn, a mime was executed by three youths, and around them and the tower there danced a circle of some twenty young men of Nola. During the procession, the populace, reinforced by merry-makers from all the surrounding Campania, shouting, singing, screaming, surged down the decorated streets and purchased from the numerous booths lining them. While the dance took place in the Cathedral square, a devout congregation within the Cathedral partook of the Sacrament. After

---

[10] The towers are named *guglie* or steeples of San Paolino. Mr. Sitwell describes them as follows: "Each obelisk is in the pattern of the guglia, that Neapolitan invention which was derived from the great machinery of the old Italian theatre, with its 'clouds' and the 'heaven' or 'Parnassus' of its transformations. The guglia belongs, in fact, to the school of Bibbiena, and is related to the huge funeral catafalques, or to the staged mysteries of the Passion erected in their churches by the Jesuits. But here, at Nola, the guglia is not static. It has been given movement." Mr. Sitwell has seen somewhat similar *guglie* at Naples. There they are permanent edifices, one outside the church of il Gesù nuovo, one in the Piazza San Gennaro and one outside the church of San Domenico. All three, however, are attributed to the seventeenth or eighteenth century and therefore cannot have been seen by Bruno. Cf. also Mary Hamilton, *Greek Saints and Their Festivals* (London, 1910), p. 111, where the *ceri* or dancing images of Gubbio and the *guglie* (sometimes translated lilies) of Nola are traced to Dionysiac revels.

this service, there was a procession round the city of clergy, led by their bishop and followed by the shouting populace.[11]

What bizarre images must have been graved on the mind of the Nolan child who witnessed this celebration in successive June months? The answer as regards at least one child is given by the overwhelming prolixity of images that pursue one another through the pages of Bruno when he is writing in his native language. Above all in the *Expulsion of the Triumphant Beast* we shall be bewildered by the successive figures; and the exhausting elaboration of his similes in all the Italian works may well be not unconnected with his recollections of the annual Feast of St. Paulinus of Nola. We have found no direct reference to the Feast in Bruno's writings. Reference to early childhood acquaintances in Nola have, however, been traced in some of his Italian works.[12]

It is not unlikely that in early youth, Bruno had contact with the poet Luigi Tansillo (1510-1568), who was sprung from a Nolan family. Tansillo appears as a character in Bruno's play, *The Torch-Bearer,* and in the *Heroic Frenzies,* and his poems are quoted by Bruno—not always with acknowledgement.[13] Tansillo's lyrics have great beauty and it may be surmised that they exercised influence on Bruno. The favourite

---

[11] Interesting accounts of Nola and of its varied celebrations will also be found in Thomas Ashby, *Some Italian Festivals* (London, 1929), which has information on the *guglie* or *gigli;* and in J. Beloch, *Campanien in Altertum* (Breslau, 1890). F. Ughelli, *Italia sacra sive de episcopis Italiae et insularum adjacentium* (2nd ed., revised by Nicolus Coletus, Venice, 1720) has much of interest concerning Nola in Vol. VI. This work mentions a Johannis Franciscus Bruno, "apostolicus protonotharius successit Orlando" (Ursino) 4 July, 1503. This bishop has not been shown to be connected with Giordano Bruno's family. Further information is in A. Ferraro, *Del cimeterio Nolano* (Naples, 1644).

[12] Detailed references to identifications and conjectures will be found in Giovanni Gentile, *Opere italiane di Giordano Bruno* (Bari, 1908 [Vols. I and II by Gentile, Vol. III by Spampanato]). This work will be cited as Gentile, *Op. ital.;* and Lagarde's edition of the Italian works (2 vols., Göttingen, 1888 [a literal transcription without notes]) will be cited as Lagarde, *Op. ital.*

[13] Luigi Tansillo, poet and soldier, was born at Venosa. His *Life and Lyrical Poems* was published by Fiorentino, Naples, 1882. He was the author of many poetical works. The first was condemned as licentious and placed on the Index, but at the end of his life Tansillo's name was removed from the Index by Pope Paul IV.

humanist theme of man's mastery of his destiny is echoed in the verses of Tansillo that inspired Bruno's lines attached to his Dedication of the work here translated.[14]

Perhaps Tansillo introduced the lad to the writings of an earlier and more famous poet whom Bruno quotes also in the present work, Ludovico Ariosto (1474-1533), whose *Orlando Furioso* had immense success both in his own lifetime and in the next generation. This epic is in the succession of broad Italian tales in which must be placed also Bruno's *Torch-Bearer*.

Bruno was sent for education to Naples. He was certainly an avid student and he described himself as pursuing in Naples "humanity, logic and dialectic." He attended at the ***Studium Generale*** the public lectures of Vincenze Colle of Sarno, and he studied privately with Teofilo de Vairano of the Augustinian monastery in Naples. Vairano subsequently taught in several colleges and was tutor to the son of Prince Marco Antonio Colonna. No work by him has come down to us.

In 1565 Filippo, then only seventeen years old, made the gravest mistake of a career that was uniformly unfortunate. He entered the Dominican monastery of San Domenico in Naples.[15] He was given the monastic name of Giordano[16] and after the usual year of probation he took the first vows. In the course of his training he passed through other monasteries of the Order, and at his trial, he stated to the Venetian Inquisition that he had sung his first Mass at the Convent of San Bartolomeo in the city of Campagna.[17] A revolting picture of the monastic life is given in his play *The Torch-Bearer*.

---

[14] Cf. pp. 247-9.

[15] The Venetian deposition states: "at fourteen or fifteen when Master Ambrosio Pasqua was prior." Spampanato has pointed out that the records of the Monastery show that Bruno was received in June 1565. He would then have been about seventeen years old. (Cf. *Archivio di Stato di Napoli, monasteri soppressi,* Vol. 581, "Catalogo de 'ricevuti all' abito dal 1524 al 1622," f. 31). Pasqua did not become prior till April 1565 (cf. *Monasteri soppressi,* Vol. 582, f. 46v).

[16] In accordance with the usual custom of adopting a "name in religion," the young Filippo was given the religious name of the second head of the Dominican Order.

[17] About ten miles from Salerno.

Bruno's studies in the monastery seem to have been fairly wide.[18] He had, naturally, the usual course of scholastic philosophy based on the works of St. Thomas whom he always held in great reverence.[19] In the convent libraries, too, Bruno no doubt laid the foundation of his intimate knowledge not only of many of the works of Aristotle (with the exception of the biological works, which he does not cite) but also of the literature of Aristotelian commentary, including those Arabic and Hebrew writers whose works had been translated into Latin. Here too he would certainly find Virgil and some other classical writers. Among classical writers cited by him are, besides pre-Socratic philosophers (of course at second hand), Cicero, Virgil, Lucan, Seneca and Ovid. In the monastic libraries Bruno may have made his first acquaintance with the works of Raymond Lull. Euclid may well have been found on the shelves, and also Ptolemy. He must have read some astronomy, as he was teaching the subject at Noli in 1576.

He often cites the *Timaeus* as well as Neo-Platonic writers. The general character of his knowledge suggests that while well-grounded in mediaeval Aristotelian philosophy, he regarded Platonic thought as somewhat an innovation, though it was the staple of the Italian humanists of his day.[20] Some Renaissance influence had, however, entered his monastery where a striking series of curious mythological reliefs, representing celestial bodies, may still be seen. Mythological imagery is a conspicuous element in Bruno's ethical works. This use of myth was of course a Renaissance habit, but no doubt the early impression on his mind at Nola and at Naples helped to mould the form of Bruno's later writings. Not only are whole works of Bruno permeated by classical mythology, but in true Renaissance style, mythological imagery is intro-

---

[18] Cf. F. Tocco, "Le fonti piu recenti della filosofia del Bruno" in Reale Accad. Naz. dei Lincei *Rendiconti della classe di scienze morali, storiche e filologiche,* I, Ser. V (Rome, 1892), 503-38, 585-602.

[19] There is a record that Bruno's Roman judges, having visited him after two years' imprisonment, granted him a coat, a pillow and a copy of the *Summa* of St. Thomas (cf. *Doc. Rom.* I [Spampanato, *Documenti della vita di Giordano Bruno,* p. 154]).

[20] Cf. R. Klibansky, *On the Continuity of the Platonic Tradition* (Warburg Institute, London, 1939).

duced even, for example, into his expression of gratitude to the University of Wittenberg. We know also from his statements at his trial that during his monastic period Bruno managed to read such modern authors as Erasmus who led him to examine the new religion.

In the monastery, Bruno must have been distinguished as of outstanding ability. Of his actual life there, however, we have record of only one incident of importance. In or about 1571, when he was but twenty-three, he had already made his mark to such an extent that he was summoned to Rome by the saintly Dominican Pope Pius V (d. 1572) and his *Inquisitor fidei* Cardinal Rebiba (1504-1577). It was his system of mnemonics that he was invited to expound to His Holiness. He mentions, however, several times that the Pope accepted the dedication to him of his (lost) work *On the Ark of Noah*.[21] But as with so many of his contacts, the interview at the Vatican came to nothing.[22]

The next stage in Bruno's career was inevitable. His tempestuous personality, fed to a fever with omnivorous reading, could not fail to lead him into trouble with the monastic authorities. It was indeed remarkable that the crisis was delayed for eleven years. He admitted to the Venice Inquisitors that proceedings were twice taken against him in the Naples convent "first for having cast away certain images of the Saints and retained only a Crucifix, thus coming under suspicion of despising the images of the saints. And another time for having . . . recommended a novice who was reading the *Istoria delle sette allegrezze* [*The Tale of the Seven Joys*] in verse that he should throw this away and read some other work such as the *Lives of the Holy Fathers*." [23] His repudiation of intellectual restraint is constantly expressed and might be regarded as the theme of his life.

The final event was precipitated by a report that Bruno defended the Arian heresy. (Indeed he states in his works and repeated at his Venice trial his conviction that Arius had been "misunderstood.") We can well believe that plenty of tales of Bruno's strange views and behaviour were

---

21 See App. I, i.

22 Our authority for the episode of Bruno's visit to the Pope is the diary of his friend Cotin, to whom it was related by Bruno. See *Doc. Par.* V.

23 *Doc. Ven.* VIII.

current among the conventual brethren. He managed somehow to get to Rome to the headquarters of his Order, but there he learned that a formidable indictment was being prepared against him in Naples, based on the discovery of an indiscreet attempt to conceal certain writings of Erasmus in the convent privy. Bruno determined to flee.[24] Most unwisely, he shed his monastic habit and thus debarred himself from hope of reconciliation with his superiors.

b. First Years of Wandering (1576–81) (See Fig. 13)

Bruno had led eleven years of monastic life when in 1576 his wandering career began its homeless course. He had but sixteen years before the prison doors would close upon him. During that time, between the ages of twenty-eight and forty-four, he produced his voluminous works. Halfway through this active course he had a brilliant period of illumination. It was the year 1584 passed in London.

Bruno's first sojourn was at the tiny port of Noli in Genoese territory. Perhaps the name, reminiscent of home, appealed to him. He spent only some four months there, occupied in teaching "the Sphere," i.e., astronomy, to "certain gentlemen" and instructing small boys in grammar. His impatience and his highly involved symbolic and allusive mode of expression must have made him a superlatively bad instructor of children, and it is no wonder that his pedagogic career was brief. Yet to groups of youth, avid for the new learning, he never failed to appeal as he passed from town to town. Always he was encouraged; always his difficult temperament led him into trouble and he was passed onward.

Bruno's wanderings next took him up the coast to Savona, but eight miles away. His stay there was brief, and he went to Turin whence he

[24] An additional danger to Bruno appears to have been confided by him to Cotin, who, in his diary, states of Bruno: "Est fuitif d'Italia jà par huict ans, tant pour un mertre commis par un sien frère, dont il est odieux et en peril de sa vie, que pour éviter les calumnies des inquisiteurs qui sont ignorans, et, ne concevans sa philosophie, le diroyent hérétique." Since there is no mention of this murder during the gruelling cross-examinations at the Venice trial, we may assume that no fragment of responsibility had attached to Bruno for this crime.

turned eastward, followed the long course of the Po and came to Venice. He was not yet regarded as excommunicate, for (according to his own testimony at the Venice trial), he received in Venice permission from the Dominican Remigio Nannini Fiorentino to publish a work—now lost—*On the Signs of the Times*.[25] We know little of his movements at Venice except that he lodged close to the square of St. Mark in the centre of the town.

From Venice he turned back to Padua where he fell in with some fellow Dominicans who persuaded him to assume again the Friar's habit. They befriended the wanderer, but none pressed him to prolong his stay. Perhaps they feared contact with the strangely attractive, yet dangerous creature. Following the northern route back through Brescia, Bruno came to Bergamo where he resumed the monastic habit. He perhaps visited Milan, and then leaving Italy he crossed the Alps by the Mont Cenis pass, and came to Chambéry. He describes his hospitable reception there by the Dominican Convent, but again he received no encouragement to remain, and he journeyed on to Lyons.

Bruno's next movements are obscure. In 1579 he reached Geneva. Here again he received kindness, not unduly pressed, this time from the Marchese de Vico of Naples. This nobleman was accustomed to render help to Italian refugees who drifted to Geneva by reason of their adherence to the Calvinist faith. Bruno described at his Venice trial, more than twelve years later, how the Marquis had interrogated him and had received the reply, "I did not intend to adopt the religion of the city. I desired to stay there only that I might live at liberty and in security." Bruno was in his incurable mental detachment in fact completely indifferent to the quarrels between Catholic and Protestant, regarding them

---

[25] Remigio Nannini (or Nanni) Fiorentino (d. 1580 or 1581), one of the great Dominican figures of the sixteenth century, was a humanist scholar and a voluminous writer. He made translations from classical writers, as well as of the *De remediis utriusque fortunae* of Petrarch and other works. From 1569 to 1578 he was employed by Pope Pius V on the great annotated edition of Thomas Aquinas. For details of the life of Remigio Nannini, see Quétif-Échard, *Scriptores ordinis praedicatorum* (Paris, 1719-21), II, 259-60 and 825; *Monumenta ordinis praedicatorum,* IX, 355 and X, 67; and G. Negri, *Istoria degli scrittori fiorentini* (Ferrara, 1722), pp. 481-83.

as irrelevant to the high philosophic problems that occupied his mind to the exclusion of all worldly wisdom and even of the commonest prudence.

Bruno admitted that the Marquis persuaded him finally to renounce his habit and that he presented him with a new outfit.[26] The question has sometimes been raised as to whether Bruno became a Protestant, but it is intrinsically most unlikely that he accepted membership in Calvin's communion. We may be sure, however, that he was eager to hear and consider for himself expositions of the faith that had commanded the sympathy of Erasmus whose writings had been the subject of his forbidden study in the Naples convent.

Bruno was no more prepared to exercise tact or reticence toward academic than toward ecclesiastical authority. It was in May 1579 that he inscribed his name in the *Rector's Book* of Geneva University, and in August we find him publishing a violent attack on Antoine de la Faye, a distinguished professor of philosophy at the University, a close friend of the rector, and a learned translator of the Bible. Bruno felt it incumbent on him to expose at the earliest possible moment twenty errors in a single lecture of this influential professor.

The result was as might have been expected. Both Bruno and his printer were promptly arrested. The printer pleaded that he had been "misled by the monk" and was sentenced to a small fine. Bruno apologized, but was consigned for further trial to the theological Consistory. Here he considered himself called to argue again the merits of the discussion. He protested that the ministers of the Geneva Church were mere pedagogues and that his own writings had been totally misunderstood. Such pleading, equally unwise and disingenuous, naturally counteracted any grace that he might have won by his apology. Yet at the end of the month, he was petitioning at Geneva for the reversal of a sentence of deprival of the right of participation in the Sacrament. The reversal was granted, but Geneva was no longer a secure resting-place for him.

---

26 Bruno's name appears in a list, compiled one hundred years later, of Italian refugees who had belonged to the Protestant church of Geneva. Such evidence is of little value.

He now turned his face toward France. He decided to try Lyons, the great book centre where he might hope to find some sort of literary employment. But he was unable to gain a livelihood there and he passed on—probably following the Rhone valley down to Avignon and then turning west through Montpellier—until at length he reached Toulouse.[27] Here for some eighteen months Bruno found congenial occupation. As in Noli, he was at first engaged to lecture to a group of scholars on "the Sphere" and other philosophical matters.

France was at this period in the throes of the religious wars, and Toulouse, a stronghold of Protestantism, had been the scene of grim struggles culminating in 1572 in a minor St. Bartholomew following on the Paris massacre. But in 1580-81, the years of Bruno's visit, the university achieved a respite of comparative calm, and the usual regulation that the holder of a university post must participate in the Sacrament was not in force. Thus Bruno was under no special disability when a vacancy arose for a teacher of philosophy. The teachers at Toulouse were chosen by the students. Bruno must have speedily gained some popularity among them for, having hastily acquired his doctorate in theology, he was forthwith elected.[28]

Among his philosophical lectures at Toulouse was a course on the *De anima* of Aristotle, on which he wrote a book. Neither this nor a volume on mnemonics perhaps produced there has come down to us.[29] The subject of artificial memory was one of special interest at the time, and it had been stimulated by the recent publication in Paris of two works of Raymond Lull (1578); Bruno wasted a great part of his energy and of his active career on this barren topic. But the Civil Wars again advanced toward Toulouse and Bruno was forced to resume his wanderings.

---

27 The route is well conjectured by Spampanato.

28 Unfortunately, the University Registry prior to 1682 has not survived, so our only source concerning Bruno's sojourn in Toulouse is his evidence at the Venice trial.

29 The latter work, *Clavis magna,* written either in Toulouse or Paris, is frequently cited by Bruno, and a section of it is probably represented by the *Sigillus sigillorum* published in London in 1583. (Cf. p. 34, n. 19, and cf. App. I, vi and vii.)

6. First Visit to Paris (1581–83)[30]

This time he journeyed to Paris, and at once made a bid for notice with a course of thirty lectures, each on one of the thirty divine attributes as treated by St. Thomas. Here he had an immediate success, the greatest granted him in the academic field, and one less ephemeral than in his other sojourns. The repute of his teaching and especially of his powers of memorization reached even King Henry III.

The Sovereign (so Bruno stated in Venice) sent for him to enquire whether his marvellous memory was natural or was achieved by magical art. Henry was in fact less interested in this distinction than in becoming master of the remarkable memory that he believed to be the source of the Italian's power. This search for power and knowledge by occult means (a theme set out for example in Goethe's *Faust*) was a real impelling force at that time when the nature of the scientific process was only very vaguely appreciated. It represents a naïf stage in the slow passage of the human mind toward an experimental standpoint. All evidence shows that Bruno had a most tenacious memory. Was his capacity directly provided and his knowledge communicated by the Evil One? Or were his power and knowledge derived from the intervention of kindly spirits? Or were they after all attained through those scarcely understood but harmless processes which we now call scientific? Was it a case of Black Magic, White Magic or Natural Magic? These were normal questions of the time. There was among Bruno's contemporaries

---

[30] Bruno stated before the Inquisitors that he stayed "perhaps five years" in Paris. But the *Rector's Book* of Geneva University gives May 1579 as the date for his visit there, which was followed by the period in Toulouse. Bruno's statement gives six months of private lectures and eighteen months in the occupation of his Chair at Toulouse. Spampanato would allow twenty months for the sojourn in Toulouse, which brings Bruno to Paris in 1581. By the summer of 1583, he was in Oxford. While this book is passing through the press, there appears Frances Yates, *The French Academies of the Sixteenth Century* (*Warburg Institute Studies*, Vol. 15, London, 1947). This most penetrating and learned work traces the relationship between Bruno and these Academies. It also suggests that Bruno had certain political activities and connections in Paris leading to a secret political mission to London.

some scepticism as to both the safety and the legitimacy of any of these aids, and no clear knowledge as to their frontiers. There was then, as indeed there is now, every gradation between a search for magical intervention and a frank acceptance of natural law. Some of the faith in magic was transmuted to belief in a vaguely apprehended system, a system which, it was thought, would enormously enhance human power and which partook of the nature of harmless or *natural magic*.[31] Sometimes the judicial examination of one charged with magical practices was in fact an attempt of the judge to gain for himself that power-bringing knowledge that the prisoner was thought to be concealing. The hope of a short cut to mastery over nature is quite in keeping with the attitude of the age.

This desire of the great to sap the source of his knowledge, this belief in a supernatural access to knowledge and power was, as we shall see, destined in the end to ruin Bruno. On this occasion, however, all went well. Bruno not only satisfied His Majesty but was permitted to dedicate to him the first of his surviving publications, *On the Shadows of Ideas*.[32] The first part of the work propounds the Platonic Ideas as the realities of which human beings and all material phenomena are but shadows. Bruno cites his favourite sources, the Wisdom literature and obscurer Greek writers, pre-Socratics and Neo-Platonists. He proceeds to his system of mnemonics as Shadows of Ideas.

The mnemonic methods of Bruno are in fact based on the system of Raymond Lull. The mastery of Lull's ridiculous and elaborate "systems" would appear to the modern mind as a proof rather than a cause of exceptional memory. But the royal patron was delighted with what seem to us mere childish devices. It was impossible to appoint Bruno to the Sorbonne where his appearance would have been forbidden by ecclesiastical authority, but a place was found for him by the King at the Collège de France, refounded some twenty-three years earlier by Francis II.

There followed for the wanderer a period of peace. The royal patron-

---

31 *Natural Magic* was a common book-title as late as the eighteenth century. It corresponded somewhat to the popular works that now appear on the *Wonders of Science*.

32 *De umbris idearum* (Paris, 1582). Cf. App. I, (a).

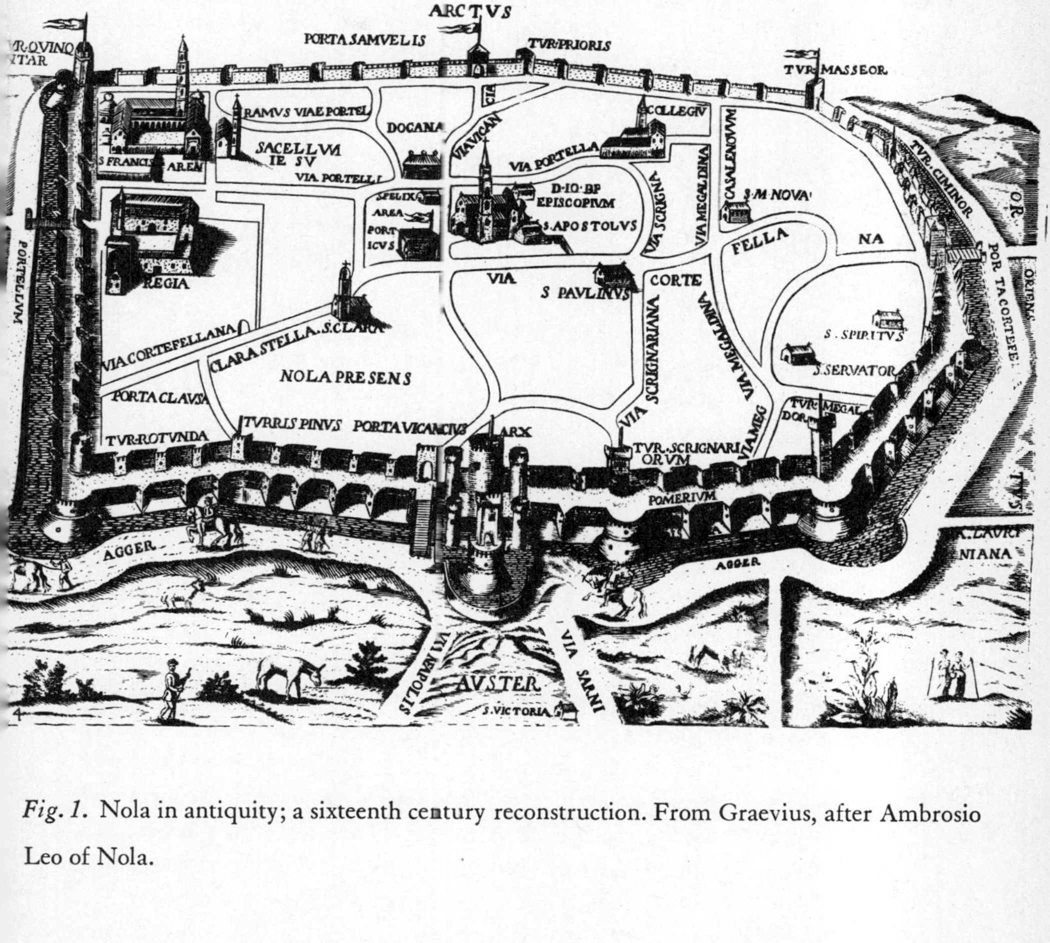

Fig. 1. Nola in antiquity; a sixteenth century reconstruction. From Graevius, after Ambrosio Leo of Nola.

MICHEL DE CASTELNAV SEIGNEVR DE MAVVISSIERE
L'obiect de ce portraict, fera veoir au Lecteur
du visage les traicts bien formez de Lauteur
mais son esprit diuin cogneu en son histoire
Luy fera beaucoup plus estimer sa memoire
Iaspar Isac fecit

En virtute suâ contentus, nobilis arte,
Italus ore, Anglus pectore, vterq; opere
Floret adhuc, et adhuc florebit; floreat vltra
FLORIVS, hâc specie floridus, optat amans.

Fig. 2. Michel de Castelnau, Marquis de Mauvissière. Engraved by Jaspar Isac. From *Les Mémoires de Messire Michel de Castelnau . . .* (Paris, 1621).

Fig. 3. John Florio, aged 58. From the engraving by William Hole in Florio, *Queen Anna's New World of Words* (London, 1611).

age no doubt facilitated publication of his works, of which three more appeared while he was in Paris. Among his Paris hearers, at least one became a faithful disciple. This was a young Czech nobleman, John â Nostitz. The mnemonic system of Bruno was as yet inextricably mingled with his philosophy that was at last taking shape. In 1615, thirty-three years after the delivery of the lectures and fifteen years after Bruno's death, the impressions of â Nostitz concerning his teacher were published in a small octavo volume printed at Brieg in Silesia, bearing a title which may be rendered: *The Artifice According to Aristotle, Lull and Ramus Set Forth by John â Nostitz, Genuine Disciple of Jordanus Brunus, and Enlarged by Conrad Berg.* The book is lost, and we know of it only from its entry in a sales catalogue [33] of books in which is

---

[33] J. L. Bünemann, *Catalogus MSStorum membranaceorum et chartaceorum item librorum ab inventa typographia. . . .* (Minden, 1732), pp. 117-18. It appears from the entry that lot 72 in Bünemann's sale included:

1) Artificium Aristotelico—Lullio Rameum in quo per artem intelligendi *Logicam;* Artem agendi practicam; Artis loquendi partem de Inventione *Topicam* methodo et terminis Aristotelico—Rameis CIRCULIS modo LULLIANO inclusis via plura quam CENTIES MILLE argumenta de quouis themate inueniendi cum usu conveniens ostenditur, ductu Io. a. NOSTITZ, IORDANI BRUNI genuini discipuli elaboratum a CONRADO BERGIO. Bregae typis Sigfridianis 1615. Opus RARISSIMUM lectu dignissimum cum figuris.

Jo. a NOSTITZ lectori Sal. *Annus nunc agitur tertius et tregesimus, cum Lutetiae Paris.* primum IORDANUN BRUNUM *arte Lulliana et Mnemonica —MULTOS ad se discipulos atque auditores allicere memini. Quo factum ut ego quoque, quid illud esset mirificae artis cogniturus, non semel interfuerim. Ac. IPSIUS—IORDANI peritiam et promtitudinem, quam postulato quouis disputandi et ex tempore copiose de eo perorandi argumento ostentabat, vehementer admirabar—quae iuuenis olim propter obscuritatem neglexeram, gestiebam nunc maturiori aetate—recognoscere. Neque me facti poenitet—quem olim obieceram IORDANI BRUNI NOLANI libellum, de COMPENDIOSA ARCHITECTURA ET COMPLEMENTO ARTIS LULLII.* anno 1582 Parisiis editum quorum *το* IRUM, ILE, ARE, et bonificabilitates—reseram, ita mihi charos reddidi ut quamuis illos delicatos Ciceronianos sermones horriditate offendant, artis tamen ipsius iucunditate non parum in legendo me retinuerint etc. Dat in Domo mea Glumbovitze prope Strenitzium maius sita 10 Nov., 1615.

2) IORDANUS BRUNUS NOLANUS de Progressu et Lampade Venatoria Logicorum ad promte atque copiose de quocumque propos. problemate disputandum A. 1587 cum figur, rar.

3) IORD. BRUN. NOLANUS de Lampade Combinatoria Lulliana.

printed an extract from the Preface of â Nostitz describing the impression created by Bruno and by his Lullian views and works in Paris in 1582.

Bruno's second published volume *The Song of Circe,* deals with "that practice of Memory which [the author] terms *Judicial.*" [34] It again had exalted patronage, and is dedicated to Henry of Valois, Duke of Angoulême.[35] The Dedication is signed by one Jean Regnault, Councillor

---

4) IORD. BRUNI. Nolani summa Terminorum Metaphysicorum.

5) EIUSD. PRAXIS Descensus, Applicatio Entis ex Manuscripto Marp. Catt. ea off. Rodolphi Hutwelcker rar.

6) NICOL. TAURELLI. . . .

7) WENCESL. SCHILLINGII. . . .

8) Ei WENCESL. SCHILLINGII. . . .

It will be noticed that item 4 of the sales catalogue is a posthumously published work of Bruno, presumably the 1609 edition to which the editor Raffaele Eglinus joined the *Scale of Practise* here given as item 5. Cf. App. I, xxix.

John â Nostitz died in 1619. There survives in the British Museum a small volume of funeral elegies of John â Nostitz. The family Library was still extant at Prague at least until 1938. A holograph of the work of Copernicus is its greatest treasure. The complicated â Nostitz family genealogy is given in Quido Vetter, *Sur les destins du manuscrit prajois, de Kopernik, "De revolutionibus orbium calestium libri sex,"* in *Mémoires de la Soc. Roy. de Bohème, Classe des Sciences* (Prague, 1931). Conrad Berg (1592-1614), theologian and Lutheran pastor, had a varied career. After travelling as tutor to various young noblemen through France, Holland, Italy and Germany, he succeeded an elder brother as professor of theology at Frankfurt on the Oder where he also became pastor. Later he became professor of theology at Bremen, and also Dean and Pastor of the Collegiate Church of St. Ansgar. Besides the *Artificium* he published several theological works.

Johann Ludolph Bünemann (1687-1759) was a theological scholar and bibliographer, and Director of the State School of Hanover.

[34] "Ad eam memoriae praxim ordinatus quam ipse Judiciariam appellat." The adjective *judicial* is used as in *judicial astrology.*

[35] Henry of Angoulême, illegitimate son of Henry II of France, had been created Duke of Angoulême and given high office by his half brother King Henry III. The Duke's mother belonged to the Scotch family Fleming of Leviston, and was maid of honour to Mary of Scots. Cf. L. Legré, *Le Grand Prieur Henri d'Angoulême, épisode de l'histoire du XVI siècle* (Marseilles, 1861); T. L. Hôte in *Malherbe et la Provence* (Rouen, 1933), p. 3; and W. Hunter, *Biggar and the House of Fleming* (1862). It is tempting to surmise that Mauvissière's interest in Bruno might first have been aroused through Angoulême and Mary Queen of Scots.

to the Duke, who sponsors both the work and Jordanus himself, stating that the author has entrusted him with the completion of the work. He writes that Giordano has "subsequently" completed another work on Memory dedicated to the King himself. Moreover, Regnault introduced Bruno to his friend the Venetian Ambassador to the French King, John Moro, to whom is dedicated yet another Lullian volume, *The Compendious Building and Completion of the Lullian Art.*[36] In the title of both these works, Bruno prefixes to his name the title *Philotheus* which reappears in several of his works published in London.[37]

Further works on mnemonics and Lullian logic were followed by the play *The Torch-Bearer by Bruno the Nolan, Graduate of No Academy, Called the Nuisance.* This may well have been his nickname and it is not unlike him to quote it, for he did not number humour among his qualities, though he had a fund of vituperative eloquence which almost took its place. On the frontispiece appears for the first time that phrase "In tristicia hilaris in hilaritate tristis" ("Joyful in grief, in gaiety sad"), which appears at intervals in Bruno's later works. The title *Candelaio* (*The Torch-Bearer*) suggests, in the Italian idiom of the day, the outspokenness which we should regard as obscenity pervading the work. This was a commonplace of the period, but is worth notice since it is associated in the play with characters who have been identified with Bruno's convent life. The work betrays Bruno's almost frantic detestation of hypocrisy and quackery in morals as in learning, and the beginnings of his formulation of a new ethic and a new philosophy:

> This is a kind of fabric in which warp and woof are one: he who can, will understand. . . . You must imagine yourselves in the most royal city of Naples near the Nile Square.[38] . . . Contemplating the action and speech with the mind of a Heraclitus or a Democritus, you will find cause to laugh, or rather to weep.[39]

There are three principal themes woven into this comedy: the love of

---

[36] For bibliography of Bruno's works, see App. I.

[37] Cf. p. 39 and Chapter 4, *a*.

[38] This was close to San Domenico, Bruno's convent. Cf. Benedetto Croce, "I seggi di Napoli" in *Nuove curiosità storiche* (Naples, 1922), p. 50.

[39] "Proprologo" (Gentile, *Op. ital.*, III, 21, 23; Lagarde, *Op. ital.*, I, 13, 14).

Bonifacio, the alchemy of Bartolomeo and the pedantry of Mamphurio. . . . We present the savourless and laggard lover, the niggardly miser, the foolish pedant. The laggard is not without stupidity and foolishness; the miser similarly is savourless and foolish; while the fool is no less niggardly and savourless than he is foolish.[40]

You will see, in mixed confusion, snatches of cutpurses, wiles of cheats, enterprises of rogues; also delicious repulsiveness [*disgusti*], bitter sweets, foolish decisions, mistaken faith and crippled hopes, niggard charities, judges noble and serious for other men's affairs with little ruth in their own; virile women, effeminate men and voices of craft and not of mercy so that he who believes most is most fooled—and everywhere the love of gold. Hence proceed quartan fevers, spiritual cancers, light thoughts, ruling follies . . . thrusting will, advancing knowledge, fruitful action, purposive industry. In fine you will see throughout naught secure, sufficiency of dealings and of vice, little beauty and nothing of good. I think I hear the persons of this play —Heaven keep thee.[41]

Bruno's play mirrored not only his convent experiences but also his observations in the universities that he had visited. It cannot have been conducive to friendship with those academic "pedants" whom his irony flagellates. The publication of what might have been rather circulated in manuscript among his friends was the tactless act of a man devoid of the wisdom of human relationships.

None of Bruno's important philosophical works had yet appeared. Nevertheless, his Paris sojourn and especially French Platonism must have stimulated his thought. He must surely have heard discussion of the great French anti-Aristotelian Pierre de la Ramée who was a victim of the massacre of St. Bartholomew (1572). Bruno refers to him as "that arch pedant of a Frenchman who has brought his scholasticism to the liberal arts."[42] We may speculate whether Bruno's apostrophe of the Dual in Nature could nevertheless have been suggested by De la Ramée's emphasis on dichotomy in logic, or perhaps by the views of Telesio.[43]

---

40 "Argumento ed ordine della comedia" (Gentile, *Op. ital.*, III, 8; Lagarde, *Op. ital.*, I, 6).

41 "Proprologo" (Gentile, *Op. ital.*, III, 27, 28; Lagarde, *Op. ital.*, I, 16).

42 Cf. *De la causa, principio et uno*, Dial. III, p. 62 (Lagarde, *Op. ital.*, I, 246; Gentile, *Op. ital.*, I, 202).

43 Cf. pp. 75-6.

A Platonist scholar who had occupied the Chair of Greek at the Collège de France and was surely still discussed in Paris at the time of Bruno's first sojourn there was Louis le Roy (d. 1577). He was known as a vitriolic critic as well as a prolific writer. Yet he is in the tradition of those Renaissance writers who pleaded for toleration and a sense of human brotherhood. As we shall see in considering the influence on Bruno of some other writers, this bias toward toleration of different schools of thought and even of different religion was connected with the philosophical view of the Coincidence of Contraries.[44] Le Roy published in 1570 an *Exhortation en françois pour vivre en concorde et iouir du bien de la paix,* dedicated to the King.

A considerable sensation was created by another work which le Roy dedicated to Henry III, the *Douze livres de la vicissitude ou varieté des choses de l'univers et concurrence des armes et des lettres par les premières et plus illustres nations du monde.*[45] The first eleven books give a general philosophical survey of history. In book XII he expatiates on the necessity of preserving a record of the achievements of civilization lest all be lost in the current disasters and wars. "Faisons pour la posterité ce que l'antiquité a fait pour nous à fin que le scavoir ne se perde mais prenne de iour en iour accroissement." His thesis is that "everywhere contraries balance one another." He is thus very near to the *Coincidence of Contraries.* Another element in Bruno's philosophy, that which we shall call *Cosmic Metabolism,* is foreshadowed in this work of Le Roy. Though accepting the Aristotelian Spheres,[46] he expounds that "It seemed unto Plato that the world was nourished by the consumption and decay of itself producing alwayes new creatures from the old." He also emphasizes the relativity of our conventional description of positions, "upper," "lower," etc.

It is tempting to imagine that Bruno during his sojourn in Paris may

---

[44] Cf. Chapter 3, *f.*

[45] Paris, 1576. The author *R.A.* of the English translation *Of the Interchangeable Course of Things in the Whole World* (London, 1594), is identified in the *Short Title Catalogue* (15488) as Robert Ashley.

[46] Cf. Chapter 3, *a.*

have met Jean Bodin (1530-1596) who was also for a time befriended by Henry III, though he held the dangerous view that sovereignty is inalienable from and belongs to the people as a whole as distinguished from the governmental power which they delegate to their rulers. Already we may conceive there was discussion in Paris literary circles leading to the remarkable work which Bodin wrote in 1599—when Bruno was beyond its cheering message. The title is *The Colloquy of Seven Men*—of various religions who each contribute to the formulation of an exalted philosophy.[47]

Doubtless discussion of such matters had its part in the formation of Bruno's philosophy. But whether on account of his play *The Torch-Bearer* or owing to the Civil War in France, Paris became uncomfortable for him. The time had come when his Catholic Majesty, like Bruno's other patrons, was readier to recommend him to others than to retain his services. Bruno turned his eyes across the Channel. That his reputation for dangerous views on matters spiritual had preceded him in England we learn in a side light from Sir Henry Cobham, the British Ambassador in Paris. He writes to Walsingham on 28th March, 1583:

---

[47] Joannes Bodinus, *Colloquium heptaplomeres de rerum sublimium arcanis abditis*. Each of the seven men expounds his views with a friendly frankness. Presently some artificial apples mixed with the fruits on the table deceive at least the Lutherans, and they decide that since the senses can be so easily deceived, it is rash to hope that the spirit, imprisoned in the senses, can reach a certain knowledge of exalted things. Their meeting ends with the singing in harmony of the verse, "Behold how good and how pleasant it is for brethren to dwell together in unity" (Psalm CXXXIII). The work circulated in manuscript and aroused much discussion. Both the Jew and the universal theist are represented with special sympathy. Höffding refers to an extant letter from Bodin written some years earlier than the *Colloquium* in which he says: "Do not let thyself be led astray by different views on religion. Hold fast in thy spirit to this only, that true religion is nothing else than the turning of a purified soul to God. That is my, or rather Christ's religion." This impulse to religious toleration is characteristic of one aspect of Renaissance thought. For example, in an interesting little work on the Koran, Nicolaus of Cusa expounds how the name God has been given by different men differently to their greatest and most exalted conceptions. On this view he bases a plea for religious toleration and for the spread of Christianity by teaching rather than by force.

"Dr. Jordano Bruno Nolano, a professor in philosophy, intendeth to pass into England whose religion I cannot commend." [48]

---

[48] Cf. O. Elton, *Modern Studies* (London, 1907), p. 334, n. 9; Spampanato, *Vita di Giordano Bruno*, p. 329. Sir Henry Cobham (1538-1605?) had seen service at the Madrid embassy as well as in Antwerp and Brussels before his appointment as Ambassador to Paris in 1579. He was recalled to England in 1583.

CHAPTER TWO

BRUNO IN ENGLAND (1583-85)

a. A Haven in London

BRUNO landed in England with royal letters of recommendation to the French Ambassador in London, Michel de Castelnau, Marquis de Mauvissière (1520-1592) (Fig. 2). This remarkable man is one of the most attractive characters of the period. Like his compatriot Ambroise Paré, his humanity transcended the religious cleavage of the times. Bruno's period of residence in London was closely bound up with his relations to this humane, tolerant, and intelligent man and was the most fruitful of his whole career.

Mauvissière sprang from a noble family of Touraine. The manner of his first emergence into prominence throws light on the France of that day. The great Cardinal de Lorraine had expressed in his presence regret that he had not heard a certain sermon. Straightway the youth recited the sermon from memory. His fortune was made, and for the remainder of his long life he was in the service of his country, first with the armies but later more often in diplomacy. Probably he first visited England with the Cardinal's niece, Mary Queen of Scots, on her journey back to Scotland in 1561 after the death of her husband Francis II. Mauvissière was subsequently in constant correspondence with the unhappy Queen, who became godmother to his daughter.[1] He was in France again in

[1] Cf. Le Laboureur, *Mémoires de Michel de Castelnau* (2nd ed., Brussels, 1731), III, 109. Le Laboureur prints a charming letter sent by Mary of Scots with a gift to her god-daughter. Queen Elizabeth was godmother to one of the children of Mauvissière who died in childhood.

1562 serving under the Chancellor, Michel de l'Hôpital, who tried to mediate between the opposed religious parties, supporting the royal power but pleading for religious tolerance. In 1562 Mauvissière, a pious Catholic but known for his human sympathy, was sent by the King to advise the *Parlement* of Normandy to spare the lives of the Huguenots who fell into their hands. Later he was imprisoned by the English Army occupying Le Havre but was exchanged and sent again on diplomatic missions. During the Civil Wars, he always counselled mercy. Mauvissière was sent more than once to negotiate with Queen Elizabeth whom he reports as uniformly insincere and unreliable. His *Mémoires* end after the massacre of St. Bartholomew's night with a plea to his son to enforce right religion by example rather than by bloodshed.[2] Mauvissière was again sent to England in 1572 to appease Elizabeth's indignation at the massacre, and in 1575 he became ambassador in London, a post he held for ten years.

England was at this time a natural refuge for such a man as Bruno, especially since he had the opportunity of entering the suite of an ambassador. This gave him access to a brilliant circle in which scientific and philosophical ideas were being canvassed. Discussion on such topics in London was fairly free. Theological regulations were usually enforced there only when political opinions also were suspect. At Court literary interests were active, and it was of advantage to be an Italian. Englishmen of literary, scientific and philosophic taste looked for light from Italy.

[2] "My son, you may judge from hence, and all People that shall read these Memoirs, in case they should at any Time come to light, to whom the Breach of the Treaties is to be imputed on both Sides; and likewise see by the Events, that the *Spiritual* Sword, that is, the good *Example* of the *Pastors* of the Church, their *Charity, Preaching,* and other *pious Works,* are better means to extirpate Heresies, and restore those who have erred, to the right way, than the *Temporal one,* which destroys and sheds our Neighbours Blood; especially when Matters are come to that Extremity, that the more People endeavour to remove the *Evil* by violent Means, the more they increase it." *Les mémoires de Monsieur de Castelnau seigneur de Mauvissière* were first edited by his son J. de Castelnau, Paris, 1621, from whose volume our portrait is reproduced. The *Mémoires* were republished with copious additions by J. le Laboureur in three vols., Brussels, 1731. An English translation, from which we have copied these closing words, appeared in London in 1724.

Moreover, England and especially London was a recognized haven for foreigners persecuted for their opinions. Thus Flemings were numerous, and their skill in cloth and silk manufacture brought much prosperity to their adopted country. Huguenots also established important industries. A list of foreigners in his diocese drawn up by the Bishop of London in 1567 enumerates 3,760 in London proper, besides 1,091 in "out-parishes," excluding Southwark.[3] Some 3,000 of these were refugees from the Netherlands. France's religious wars were responsible for 512, while 138 were Italians.[4] A certificate by the Lord Mayor to the Privy Council in 1568 shews that the number was rapidly rising. There were then no less than 6,704 strangers in London, the Liberties adjoining, and Westminster.[5] At Elizabeth's own order these strangers were given considerable liberty of worship. The Queen wrote a gracious letter to the French Church promising protection.

During Elizabeth's reign, moreover, many great English nobles harboured Continental refugees in their palaces. Sometimes these were useful for foreign correspondence while some acted as spies or as accredited emissaries in the interminable intrigues that resulted from the disturbed state of Europe.

By the Court circle Italian refugees were specially cultivated. About the year 1580 there were in London some scores of distinguished Italians. The Queen liked to talk their language in public, and extended welcome to them.

b. The Oxford Incident

Before Bruno settled finally in the home of his benefactor in London, he was involved in a curious incident at Oxford. How did he reach the uni-

[3] R. E. G. Kirk and E. F. Kirk, *Returns of Aliens Dwelling in the City and Suburbs of London from the Reign of Henry VIII to that of James I,* Publication of Huguenot Society of London (Aberdeen, 1900), Vol. X, Parts i-iv, p. xv.

[4] Samuel Haynes, *Collection of State Papers . . . from the Year 1542 to 1570, . . . left by William Cecil Lord Burghley at Hatfield House* (London, 1740), p. 461. It may be noted that 36 of the strangers were "Scottes."

[5] Kirk, *op. cit.*, p. xvi, quoting John Strype, *Annals.*

versity? It is hard to imagine a less congruous figure in the Oxford of that day, the home of the most conservative Aristotelian study. Bruno may have been invited by the Chancellor of the University, the Earl of Leicester, a great patron of the Italians in England, uncle of Sir Philip Sidney, and a member of the circle in which Bruno was known. Or the introduction may have been through John Florio (Fig. 3),[6] secretary to Mauvissière and tutor to his daughter, and thus a fellow member with Bruno in Mauvissière's suite.

John Florio is one of the fixed points in Bruno's career, and we must devote some space to him. His father, Michael Angelo Florio, was the son of an Italian Jew who had been converted to Christianity. Michael Angelo Florio had joined the Franciscans but had thrown off the friar's habit and had fled his native country. He became a Protestant, and found asylum in England, where he was befriended by Lord Burghley and was appointed preacher to the Italian Protestant congregation. His son John (1553-1625), the friend of Bruno, was born in England and was a well-known London character who produced writings that are important for the development of the English language. John Florio published in 1578 an attractive phrase book in the Italian and English tongues, *The First Fruites of Florio*. A similar work is *Florio's Second Fruites to be Gathered of Twelve Trees* (1591), which contains 6,000 Italian proverbs. In it appear two characters, Torquato and Nundinio. These were the names given to the two Oxford doctors whom Bruno held up to ridicule in the first philosophical work which he published in England, *The Ash Wednesday Supper* (1584).[7] "The Nolan" himself has a Dialogue with Torquato in the *Second Fruites*. John Florio is best known for his excellent Italian and English dictionary, *A Worlde of Wordes or Dictionarie in Italian and English* (1598). The second edition of this work cites Bruno as a source.[8]

Florio was probably the original of Menalcas in Spenser's *Shepherds*

---

[6] For fuller details concerning John Florio, see Frances Yates, *John Florio* (Cambridge, 1934).

[7] Cf. pp. 35-6.

[8] *Queen Anna's New World of Words or Dictionarie of the Italian and English tongues* (London, 1611).

Calendar (1579) and is probably satirized as Holofernes in Shakespeare's *Love's Labour's Lost* (perhaps written in 1591) and as Parolles in *All's Well that Ends Well* (perhaps written in 1595).[9] He was intimate with Raleigh and Sidney, both educated at Oxford and with both of whom Bruno came in contact.

Another important work of Florio was his English translation of the *Essays* of Montaigne (dedicated to Sir Philip Sidney's daughter, the Countess of Rutland). Though this did not appear until 1603, Bruno may well have been introduced to Montaigne's work by Florio. Like Florio, Montaigne had Jewish ancestry. Michel de Montaigne (1533-1592) had the advantage of travel in Italy and a leisured life on his estates in southern France. He thus developed a strong vein of individualism as well as tolerance.[10] Though far from the mood of a rebel, he observed the relativity of the findings both of sense and of reason and was therefore led to a philosophy of Nature not entirely remote from Bruno's views:

---

[9] First suggested by Croce (in the *Nuove curiosità storiche,* pp. 121-22). The temptation to find association with Shakespeare is almost irresistible to writers on characters in Elizabethan England. Such suggestions concerning Bruno are made by W. König, "Shakespeare und Bruno," in *Jahrbuch der deutschen Shakespeare Gesellschaft,* XI (Weimar, 1876), 97-139. Florio has even been suggested as the original of Falstaff! (See Arthur Acheson, *Shakespeare's Last Years in London* (Quaritch, 1920).

Reminiscences in Shakespeare of the works of Bruno have been sought by Spampanato, *Soglia del secento* (Milan, 1926), pp. 57 *seqq.* He finds echoes of the *Candelaio* in the etymology of *mulier* in *Cymbeline,* V, 5; the necessity of a ring in *As You Like It,* III, 3 and IV, 2; the attribution of ills through pride to Fate or stars in *King Lear,* I, 2; the distinction between sharp and gentle madmen in *King Lear,* I, 4; the view of sorcery in *Macbeth,* IV, 1; the discourse of the Queen with two gentlemen in the Duke of York's garden, in *Richard II,* III, 4; the pun against Holofernes in *Love's Labour's Lost.* Croce first threw out the suggestion that Berowne in *Love's Labour's Lost* may have been intended for Bruno. The relation of the Italians in London with the characters in this play has been elucidated by Frances Yates, who discusses also the relation of the play to Raleigh's "School of Night" (*A Study of "Love's Labour's Lost"* [Cambridge University Press, 1936]).

[10] Cf. especially the *Essays of Montaigne done into English by John Florio,* ed. G. Saintsbury (London, 1878), Book II, Chap. XII, pp. 131, 133, 135. Cf. also Book I, Chap. XXV, p. 167.

But whatsoever shall present unto his inward eyes, as it were in a Table, the Idea of the great image of our universall mother Nature, attired in her richest robes, sitting in the throne of her Majestie, and in her visage shall read, so generall, and so constant a varietie; he that therein shall view himselfe, not himselfe alone, but a whole Kingdome, to be in respect of a great circle; but the smallest point that can be imagined, he onely can value things according to their essentiall greatness and proportion. This great universe (which some multiplie as Species under one Genus) is the true looking-glasse wherein we must looke, if we will know whether we be of a good stamp, or in the right byase.[11]

Florio was in a position to introduce Bruno to Oxford. He had resided there and in 1578 he dedicated his *First Fruites* to the Earl of Leicester, Chancellor to the University. In 1582, a year before Bruno's arrival, he had joined the staff of Mauvissière.

Bruno's visit to Oxford may also have been facilitated by the most distinguished of the Italian émigrés in England, Albericus Gentilis (1552-1608), "the grandfather of International Law," who reached England in 1580 and settled in Oxford. He had great influence with Elizabeth, and was able to persuade her on one occasion to refrain from inflicting punishment on the Spanish Ambassador. He held strongly to the view that force should never be an instrument of religious conversion.[12] Among his friends were Sir Philip Sidney, Sir Thomas Walsingham, the Earl of Leicester, and Lord Burghley. His friendship with Florio, at least in later life, is attested by his Italian poem to the Queen in Florio's *Queen Anna's New World of Words.*

---

[11] *Ibid.,* Book I, Chap. XXV, p. 165.

[12] In this opinion he was supported by John Hotmann. John's father Francis had been his teacher in Switzerland and perhaps John was now teaching the son of Gentilis. Writing from Oxford to Gentilis, then in London, John Hotmann exclaims in February 1581, "I greatly honour your singular doctrine and piety of which I hear much spoken" ("Magni facio tuam singularem et doctrinam et pietatem, de qua multa audivi praedicari"), *Francisci et Joanni Hotomanoreum epistolae* (Amsterdam, 1700), Epist. II, p. 261, and Epist. 85, p. 333. For Albericus and Bruno, see also pp. 43 and 140. It should, however, be mentioned that a character *Albericus,* an attractive recipient of the Lullian method, appears in the *Cantus circaeus* of 1582 (cf. p. 20). Cf. also Chapter 4, *e.* A Gentilis Albericus is mentioned by Ambrosio Leo as having pronounced most eloquent funeral orations in Nola in 1512. This figure we are not now considering.

A close friend of Florio who was in Oxford in 1583 was Matthew Gwynne (1558?-1627), "il Candido," with whom Florio shared a love of music as well as of letters. This versatile man had lectured on music in the university. Later, having studied medicine, he became one of the earliest professors at Gresham College in London.

In June 1583 Oxford prepared entertainment for a Polish noble, Albert a Laski, who was on a mission to England.[13] This Albert a Laski was subsequently introduced by the Earl of Leicester to John Dee. The Queen herself is stated to have sent money to Dee to enable him to entertain the Earl and his Polish guest at dinner on 31st July, 1583. A Laski became involved in the experiments of John Dee to obtain the "Philosopher's Stone." On leaving England in September 1583 he took with him both Dee and his pupil Kelly. They worked at their chemical experiments at a Laski's castle near Cracow. Ultimately he tired of them, and their subsequent travels to princes who entertained them and passed them on with a gift recall the experiences of Bruno himself. They were able to return to the care of their own monarch, but no such haven awaited Bruno.

Gwynne was among those who made "disputations" at the Oxford entertainment in 1583 in honour of Albert a Laski, and it may have been at Gwynne's suggestion that Bruno was invited to take part. In any

---

[13] Cf. William Camden, *History of Annals of England,* Book III, 1583, Ann. 26. "Out of *Polonia* a country bordering upon *Russia,* came this Summer into *England* to see the Queen, *Albert Alesco palatine of Siradia* [i.e., Voivode of Sieradz], a learned man, well shaped, with a long beard, and very comely and decent apparel: who being graciously welcomed by her, and entertained by the Nobility with great Respect and Feasting, as also by the University at *Oxford* with learned Divertisements and several Comedies, after four months stay here, withdrew himself privately, being run far in Debt."

Strype gives an interesting passage which may provide a sidelight on the visit of a Laski: "These strangers who consisted chiefly of Low-Dutch and Germans had once the West Part of the Church of the Augustine Friars in Broad Street granted to them by King Edward VI . . . whereof Joannes a Lasco a noble Polonian was their Minister with the title of Superintendent. But under Queen Mary they were dissolved and glad to flee into foreign parts. . . ." The Church was restored to them by Elizabeth (*Annals of the Reformation* [London, 1709], p. 119, under Chap. VIII, Anno 1559). This Johannes a Lasco (d. 1560) was an important leader of the Polish Protestants. He was perhaps an uncle of Albert a Laski.

event the result was disastrous. It could hardly have been otherwise.

Here is Bruno's impression of the general characteristics of members of the university:

> They spoke Latin well, [were] proper men, . . . of good reputation . . . fairly competent in learning but mediocre in education, courtesy and breeding. . . , well furnished with titles . . . for 'tis *yes my master; yes my Father, or my mistress; yes sir forsooth;* . . . elect indeed, with their long [academic] robes, clad in velvet. One wore two shining gold chains about his neck while the other, by God, whose precious hand bore twelve rings on two fingers, had rather the appearance of a rich jeweller who would wrench eyes and heart from the amorous beholder. . . . Did they know aught of Greek? Aye and also [14] of beer. . . . One was the herald of the idol of Obscurity and the other the bailiff of the goddess of Presumption.[15]

"Go to Oxford," he says again,

> and let them recount to you what happened there to the Nolan when he disputed publicly with those doctors of theology in the presence of the Polish prince Alasco [*sic*] and others of the English nobility. Would you hear how they were able to reply to his arguments? How fifteen times by means of fifteen syllogisms, a poor doctor whom on this solemn occasion they had put forward as a very Corypheus of the Academy, was left standing like a chick entangled in tow? Would you learn with what incivility and discourtesy that pig comported himself, and the patience and humanity of him who shewed himself to be born a Neapolitan and nurtured under a more benign sky? Are you informed how they closed his public lectures, both those on the Immortality of the Soul and on the Five-fold Sphere? [16]

"That pig" was Doctor John Underhill, Rector of Lincoln College and Chaplain to Her Majesty.[17] In the Oxford archives there is no rec-

---

[14] *Etiamdio.* A speaker immediately interrupts to point out that this word is obsolete!

[15] *La cena de le ceneri,* Dial. I, pp. 1-2 (Gentile, *Op. ital.,* I, 15-17; Lagarde, *Op. ital.,* I, 120-21).

[16] *Ibid.,* Dial. IV, pp. 92-93 (Gentile, *Op. ital.,* I, 101-2; Lagarde, *Op. ital.,* I, 176).

[17] The record leading to this identification we owe to Gabriel Harvey, who was in the habit of making marginal scribbles in his books. In one of them occurs the following: "Jordanus Neapolitanus (Oxonij disputans cum Doctore

ord of Bruno's visit, which evidently created less impression on the officials than on himself. It may be that his discourses were given in private. But clearly Oxford was no place for him,[18] and he returned or was returned promptly to his refuge under the more tolerant roof of the long-suffering Mauvissière.

In a little book surreptitiously printed by Bruno in London, probably in 1583, there is a curious brief Epistle addressed by him "to the most excellent Vice-Chancellor, the most renowned Doctors and most celebrated Masters of Oxford University."[19] It sets forth, in Bruno's most bombastic style, both his own claims and the imbecility of those who reject his message. It is he who is "lover of God, doctor in a harder theology, professor of a most pure and harmless wisdom, a philosopher known, accepted and honourably received in the foremost academies of Europe." He is "the vanquisher of presumptuous and persistent

---

Vnderhil) tam in Theologia, quam in philosophia, omnia reuocabat ad locos Topicos, et axiomata Aristotelis; atque inde de quauis materia promptissime arguebat. Hopperi principia multo efficaciora in quouis argumento forensi." See G. C. Moore Smith, *Marginalia of Gabriel Harvey* (Stratford, 1913). For Gabriel Harvey, see p. 41.

[18] Miss Frances Yates suggests that Bruno's quarrel with Oxford was based on the repudiation by Oxford of scholastic Aristotelian studies and on his own devotion to mediaeval philosophy. She intimates that "Bruno prefers the metaphysics of mediaeval Oxford to the grammar of Renaissance Oxford." ("Giordano Bruno's Conflict with Oxford" in *Journal of the Warburg Institute* [London, January, 1939]; our quotation is from p. 233.) This view is further developed by Miss Yates in "The Religious Policy of Giordano Bruno," *Journal of the Warburg and Courtauld Institutes* [April-July, 1939-40], III, 181-207. Certainly Bruno expresses his contempt for the fashionable preoccupation with grammar and style. He also declares his admiration for St. Thomas Aquinas. On the other hand, he can assuredly be claimed by no single group or creed, least of all by the Schoolmen. Nor was it too great a zeal on his part for mediaeval metaphysics that impelled his judges to condemn him to be burnt alive.

[19] *Epistola ad excellentissimum Oxoniensis academiae Procancellarium, clarrissimos doctores atque celeberrimos magistros* (*Op. lat.*, II, ii, 76). The Epistle is incorporated in some, though not all, copies of a volume on mnemonics, *Recens et completa ars memorandi . . . explicatio triginta sigillorum . . . sigillus sigillorum* (*Recent and Complete Art of Memory . . . with Explanation of the Thirty Signs . . . to Which Is Added the Sign of Signs*) (without place or date of printing). It is dedicated to Mauvissière, in whose house it was composed and to whom as always the author expresses passionate gratitude. Cf. App. I, 5 (a) to (e).

ignorance who yet protests that in all his actions there is love of all his fellow beings, of the Briton, no less than the Italian, of women no less than men, of sovereigns no less than prelates." On the title-page of this tactless effusion, issued after the unfortunate Oxford episode, Bruno again prefixes to his name the title Philotheo which he used in the next three works, published in London.[20] Perhaps it is this work, perhaps another, which as "My *Mnemosine,* hidden under Thirty Seals and confined in the pitchy jail of the Shadow of Tears," is invoked in the first of the important Italian works which quickly followed his return to the kindly atmosphere of the French Embassy (Figs. 4, 5, 11).

c. Bruno's Circle in London

We have now to consider Bruno's circle in London in so far as it can be traced. Like all that concerns his career, the details are obscure and can often be presented only tentatively. Of the closeness of his friendship with Florio we have many indications. In contrast to all other evidence, Bruno is presented by Florio in the *Second Fruites*[21] as urbane and gentle. In Florio's picture, Bruno's feud with Torquato[22] has melted into something like amused tolerance. The Nolan mildly chaffs Torquato on his late rising and luxurious habits, waits patiently during his robing, and mentions that he himself is an early riser and that he "rarely drinks except at meals." In a later chapter Florio summons up Nundinio, though the Nolan has retired. Could the name *Nundinio* be a pun on the name of George *Chapman* (1559-1634)?[23] It is reasonable to think that Bruno may have known the poet George Chapman, author of the English translation of the *Iliad* and an enthusiastic member of the "School of Night." His friend Matthew Royden (1580-1622) shared his interests. Nor is it very hazardous to suggest that the name *Torquato* is a pun on George *Turner* (1569-1610), who in the year 1584 was admitted

[20] Cf. p. 21, n. 27; p. 39, n. 39. [21] Cf. p. 29. [22] Cf. p. 29.

[23] But Miss Yates draws my attention to the suggestion both in the *Cena* and in Florio's *Second Fruites* that Nundinio is connected with Scotland. Chapman was born at Hitchin in Hertfordshire.

a "Candidate" of the Royal College of Physicians, occupying successive offices after his election to the Fellowship in 1584. The circumstances of his election as an "Elect" of the College in 1602 suggest an association with unorthodox philosophy, for a letter has survived "To our very loving Friends Mr. Dr. Forster, President of the Physicians in London and to the rest of the Electors" from J. Stanhope and Robert Cecyll,

> to pray you (now at your election) to admytt Mr. Dr. Turner who is now the senior, into that place, and not to exclude him by preferring his junior, seeing we are informed that there is no other exception to be taken but his backwardness in religion, in which he is no way tainted for malice or practice against the State . . . seeing he is for his knowledge and practice so well esteemed by divers noblemen and others in this place, and her Majestie herself, as it were to be, wished he might not be so disgraced, especially seeing his election as we are informed is not against the Statute and that it may be God may open his eyes hereafter to see his error, which we do wish with all our hearts.[24]

Among those who shewed kindness to Bruno were Sir Philip Sidney and his devoted friend Sir Fulke Greville. The latter appears as the host in Bruno's *Ash Wednesday Supper,* and two others of Bruno's Italian works are inscribed to Sidney. In the Dedication to Sidney in the *Expulsion of the Triumphant Beast,*[25] Bruno complains that enemies have interposed between Sir Fulke Greville and himself, but expresses his gratitude and affection for both patrons "before turning my back on your beautiful, fortunate and most courteous country." In the Dedication of the *Heroic Frenzies,* Bruno exalts the love of philosophy above that of woman, seemingly daring to remonstrate with Sidney's preoccupation with Stella.

There is evidence that Sir Walter Raleigh was a friend of Mauvissière. One of the Ambassador's letters to Florio instructs him to call on Raleigh and present an invitation to supper on the following day.[26] The same

---

[24] W. Munk, *Roll of the Royal College of Physicians of London* (London, 1878), I, 89-90.

[25] Cf. pp. 117-18.

[26] Public Record Office, S.P. 78, 14, No. 119, f. 245. Cf. *Cal. S.P. Foreign,* p. 260. Messages to Raleigh are also in a letter from Mauvissière from Paris to Florio, S.P. 78, 14, No. 118, f. 225. Cf. *Cal. S.P. Foreign,* p. 175.

letter sends remembrances to Lord Howard of Effingham who was also in relationship with Italians in London.[27] From France Mauvissière wrote again to Florio sending special messages to Raleigh. There were certainly discussions between Mauvissière and Raleigh and other members of what came to be called Raleigh's "School of Night." [28] The setting of Bruno's *Ash Wednesday Supper* suggests such a symposium. Though he places it in Sir Fulke Greville's house, he afterwards stated [29] that it was under Mauvissière's roof. Doubtless the book was suggested by gatherings in both houses. We have undoubted evidence that Bruno's work was known to Thomas Hariot (1560-1621), the mathematician and astronomer who was the scientific leader of the group.[30]

In *La cena de le ceneri* Bruno, on his way to Sir Fulke Greville, notes the palace of Lord Buckhurst to whom at the Supper, he is introduced by Florio. This is Sir Thomas Sackville (1536-1608), who became Lord Buckhurst (1567) and later first Earl of Dorset. He was a poet and patron of Florio. Another character in this same work bears the familiar name of Smith. This benevolent onlooker holds the course for the discussion and is ultimately converted to the Nolan's view. He can perhaps be identified with Sir Thomas Smith [31] (1556-1609), Public Orator at Oxford in 1582, Proctor in 1584, and subsequently Secretary to Essex. Can he as Junior Proctor have befriended Bruno in the Oxford episode?

In Bruno's next work, *On Cause, Prime Origin and the One,* Florio

---

[27] Cf. p. 43, n. 54.

[28] See Yates, *A Study of "Love's Labour's Lost"* and M. Brabrook, *The School of Night* (Cambridge, 1936) for discussion of Bruno's relationship with members of the School.

[29] Cf. *Doc. Ven.* XIII (Spampanato, *Documenti della vita di Giordano Bruno,* p. 121). When interrogated before the Venice Inquisition, Bruno stated that the supper took place under the roof of Mauvissière. Probably in his work he was following historical fact regarding one such gathering in Sir Fulke Greville's palace, while we may well believe that they took place many times in the French Embassy. Since Mauvissière was a Catholic, Bruno would expect the Inquisition to look with less suspicion on assemblies held under his auspices.

[30] Cf. p. 67.

[31] Cf. p. Sir T. Smith was both undergraduate at Christ Church and subsequently student there. For other Christ Church connections with the Oxford incident, see p. 97, n. 13.

perhaps figures again as the understanding friend under the pseudonym of "Eliotropio,"[32] a flower which formed part of his coat of arms. It may be that this figure is partly drawn from Florio's young friend, the poet Samuel Daniel (1562-1619). In dealing with this euphuizing group, it is not extravagant to note that Eliotropio's first long speech opens by calling Bruno's task "La impresa che hai tolta,"[33] and to recall that *Impresa* (personal emblem) was the title of Samuel Daniel's first published work (1584), a translation from the Italian of Paolo Giovio. Daniel had just left Magdalen Hall, Oxford.[34] A certain *N.W.* attached a laudatory preface to this work, recalling "that which Nolanus (that man of infinite titles amongst other phantastical toys) truly noted by chance in our schools, that by the help of translations all science had their offspring."

Another contemporary Englishman who appears in the work *On Cause, Prime Origin and the One* is one Alexander Dicson, "learned, upright, loveable, well-nurtured and faithful friend whom the Nolan loveth as his own eyes."[35] This Dicson or Dickson was Bruno's disciple in mnemonics and published in 1583 a volume *On the Shadow of Reason and Judgement,*[36] dedicated to the Earl of Leicester and obviously inspired by Bruno's *On the Shadows of Ideas* of 1582. Dicson's work was promptly answered in 1584 by "Antidicsonus cuiusdam Cantabrigiensis G.P.; accessit libellus in quo dilucide explicatur impia Dicsoni artificiosa memoria." In a dedication to Thomas Moufet, *G.P.* gives a list of writers on mnemonics "memoriographae ostentatores Metrodori,[37]

---

[32] First noted by F. A. Yates, *John Florio,* p. 102. Miss Yates points out in the speeches of Eliotropio other indications of Florio's coat of arms as well as of his motto, "Chi si contenta gode."

[33] "The enterprise which thou hast undertaken," using the word *impresa,* which means both enterprise and personal emblem. Miss Yates (*ibid.,* p. 102) thinks this phrase may be intended to remind the reader of the heliotrope in Florio's coat of arms.

[34] Now Hertford College.

[35] Cf. p. 39, n. 39. In Dial. II of *On Cause, Prime Origin and the One,* Dicson is given the first name of "Arelio."

[36] *De umbra rationis et iudicii sive de artificiosa memoriae quam publice profititur vanitate* (T. Vautrollier, London).

[37] A figure mentioned by Cicero and Pliny as famous for memory.

Rosseli,[38] Nolani, Dicsoni repellantur." Mnemonics were in the fashion in England, for *G.P.* produced another and similar work later in the year, and we shall notice Thomas Watson's volume on the subject.[39] It is unfortunate that we know no more of this Dicson.

It would appear that not all Bruno's encounters in Oxford had been unfortunate. In the work, *On Cause, Prime Origin and the One,* two names are mentioned as distinguished for their courtesy. One of these is Dr. Tobie Matthew, the very Protestant Dean of Christ Church who was subsequently Bishop of Durham and Archbishop of York. The other is a certain Culpeper, presumably the then Warden of New College.[40]

Can we identify among Bruno's circle any of the speakers in the work here translated, *On the Infinite Universe and Worlds*? Theophilo or Philotheo, who appears in all three of the Italian philosophical works, is of course the Nolan himself. "How can I speak of the Nolan? Perhaps, since he is as near to me as I am to myself, it beseemeth me not to praise him." [41] Elpino or Alpino is perhaps a punning name for Thomas Hill, a contemporary who sometimes called himself Mountain. Hill was a voluminous and miscellaneous writer interested in mathematics, astrology, dreams, magic, physical devices, etc., and was moreover an Italian scholar.[42] While treating the theory of Copernicus with respect, Hill does not accept it, but in Bruno's work Elpino is gradually converted to the new views. Of Gentilis and Florio we have already spoken.

If some of the identifications seem far-fetched, it must be remembered

[38] Cosmas Rossellus, *Thesaurus artificiosae memoriae, concionatoribus, philosophis, medicis, juristis, oratoribus, caeterisque bonarum litterarum amatoribus* (Venice [apud Paduanium florentinum] 1579).

[39] Cf. p. 40.

[40] Cf. p. 97, n. 13. We suggest that *Armesso,* a sceptic character in the Dialogue, *De la causa, principio et uno,* may be the *Mercurius* of Dicson's work, but we have not identified a prototype.

[41] *La cena de la ceneri,* Dial. I, p. 7 (Gentile, *Op. ital.,* I, 23; Lagarde, *Op. ital.,* I, 125). Cf. p. 93, n. 2.

[42] The scholarship of Hill is attested by his numerous translations of surgical, medical and chemical works from Italian as well as from Latin, and from the German of Paracelsus. It is possible that the works on gardening are from a different writer. Gentile (*Op. ital.,* I, 287) notes that a character in Tasso's *Aminta* (first published in 1580) bears the name Elpino, but we find no resemblance between the Elpino of *Aminta* and Bruno's speaker.

that Bruno's cryptic allusion to names was simply "playing the game" as practised by his circle in England. The aim was not secrecy, but rather a display of fancy and "precious" skill in the allusive indication of the familiar members of the Anglo-Italian circle. It was akin to the choice by continental humanists of allusive classical names.

Bruno may have first met in Paris the poet Thomas Watson (1557-1592) who was there in 1581. Watson was deeply influenced by Italian literature. In 1582 he had published *Hekatompathia or Passionate Centurie of Love,* poems inspired by or translated from ancient classical French and Italian writers; and his Latin poem *Amyntas* (1585) was based on Torquato Tasso. In 1590 appeared his *Meliboeus . . . siue ecloga in obitum . . . Francisce Walsinghami.* Now the name Meliboeus, as well as many of those connected with the *Hekatompathia,* occurs beside that of the Nolan in Florio's *Second Fruites.* Watson is also known for his *First Sett of Italian Madrigals Englished,* which brings him further into relationship with the musicianly Florio and Gwynne. But Watson himself points out a friendly connexion with Bruno. For in the Dedication to the *Compendium memoriae localis* which bears his name, he writes: "I very much fear if my little work is compared with the mystical and deeply learned *Sigillis* of the Nolan or with the *Umbra artificiosa* of Dicson, it may bring more infamy to its author than utility to the reader." [43]

From those known to have had relations with Bruno in London we turn to certain of those who probably met him. Their consideration will help to obtain a picture of the society in which he found himself.

Among Bruno's contacts was probably that delightful Cornishman, Richard Carew (1555-1620), whose gentle wit would soften irate spirits and whose scholarship must have impressed the critical Italian.[44] Carew

[43] Vautrollier? London? 1585? Watson's volume is dedicated to Henry Noel (d. 1597).

[44] Richard Carew, best known for his *Survey of Cornwall* (1602), published in 1594 two volumes translated from the Italian in which he "clad in a Cornish gabardine" the Italian translation by Camillo Camilli of John Huarte's *Examen de ingenios.* Carew also made a translation in verse of Tasso's *Godfrey Bulloigne or the Recouerie of Jerusalem.* Only the first five cantos appeared in 1594, but the whole work, edited by A. B. Crosart, was published in 1881.

one Albertino who may well be intended to represent the great jurist Alberico Gentilis.[52]

There is a letter from Gentilis written from Oxford to his friend Hotmann, obviously referring to lectures of Bruno though not mentioning him by name. It reflects the impression of the fascination exercised by Bruno on the groups of scholars who assembled to hear him successively in Noli, in Toulouse, in Paris, perhaps even in Oxford, and certainly in London. "I heard," writes Gentilis, "from the greatest of men assertions strange, absurd and false, as of a stony heaven, the sun bipedal, that the moon doth contain many cities as well as mountains, that the Earth doth move, the other elements are motionless and a thousand such things." [53]

Bruno doubtless came into some contact with the more prominent Italians in London. He could not fail to have met the musicians Ferrabosco, father and son, nor Petruccio Ubaldini (1524-1600?), the prolific writer of both Italian and English prose and verse who dedicated to Lord Howard of Effingham a magnificently illustrated account of the defeat of the Armada.[54]

---

[52] Cf. pp. 31 and 140. Neither Spampanato (*Vita di Giordano Bruno,* pp. 416-17) nor Gentile (*Op. ital.,* I, 387) accepts this view, though of course aware that Gentilis was at Oxford in 1583 and that he subsequently befriended Bruno in Wittenberg. They indicate somewhat unconvincingly that perhaps Bruno intended to honour a certain Geronimo Albertino of Nola who was the father of a fellow soldier of his own father Giovanni Bruno.

[53] Cf. p. 31, n. 12.

[54] Within a few months of the defeat of the Armada by Lord Howard of Effingham, an account of the victory was written in Italian by Petruccio Ubaldini. The original work (British Museum Royal MS 14. A X) was not published, but an English translation appeared in 1590 with plates engraved by Augustine Ryther from drawings by Robert Adams, "surveyor of the Queen's buildings." Lord Howard employed Cornelius Vroom of Haarlem to make ten designs based on these plates for tapestry panels, which were woven by Francis Spiring of Haarlem and hung in Arundel House Strand until in 1616 Lord Howard, now Earl of Nottingham, sold them to James I who hung them in the House of Lords, where they remained until destroyed in the great fire of 1834. Cf. H. Yates Thompson, *Lord Howard of Effingham and the Armada* (Roxburgh Club, 1919). Ubaldini had come to England from Florence in 1545 but he did not finally settle there until 1562. He enjoyed the favour of the Court and was given a pension by Elizabeth. He was a skilled illuminator and a number of beautiful manuscripts from his hand have survived. His writings are all in Italian.

Besides literary circles, Bruno may reasonably be supposed to have met certain English astronomers and mathematicians. These we consider separately.[55]

The interest of Bruno's wanderings after he left London centre in his writings and philosophy. We shall therefore consider in turn the works which he produced at each of his successive places of sojourn, beginning with the London works.

d. The London Years of Illumination (1583–85)

Bruno is now in his thirty-sixth year. Suddenly there appears the fruit of these long years of study and reflection that he had incredibly combined with his wanderings, his privations and the constant uncertainty of livelihood.

Six works on philosophy and ethics issued from Bruno's pen during the years 1584-85. In them are set forth his thought on the Infinite Universe. All are in Italian. The prose style is sometimes almost uncouth and is full of repetition, but there are noble prose passages, and interspersed in the works are verses in which he succeeds in conveying something of the harmony and beauty which he apprehends in the infinite universe.

It is interesting that Bruno chose the Italian for these works. The use of the vernacular for philosophical writings was in its infancy and in this matter Bruno was something of a pioneer. English had been used for scientific purposes but Bruno confesses that he never mastered that language. The circle that received him in London was familiar with Italian, and that tongue, flexible and still developing, was certainly better adapted than Latin to express the tumultuous flow of his thought. That he had a rhetorical mastery of Latin is well shown by his later works. His Latin philosophical works are to a considerable extent expansions of the three little London volumes and are distinguished by similar qualities—a rush of language sometimes hardly coherent, sometimes, and especially in the verse passages, attaining true eloquence and

[55] Cf. Chapter 3, *c*.

exaltation. Some of the Latin chapter headings on the other hand exhibit a remarkable power of epitome. This is especially shown for example in the Table of Contents attached to the *Acrotismus*.[56] But in many respects the six brief Italian works are Bruno's masterpieces.

The three Italian philosophical works bear the imprint "Venice, 1584," while the three Italian ethical works are all ascribed on their title-page to Paris. Nevertheless, all six works were published in England. In spite of the comparative tolerance that prevailed in England, there is no doubt that too intimate connection with Bruno's views would have entailed difficulties for the printers. So the false imprints were used without printers' names. Not only, however, can the type be recognized as of English origin, but at his trial before the Inquisition at Rome, Bruno admitted that these volumes had all in fact been printed in London. Moreover, two of the Italian ethical works are dedicated to Sir Philip Sidney. Bruno at his trial averred that his printers had advised him that the imprints of Venice and of Paris would increase the sale of his books.[57]

It is noteworthy that all the six Italian works were concerned with Bruno's original thought. While he drew for illustration on his amazing knowledge of writers from the ancients right on to his own contemporaries, we fortunately hear no more of Lull during the remainder of this happy interval. Before we can consider these Italian works written in London, it is necessary to make a preliminary survey of their author's cosmology and philosophy.

---

[56] See App. I, 18.
[57] See App. II.

CHAPTER THREE

COSMOLOGY AND PHILOSOPHY OF BRUNO

a. The Mediaeval Cosmic Scheme

COSMOLOGY and philosophy are in all ages very closely linked, and Bruno's cosmological views are crucial to all his thought. It is therefore convenient before attempting a survey of his own philosophy to consider the cosmic scheme current in his day.

For many centuries "Aristotelian" cosmological conceptions had, with little modification, dominated European thought. In that tradition, the universe is treated as a series of concentric spheres with a central motionless earth. Immediately enwrapping the earth are "Spheres" of the three other elements, arranged from within outward in order of decreasing density—Water, Air, Fire. The outermost limit of these is the limit of the mundane or sublunary sphere. Beyond is a further series of seven concentric spheres, each the abode of one planet, moon and sun being reckoned as planets. Outside these planetary spheres is the sphere of the fixed stars. Beyond this again is the sphere of the *Primum mobile* which has motion imparted to it by divine power, thus causing it to move each of the spheres within.[1]

In several passages accessible to mediaeval writers, Aristotle gives this

---

[1] In mediaeval Christian versions of the scheme, divine power is sometimes shewn acting through the labour of angels imparting motion by cranks (cf. Israel Abrahams, Edwin Bevyn, and Charles Singer, *The Legacy of Israel* [Oxford, 1927], Fig. 25 from a fourteenth century manuscript).

general view of the universe.[2] He devotes much space to explaining the perfect nature of circular movement,[3] the natural position of the earth as central to the universe and of the elemental spheres just outside it,[4] as well as to the necessity of an unmoved mover beyond the whole.[5] He also explains that the heavenly bodies must themselves be firmly attached to the rotating spheres.[6] In discussing the motions of the planets, he propounds the view that each planet must be moved by several concentric spheres whose equators are, however, not parallel but inclined one to another. He thus attributes fifty-five spheres to the planets (or by another calculation forty-nine).[7]

Aristotle was neither astronomical observer nor mathematician. His relatively simple scheme, integrated into his philosophy, which had become current in the Middle Ages, had been elaborated by certain of his successors among the ancients who were both astronomical observers and constructive mathematicians. Early thinkers right up to Kepler (1609)[8]—including Copernicus and Tycho Brahe—believed that all heavenly bodies move in circles. They believed this motion to be "perfect," that is, travelling always equal distances in equal times.

But the Aristotelian scheme in its various presentations was soon found inadequate to explain all the observed motions of the planets. For this purpose two mathematical devices were invoked, the excentric or circle with a movable centre, and the system of the epicycle on a deferent. The excentric circle was the name given to the path of a planet which revolved uniformly about a centre that itself moved in a relatively small circle around the earth. A fundamentally similar device provided for

---

[2] *De coelo,* 113-14, 286b 10–287b 21, and see below.

[3] *De gen. et corr.,* II, 11, 338a; *Physica,* VIII, 8, 264b; *De coelo,* II, 3, 286a.

[4] *De coelo,* IV, 3-4, 310a-312a.

[5] *Physica,* VIII, 6, 258a-259b.

[6] *De coelo,* II, 8, 289b.

[7] *Metaphysica,* XII, 8, 1074a, 13. In *De gen. et corr.,* II, 2, Aristotle distinguishes between the elements as perceptible bodies which are always encountered by us in "alteration" or mixture with one another, and the originative sources of these elements "which are equal in number (four) and identical in kind with those in the sphere of the eternal and primary things" (Cf. *De gen. et corr.,* II, 9, 335a).

[8] Date of publication of Kepler's *Astronomia nova.*

each planet a small circle, known as the epicycle, on which the planet revolved around a centre which was itself carried around a larger circular orbit called the deferent. Thus every point along the circumference of the deferent became in turn the centre of the epicycle.

This mathematical scheme had been brought to highly complicated form by Claudius Ptolemy, the astronomer, geographer and mathematician who lived in Alexandria in the first half of the second Christian century. Ptolemy gave a complete and lucid compendium of the whole range of astronomical science in his time in his *Mathematical Syntaxis,* better known by the title of the Arabic version, as the *Almagest*. Ptolemy specifically explains that either of the two mathematical devices described above can be used indifferently, but that where it is necessary to explain two divergent movements, the two methods can be combined (Fig. 6).[9]

During many centuries Ptolemy's scheme worked satisfactorily for astronomical prediction. But with the passage of time, the errors in his Tables gradually accumulated so as to make them seriously inaccurate for astronomical prediction. The difficulty was tackled by a group of astronomers assembled at Toledo by King Alphonso of Castille. They made a fresh series of observations on which were based the "Alphonsine Tables" which were issued about 1270. Thus modified, or with small further modifications, the scheme of Ptolemy remained the generally accepted conception of the universe until Copernicus (1543) (Fig. 7). It is assumed by Elpino in the work here translated, until after his conversion.

---

[9] Ptolemy, *Almagest,* III, 3 and XII, 1. The text was first introduced to the Latin-speaking world by Gerard of Cremona (1114-1187) who translated the Arabic version. Gerard's translation was first printed at Venice in 1515. Ptolemy's Greek text was printed 13 years later in 1528. The systems of excentric and deferent are very clearly and summarily shewn in Angus Armitage, *Copernicus the Founder of Modern Astronomy* (Allen and Unwin, 1938), p. 28. An interesting survey of the stages in the development of the Ptolemaic system is in Grant McColley, "Humanism and the History of Astronomy" in *Studies and Essays in the History of Science and Learning Offered in Homage to George Sarton on the Occasion of His Sixtieth Birthday 31 Aug. 1944* (New York, 1946), edited by M. F. Ashley Montagu, pp. 323 *seqq*. Cf. also by the same author "A Facsimile of Salusbury's Translation of Didacus à Stunica's *Commentary upon Job*" in *Annals of Science* (London, 1937), II, ii, 179-182.

What modifications were introduced by Copernicus? His great book was, in fact, much less revolutionary than is often supposed. He still maintained the general Ptolemaic view of a series of concentric spheres in circular motion around a motionless centre and limited by a sphere of fixed stars, though he placed the sun instead of the earth as the motionless centre of the universe, and he conceived the earth as occupying one of the rotating planetary spheres. But neither mathematically nor philosophically was the change profound. Copernicus still regarded the stars as really motionless and "fixed" in their unchanging position in the eighth sphere. The universe remained finite and an affair of circles and geometrical constructions. Copernicus believed that the rotation of the earth's sphere carried the earth to perform one revolution around the sun in the course of a year. He further ascribed to the earth a spinning motion around her own centre as the cause of the phenomenon of alternating day and night. All this was accepted by Bruno, but for him it was only a step in the search for a completer and more revolutionary cosmological conception. Bruno writes of Copernicus: "This important, subtle, diligent and mature mind" was ordained to be as the dawn heralding the re-emergence of the sun of the true philosophy.[10] Nevertheless, the universe conceived by Bruno was not merely of different structure but of a completely different order to that pictured by Copernicus.

It was a truly marvellous intuition of Bruno that the new framework which Copernicus had sketched was but a part of a great cosmological pattern. It is true that this pattern had been glimpsed by certain earlier writers. But both critics and followers of Copernicus in the sixteenth century saw in his work a rearrangement of the well-established world scheme. Some might regard the rearrangement with contempt, and some with admiration. To Bruno and to Bruno alone the suggestion of Copernicus entered into the pattern of a completely new cosmological order. In this sense Bruno not only anticipated Galileo and Kepler, but he passed beyond them into an entirely new world which had shed all

---

[10] Cf. *La cena de le ceneri,* Dial. I, pp. 5-7 (Gentile, *Op. ital.,* I, 22; Lagarde, *Op. ital.,* I, 124, 125); also *De immenso et innumerabilibus,* Lib. III (*Op. lat.,* I, i, especially p. 395, where Copernicus is criticized, "non mathematicus sed physicus").

the dross of tradition. It was a great vision which, from the very nature of the case, could be shared in full neither by his own nor by the succeeding generation.

b. An Infinite Universe and Infinitely Numerous Worlds

The whole of Bruno's philosophy is based on his view of an infinite universe with an infinity of worlds. He conceived the universe as a vast interrelationship throughout space and time, comprehending all phenomena, material and spiritual. Thence he was led to contemplate the parts under the mode of relativity. The conception of the infinity of the universe renders meaningless the ascription to it of motion, but Bruno conceives each of the infinitely numerous worlds to be moving on its course in relation to other worlds, impelled by its own twofold nature as individual and as part of the whole. All estimates of direction, position and weight within the whole must be relative. Moreover, the cosmological system is illumined by the properties of number.[11]

Bruno was not entirely original in these conceptions. But he saw new implications in them and revealed them with a new vividness. Paradoxically, the two writers who most influenced his cosmological views, Lucretius and Nicolaus of Cusa, occupy opposite philosophical poles. Lucretius denied the validity of theological or metaphysical thinking; Nicolaus sought in his cosmology and even in his physical experiments a reinforcement of his theological views. Bruno was neither astronomer nor mathematician and he was exceptionally devoid of experimental understanding; but contemporary astronomical and mathematical views provide the very fabric of his philosophical system.

The conception of an infinite universe embracing infinitely numerous worlds is familiar in Lucretius. The insurgent fury of the search for truth, the vision of mighty forces uniting in the infinite universe, the passionate rejection of religion imposed by authority, the magnificent diction of the Latin poet are all qualities shared by the Nolan. Bruno's

[11] For relativity of time, cf. *De immenso,* Lib. I, Cap. 12, and for analogy of number, Cap. 13 (*Op. lat.,* I, i, 244, 248, etc.).

. 4. House in Butcher Row bearing emblems of crown and fleur-de-lis. In 1582-4 it s the French Embassy. From E. Walford's *London* (1875-8).

. 5. Butcher Row. From Walford and Knight's *London*.

Fig. 6. The Ptolemaic universe. From Andraeus Cellarius, *Harmonia macrocosma seu atlas universalis et novum totius universi creati cosmographiam generalem et novam exhibens* (Amsterdam, 1660), Pars Prior.

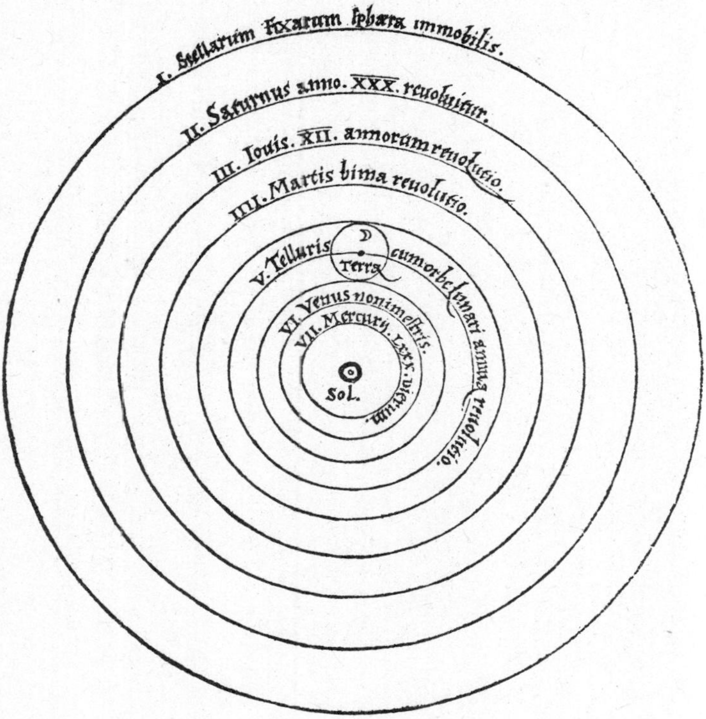

Fig. 7. The Copernican universe. From *De revolutionibus orbium coelestium* (Nuremberg, 1543).

Folio.43

A perfit description of the Cælestiall Orbes,

according to the most auncient doctrine of the Pythagoreans. &c.

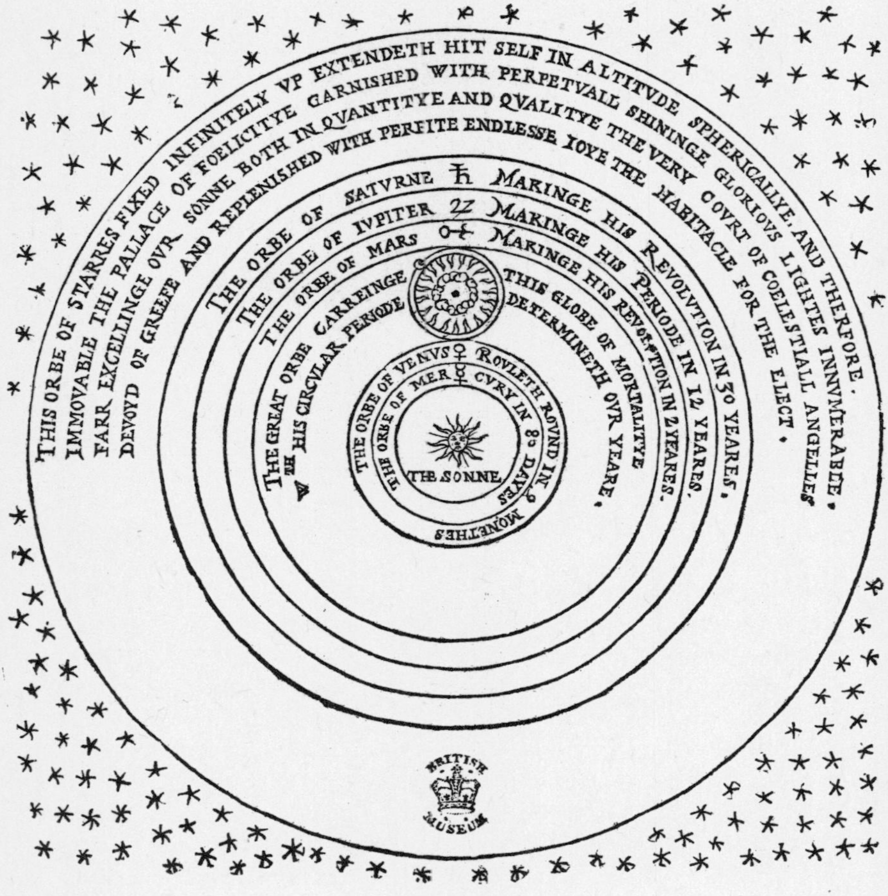

Fig. 8. Thomas Digges' representation of the universe. From his enlarged edition of Leonard Digges, *Prognostication Euerlasting* (London, 1576).

Latin verse constantly echoes the majesty of the Lucretian lines. To Bruno, Lucretius was as a living teacher, and many elements in his philosophy were direct developments from Lucretius. Thus the behaviour of the Lucretian atoms provided something closely akin to Bruno's view of cosmic metabolism[12] and suggested to Bruno the "minimum" and the "discrete continuum." On another level, Bruno received from Lucretius the vision of the dignity of the human soul. But especially the view of an infinite universe which constituted the field of the ceaseless motion of the Lucretian atoms foreshadows some of Bruno's arguments:

> But since I have taught that the most solid bodies of matter fly about for ever unvanquished through the ages, come now, let us unfold, whether there be a certain limit to their full sum or not; and likewise the void that we have discovered, or room or space, in which all things are carried on, let us see clearly whether it is all altogether bounded or spreads out limitless and immeasurably deep.
>
> The whole universe then is bounded in no direction of its ways; for then it would be bound to have an extreme point. Now it is seen that nothing can have an extreme point, unless there be something beyond to bound it, so that there is seen to be a spot further than which the nature of our sense cannot follow it. As it is, since we must admit that there is nothing outside the whole sum, it has not an extreme point; it lacks therefore bound and limit. Nor does it matter in which quarter of it you take your stand; so true is it that, whatever place every man takes up, he leaves the whole boundless just as much on every side. Moreover, suppose now that all space were created finite, if one were to run on to the end, to its furthest coasts, and throw a flying dart, would you have it that that dart, hurled with might and main, goes on whither it is sped and flies afar, or do you think that something can check and bar its way? For one or the other you must needs admit and choose. Yet both shut off your escape and constrain you to grant that the universe spreads out free from limit. For whether there is something to check it and bring it about that it arrives not whither it was sped, nor plants itself in the goal, or whether it fares forward, it set not forth from the end. In this way I will press on, and wherever you shall set the furthest coasts, I shall ask what then becomes of the dart. It will come to pass that nowhere

[12] Cf. p. 71.

can a bound be set, and room for flight ever prolongs the chance of flight. Lastly, before our eyes one thing is seen to bound another; air is as a wall between the hills, and mountains between tracts of air; land bounds the sea, and again sea bounds all lands; yet the universe in truth there is nothing to limit outside.[13]

The poem of Lucretius had been rediscovered in the youth of Cusanus[14] and had doubtless exercised its influence on him. Thus the Lucretian conception of the essential unity and infinity of the universe reached Bruno both directly and through Cusanus. Before considering Nicolaus of Cusa's vision of infinity we will turn for a moment to earlier thinkers. Lucretius himself looks back to Democritus, and there persisted from early Greek thinkers right through to the late Middle Ages a form of thought very different from Aristotelianism and especially from its cosmology as developed by Ptolemy.

From land to land, from century to century, for the most part vaguely or in the form of confused and contradictory rumours, there had travelled the view of a universe infinite and without bound, yet One, a single Whole, embracing an infinity of interrelated parts. Some ancient thinkers had had glimpses of this vision, as had later thinkers, Moslem, Jewish and Christian. Their thought was not unknown to Bruno.

The development of this thought suited well the attitude to which a special appeal was made by the *Timaeus* of Plato, a work familiar in

---

[13] *De rerum natura,* I, 951-80 *seqq.* Cf. also I, 1008-13 (the Infinite Universe compounded of Matter and Void); II, 1048 *seqq.;* VI, 648-79, etc.

That Bruno carried Lucretius round with him we know from the remark of Cotin (cf. p. 136) that Bruno had hired out his copy to John Sambucius, "domesticus aulae Caesaris." Sambucius, physician, poet and humanist, died in 1584.

[14] The poem of Lucretius was rediscovered in 1417 by Poggio Bracciolini (1380-1459) on an expedition during the Council of Constance. He had a copy made and sent to Niccolo Niccoli, who apparently kept it till 1434, making meanwhile the beautiful transcript now in the Laurentian Library. Cf. R. Sabbadini, *Le scoperte dei codici latini e greci ne' secoli XIV e XV* (Florence, 1905); and J. E. Sandys, *History of Classical Scholarship* (Cambridge, 1908), I, 79-80, citing Lehnerdt, *Lucretius in der Renaissance* (1904). The poem was printed s.l. et a. perhaps at Brescia, 1470. It appeared again at Verona in 1486 and the Aldine edition was printed in 1500. The work exercised a great influence on late fifteenth and especially on sixteenth century writers.

monastic libraries at least in the partial version of Chalcidius. The *Timaeus* presents a pantheistic view of the universe as a living creature pervaded by immanent divine soul. The universe of *Timaeus* was created by God, though a certain antecedent substance is postulated: "Why did the Creator make the world? . . . He desired that all things should be like himself. Wherefore he set in order this visible world which he found in disorder."[15] This immanent-transcendent view was especially influential on the Moslem culture that had itself determined much of Western thought in the later Middle Ages.

The Judaeo-Arabian presentation and development of Greek science was of the utmost importance to the rise of science among the Latins. Astronomy, chemistry, mathematics and medicine in Europe bear to this day the imprint of this influence exerted during many centuries. Even more crucial to the development of European thought than any direct achievement of "Arabian" science was the influence of "Arabian" philosophy (the work of Arabic-speaking Persians, Moors, Jews and Christians), and especially the discussion of questions concerning the human soul in its relation to the divine soul and to the universe around man. Free will and predestination, the separate individual existence and the immortality of the soul, the cosmic function of man's spirit, were among the questions that exercised philosophers who used the Arabic tongue.

The consideration of these problems was intimately linked by many of these thinkers with profound changes in the conception of the physical environment of man. The infinity of time and space had been rejected by orthodox Christian thought in mediaeval Europe, but was more or less cautiously set forth in a whole body of Moslem and Jewish writings which were translated into Latin between the twelfth and fifteenth centuries. These conceptions were widely canvassed in the universities of North Italy and France and especially in Padua and Paris. Bruno refers to the Aristotelian commentaries of the Persian Muslim Avicenna (980-1037). Often cited by Bruno is the *Fons vitae* of Avicebron (at that time believed to have been a Moor and now recognized as the Spanish Jewish

[15] *Timaeus*, 29-30. Cf. Jowett, *Dialogues of Plato* (3rd ed., 1892), III, 353.

poet, statesman and philosopher Solomon Ibn Gabirol (1021-1058). This author's neo-platonism was very congenial to Bruno. Again, Bruno often cites the Spanish Moor Averroes (1126-1198). Averroes practised medicine and held the office of judge, but it is his philosophy that has exercised a profound influence on the course of European thought. His view both of the eternity of the world and of the unity of intellect or soul fitted well with Bruno's cosmological thought.

Most remarkable among the students at Padua and most crucial for the development of Bruno's thought was Nicolaus, born in 1401 at Cues in the Rhineland, and usually known as Nicolaus of Cusa or Cusanus (d. 1464). Educated in the Platonic tradition by the *Brothers of the Common Life* of Deventer, Nicolaus passed at the age of seventeen to Padua, and availed himself of every aspect of the very active intellectual life of that university. He studied law and mathematics, learnt the Greek language and became familiar with much classical literature. He also entered into the study of Arabian scholasticism. He passed to an ecclesiastical career and became Bishop of Brixen in the Tyrol and also Cardinal.

The contrast between the modern bias toward observation and the scholastic interest in ratiocination had declared itself at Padua.[16] No less is the contrast between the mind of Cusanus as revealed in his writings and his actual life course.[17] An ardent advocate of reform in ecclesiastical institutions and of the widest tolerance, he found himself at the Council of Bâle in 1436 forced to decide between loyal acceptance of the Papacy or uncompromising revolt. He decided to support the Papacy and never swerved from this position, though it involved him often in action little in harmony with the exalted thought reflected in

[16] It is noteworthy that Padua, the one Italian university without effective religious tests either for students or for professors, was also the home of the scientific movements of the sixteenth and seventeenth centuries. Yet we shall not be surprised to find that this great institution, freed from theological orthodoxy, nevertheless developed an academic orthodoxy that prevented too easy a path for the great innovators in her midst.

[17] But see a very interesting comparison between the thought of Cusanus and that of Spinoza by Fiorentino in *Bernardino Telesio ossia studi storici su l'idea della natura* (Florence, 1874), II, especially 73 *seqq.*

his writings. His value was at once recognized in Rome, and henceforward he was continuously preoccupied with political and administrative work. Yet he found time for a vivid intellectual life, the record of which remains for us in his books. His philosophy fertilized the course of thought in Europe, and especially through the works of Bruno. In his exquisite little work, the *Vision of God,* Cusanus sets out his view of a universe, limitless beyond conception, informed throughout by the spirit of beauty and of perfection. The further the insight he gains into the nature, physical and spiritual, of any part of the boundless universe, the more he is exalted by the vision, the further he is impelled to pursue his adventure of discovery.

The range of the intellectual interests of Cusanus is remarkable. He was widely read in all literature available in his time, of Christian, pagan, Moslem or Jewish writers. He made great though fruitless efforts toward the reform of the Church. He wrote on the calendar, shewing familiarity with a number of astronomical records and writers on the subject. He was deeply involved in the humanist movement and in the revival of classical learning. He had an inkling of the principles of palaeography, and a surprisingly modern taste in manuscripts. Even more remarkable is it that he had an experimental bias, and in his view of the estimation of weight as an instrument to be applied to the systematic investigation of matter, he was one of the pioneers of the experimental era.[18] Despite all this, Cusanus is a true mediaeval in his pre-

[18] In a work *On Static Experiments* (the fourth Dialogue of his *Idiotae de Sapientia* or *Wisdom of the Simple Man*), he describes experiments that he himself carried out on the floating property of pieces of wood of different sizes and different shapes. Cusanus is the very first in the Western world who employed weighing as a method for discovery of natural laws. Lynn Thorndike has pointed out that in this respect, Cusanus was partially (though only partially) anticipated by Blasius of Parma (fl. 1377) (cf. *History of Magic and Experimental Science,* IV, 75-76 and App. C). Cusanus describes a crucial experiment by which he placed 100 pounds of earth in a pot in which he then planted seeds. He observed that as the seeds grew, the weight of the earth diminished, shewing that they had extracted considerable matter from the earth. The same experiment he repeated, planting growing herbs instead of seeds. He suggests that it is water which is thus extracted from the earth. Moreover, he carried the experiment further by burning the plants in a closed vessel and weighing the ashes. He opines that all the "virtues" of the water must have weight. He suggests that the fertility of soils might be appraised by comparing

occupation with theological analogy in the interpretation of phenomena.

The most important work of Cusanus is called *On Instructed Ignorance*[19] and is concerned with the limits of the knowable. In it he constantly returns to the consideration of an infinite universe. Cusanus is fascinated by the infinite in number and by the conception of continuous subdivision. But especially, when he casts his gaze on the heavens he can conceive no limit to them. The universe, he declares, can have no circumference and no centre, for if it had centre and circumference it would be constrained within a limit, and this is totally impossible. Just as the earth cannot be the centre of the infinite universe, so neither can the sphere of the fixed stars nor any other sphere be its circumference, however much, comparing earth and sky, the earth may appear nearer to the centre, and the heaven nearer to the circumference. Therefore, the earth is not the centre of the eighth or of any other sphere. Nor indeed is the very centre of the universe more within our earth than without it. God is both centre and circumference of the universe. Cusanus assures the reader that wherever the observer is placed in the universe, that will appear to him the centre, so that in our minds we must combine centre and zenith. Moreover, the ancients suffering from uninstructed ignorance, could not apprehend that this earth moves. The earth, he further tells us, is not a mathematical measurable part of the universe any more than a hand is an aliquot part of a man. Each is an integral and necessary part of a whole. Just as light, so also does influence pass from star to star. He assumes that other celestial bodies are inhabited. While rejecting the arrogation of a supreme position for our earth, he sees no reason to esteem it altogether vile. "It is impossible," he says, "for man to know whether the region of earth is more or less noble than

---

their respective weights. Moreover, he suggests that by properly devised experiments, the weight of the whole earth may be ascertained. Again he suggests that the force of the wind could be estimated by the weight it is capable of moving. The passage of time throughout both the day and the year he proposes to record by a method of weights.

[19] *De docta ignorantia.* First published in *Opuscula varia,* s.l. et d., perhaps *circ.* 1489. The most accessible edition is that of Basle, 1565 (in the *Opera omnia*). The views described above will be found also in other works of Cusanus.

another [region of the universe]. . . . Perhaps the inhabitants of other stars are nobler than ourselves. We imagine the inhabitants of the sun to partake of its fiery nature and to be more spiritual than the inhabitants of the aqueous moon." The denizens of each, he surmises, are fitted to their habitation.[20] From the *Timaeus,* Cusanus draws the conception of the whole universe as animated by a single Soul emanating from the Godhead.[21] In the interpretation of this conception, he utilizes the symbolism of the Trinity.[22]

We shall find the influence of Cusanus constantly permeating Bruno's thought.[23] It is noteworthy in connection with Bruno's relation to Copernicus that the latter was quite unaffected by the writings of Cusanus. The cast of mind of Copernicus was utterly different from that of Cusanus. Bruno too had neither the experimental bias nor the Christian mysticism of the Cusan. Moreover, in worldly outlook as in temperament, the ecclesiastical statesman was poles apart from the wandering fugitive, nor was it solely untoward fate that determined Bruno's very different fortune. Yet the cosmic view that evoked those paeans of Bruno was, in essence, the cosmic view of Cusanus. Bruno uses the very phrases of Cusanus and we must believe that he drew from him the first apprehension of his impassioned vision of infinity. The vision is

---

[20] Cf. especially *De docta ignorantia,* Lib. II, Capp. 11-12, for these views.

[21] Cf. especially *De docta ignorantia,* Lib. II, Capp. 8-10. Again, "Intellectus autem iste in nostra anima eapropter in sensum descendit, ut sensibile ascendat in ipsum. Ascendit ad intellectum sensibile ut intelligentia ad ipsum descendat. . . ." (*De coniecturis,* Lib. II, Cap. 16); and "Quia mens est quoddam divinum semen sua vi complicans omnium rerum exemplaria notionaliter: tunc a Deo, a quo hanc vim habet, eo ipso quod esse recepit est simul et in convenienti terra locatum, ubi fructum facere possit et ex se rerum universitatem notionaliter explicare, alioqui haec vis seminalis frustra data ipsi esset, si non fuisset addita opportunitas in actum prorumpendi" (*Idiotae,* Lib. III, Cap. 5). Cf. Ernst Cassirer, *Individuum und Kosmos . . .* (Leipzig, 1927), pp. 47 *seqq.* Cf. also *infra* p. 86.

[22] Cf. especially *De docta ignorantia,* Lib. II, Cap. 7. Cf. also *De coniecturis,* Lib. I, Cap. 11 with figure.

[23] A good study of the relation between the philosophies of Cusanus and of Bruno will be found in F. Fiorentino, *Il panteismo di Giordano Bruno* (Naples, 1861), Chap. 2. Cf. also M. M. Gorce, *L'essor de la pensée au moyen age* (Paris, 1933).

repeated many times in his works.[24] Following Cusanus again, Bruno is clear that in an infinite universe there can be no absolute position, neither higher nor lower, neither centre nor circumference:

To a body of infinite size there can be ascribed neither centre nor boundary. . . . Just as we regard ourselves as at the centre of that [universally] equidistant circle, which is the great horizon and the limit of our own encircling ethereal region, so doubtless the inhabitants of the moon believe themselves at the centre [of a great horizon] that embraces this earth, the sun and the other stars, and is the boundary of the radii of their own horizon. Thus the Earth no more than any other world is at the centre; moreover no points constitute determined celestial poles for our earth, just as she herself is not a definite and determined pole to any other point of the ether, or of the world space; and the same is true of all other bodies. From various points of view these may all be regarded either as centres, or as points on the circumference, as poles, or zeniths and so forth. Thus the earth is not in the centre of the universe; it is central only to our own surrounding space.[25]

With Cusanus too, Bruno accepts the Averroan doctrine of the eternity of the universe. "There are not," Nicolaus had said, "three Times, past, present and future, but one perfect Time."[26] Infinite Time was for Bruno a mode of Infinite Space.

"It is then unnecessary," says Bruno,

to investigate whether there be beyond the heaven Space, Void or Time. For there is a single general space, a single vast immensity which we may freely

[24] Cf. *Op. lat.*, I, i, 68, 70 *seqq.* Many such passages might be quoted from all Bruno's works, including the one here translated. Cf. *De immenso,* Lib. I, where especially Cap. 1 unfolds a magnificent vision of the infinity of the universe, and of the vast range and virtue of the mind which informs this universe (*Op. lat.,* I, i, 202-6, etc.). Or again those wonderful lines in Cap. 7 (*Op. lat.,* I, i, 226). Cf. also p. 370. But we have not space here even to refer to a tithe of the noble passages in which Bruno's spirit soars toward apprehension of the infinite.

[25] *De l'infinito universo et mondi,* Dial. II, pp. 40-41 (Gentile, *Op. ital.,* I, 316; Lagarde, *Op. ital.,* I, 328, 329).

[26] *Liber excitationum,* Lib. I (*Op. omnia* [Basle, 1565], pp. 367-68). Cf. *De immenso,* Lib. I, Cap. 12 (*Op. lat.,* I, i, 244). Cf. also Cusanus, "ut infinitus et aeternus mundus cadat absque proportione, ab absoluta infinitate et aeternitate, et unum ab unitate," *De docta ignorantia,* Lib. II, Cap. 4 (*Op. omnia,* p. 28).

call *Void;* in it are innumerable globes like this on which we live and grow. This space we declare to be infinite; since neither reason, convenience, possibility, sense-perception nor nature assign to it a limit. In it are an infinity of worlds of the same kind as our own. For there is no reason nor defect of nature's gifts, either of active or of passive power, to hinder the existence of other worlds throughout space, which is identical in natural character with our own space. . . . Beyond the imaginary convex circumference of the universe is Time. For there is the measure and nature of motion, since similar moving bodies are there.[27]

Bruno thus imagined an infinity of worlds, each finite like our own, and each pursuing its own course within the infinite universe. The inhabitants of Bruno's numberless worlds are, like those of the worlds of Cusanus, in conformity with the conditions of their habitats.[28]

Bruno never uses Christian symbolism. The Wisdom literature appealed strongly to him; and his invocations of the joy and release brought by his cosmic views are reminiscent of certain Old Testament invocations of Wisdom.

In his valedictory address at Wittenberg, Bruno passes easily without any sense of incongruity from Juno and Minerva to his paean of praise of Wisdom with quotations both from the Apocrypha and from the Old Testament. He transfers to Wisdom his conception of infinite unity:

If all things are in common among friends, the most precious is Wisdom. What can Juno give which thou canst not receive from Wisdom? What mayest thou admire in Venus which thou mayest not also contemplate in Wisdom? Her beauty is not small, for the lord of all things taketh delight in her. Her I have loved and diligently sought from my youth up.

I prayed unto the Lord, and besought him and with my whole heart I said, O God of my fathers, and Lord of mercy who hast made all things by thy word, and ordained man through thy wisdom, that he should have dominion over the creatures which thou hast made;

---

[27] *De l'infinito universo et mondi,* Dial. V, p. 154 (Gentile, *Op. ital.,* I, 404; Lagarde, *Op. ital.,* I, 389).

[28] *De docta ignorantia,* Lib. II, Cap. 12 (*Op. omnia,* pp. 40-41). Cf. *De l'infinito universo et mondi,* Dial. III, p. 99 (Gentile, *Op. ital.,* I, 362; Lagarde, *Op. ital.,* I, 360).

Give me wisdom, that sitteth by thy throne and reject not thy servant. O send her out of thy holy heavens from the throne of thy glory, that being present she may labour with me, that I may know wherein I fail and what is pleasing to thee. For she knoweth and understandeth all things, and she shall lead me soberly in my doings and preserve me in her power.[29]

God, that most fertile Mind, will indeed send Wisdom, but what sort of Wisdom? Only such as can be adapted to our mental vision, in the shadow of light; as from the Sun who cannot be reached nor apprehended, who in himself continueth mysteriously and steadfastly in infinite light, yet his pervasive radiance descendeth to us by the emission of rays and is communicated and diffused throughout all things. For as firstly there is the essence of the sun that can barely be attained by the Mind alone; secondly, the substance of the sun, which occupieth and encompasseth his own orb and liveth where he liveth; and thirdly there is the action or operation of the sun, which comprehendeth all things and is comprehended by all things; in no other way is it possible to consider the threefold sun of the understanding: firstly as the essence of the divine; secondly as the substance of the universe, which is the reflection of the first; thirdly as the light of the perception of those who participate in life and knowledge.

This view is supported by citation from the Cabbala, from the "Orphic theologians," and from Job.

Listen to Job:

Where shall wisdom be found? And where is the place of understanding? Man knoweth not the price thereof; neither is it found easily in the land of the living; The depth saith, It is not in me: and the sea saith, It is not with me. It is hid from the eyes of all living and kept close from the fowls of the air.

That is from the *numina,* those stars, those fiery gods and watery orbs which course across the firmament and over the space of the ether, as though by their regular flight and speedy circling they make their own orbs.

Destruction and death said, 'We have heard the fame thereof with our ears. God alone understandeth the ways thereof, and he knoweth the place thereof.'[30]

---

[29] Cf. Wisdom of Solomon VIII, 21–IX, 2; IX, 4, 10, 11.
[30] Cf. Job XXVIII, 12-14, 21-23.

In its second mode, Wisdom is most manifest on the surface and body of all created things, for everywhere Wisdom crieth and on all sides her voice is heard.[31] For what are all those things which we see, stars, animals, bodies and the beauty thereof, but the voices and echoes [vestigia] of Wisdom, the works of the Divine Being [divinitatis] that shew forth his lofty providence, in which as in a book may be read most clearly the story of Divine Power, Wisdom and Goodness? For the invisible things of God are discovered through those things which are understood. This thou hast from Scripture. Wilt thou hear more clearly the voices of the assemblies? *The heavens declare the glory of God.*[32] . . . The third mode is within our spirit; it is situate at the helm of our soul, controlling the rudder of the ship in the wild sea of this surging century where it is a lighthouse of the spirit in the surrounding darkness. These three habitations hath divine Wisdom: the first without building, eternal, indeed the very seat of eternity; the second, which is the firstborn, our visible universe; the third, the nextborn, which is the soul of man.[33]

The infinite universe is thus the ever-recurring theme of Bruno's thought. "The one infinite is perfect, in simplicity, of itself, absolutely, nor can aught be greater or better. This is the one Whole, God, universal Nature, occupying all space, of whom naught but infinity can give the perfect image or semblance."[34] He recounts in detail the reasons for his belief that the universe is infinite, meeting every objection based on argument or observation. Whatever aspect of Bruno's thought we are considering, we shall constantly encounter this overwhelming vision. Its awful majesty alone enabled him to support the eight suffering years that culminated in his death.

---

[31] Cf. Proverbs VIII, 1.

[32] Psalms XIX, 1.

[33] *Oratio valedictoria* (*Op.lat.*, I, i, 12-14). Cf. the work here translated, Dedication to Mauvissière, p. 4 (Gentile, *Op. ital.*, I, 270; Lagarde, *Op. ital.*, I, 292) and *De la causa, principio et uno*, Dial. V, p. 122 (Gentile, *Op. ital.*, I, 252; Lagarde, *Op. ital.*, I, 280).

[34] *De immenso*, Lib. II, Cap. 12 (*Op. lat.*, I, i, 307).

c. Astronomy in the Sixteenth Century with Special Reference to England[35]

Close as was the relationship between the cosmic views of Cusanus and of Bruno, the content of their minds shewed the century that separated them. Bruno lived in the dawning age of men of science. Though he was a man of science neither by temper nor training, nor by capacity, he gives in his works several figures illustrating simple experiments. We recognize also the boy who noted the changed aspect of Mt. Cicada in the observer of the flight of birds.[36] For his close reasoning on simple phenomena must also be based on observation. This attitude is noteworthy as out of tone with his training and the academic atmosphere of his time. But we must not be led astray into the idea that his conception of the 'minimum' had any relation to the invention of the microscope, which was too late to be known to him. Doubtless he is echoing Lucretius when he exclaims concerning the tiny members of animalcula, their heart, nerves and viscera: "The minimum of nature or reality is amazingly smaller than the smallest perceptible minimum. There is no art to define it."[37] His reflections on the apparent motions of the heavenly bodies permeate his works.[38] To him the reflections were always more interesting than observations.

---

[35] It is hardly possible to observe a strictly logical sequence in dealing with the views of Bruno and the influences on him. This survey of contemporary astronomy seems, however, most appropriate here.

[36] *De immenso,* Lib. II, Cap. 3 (*Op. lat.,* I, i, 266).

[37] *De triplici minimo et mensura,* Lib. I, Cap. 9 (*Op. lat.,* I, iii, 169). Cf. Lucretius: "There are living things sometimes so small that a third part of them could by no means be seen. Of what kind must we think any one of their entrails be? What of the round ball of their heart or eye? What of their members? What of their limbs? How small are they? Still more, what of the several first-beginnings whereof their soul and the nature of their mind must needs be formed? Do you not see how fine and tiny they are? Moreover, whatever things breathe out a pungent savour . . . learn that many idols of things wander abroad in many ways with no powers, unable to be perceived" (*De rerum natura,* IV, 116-28).

[38] One of the clearest of these passages, in which it is obvious that Bruno has confirmed his views by simple experiment, is *De immenso,* Lib. IV, Cap. 5 (*Op. lat.,* I, ii, 25) but many other such passages will be found both in the Latin and Italian works, including that here translated.

In spite of Bruno's strictures on the backwardness of learning at Oxford, there is evidence of the repercussions of the new astronomy there. Thus in 1576 the question assigned for disputation by candidates incepting as Masters of Art at Oxford was: *An terra quiescat in medio mundi.* Perhaps we may even detect an echo of Bruno's visit to Oxford of 1583 in the topic of 1588, *An sint plures mundi.*[39] But London far more than Oxford was a centre of astronomical study and speculation. Copernican views had been discussed there for a generation and several mathematicians resident there had been feeling their way to a conception of a universe devoid of the traditional frontier. The earliest in whom we can trace the new astronomical views is Robert Recorde (1510-1558). His *Castle of Knowledge containing the explication of the Sphere both Celestiall and Materiall* of 1556 is in the conventional form of a dialogue between a *Master* and a *Schollar.* The former, after explaining the Ptolemaic view, glances at the Copernican system by raising the question of "the quietness of the earth" inherent in the Ptolemaic scheme. Almost echoing Copernicus, he reminds his pupil:

> Not only Eraclides Ponticus, a great Philosopher, and two great clerkes of Pythagoras schole, Philolaus and Ecphantus, were of the contrary opinion, but also Nicias Syracusius, and Aristarchus Samius, seeme with strong arguments to approue it; but the reasons are to difficulte for this firste introduction, and therefore I will omit them till an other time. And so will I do the reasons that Ptolemy, Theon and others doo alleage, to prooue the earthe to bee without motion; and the rather, bycause those reasons doo not proceede so demonstrablye, but they may be answered fully, of him that holdeth the contrarye. I mean, concerning the circularre motion; marye, direct motion of the centre of the world seemeth more easy to be confuted, and that by the same reasons, whiche were before alleaged for prouing the earthe to be in the middle and centre of the worlde.

The *Schollar* uses the term "absurdity" of the non-Ptolemaic view and the *Master* then declares, "That is truly to be gathered; howe bee it Copernicus, a man of greate learninge, of muche experience and of

---

[39] Francis R. Johnson, *Astronomical Thought in Renaissance England* (Baltimore, Johns Hopkins Press, 1938), p. 181, citing Andrew Clark, *Register of the University of Oxford* (Oxford, 1887), II, 170.

wondrefull diligence in observation hath renewed the opinion of Aristarchus Samius." He warns him, "You are to younge to be a good judge in so great a matter . . ." and even promises, "At other time, as I sayd, I will so declare his supposition that you shall not only wonder to hear it, but also peradventure be as earnest then to credite it as you are now to condemn it."

Very few months after this work of Recorde, we get a definite opinion from John Dee (1527-1608), who states in a preface to John Feild's *Ephemeris anni 1557*[40] that he had persuaded Feild to compile these tables, since the work of Copernicus, Rheticus and Rheinhald had rendered the old tables no longer satisfactory.

Dee was a friend of Leonard Digges (d. *circ.* 1571), the maker of an early form of telescope. He was also the teacher of Leonard's son Thomas Digges (d. 1595), the first professional astronomer known to us who sets forth the theory of an infinite universe. In 1573 Thomas Digges published in his *Alae seu scalae mathematicae,* dedicated to Lord Burleigh, the record of a series of observations of the new star in Cassiopeia, discovered the previous year. His exaltation at the discovery is reflected in the preface on "this stupendous creation of God." The incongruity of the Ptolemaic scheme had impressed Digges. He likens the system with its orbs and epicycles to a monstrous picture of a man with head, feet and limbs each taken from the representation of a separate individual. He insists on the need of careful observations to construct a more seemly anatomy of parts joined in perfect proportion and symmetry, and he prophesies that "the paradox of Copernicus" (Paradoxum hactenus explosum) concerning the earth's motion will be firmly demonstrated by observation and not by argument. He is uncertain whether the earth's motion is the sole cause of apparent change of size of the new star. His work is typical of that twilight between the ratiocinatory and the demonstrative, the scholastic and the scientific, the mediaeval and the modern, in which Bruno's stormy and contradictory life-span was passed.

In 1576 came the pronouncement by Thomas Digges for an infinite

[40] *Ephemeris anni 1557 currentis iusta Copernici et Reinhaldi canones . . . supputata ac examinata ad meridianum Londinensem* (London, 1556).

universe. This was in an "Addition" to a new edition of the *Prognostication Everlastinge* of his father Leonard Digges. The work of Thomas Digges is introduced by a figure (Fig. 8) showing a universe with central sun, and stars "fixed infinitely up." The figure is followed by a preface "To the Reader" in which Digges explains that among "Sondry faultes that by negligence in printing have crept into my father's Generall Prognostication . . . I found a description or Modill of the world and situation of Spheres Caelestiall and Elementare according to the doctrine of Ptolome," and he decides to give the Copernican scheme. He is certain that "Copernicus mente not as some have fondly excused him, to deliuer these grounds of the Earthe's mobility onely as Mathematicall principles, fayned and not as Philosophicall truly auerred." Moreover, Digges declares, "This ball euery 24 hours by naturall, uniforme and wonderfull slie and smooth motion rouleth rounde, making with his Periode our naturall daye, whereby it seems to us that the huge infinite immoueable Globe should sway and tourne about."[41]

The "Addition" itself is entitled *A Perfit Description of the Caelestiall Orbes according to the most aunciente doctrine of the Pythagoreans, latelye reuiued by Copernicus and by Geometricall Demonstrations approued.* In it Thomas Digges sets forth the Copernican theory of a universe of concentric revolving spheres. But he interpolates a somewhat confused exposition, which is in no way derived from Copernicus, of an infinite universe with stars stretching through endless space (Fig. 8):

Heerein can wee neuer sufficiently admire thys wonderfull and incomprehensible huge frame of goddes woorks proponed to our senses, seinge fyrst thys baull of the earth wherein we moue, to the common sorte seemeth greate, and yet in respecte of the Moones Orbe is very small, but compared with *Orbis magnus* wherein it is caried, it scarcely retayneth any sensible proportion, so merueilously is that Orbe of Annuall motion greater than this little darcke starre wherein we liue. But that *Orbis magnus* beinge as is before declared but as a poynct in respect of the immensity of that immoueable heauen, we may easily consider what little portion of gods frame, our Elementare corruptible worlde is, but neuer sufficiently be able to admire the immensity of the Rest. Especially of that fixed Orbe garnished with lightes

[41] Fol. M. 2.

innumerable and reaching up in *Sphaericall altitude* without ende. Of whiche lightes Celestiall it is to bee thoughte that we onely behoulde sutch as are in the inferioure partes of the same Orbe, and as they are hygher, so seeme they of lesse and lesser quantity, euen tyll our sighte beinge not able farder to reache or conceyue, the greatest part rest by reason of their wonderfull distance inuisible unto us. And this may wel be thought of us to be the gloriouse court of the great God, whose unsearcheable worcks inuisible we may partly by these his visible coniecture, to whose infinit power and maiesty such an infinit place surmountinge all other both in quantity and quality only is conueniente.[42]

While this passage establishes the priority of Thomas Digges among astronomers, it must be remembered that the infinity of the universe had been postulated a century earlier in the philosophical works of Nicolaus of Cusa.

The work of William Gilbert (1540-1603) *On the Magnet,*[43] which appeared in London in 1600, is usually regarded as the first major work of experimental science by an Englishman. The last part of this book is devoted to a general consideration of the solar system, and Gilbert comes to the conclusion that there is a "magnetic diurnal revolution" of the earth. He postpones discussion of the orbital motion of the earth, though referring to Copernicus as "the first who attempted to illustrate the phenomena of moving bodies by new hypotheses."

While avoiding Copernican discussion, Gilbert betrays that he had been reading Bruno or had held discussion with him or with someone who held similar views concerning the nature of the heavenly bodies. "Who," he asks,

has ever made out that the stars which we call fixed are in one and the same sphere, or has established by reasoning that there are any real and, as it were, adamantine sphaeres? No one has ever proved this, nor is there a doubt but that just as the planets are at unequal distances from the earth, so are these vast and multitudinous lights separated from the Earth by vary-

[42] The whole of the *Perfit Description* is printed by Francis R. Johnson and Sanford V. Larkey in "Thomas Digges, the Copernican System, and the Idea of the Infinity of the Universe in 1576," *Huntington Library Bulletin,* No. 5 (April 1934).

[43] *De magnete magnetisque corporibus et de magno magnete tellure philosophia nova plurimis argumentis demonstrata* (London, 1600).

ing and very remote altitudes; they are not set in any sphaerick frames or firmament. The intervals of some are from their unfathomable distance matter of opinion rather than of verification; others less than they are yet very remote, and at varying distances, either in that most subtle quintessence the thinnest aether or in the void. . . . How immeasurable then must be the space which stretches to those remotest of fixed stars! How vast and immense the depth of that imaginary sphere! How far removed from the Earth must be the most widely separated stars and at a distance transcending all sight, all skill, all thought! How monstrous, then would such a motion be!

It is evident then that all the heavenly bodies, set as if in destined places, are there formed unto spheres, that they tend to their own centres, and that round them there is a confluence of all their parts. And if they have motion, that motion will rather be that of each round its own centre, as that of the Earth is; or a forward movement of the centre in an orbit, as that of the Moon; . . . But there can be no movement of infinity and of an infinite body, and therefore no diurnal revolution of that vastest *Primum mobile*.[44]

In a work that appeared long posthumously in 1651,[45] Gilbert refers to the same theme. In it he wavers between the schemes of Copernicus and of Brahe, inclining to the latter. Two pages of the book are devoted to a discussion of Bruno's astronomical views but the question of infinite space is now hardly mentioned. The book adds something, however, to our knowledge of the relation of Bruno and Gilbert, for it gives a diagram (Fig. 9), undiscussed in the text, which recalls both Bruno's views and the diagram of Digges.

In the minds of some at least of his contemporaries, Gilbert's views were closely associated with those of Bruno. Thus in a letter to Thomas Hariot (1560-1620) from Sir William Lower, dated 21st June, 1610:

Wee . . . were a consideringe of Kepler's reasons by which he indeauors to ouerthrow Nolanus and Gilberts opinions concerninge the immensitie of the spheere of the starres and that opinion particularlie of Nolanus by which he affirmed that the eye beinge placed in anie parte of the universe, the apparence would be still all one as unto us here. When I was a sayinge that although Kepler had sayd somethinge the most that mighte be urged for

---

[44] Gilbert, *On the Loadstone,* trans. from the Latin by Silvanus P. Thompson (London, Chiswick Press, 1900), pp. 215-16.

[45] *Philosophia nova* (Amsterdam, 1651).

that opinion of Nolanus, yet of one principall thinge he had not thought.[46] . . .

Among Hariot's papers there is one on which are noted the words "Nolanus de immenso et mundi." [47] Hariot has been claimed as anticipating Kepler (with whom he corresponded) in speculations concerning the ellipticity of planetary orbits, and as anticipating Descartes on quadratic equations. He was perhaps the first to bring all terms of an equation to one side and equate to zero, and he pointed out that an equation has as many roots as it has powers or dimensions. Hariot made improvements too in mathematical notation. His telescope was said to have a magnification by 50, and he made a great many observations with it. He was a leader of the group that ultimately became the "School of Night." We are thus not surprised to find him considering Bruno's views. Much of Hariot's work remained unpublished, and has been discovered only in the present century.

Turning now to Continental writers on astronomy, we consider first Girolamo Fracastoro, whose name is given to a speaker in the work here translated. Fracastoro was a very influential humanist and physician.[48] He had been a fellow student of Copernicus at the University of Padua. Bruno cannot have met him, as he died when the Nolan was a small child. Though best known for his medical works, Fracastoro made varied contributions to scientific thought. In his work on *A Single Centre of the Universe* (1538) he opposes certain details in the current Ptolemaic epicyclic scheme of planetary movement.[49]

---

[46] Quoted by Yates in *A Study of "Love's Labour's Lost,"* p. 94, from B. M. Additional MS 6789, ff. 425-26. Miss Yates notes that this passage was first observed by Henry Stevens, *Hariot and His Associates* (London, 1900).

[47] This was first brought to notice by Miss Ethel Seaton in a paper read before the Elizabethan Literary Society in February 1933.

[48] Cf. Charles and Dorothea Singer, "The Scientific Position of Girolamo Fracastoro (1478?-1553)," *Annals of Medical History,* Vol. I, No. 1 (New York, 1917).

[49] *Homocentrica sive de stellis,* first published in 1538. Cf. especially § 2, Chap. 2. For Fracastoro's cosmological and astronomical views, see J. L. E. Dreyer, *History of Planetary Systems* (Cambridge, 1906), and G. Rossi, *Fracastoro in relazione all' Aristotelismo e alle scienze nel rinascimento* (Pisa, 1892). For other passages where Bruno draws on Fracastoro, see F. Tocco, *Le opere latine di Giordano Bruno esposte e confrontate con le italiane* (Florence, 1889). Cf. also *infra* p. 102.

Bruno cites as sympathetic to the new insurgent astronomical views Palingenio (whom he imagines to be a German), author of the *Zodiac of Life*.[50] Among eminent Germans Bruno mentions also Paracelsus, "that prince of physicians who ranks alone with Hippocrates."[51] Bruno cites too Cornelius Agrippa (1486-1535), a figure not unlike Paracelsus and Bruno himself in the unhappiness and misadventures of his life and in the extravagance of his writings.[52]

Bruno adopts the revolutionary deduction of Tycho from the observations in 1572 of a new star and in 1577 of a great comet far more distant than the moon. That such ephemeral bodies could suddenly appear at these distances disproved the current view of the immutable character of the "ethereal regions" and of the bodies within them. "All the stars," says Bruno, "have motion, even those 'fixed' stars of which our sun is one. Nor are the comets in anywise different from other planets but for their apparent difference of position. Whereby their light is sometimes as though exposed to us in a slanting mirror." He even declares, "These things were discovered by me some lustres back and were proved by reason ('interior sense'). But now at last I may accept that they are confirmed by the learned Dane Tycho who by his wise talent hath discov-

---

[50] Cf. Bruno's *Valedictory Oration* to the professors and the audience at Wittenberg University, 1588 (*Op. lat.*, I, i, 17). Palingenio's poem is dedicated to Ercole d'Este, Duke of Ferrara, and he himself is identified with Pietro Manzoli of Ferrara. The *Zodiacus vitae* appeared first in 1530 and again at Lyons, 1552, and in many subsequent editions. The author propounds eight finite spheres and an infinite *ninth* sphere beyond. Palingenio is cited also in *De immenso*, Lib. VIII, Cap. 2, and again in Cap. 4 in connection with the views of Plato and those of Pseudo-Dionysius the Areopagite. Cf. *Op. lat.*, I, ii, 292 *seqq.*

[51] *Op. lat.*, I, i, 17 (see above, note 50), and again in the Preface to the Lullian *De lampade combinatoria* dedicated to the Rector and Senate of Wittenberg University. *Op. lat.*, II, ii, 234.

[52] *Op. lat.*, II, ii, 235 (see above, note 51). Agrippa started life as a soldier, but soon turned to teaching, and held a series of posts; he lectured on Hebrew, on theology, and on the writings of Hermes Trismegistus; he was Syndic and Orator to the city of Mainz, practised medicine in Lyons, entered the service of Margaret of Austria and finally was historiographer to the Emperor Charles V. Bruno remarks that Agrippa comments on himself rather than on Lull! Agrippa holds an honourable place among the heralds of "Nature Philosophy" and was one of the earliest to take up the defence of the hapless victims accused of witchcraft.

ered many things." [53] He quotes Cornelius Gemma's remark in the same sense concerning the comet and cites Roeslin (whom he calls the German physician Helyseus).[54] He refers also to Cardan (1501-76).[55]

He cites too the information of Pico della Mirandola that Leo Hebraeus had invented an instrument whereby he had observed two "motionless" stars occupying positions differing by two degrees from their positions observed later in the same year.[56] For the understanding of such things, says Bruno,

> The difficulty proceedeth from a false method and wrong hypothesis—namely of the weight and immobility of the earth, the position of the *primum mobile* with the other seven, eight, nine or more [spheres] on which stars are implanted, impressed, plastered, nailed, knotted, glued, sculptured or painted—and that these stars do not reside in the same space as our own star, named by us Earth.[57]

---

[53] *De immenso,* Lib. I, Cap. 5 (*Op. lat.,* I, i, 218-19). Tycho Brahe (1546-1601), Danish astronomer, opened his career by observing a new star in Cassiopeia on 11th November, 1572, of which he printed an account in the following year. From 1576 he systematically studied the heavens for 21 years at his famous laboratory *Urania* on the Baltic island of Hveen. In 1588 Tycho published his own system of the world. The earth is the centre of it and centre also of the orbits of sun, moon and fixed stars. The sun is centre of the orbits of the five planets. This system is a mere alternative to that of Copernicus, since all the computations of the positions of heavenly bodies are identical for the two. In Tycho's diagram of the universe, the stars are represented in a sphere. His universe was thus Ptolemaic *and* Copernican.

[54] *De immenso,* Lib. IV, Cap. 13 (*Op. lat.,* I, ii, 70-74). Cornelius Gemma (1535-1577) was born and passed his life at Louvain, where he occupied the chair of medicine. He occupied himself largely with astrology and mathematics but is remembered for his observations of an eclipse of the moon in 1569 and of the new star in Cassiopeia, which appeared in 1572. He recorded this star on 9th November, two days before it was seen by Tycho Brahe. His work attracted the attention of Galileo.

Helisaeus or Elyseus Roeslin of Strassbourg became physician to the Count of Hanover. He published several astronomical works of which the first was *Theoria nova coelestium meteorum* (Strassbourg, 1578). He was also the author of a work on medical astrology, 1609.

[55] Cf. below, p. 196.

[56] *De immenso,* Lib. III, Cap. 10 (*Op. lat.,* I, i, 395). Leo Hebraeus, the inventor of "Jacob's staff" for measuring the position of stars, was the French Jew Levi ben Gerson (1288-1344), philosopher and astronomer.

[57] *De l'infinito universo et mondi,* Dial. IV, pp. 151-52 (Gentile, *Op. ital.,* I, 402; Lagarde, *Op. ital.,* I, 388).

Bruno also recalls the observation of a new star in 1585 by Olaus Cimber, and the Landgrave William of Hesse's "renewal to memory" of the observations of Rothmann ten years earlier. In this connection Bruno, who cites both ancient and mediaeval observations, remarks that this confirms Pliny's report of the star seen by Hipparchus in 125 B.C. "Veritas temporis filia," exclaims Bruno, recalling that Aristotle, Aeschylus and Hippocrates of Chios had all asserted that comets are planets. "We now see that comets, planets, and our earth are all one kind." [58]

d. Cosmic Metabolism

We turn from the more astronomical to the more philosophical elements of Bruno's cosmic views.

From Lucretius and certain Renaissance Lucretians such as Fracastoro,[59] Bruno drew his conception of what he calls the *Minima* from which all things are formed. The diverse multiplicity of phenomena he attributed to the grouping of these "minima" which are in eternal motion, constantly leaving yet constantly tending to return to "their own natural body and place." Thus he envisaged an eternal process of what we may call *cosmic metabolism*. Death was but a stage in this process, while life was a quality inherent to a greater or lesser degree in every part of nature. "From the Minimum everything groweth and every magnitude is reduced to the minimum"; and "the Minimum buildeth up to the many and to the innumerable and infinite." [60]

As Semina are aggregated around bodies, atoms are added to adjacent parts, so the body with its members takes its rise; but as these parts are expelled from the centre, so the bodies, however well knit, are gradually dissolved.[61]

---

[58] *De immenso,* Lib. VI, Cap. 19 (*Op. lat.,* I, ii, 228-29). For the Renaissance illustrations of this phrase, *"Veritas temporis filia,"* see F. Saxl in *Philosophy and History: Essays Presented to E. Cassirer* (Warburg Library, London, 1936).

[59] Cf. pp. 68 and 102.

[60] *De minimo,* Lib. III, Cap. 2 and Lib. IV, Cap. 1 (*Op. lat.,* I, iii, 237 and 269).

[61] *De immenso,* Lib. II, Cap. 5 (*Op. lat.,* I, i, 273).

When we consider . . . the being and substance of that universe in which we are immutably set, we shall discover that neither we ourselves nor any substance doth suffer death; for nothing is in fact diminished in its substance, but all things, wandering through infinite space, undergo change of aspect.[62]

The universe being infinite, and the bodies thereof transmutable, all are therefore constantly dispersed and constantly reassembled; they send forth their substance, and receive within themselves wandering substance. Nor doth it appear to me absurd but on the contrary most fitting and natural that finite transmutations may occur to a subject; wherefore particles of [elemental] earth may wander through the ethereal region and may traverse vast space now to this body, now to that, just as we see such particles change their position, their disposition and their form when they are yet close to us. Whence we deduce that if this earth be eternal, it is not so by virtue of the stability of any one part or individual, but through vicissitudes of many parts, some being expelled therefrom and their place taken by others. Thus soul and intelligence persist while the body is ever changing and renewed, part by part. This may be observed also in animals which survive only by absorption and evacuation. Whoever considers well, will recognize that we have not in youth the same flesh as in childhood, nor in old age the same as in youth: for we suffer perpetual transmutation, whereby we receive a perpetual flow of fresh atoms, while those that we have received are ever leaving us.[63]

The world is made up of "minima" or "monads" which, though sometimes equated with atoms, are a philosophical rather than a material conception and have in them some of the qualities of the whole. They bear some resemblance to the *semina* of Bruno's predecessor Fracastoro, being associated with some of the qualities of life. They perhaps provided a suggestion to Leibnitz for his Monads:

Concerning those prime indivisible bodies from which the whole universe was originally composed, we must believe that they undergo certain vicissitudes through the immensity of space whereby they ebb and flow hither and

[62] *De l'infinito universo et mondi,* "Introductory Epistle," (Argument of the Fifth Dialogue) p. 24 (Gentile, *Op. ital.*, I, 282; Lagarde, *Op. ital.*, I, 303).

[63] *Ibid.*, Dial. II, pp. 47-48 (Gentile, *Op. ital.*, I, 321; Lagarde, *Op. ital.*, I, 332).

thither. And if, by divine providence, they do not form new bodies nor dissolve the old, they are at least able to do so. For mundane bodies are in fact dissoluble; though either on account of intrinsic quality or through external influence they may persist to eternity, suffering a balanced influx and efflux of atoms; and thus they may remain constant in number, though their corporeal substance be like ours renewed from day to day, from hour to hour, from moment to moment, by the processes of attraction and metabolism [64] of all the parts of the body.[65]

Bruno does not seem consistently to envisage the monad with the specific varied shapes of the Lucretian atoms.[66] In the work here translated, Theophilus asserts that the infinite may contain dissimilar finites, such as earth, water, etc., which unite by the concourse of their innumerable minimal parts or atoms:

There are many dissimilar finite bodies within a single infinity. . . . Many continuous parts form a unity; . . . as with liquid mud. There throughout and in every part, water is continuous with water, earthy matter with earthy matter; wherefore, since the concourse of the atoms of earth, and the atoms of water, is beyond our sensible apprehension, these *minima* are then regarded as neither discrete nor continuous; but as forming a single continuum which is neither water nor earth . . . ; the infinite universe may be regarded as a single continuum in which discreteness is no more introduced by the interpolation of ether between the large celestial bodies than it can be within the mud, by the interposition of air among the dry and the watery particles; the difference being solely in the fineness and subtlety of the parts of the mud exceeding our sensible apprehension, as against the greatness, size and sensible qualities of the members of the universe. And thus contrary and diverse mobile parts converge to constitute a single motionless continuum.[67]

---

64 "Digestione."

65 *De l'infinito universo et mondi,* Dial. IV, pp. 112-13 (Gentile, *Op. ital.,* I, 373; Lagarde, *Op. ital.,* I, 367).

66 But many passages in Lucretius suggest a cosmic metabolism in which every sort of atom is combined. Cf. *De rerum natura,* I, 208-37, 296-326, 498-502; II, 62-79, 991-1022; V, 828-36. The motion of the parts within the motionless whole, in II, 317-32, just fails to suggest a *discrete continuum.*

67 *De l'infinito universo et mondi,* Dial. II, pp. 51-52 (Gentile, *Op. ital.,* I, 323-24; Lagarde, *Op. ital.,* I, 334).

Bruno's conception of matter is, like that of Cusanus, illuminated by analogy both from geometry and from number. Following the fantasy of Raymund Lull, he uses as symbols of thought geometric figures with numbers. Congenial to Bruno too are the analogies drawn by Cusanus from the growth of endless mathematical series, arising from Unity.[68] Bruno finds in mathematical theory support for his conception of the indivisible atom or monad.[69] His vision is most clear in the great poems.

The minimum is the substance of all things, and thou wilt at length find it the same and the greatest of all. Here is the monad, the atom: and the whole Spirit extending hence upon every side; it is without bulk, its whole essence constituting all things by its symbols. If thou examinest the matter, this it is, with its substances. Since indeed the minimum thus reneweth all things, so that nothing is spread beneath it nor is there aught else. Were there no monad, there would be nought of number for it doth constitute species, building up every kind. For it is the prime basis in all things, that as it were whence God and the parent nature and art do elaborate on high, that which reigneth over every kind and resideth in every kind. . . . Number is the accident of the monad but the monad is the essence of number; thus the atom entereth into composition and the atom is the essence of the composite. . . . For the substance for the building of all bodies is the minimum body or the atom, and for building a line or a surface, the minimum is the point.[70]

e. Inherent Necessity

All motion, and indeed all changes of state, Bruno ascribes to the inevitable reaction of a given body to its environment. He does not conceive

---

68 For example, cf. Cusanus, *De docta ignorantia,* Lib. I, Capp. 2, 5, 11; Lib. II, Cap. 3, etc. (*Opera,* pp. 2, 4, 8, 26, etc.); *De coniecturis,* Lib. I, Capp. 4, 11; Lib. II, Cap. 6 (*Opera,* pp. 77, 85, 99); *De filiatione dei* (*Opera,* pp. 156, 162-63, 171); *De ludo globi,* Lib. II (*Opera,* p. 231); *De beryllo,* Cap. 17 (*Opera,* p. 272); *De venatione sapientiae,* Capp. 21, 36 (*Opera,* pp. 314, 328); *Liber excitationum,* Lib. X (*Opera,* p. 676); *Complementum theologium,* Cap. 9 (*Opera,* pp. 1114 *seqq.*).

69 Cf. especially *De minimo* (*Op. lat.,* I, iii, 119-361) and *De monade, numero et figura* (*Op. lat.,* I, ii, 320-473).

70 *De minimo,* Lib. I, Cap. 2 (*Op. lat.,* I, iii, 138-40).

merely an external environment acting on an inner nature, but rather regards the force leading to change in a given body as a function of the nature of the body itself, a nature which, of course, includes reaction in a particular manner to a particular environment. He thus conceives the phenomena of the universe or Nature as a synthesis of freely developing innate forces impelling to eternal growth and change.

He speaks constantly of the heavenly bodies as "animalia" pursuing their course through space. An "animal" for Bruno is that which is endowed with *anima.* Not only all life but all being he regards as in some sort animated. In the work here translated he expounds his view that this *anima* constitutes the *raggione* or inherent law which, in contradistinction to any outward force or constraint, is responsible for all phenomena and above all for all motion. It is true that the *raggione* of every part is influenced by the *raggione* of all other parts. But it is this ultimate nature, rather than the detailed behaviour, of each part which suffers this influence.

> The individual,[71] whether corporeal or incorporeal, is never completed; and among eternally pursuing individual forms, seeking eternally nevertheless those to pursue, resteth never content. . . . Thus is the infinity of All ever bringing forth anew, and even as infinite space is around us, so is infinite potentiality, capacity, reception, malleability, matter.[72]

All motion and all matter in its diverse modes are the expressions of a rigorous Necessity but this Necessity is an inward force, not an outward constraint. This is Bruno's version of the Nature Philosophy that made such an appeal to the men of the Renaissance. Often cited with admiration by Bruno is the work of Bernardino Telesio (1509-1588) who founded the Academy at Cosenza. His great work was entitled *On the Nature of Things.*[73] Telesio had his own version of the conceptions of

71 Literally: Individual matter (materia particularis).

72 *De immenso,* Lib. I, Cap. 1 (*Op. lat.,* I, i, 204).

73 Part I, Rome, 1565; Part II, Rome, 1587. Cf. *De la causa, principio et uno,* pp. 62-63 (Lagarde, *Op. ital.,* I, 246). A correspondence has survived between Telesio and Francesco Patrizzi (1529-1597) who objected that the universal elemental "matter" of Telesio cannot be apprehended by the senses, which reveal it only under changing manifestations. He begged Gregory XIV to forbid the study of Aristotle at

the pre-Socratics; he cites the authority of Parmenides for his view that Cold and Heat are the ultimate fundamental elements. Telesio rejects the Aristotelian distinction between Form and Matter. This and his vitalism—the view that every material thing is endowed with power of feeling—brings him near to Bruno's Nature Philosophy. He says too that the heavenly bodies rotate because it is their nature to do so.

Bruno resolves problems of individual will in something like a universal pantheism. He remarks that David of Dinant [74] was no fool to regard matter as divine. We may recall that Bruno at his final trial was pathetically certain that if only he himself could make his judges understand, they would welcome his philosophy:

> If then spirit, soul, life, is in all things, and to a varying extent filleth all matter, it must assuredly be the true act and the true form of all things. . . . Thus only the external forms of things change and dissolve again, for they are not things in themselves but appertain to things, not substance but accident, and circumstance of substance.[75]

> The Prime Origin is not that which moveth, but itself still and immobile, it giveth the power to generate their own motion to innumerable worlds, to great and small animals throughout the vast space of the universe, each with a pattern of mobility, of motion and of other accidents, conditioned by his own nature.[76]

---

the universities, maintaining that Platonism was consonant with the Catholic faith! See Fiorentino, *Bernardino Telesio* (Florence, 1874), II, 2 *seqq.* Bruno stigmatizes Patrizzi as a *rotten Italian pedant,* bracketing him with "the arch-pedant Frenchman" Ramus (*De la causa, principio et uno,* Dial. III, p. 62 [Lagarde, *Op. ital.,* I, 246; Gentile, *Op. ital.,* I, 202]). Cf. Bruno's attack on Ramus in the *Eroici furori* (Gentile, *Op. ital.,* II, 436). As Gentile points out, Bruno was concerned only to refute the Aristotelian cosmology—not the other Peripatetic views, all of which were opposed by Ramus.

[74] Works condemned to be burned, Paris, 1210. Cf. *De la causa, principio et uno,* p. 10, "Argomento del terzo dialogo" (Lagarde, *Op. ital.,* I, 203) and cf. below pp. 98-9, n. 19.

[75] *De la causa, principio et uno,* Dial. II, pp. 50-51 (Gentile, *Op. ital.,* I, 189-90; Lagarde, *Op. ital.,* I, 238).

[76] *De l'infinito universo et mondi,* Dial. I, p. 24 (Gentile, *Op. ital.,* I, 304; Lagarde, *Op. ital.,* I, 319-20). Cf. also among many passages *Spaccio de la bestia trionfante,* p. 12, "Epistola esplicatoria" (Lagarde, *Op. ital.,* I, 408).

Bruno's vision of all things impelled to action according to their essential nature fitted his assertion of man's inborn right to follow the dictates of his own soul:[77]

So thou mightest say that the atom in nature is constant and that no one figure appertaineth thereto. Thus the divine nature of the soul is perceived, nor doth any passion or change take place therein. To whatever fate she is subject, coming to the part of a composite whole, she hardly remaineth for one moment affected by the same fate, yet she remaineth steadfast as a single entity . . . for the judgement-halls of inexorable fortune dwell in the soul.[78]

Such passages manifest the contemporary mood of individualism that found expression in religion, in politics, in observation of nature and in philosophy.[79]

These views had spread from Platonist humanism in Italy to Aristotelian humanism in France. They profoundly influenced the mathematician and theologian, Jacques Lefèvre of Étaples (1455-1537), who edited the first complete edition of Cusanus[80] which Bruno declares to be "a glory to France."[81] Lefèvre had also edited the works of Pseudo-Dionysius the Areopagite.

The forces assailing the autonomy of the human will were on the one hand ecclesiastical authority, and on the other, belief in astrology and in the pagan conception of *Fortuna* or Fate. To none of these did Bruno yield obedience. His doctrine of *Inner Necessity* is, of course, incompatible with the cruder astrology.[82] His use of personification of the heav-

---

[77] Cf. p. 3.

[78] *De minimo,* Lib. II, Cap. 6 (*Op. lat.,* I, iii, 208-9).

[79] For a masterly review of this subject, see Cassirer, *Individuum und Kosmos.* Cf. also Jacob Teicher, "Il principio VERITAS FILIA TEMPORIS presso Azarjah de Rossi" in Reale Accad. Naz. dei Lincei *Rendiconti della classe di scienze morali, storiche e filologiche,* IX, Ser. VI (May 1933), 5-6.

[80] Paris, 1514.

[81] Cf. Preface to *De lampade combinatoria* (*Op. lat.,* II, ii, 235). It is entertaining to find the ebullient Bruno awarding the palm to de Bovelles for a more modest style than that of Lefèvre.

[82] But many Renaissance thinkers did not perceive the irreconcilable opposition between astrology and man's free will. We are startled to find astrology as part of the world picture of such figures as, for example, Kepler (1571-1630) and Prince Cesi (1585-1630), founder of the *Academy of the Lynx.*

enly bodies is merely parable and symbol, "the Shadows of Ideas."[83]

Bruno greatly praises a pupil of Lefèvre, Charles de Bovelles (1470-1533) who was also deeply under the influence of Lull. Like his teacher, De Bovelles was a prolific writer of diversified talent. He produced the first Geometry published in the French language. His work *On Wisdom* presents an extraordinary combination of mediaeval thought with insurgent humanism. The discussion of macrocosm and microcosm and of the functions of the angelic hosts is in full mediaeval style. Elaborate figures and tables of qualities are reminiscent of Lull while the use of symbolism based on the Trinity often recalls Cusanus. De Bovelles strengthens his argument with quotations from Pseudo-Dionysius the Areopagite. But the grand theme of the work is that Man has been endowed by God with Mind whereby he may through Wisdom attain to unity with the Godhead himself.[84]

Bruno may have derived from these writers and from Lucretius inspiration toward his doctrine of *Inherent Necessity,* though surely he had need of naught beyond his own burning conviction of the human birthright. In the work here translated, the conception is revealed that not merely man, nor even only living things, are imbued with this inward urge. In Bruno's thought everything on earth, everything throughout the universe, is endowed with an immanent urge or impulse in conformity with its own inward nature. This which we have called

---

[83] Cf. *On Shadows of Ideas,* p. 18 and App. I, 1 (a).

[84] Carolus Bovillus, *Liber de sapiente* in *Opera* (Paris and Amiens, 1510-11). The thesis is propounded at once in the Dedication to Guillaume Breçonnet (or Briçonnet, Bishop of Lodève and subsequently of Meaux, a former pupil and faithful disciple) which is illustrated by a most interesting woodcut replete with messages signifying that man must by knowledge be master of his fate. In the foreground are the seated figures of *Fortuna* and *Sapientia.* Fortuna is blindfolded and bears a revolving wheel in her hand. Her seat is an unstable sphere and above her the head of *Insipiens* announces: "Thee, O Fortune, do we make our goddess and place thee in heaven." Wisdom, on the other hand, is seated on a four-square throne and gazes serenely into the Mirror of Wisdom which she bears in her hand. Above all is a head labelled *Sapiens* who proclaims: "Put thy faith in thine innate virtue [virtuti]: fortune is more fleeting than virtue." The *Liber de sapiente* with figures, edited by Raymond Klibansky from the *Opera* (1510-11), is appended to Cassirer, *Individuum und Kosmos.*

Inherent Necessity impels it to mould its own development, its environment, its destiny.

> That which resideth in the small, may be seen in the great, and it appeareth that the part hideth everywhere in the whole.[85]
>
> Necessity, Fate, Nature, Design, Will all ordered justly and without error converge in the One.[86]
>
> God, since his nature is utterly perfect . . . and since he acteth without restraint, he acteth freely; thus will concurreth with goodness, and goodness with necessity. Wherefore since the best doth exist in every species, he impelleth [agit] of necessity one and no other; and since he cannot be other than good, he cannot work [facere] otherwise than as he worketh. Therefore by the necessity of his nature he worketh good, and yet better; and of two contraries, the worse could not be object or subject either of his power or of his will or of necessity. Beware then that priest who would rank either divine freedom or our own freedom as merely contingent and possible.[87]

This theme of immanent necessity is, it will be noticed, one of Bruno's arguments for the infinity of the universe, since he cannot accept that the Infinite Nature of God is consistent with the creation of a finite universe. His majestic conception gives a universal cosmic free will. As regards man, it links the problem of free will with the problem of knowledge. For the spontaneity and productivity of knowledge become the ultimate guarantees of human creative power. We are thus introduced also to a new ethic. In the *Expulsion of the Triumphant Beast* the old celestial bodies are banished from heaven. A new moral philosophy is heralded, and the basis will be "Sinderesi," [88] as Bruno calls it. His supreme law is in fact the *Inner Light.*

---

85 *De immenso,* Lib. IV, Cap. 9 (*Op. lat.,* I, ii, 146).

86 *De gl' heroici furori,* Dial. III, i, 83 (Gentile, *Op. ital.,* II, 372; Lagarde, *Op. ital.,* II, 650).

87 *De immenso,* Lib. I, Cap. 12 (*Op. ital.,* I, i, 246-47).

88 Cf. p. 117. *Synteresis,* a term used by St. Thomas and by Jerome to signify the preservative or directive action of conscience. In 1483 Lydgate, translating the version by Jean de Gallopes of Guillaume de Deguilleville's *Pylgremage of the Sowle,* wrote: "Synderesys . . . the hiher party of Resoun; whereby a man shall best discerne Hys conscience to governe." In modern mystic literature the word is used to denote "the divine nucleus, the point of contact between man's life and the divine life (E. Underhill, *Mysticism,* I, iii, 64).

f. Coincidence of Contraries

For the further elements of Bruno's philosophy his most important source was Nicolaus Cusanus. Again we observe the same views submitted to the crucible of two very different minds. In both writers, closely associated with belief in the infinity of the universe was the doctrine of the Coincidence of Contraries. The subject-object relationship similarly was envisaged by both writers as a process of admixture culminating in identity. They both cite Pseudo-Dionysius (fifth century) who held that God transcends all contraries.[89] His work was commented on by Johannes Eriugena (d. 877); by St. Thomas (1225-1274); by Albertus Magnus (1193-1280); by Meister Eckhart (d. *circ.* 1327) and by Marsillio

[89] Cf. *De divinis nominibus,* Capp. 4-13, ff. 43-62, of the edition of Paris, 1566. An edition of the *Opera omnia* in terribly crabbed print appeared at Strassbourg in 1602. It has attractive figures (ff. XLVIII, LVI, LXXVIII) of the various souls all gathered into the world soul—cf. especially the circles all intertwining and their lines converging in the largest circle which bears the legend "Providentia desideratur" on f. XLVIII. This edition has Commentaries by all the above named as well as by Hugo (of St. Victor), Grossetête and Leo of Vercelli, and a new translation by Ficino of the *De mystica theologica* and the *De divinis nominibus.* For these writers in this connection, see F. Morel, *Essai sur l'introversion mystique, étude psychologique de Pseudo Denys l'Aréopagite* (Geneva, 1918), Part II; E. Cassirer, *op. cit.;* F. Überweg, *Grundriss der Geschichte der Philosophie,* Part II, "Die patristische und scholastische Philosophie" (11th ed. by E. Geyer, Berlin, 1928). The Commentary of Thomas is really an Epitome. He is dubious of this element in the thought of Ps.-Dionysius and notes that the latter "follows Plato when writing *de speciebus naturalibus separatis* but is entirely true and Christian when declaring God to be the First Principle." For an interesting discussion of Thomas and Albert and Averroist thought, see M. M. Gorce, *L'essor de la pensée au moyen age.* Ficino in his Introduction to his translation of *De divinis nominibus* equates the doctrine of Convergence of Contraries with Identity in the World Soul: "Soluta iam totaque surgit in unitatem suam per quam cum ipso uno rerum principio inexistimibalem consequetur unionem" (Part III, f. XX). In his work *De sole et lumine* (Venice, 1503), Ficino uses the Neo-Platonic conception elaborated by Dionysius of God as the Sun. Cusanus and Bruno both compare the One, the World Soul, to Light. The philosophy recently propounded by Lance Whyte as *unitary process thought* has also ancestry from the conception of convergence of contraries. Mr. Whyte recognizes Bruno among its forerunners and indeed takes it back to Heraclitus, but does not mention Cusanus or Pseudo-Dionysius.

Ficino (1433-1499). All these writers except Eckhart are cited by Bruno. Cusanus gave the doctrine a new slant and a new emphasis. Following but developing the views of Pseudo-Dionysius on the Hierarchy of the Cosmos, Cusanus saw Salvation as the Line of Unification between Contraries.

The usual mediaeval view of the Cosmos was a hierarchy from God, through the world of Pure Intelligences and Heavenly Powers (comprising the Circle of Seraphim, Cherubim and Thrones; the Circle of Dominations, Virtues and Powers; the Circle of Principalities, Archangels and Angels) down to Man. All Being, it was conceived, radiates from God through the Intelligences and Heavenly Powers to Man, and thence back to God. This cosmic hierarchy is expounded in detail by Moses Maimonides (1135-1204) from whom it is quoted by Albertus. It had, however, been set forth centuries earlier by Pseudo-Dionysius and interpreted by Eriugena. The cosmic hierarchy came to be regarded as the archetype of the ecclesiastical hierarchy.

Cusanus accepted this usual mediaeval view but here too we find the extraordinary dualism which pervaded his whole life. For he sought to combine the mediaeval conception of a cosmic hierarchy with an entirely different cosmic conception with which he came at last to be entirely imbued. In *De docta ignorantia* and in *De coniecturis* he considers how man may attain to knowledge of God—the Infinite, the Maximum. Between finite and infinite, he reiterates, there can be no proportional relationship. Therefore the finite intellect cannot attain to ultimate truth.[90]

So Cusanus turned from the rational theology of the schoolmen to that mystical theology wherein he found expression for the poetical and emotional side of his nature. Yet he did not wholly submerge his powerful intellect in his ecstatic vision. "Wisdom is the son of God and where it is received there is received also Filiation to God." [91] He propounded the view that since infinity cannot be grasped by mere feeling, there is needed the *amor dei intellectualis,* the love of that which we have recog-

---

[90] *De docta ignorantia,* Lib. I, Cap. 3 *seqq.* (Opera, p. 2 *seqq.*). The views briefly described here are expounded many times throughout the works of Cusanus.

[91] *Liber excitationum,* Lib. V (*Opera,* p. 482).

nized and known as good. Thus, he says, knowledge and ignorance become One and at last by the *Visio intellectualis* we even attain to a glimpse of Infinity.[92] Now for Cusanus the instrument of this *Visio intellectualis* is Mathematics, which provides a new logic applicable to the infinite.[93]

As old at least as Aristotle is the problem: How can there be a relation between finite and infinite? Between physical and metaphysical, between experience and thought? Finite understanding, says Cusanus, can never reach absolute truth, but can approach ever nearer thereto even as a triangle by infinite multiplication can approach ever nearer to the perfection of circular form.[94] Empirical knowledge, he observes with Plato, is founded on ideal conception, yet it never comprises the whole truth of the ideal conception. The conditioned and finite tends toward the infinite which it never reaches. Thus may be realized "how the Providence of God uniteth Contraries." [95]

As regards theology, Cusanus found that this process leads to informed (that is conscious) ignorance; as regards experience, it leads to ignorant knowledge. For experience forbids true knowledge, and true knowledge is itself relative, always aiming at greater truth. Experience, says Cusanus, is really hypothesis, conjecture. In this conception of *Conjecture* he finds the link between Creator and Creation, Idea and Manifestation. "Conjecture is a positive assertion in place of truth, having some part in

---

[92] "Hic amor dei cum intelligentia conditus inebriat mentem," *Liber excitationum,* Lib. IV (*Opera,* p. 460);
"Bibitur quasi aqua spiritus dei per spiritum nostrum intellectualem . . . ," *ibid.,* Lib. VII (*Opera,* p. 585);
"Spiritus dei . . . sicut amor veritatis est forma, animam intellectiuam formans et uiuificans atque in motu ponens," *ibid.,* Lib. VII (*Opera,* p. 586);
"Spiritus rationis est uis libera intellectualis desiderii quae inhabitatio est ipsi spiritui possessio Dei seu vitae aeternae . . . ," *ibid.,* Lib. VIII (*Opera,* p. 591);
"Idem est intelligere et amare," *ibid.,* Lib. X (*Opera,* p. 672).

[93] Mathematics are used to illustrate the coincidence of contraries in many passages of Cusanus. The conception is formulated in the opening of *De mathematica perfectione* (*Opera,* p. 1120).

[94] *De docta ignorantia,* Lib. I, Capp. 10, 12 *seqq.* and especially Cap. 23 (*Opera,* pp. 7, 9, 18, etc.).

[95] *De docta ignorantia,* Lib. I, Cap. 22, and in many other passages (*Opera,* p. 17, etc.).

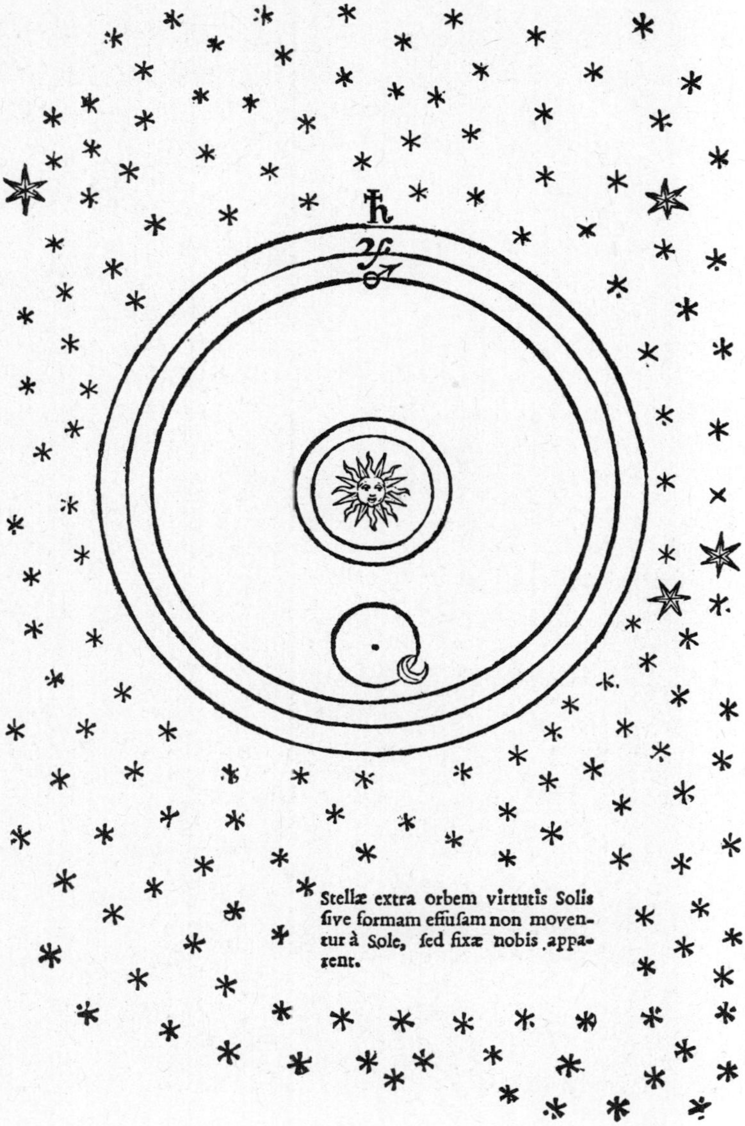

Stellæ extra orbem virtutis Solis
ſive formam effuſam non moven-
tur à Sole, ſed fixæ nobis apparent.

Fig. 9. William Gilbert's representation of the universe. From his posthumous *De mundo nostro sublunari* (Amsterdam, 1651).

Fig. 10. Portrait of Fulke Greville by P. van Somer. Photograph kindly given by the late Lord Willoughby de Broke.

truth." Single truth can only be manifested to us in difference, but there is no difference which does not in some sort attain to and have part in this unity.[96] Thus instead of identity or opposedness, we have infinite interrelationship.

From these thoughts and not on physical but on metaphysical grounds, the *De docta ignorantia* and the *De coniecturis* develop the idea both of the motion of the earth and of the relativity of all motion. The infinity of the universe is envisaged as bound up with the identity of contraries. The same thought recurs repeatedly in his works. In the *De pace fidei* the conception is applied to differences of belief. Cusanus describes the vision "of a certain man in Constantinople" who prayed to the Creator that persecution on account of difference in religious rite should be moderated. The King of Heaven and Earth spoke, saying that the groans of the oppressed had reached him as sad ambassadors from the kingdom of this world. The Archangel pointed out that the whole earth is populated by the descendants of one man: "There cannot be a great multitude without great diversity. . . . Thou didst send to the nations various Prophets and masters, some at one time, some at another."[97] In the vision, representatives of many peoples speak in turn, and finally there is concluded a "concord of the mode [rationis] of all religions."[98] Several times Cusanus refers to the promise that through Abraham all peoples of the earth shall be blessed: "Therefore the children of Abraham are those who believe in God in so much as they are justified by Faith."[99]

---

[96] *De coniecturis,* Lib. I, Cap. 13 (*Opera,* pp. 88 *seqq.*). Cf. also *De venatione sapientiae,* Cap. 36 (*Opera,* p. 327) and many other passages.

[97] *De pace fidei* (*Opera,* p. 862).

[98] *Ibid.* (*Opera,* p. 879).

[99] *Cribrationis Alchoran,* Lib. III, Cap. 13 (*Opera,* p. 924). This phrase gives us again an example of the tragic contrast between Cusanus the thinker and Cusanus the administrator. For while his episcopal rule was sullied by none of the sadistic violence which has periodically disgraced central Europe, yet there is no doubt that he inflicted the humiliating badge on Jews within his episcopal jurisdiction. To the all-knowing God he prays, "Thou remainest unknown to all and ineffable . . . for there is no proportion between finite and infinite . . ." "Be thou gracious and shew thy face and all peoples will be saved . . . If thou wilt deign to do so, the sword will cease and the malice of hatred and suchlike evils, and all will know that there is but one religion in the variety of rites" (*De pace fidei,* Cap. 1

The identity of contraries culminating in the godhead is set forth again and again by Cusanus.[100] He found in the Christ idea the reconciliation between all contraries, between finite and infinite, between sense-perception and soul. "Unus Christus ex omnibus," he exclaims.[101]

Bruno's teaching on the coincidence of contraries was closely similar to that of the Cusan, though presented without mystic theological interpretation:

Our philosophy . . . reduceth to a single origin and relateth to a single end, and maketh contraries to coincide so that there is one primal foundation both of origin and of end. From this coincidence of contraries, we deduce that ultimately it is divinely true that contraries are within contraries; wherefore it is not difficult to compass the knowledge that each thing is within every other—which Aristotle and the other Sophists could not comprehend.[102]

All power and act which in origin is complicated, united and one is in other things explicate, dispersed and multiple. The universe, the great image, the figure, the only-begotten nature, is also all that it can be through the species and principal members and content of all matter; to which naught can be added and from which naught is wanting, of form complete and unique. But it is not yet all that it can be owing to differences, modes, qualities, individuality: [103] indeed it is but an *umbra* of the primal act and primal power. Wherefore power and act are not in it absolutely the same, for no part thereof is all which it can be. . . .[104]

Among many passages we may recall from the *De immenso* Bruno's magnificent lines proclaiming that the potentiality of all parts is in the

[*Opera,* p. 863]). In the *De visione dei,* he perceives every individual as directly under the loving care of God and recalls in illustration certain portraits that appear to gaze directly at every beholder. Among these he mentions the portrait of himself by Roger van der Weyden (*circ.* 1390-1464), cited also by Bruno in the work here translated.

[100] It is impossible to cite all the passages. Cf. especially *De docta ignorantia, De coniecturis, De ludo globi, De pace fidei,* etc.

[101] *De docta ignorantia,* Lib. III, Cap. 12 (*Opera,* p. 60); *Liber excitationum,* Lib. IX (*Opera,* p. 639).

[102] *De l'infinito universo et mondi,* Dial. V, p. 163 (Gentile, *Op. ital.,* I, 409-10; Lagarde, *Op. ital.,* I, 393).

[103] *Individui; lit.,* individuals.

[104] *De la causa, principio et uno,* Dial. III, p. 83 (Gentile, *Op. ital.* I, 219; Lagarde, *Op. ital.,* I, 258).

Whole and in each part ("All things are in all").[105] This is the real basis of his view of the Identity of Opposites, and he fortifies himself with the support of such names as Anaxagoras, Anaxamines and "the divine Parmenides," as well as of Plato's Timaeus and the Neo-Platonists. We have seen that various works current in Paris during Bruno's first visit were in harmony with the doctrine of the coincidence of contraries.[106]

Light is thrown on Bruno's doctrine of the *Identity of Contraries* also by his cosmological speculation. At the close of Dialogue I of the work here translated, he contrasts terrestrial motion derived from the infinite First Cause with terrestrial motion from motive impulse intrinsic to the finite earth herself. The former is instantaneous and therefore, being circular, is indistinguishable from complete stillness; the latter, being "within time and in a certain succession," is "distinct from immobility." He adds, "Thus it is that we can say that God moveth all: and thus should we understand that He giveth the power of self motion to all which moveth."

Now the first half of the explanation would seem to suggest that the effects of God as First Cause are fused into an infinite effect which comprises all possible change or motion and is thus equivalent to no change or motion. The second half expresses the more usual view of God, the creator of Nature and of immutable Natural Law. In the second Dialogue of the same work, the implications of this twofold conception are further developed. Bruno refers to his work *On Cause, Prime Origin, and the One* which is concerned with the relation between Finite Cause and Infinite First Principle, the two attributes being fused in the Divine Creator.[107]

Drawing mathematical analogies, Bruno claims (for example in *On Cause, Prime Origin and the One*) that corruption of one is generation of another, hatred of opposition is no other than love of the convenient,

---

[105] *De immenso,* Lib. V, Cap. 9 (*Op. lat.,* I, ii, 146).

[106] Cf. p. 23.

[107] *De la causa, principio et uno,* Dial. I, p. 15 (Gentile, *Op. ital.,* I, 59; Lagarde, *Op. ital.,* I, 218) and Dial. II, pp. 34-5 (Gentile, *Op. ital.,* I, 175-76; Lagarde, *Op. ital.,* I, 228).

heat and cold are merely relative terms; while the physician seeks ever the contrary antidote to arrive at health:

In conclusion, he who would know the greatest secrets of nature should regard and contemplate *maxima* and *minima* of opposed bodies. For profound magistery [magia] it is to be able to reach the contrary, after having found the point of union.[108]

The One Infinite is perfect; simply and of itself nothing can be greater or better than it. This is the one Whole everywhere, God, universal nature. Naught but the infinite can be a perfect image and reflection thereof, for the finite is imperfect; every sensible world is imperfect, wherefore evil and good, matter and form, light and darkness, sadness and joy unite, and all things are everywhere in change and motion. But all things come in infinity to the order [rationem] of Unity, Truth and Goodness; whereby it is named *universum*. . . . Wherefore as rational and irrational in the animal are indifferent, being a single truth, so in the infinite, in the maximum, hot and cold are assuredly one throughout the universe; and we have often shewn them coincident in the minimum as in the maximum.[109]

In a later chapter we shall observe that a doctrine akin to the coincidence of contraries has in modern times taken a form that would indeed have surprised Pseudo-Dionysius and all those who inspired Bruno in this view. But we do not suggest that Marx was a direct disciple of Bruno! Nor indeed would we attribute to direct influence of Bruno each of the other and different streams of thought that lead to the vision of all-embracing Unity.

g. *Bruno's Synthesis of Universal Relativity*[110]

Let us consider the implication of Bruno's conception of a single infinite continuum comprising atoms discrete yet continuous,[111] an infinitely

[108] *Ibid.*, Dial. V, pp. 139-40 (Gentile, *Op. ital.*, I, 263-64; Lagarde, *Op. ital.*, I, 288-89).

[109] *De immenso*, Lib. II, Cap. 12 (*Op. lat.*, I, i, 307).

[110] An interesting study is B. Spaventa, "La dottrina della conoscenza di G. Bruno," *Atti della R. Accad. di scienze morali e politiche di Napoli* (Naples, 1865), II, 294 *seq.*

[111] Cf. p. 73.

vast cosmos whose innumerable parts exert no absolute constraint one on another. Each, in obedience to the law of its own being, obeys its own intrinsic urge. Yet all are intimately interrelated by the immanence throughout each one of the universal spirit whereby all are fused into a single universal whole. Bruno is thus led to the conception of the identity of subject-object, which to him was bound up with the coincidence of contraries.[112] All life, indeed all Being, he regards as an expression, we had almost said a free expression, of Immanent Necessity, and since the whole is infinity, we can form no absolute concept of the mode or motion of any part, but we can observe the relationship of part to part. Our world of sense-perception is then built not on absolute values, but on certain observed relationships. Once more we are with the great problems of the relationship between Cause and Effect, Subject and Object, Innate Necessity. Can we attain to a synthesis of his views on these great themes?

Bruno constantly reiterates that on the one hand the immediate interpretation of our sense-data may lead us far astray, while on the other hand our imagination, though it also may set us on a right track, may similarly be completely deceptive. Only by enthroning reason as arbiter can we reconcile imaginative experience with sense-perception and derive profit from both:

No corporeal sense can perceive the infinite. None of our senses could be expected to furnish this conclusion; for the infinite cannot be the object of sense-perception; therefore he who demandeth to obtain this knowledge through sense is as one who would desire to see with his eyes both substance and essence. And he who would deny the existence of a thing merely because it cannot be apprehended by the senses nor is visible, would presently be led to the denial of his own substance and being. There must then be some measure in the demand for evidence from sense-perception, for this we can accept only in regard to sensible objects; and even then it is not above all

[112] Olschki remarks that Bruno oscillated between theism and pantheism. I would rather say that the two views are reconciled in the single universe envisaged by him. Cf. L. Olschki, "Giordano Bruno," *Deutsche Vierteljahrhundertschrift f. Literaturwissenschaft und Geistesgeschichte,* II, Heft i (Halle, 1924), (Italian trans. by G. Zamboni [Bari, 1927]).

suspicion unless it cometh before the court aided by good judgement. It is for the intellect to judge, yielding due weight to factors absent and separated by distance of time and space. And in this matter our sense-perception sufficeth us and yieldeth us adequate testimony, since it is unable to gainsay us. Moreover, sense advertiseth and confesseth his own feebleness and inadequacy by the impression it giveth us of a finite horizon, an impression which is ever changing. Since then we have experience that sense-perception deceiveth us concerning the surface of this globe on which we live, much more should we hold suspect the impression it giveth us of a limit to the starry sphere.

Of what use then are the senses to us?

Solely to stimulate our reason, to accuse, to indicate, to testify in part; not to testify completely, still less to judge or condemn. For our sense-perceptions, however perfect, are never altogether undisturbed. Wherefore truth is in but very small degree derived from the senses as from a frail origin, and doth by no means reside in the senses.

Where then resideth truth?

In the sensible object as in a mirror. In reason, by process of argument and discussion; in the intellect, either through origin or by conclusion; in the mind, in its proper and vital form.[113]

Bruno heralds the change, which became explicit in the work both of Kepler and of Descartes, by which discussion of the nature of material reality yields place to the conception of an Order of the Universe. For Bruno's passionate assertion of the infinity of space was not merely denial of boundary. He conceived Infinite Space as the field of all motion, the vehicle of an Infinite Power which is the expression of the Infinite Life of the Universe:

Thus the heaven, the infinitely extending air [aria], though part of the infinite universe, is not therefore a world or part of worlds; but is the womb, the receptacle and field within which they all move and live, grow and render effective the several acts of their vicissitudes, produce, nourish and maintain their inhabitants and animals; and by certain dispositions and orders they

[113] *De l'infinito universo et mondi,* Dial. I, pp. 2-3 (Gentile, *Op. ital.,* I, 288-89; Lagarde, *Op. ital.,* I, 307-8). We may recall here also the magnificent poem to *Mens* at the opening of the *De immenso* (*Op. lat.,* I, i, 201).

minister to higher nature, changing the face of single being through countless subjects.[114]

It is manifest that each of these innumerable worlds which we see in the universe is not therein as in a containing position or in an interval or space; but rather in that which comprehendeth, conserveth, the universal motor and efficient cause: which cometh thus to be completely contained within each of these worlds, to be as the whole soul of every part thereof.[115]

Bruno gives much space to combating Aristotle's arguments against the Void. Nor was there in Bruno's mind any sharp distinction between the three infinities of Space, Time and Matter. They merge into one another as does his conception of Infinite Space, Nature and the Infinite World Soul.

The Minimum is the substance of all things and thou wilt await it at length as the largest of all things. This is the Monad, this is the atom, the whole spirit that is poured hence on all sides, without form, disposing all things by its tokens [signis], the total essence and substance, this it is if at length thou examinest the matter.[116]

The universal Intellect is the intimate, most real, peculiar and powerful part of the soul of the world. This is a single whole which filleth the whole, illumineth the universe and directeth nature to the production of suitable species: this is concerned with the production of natural things, as our intellect with the congruous production of rational kinds. This is called by the Pythagoreans the motive force and mover of the universe, as said the poet: *"Mind moveth the whole form and mixeth itself throughout the body."* [117]

And again:

For nature is not merely present, but is implanted within things, distant from none; naught is distant from her except the false, and that which existed never and nowhere—nullity. And while the outer face of things

[114] *De l'infinito universo et mondi,* Dial. III, p. 99 (Gentile, *Op. ital.,* I, 362; Lagarde, *Op. ital.,* I, 360).

[115] *De la causa, principio et uno,* Dial. V, p. 124 (Gentile, *Op. ital.,* I, 253; Lagarde, *Op. ital.,* I, 281).

[116] *De Minimo,* Lib. I, Cap. 2 (*Op. lat.,* I, iii, 138).

[117] *De la causa, principio et uno,* Dial. II, p. 39 (Gentile, *Op. ital.,* I, 179; Lagarde, *Op. ital.,* I, 231). The quotation is from the *Aeneid* of Virgil, VI, 726-27. These lines were quoted by Bruno at his Venice trial.

changeth so greatly, there flourisheth the origin of being more intimately within all things than they themselves. The fount of all kinds, Mind, God, Being, One, Truth, Destiny, Reason, Order.[118]

Thus the single spirit doth simultaneously temper the whole together [contemperat]; this is the single soul of all things; all are filled with God.[119]

Souls, like light or sound, are diffused in all directions through space; they do not impede one another but influence one another: [120]

It is manifest . . . that every soul and spirit hath a certain continuity with the spirit of the universe, so that it must be understood to exist and to be included not only there where it liveth and feeleth, but it is also by its essence and substance diffused throughout immensity as was realized by many Platonists and Pythagoreans. Thus it is that [the individual soul] doth apprehend most distant species, in an instant and without motion, nor doth the eye or aught therefrom suddenly advance to the stars, nor aught suddenly from the stars to the eye. The power of each soul is itself somehow present afar in the universe, inasmuch as the substance which is not included in the living body is yet exceedingly connected and attached thereto. Therefore certain impediments being removed, suddenly and at once it hath present to it the most remote species which are not joined to it by motion. Naught is mixed, yet is there some presence. Indeed experience teaches us somewhat of these things. For if a nose hath been cut off and one is implanted from another body, on the day when the first owner thereof doth die, as his body putrefieth so also doth the implanted nose putrefy.[121] Thus it is manifest that the soul can be diffused far beyond the body throughout the whole horizon of the nature thereof. Thus doth it happen that it knoweth not only the members belonging to itself but even all those with which it hath contracted

---

[118] *De immenso,* Lib. VIII, Cap. 10 (*Op. lat.,* I, ii, 314).

[119] *Ibid.,* Lib. IV, Cap. 9 (*Op. lat.,* I, ii, 51).

[120] Cf. the Lucretian view of the winds, scents, heat, cold and sound as mighty though invisible forces, "yet all these things must needs consist of bodily nature inasmuch as they can make impact on our senses" (*On the Nature of Things,* I, 302-3). Thus Bruno, "Even as light is physically poured without end into the vastness of space, the bright Spirit informeth, embraceth and filleth even those things that are guarded by the flame thereof or by flood" (*De immenso,* Lib. I, Cap. 7, [*Op. lat.,* I, i, 226]).

[121] This is recounted in many mediaeval works. For implanting operations, see *De l'infinito universo et mondi,* Dial. IV, p. 117 (Gentile, *Op. ital.,* I, 377; Lagarde, *Op. ital.,* I, 370).

any use, participation or communion. . . . Even so if a person doth prick his finger or any part of his body, he feeleth it not only in that part but throughout all his members.

Thus since the soul of the individual is continuous with the soul of the universe, it is not impossible that it may be carried to bodies which do not interpenetrate with it . . . as if innumerable lamps are lit and together give the effect of one light, nor doth the one light impede or weaken or exclude the other.

Similarly when many voices are diffused throughout the same space, even as with light [visualibus] rays. Or as we say popularly, the rays are spread out to receive the same visible whole, where all penetrate the same medium, some in straight lines and some obliquely, yet they do not on that account interfere one with another; so the innumerable spirits and souls diffused through the same space interfere not at all with one another, nor doth the diffusion of one impede the diffusion of the infinity of others.[122]

Thus the Lucretian universe of innumerable minimal parts or atoms in perpetual concourse and discourse became for Bruno the symbol of the spiritual universe of an infinity of monads, infinitely numerous elements of the universe, each pursuing the development congruent to its inner nature. And to Bruno the universe like all its parts had the quality of life. This quality the parts derive from the Whole and in some sense share with the Whole. Thus the World Soul too is for Bruno an infinite continuum in which all things partake; yet in another sense discontinuous and divisible and even (on the analogy of number though not with unvarying consistency) infinitely divisible.

This conception again was symbolic of his view of the human soul, every individual soaring to the uttermost height of thought and spiritual development congruent with his own nature, every individual imbued with the divine spirit whereby the whole infinity of discrete and independent souls is yet fused into a vast Whole, transcending their discrete separateness, a Unity encompassing time and space, comprehended within infinite space and eternal time, a universal relativity within the immensity of the World Soul, governed by Mind, or, as he sometimes says, Wisdom.

[122] *De magia* (*Op. lat.*, III, 408-10). Bruno proceeds with an interesting argument that so-called magic is consonant with the laws of Nature.

The infinite universe of Bruno's conception was inevitably regarded by him as what we may call a synthesis of infinite relativity. All things and all thoughts and all individual souls have for him their individual and absolute value, yet each can be appraised only in relationship to the others, and the absolute value of each is merged in its relationship to the infinite whole:

> These philosophers [Pythagoras and Solomon] discovered their friend Wisdom when they discovered this Unity. For Wisdom, Truth and Unity are one and the same.[123]

---

[123] *De la causa, principio et uno,* Dial. V, p. 122 (Gentile, *Op. ital.*, I, 252; Lagarde, *Op. ital.*, I, 280).

CHAPTER FOUR

THE ITALIAN COSMOLOGICAL WORKS[1]

HAVING taken a brief general view of Bruno's cosmology and philosophy, we turn to the six Italian works produced during his happy London sojourn. In them the main elements of his philosophy first found expression. The three Italian cosmological-philosophical volumes considered in the present chapter are perhaps the most important among all Bruno's writings. Each is dedicated to his beloved patron Mauvissière.

An Argument to each Dialogue of the work is incorporated in each of the three Dedicatory Epistles. These Arguments marshal the subject matter of each Dialogue under numbered headings which, however, are absent from the text of the Dialogues themselves.

a. The Ash Wednesday Supper (La Cena de le Ceneri)

We will pass quickly over the earliest of these volumes since we hope soon to have *The Ash Wednesday Supper*[1] in English translation from Miss Frances Yates. The work is in the form of a series of five Dialogues, or rather conversations, in which the lover of God, Theophilo,[2] represents the veiws of Bruno, "the Nolan" as he always calls himself, perhaps in order to avoid either the use or rejection of the monastic name. The Dialogues are in prose, interspersed with sonnets. There is much parade of learning and citation of ancient and modern au-

[1] See App. I, 6-9.

[2] Called in later works Philotheo.

thors. Certain of Bruno's London friends are introduced. Theophilo converses with Smith,[3] with Prudentio the Pedant and with a woman named Frulla.

He gives a satirical account of the persons who disputed with the Nolan in Oxford,[4] and passes to the Nolan's own views. After various digressions, compliments to England and reference to Bruno's *Shadows of Ideas,* Theophilo agrees to give an account of the colloquy of the Nolan with the doctors Torquato and Nundinio.[5] Then we hear of the invitation from Sir Fulke Greville to discourse on the Copernican theory; of the neglect of that nobleman to send word on the appointed day; of the belated arrival of the Nolan's friends Florio and Gwynne; of their hapless journey and the discourtesy of the London boatmen and loafers, almost matched by that of Greville's own lackeys and guests.

Before the Inquisitors at Venice Bruno stated that the Ash Wednesday Supper took place in the house of Mauvissière. It is therefore possible that his whole picture of the journey to Greville's house was introduced merely to express the Nolan's soreness at the unmannerly ways of the Elizabethan crowd. The discourtesy from which he suffered was common at the time. Mauvissière himself, most peaceable and gentle of men, had to remonstrate with the authorities against anti-alien manifestations, which went so far as to disturb the drainage system of the Embassy.

In the earlier part of *The Ash Wednesday Supper,* compliments to the Queen and to the English celebrities who had befriended Bruno alternate with complaints, amused, incredulous and often querulous, against English behaviour. Not until the third Dialogue do we pass to philosophy. Nundinio is cited as protagonist of the Nolan's opponents; Smith is very soon converted by Theophilo. The Dialogue opens with a glancing shot at those English gentlemen who know no language but their own, somewhat of a boomerang from one who in two years learnt no English, though incidentally we hear that Bruno had some command of French and Spanish besides Latin and Italian. Then we pass to an assurance that Copernicus not only meant what he said (in spite of the

---

[3] Cf. p. 35. [4] See p. 28 *seq.* [5] Cf. pp. 35-6.

Preface inserted in his book by Osiander)[6] but that he was right in his views as to the motions of the earth. Moreover a whole string of names is cited of those who are said to have anticipated Copernican views, from "Nicetas the Syracusan Pythagorean" to Cusanus. Simple optical experiments demonstrate how easily we may be deceived by a wrong interpretation of our sense-perception, and this is applied to the apparent motionless central position of our earth.

From Copernicus the Dialogue passes to Cusanus and others who attained to that vision of cosmic infinity which was indeed an obsession or perhaps, we should say, a constant solace and inspiration to Bruno's thought. Theophilo then discourses on the plurality of worlds and speculates as to their inhabitants.

The fourth Dialogue disclaims any opposition to "true theology." Theophilo recounts the discourtesy of Torquato, "who can hardly exceed Nundinio so much in ignorance as in presumption, foolhardiness and impudence." Philotheo describes further arguments at the Supper, and narrates that the Nolan accused Torquato of misunderstanding Aristotle and then convicted him of misinterpreting Copernicus.

The last Dialogue, again citing the support of the early Greek writers, sets forth Bruno's own cosmological belief—the infinite universe with its infinitely numerous worlds called by the ancients "*ethera,* that is runners, messengers, ambassadors who bring tidings of the magnificence of the single Highest." Their motion depends on the Necessity that is innate in them; their relative weight, lightness, motion upward or downward; cosmic metabolism which is propounded as the interpretation of the earth's local motion; [7] secular changes of the earth and considerations in

---

[6] Andreas Osiander (1498-1552), a Lutheran theologian and mathematician, was successively Professor of Hebrew at Nuremberg and of Theology at Königsberg. He risked his own position by advocating unpopular theological doctrine. But, entrusted with the publication of the work of Copernicus, of which the author had passed the proof-sheets on his death-bed, Osiander inserted a preface suggesting that Copernicus intended the work merely as a mathematical exposition and not as related to the facts of nature. Hence the indignation of Bruno.

[7] For these subjects, cf. Aristotle, *De coelo,* I, 3. *De coelo,* 270b, 24 derives *ether* from ζel θεῖν (ever-running). This derivation goes back to Plato, *Cratylus,* 410b. Cf. also θεωρέω (to act as ambassador).

relation to motions of the earth. Citing Aristotle as regards secular changes, Theophilo says:

Here he spoke as one who uttered prophecy or divination. Though he sometimes hardly understands himself, halting and mingling always somewhat of his own error with the divine frenzy, he yet speaketh for the most part and fundamentally what is true.[8]

Finally Prudentio is converted to the Nolan's views and opens a series of mighty adjurations by calling on the Nolan "by your faith in the highest and Infinite One" "to remain under the protection of the most illustrious and noble Mauvissière."

b. On Cause, Prime Origin and the One (De la Causa, Principio et Uno)[9]

The next work, again in Italian, was published in the same year and deals mainly with metaphysics. The Dialogues are represented as taking place in the house of Mauvissière. The Dedication to him, unlike the conventional adulation which we expect in writings of the period, expresses Bruno's transparently sincere affection and gratitude:

O illustrious and unique Knight, if I turn my gaze to behold the constancy of mind, the perseverance and the solicitude with which, adding service to service and benefit to benefit, you have conquered me, laid me under obligation, rendered me your prisoner: you who are wont to overcome every obstacle, to deliver from every danger, to bring to fruition all your honourable projects.

We may gain a further insight into Bruno's thought on Cause, Prime Origin and the One from the sonnets appended to the Dedication and

[8] Dial. V, p. 115 (Gentile, *Op. ital.*, I, 119; Lagarde, *Op. ital.*, I, 189). The passage quoted from Aristotle is from *Meteorologica,* I, 14, 1-10. We might almost apply Bruno's words to himself!

[9] Mrs. Linetta Richardson, former Professor of Italian in Birmingham University, has a translation of this work in preparation.

Arguments. Three Latin sonnets, "To the Origins[10] of the Universe," "To my own Spirit," and "To Time" are followed by an Italian sonnet, "On Love" as the source of illumination, and a final magnificent apostrophe of "The Cause, Origin and Sempiternal One."

The work is concerned with problems of the Aristotelian philosophy but its conclusions are of course in opposition to Aristotle.

The views of the Nolan are again represented by Theophilo.[11] The other speakers are Heliotrope (i.e., Florio) and Hermes (Armesso) to whom are added in the last four Dialogues Dicson,[12] Gervasio and Polihimnio. As in the previous work, the reader must endure many diversions before reaching the real subject matter which concerns such themes as Form, Matter and Mind.

The first Dialogue discusses the speakers and refers with praise to the learning, eloquence and courtesy of Tobie Matthew and of Culpepper; and to Nizzoli, "un lexico, un cornucopia, un Nizzolio."[13] There are apologies—not without cause—for the strictures on England in *The Ash Wednesday Supper*. The second Dialogue proceeds to a consideration of what is meant by Origin and by Cause. Bruno conceived them as the internal and external factors respectively of the single, infinite universe, informed by the universal intellect. God the divine

---

[10] It is hard to choose the correct translation of the word *principio* which conveys the idea both of *origin* and of *nature* or essential *principle*. In Bruno's thought these two meanings were transfused. Florio gives for *principio* "beginning, ground, or chief original, race and stock of a thing, origin."

[11] He is called in the first Dialogue "Philotheo" but is obviously the same character as Theophilo.

[12] See above, pp. 38-9.

[13] Cf. p. 39, n. 40. Matthew and Culpepper were among the five doctors (all either former or future Vice-Chancellors of the University) who welcomed a Laski to Oxford. Cf. Spampanato, *Vita di Giordano Bruno* (Messina, 1921), I, 340, 342; citing H. Languet, *Arcana saeculi decimi sexti* (Halle, 1699), I, 299 and II, 428-9. Tobie Matthew (1546-1628) "learned, eloquent and loved" as reported by a Wood, was at the time Dean of Christ Church. He became Bishop of Durham in 1595, and Archbishop of York in 1606. Martin Culpepper was Rector of New College 1573-99. He had been Dean of Chichester since 1577. Mario Nizzoli (1498-1566) was a very learned opponent of scholasticism. He published a *Lexicon* to Cicero and also *De veris principiis et vera ratione philosophandi contra pseudophilosophos* (Parma, 1533), Libri IV, which was reprinted by Leibnitz.

primal substance is unknowable, but may be apprehended through His works and especially by a study of the innumerable great celestial bodies. They are inhabited by living beings and are themselves endowed with life and pursue their courses through infinite space. Theophilo and his disciple Dicson emphasize that everything, however trivial, humble, minute has its part in the primal spiritual substance of the universe.

How far can we learn the nature of Cause and Origin by study of that which ensues from them? The relationship is considered of Efficient, Formal and Final Cause, and the Nolan's pantheism leads far from the usual Aristotelian interpretation of those terms. Primal origin is equated with matter, form with soul. Thus form is distinguished not by material nature, which is uniform, but by the acts and exercise of the faculties of those grades of being which it produces. Moreover, form and the soul are at once the whole and also every part of the whole.

The third Dialogue discusses "matter whose nature is conditioned by elemental origin rather than by cause or form." David of Dinant is cited that matter is excellent and divine.[14] The view is enunciated of the conservation of matter (a view elaborated in the *Infinite Universe and Worlds* as cosmic metabolism). No substantial form loses being, says the Nolan. One constant formal principle, even as one constant material principle, seeks expression through diverse, ever-changing manifestations.

Matter can be considered as Potentiality or as Subject, but the Supreme and Divine, comprehending the whole universe, *is* the total potentiality as well as the whole of Being. Parts do not fulfil their whole potentiality; hence death, corruption and vice. Intellect cannot comprehend this absolute act which is one with absolute potentiality of the universe. No eye can reach this most exalted light and this deepest abyss. But it is expressed in Holy Writ of the Divine Spirit. "The darkness hideth not from thee;

[14] See pp. 76 and 99. The name of David of Dinant is given in the "Argument," but in the text this belief is referred to its source in the *Fons vitae* of Avicebron. Like all his contemporaries, Bruno was of course not aware of the identity of Avicebron with the Spanish-Jewish philosopher Solomon ibn Gabirol (*circ.* 1021-*circ.* 1058).

but the night shineth as the day; the darkness and the light are both alike to thee."[15]

The fourth Dialogue then continues the discussion of matter. The thesis of Plotinus is cited that if in the intelligible world there is a multitude of different species there must be something in common behind the peculiarity and distinction of each. That which is in common is matter; that which is peculiar and distinct is form. Ultimately, matter is one with Act, and in incorporeal things, matter comes to coincide with Act as potential Being coincides with Being. Moreover, in absolute potentiality and absolute act there is no distinction between matter and form. For this (which is both matter and form) is the ultimate purity, simplicity, indivisibility and unity, and the whole; though if it have certain dimensions, figures and distinction, quality, it is not absolute or the whole. For the form which comprehends all quality is no single one. Thus Averroes understood the matter, and though he knew no Greek, he comprehended the peripatetic teaching better than many who read Greek. Being perceptible and explicit is not a primal quality of actuality but is an effect thereof. When, following Aristotle, we seek the perpetuity of form in Nature, we find it, not in the fixed stars nor in ideas but in the bosom of matter, for matter is the fount of actuality. Matter is ever the same, immutable, though around and within it is change. The compound is altered, augmented, diminished, changes position, suffers corruption—but never does this happen to basic matter. Matter receives nothing from form. What can the corruptible give to the eternal—what can one imperfect being, as is the form of sensible objects, always in motion, give to a thing so perfect that if rightly regarded it will be recognized as divine? Perhaps this was the meaning of David of Dinant, not understood by those who reported his views.[16] It is matter which conserves form; therefore it is form which desires matter for its conservation since, separated from matter, form loses its being.[17]

The fifth Dialogue concerns the One, completing the foundation of

[15] Psalms CXXXIX, 12.

[16] Cf. *De vinculis in genere* (*Op. lat.*, III, 696), citing both David of Dinant and Avicebron. Cf. n. 14 above.

[17] Cf. Dial. IV, pp. 99-115 (Gentile, *Op. ital.*, I, 237-46; Lagarde, *Op. ital.*, 267-76).

the edifice concerning natural and divine knowledge. Once more we learn that the universe is One, infinite and immobile. Matter and form, potentiality and action, though logically distinct, are physically one and infinite, immobile, indivisible, without distincton between whole and part, between origin and result (*principio et principiato*).

Again and again, the Nolan attempts to give expression to his vision of infinite spirit pervading the infinite universe. Ultimately, there is no specific difference between part and whole, and there is no number in the universe, for the universe is itself unity. And this is true whether we consider the mode of time, of space or of size. God [18] is in everything more intimately than its own form is in it, since He is the essence by which everything has its being. Diversity and Change express a unity embracing all formal multiplicity, for all is one in substance and in truth. Difference and numbers are not being, but are derived from being and surround being. "He who has found this Unity has discovered the indispensable key for the true contemplation of nature." [19]

Change is not toward a different being but toward a different mode of being; and the universe comprises all being and every mode of being:

> Thus you will understand that all is in all but all is not totally and in every mode within each one. . . .
>
> Moreover, just as the soul (to use the usual expression) is in the whole form to which it giveth being, and is at the same time individual; and is thus similarly in the whole and in every individual part; so the essence of the universe is One in the infinite and in every part or member thereof so that the whole and every part become One in substance. . . . That which is said of the seed as regards the limbs of animals may similarly be said of food as regards chyle, blood, phlegm, flesh and seed . . . and is similarly the case of all things, rising from the lowest grade of nature to the supreme highest thereof, from the physical universe known to philosophers to the height of the archetype in whom theologians believe . . . until we reach an original and universal substance, identical throughout the whole, which is Being, the foundation of all kinds and of all forms—just as in the carpenter's art there is a substance, wood, subject to all sizes and shapes but

---

[18] "Jove" (p. 120; Lagarde, *Op. ital.*, p. 279). In the Argument, Bruno has "Jove as they call him" (p. 16; Lagarde, *Op. ital.*, p. 207).

[19] "Argument," pp. 16-17 (Gentile, *Op. ital.*, I, 143; Lagarde, *Op. ital.*, I, 207).

these are not wood, they are in, of, or around wood. Thus everything which maketh diversity of kinds, species, differences, properties, everything which dependeth on generation, corruption, alteration and change is not being or existence but is a condition and circumstance of being or existence which is one, infinite, immobile, subject, matter, life, soul, truth and good.[20]

When we aspire and strain to an origin and substance of things, we progress toward the indivisible, and we can never believe that we are united to the primal Being and universal substance until we understand indivisibility. . . . The Peripatetics and the Platonists reduce infinite indivisibles to one indivisible nature comprehending many kinds . . . and many determinate kinds to one being which they reduce to a name and word, a logical abstraction and ultimately vanity.[21]

"The infinite dimension, being no magnitude, coincides with the individual." This is illustrated by geometric figures. Thus we are again brought to the coincidence of contraries. Contemplating the infinite One which lies behind all phenomenal manifestations, we recognize that

even in the two extremes of the scale of nature, we contemplate two principles which are one; two beings which are one; two contraries which are harmonious and the same. Therefore height is depth, the abyss is light unvisited, darkness is brilliant, the large is small, the confused is distinct, dispute is friendship, the divided is united, the atom is immensity. . . . Here are the signs and proofs whereby we see that contraries do truly concur; they are from a single origin and are in truth and substance one. This, having been seen mathematically is accepted physically. . . . Here as in a seed are contained and enfolded the manifold conclusions of natural science; here is the mosaic, the disposition and order of the speculative sciences.[22]

---

[20] Dial. V, pp. 121, 124-26 (Gentile, *Op. ital.*, I, 251, 253-54; Lagarde, *Op. ital.*, I, 279, 281-82).

[21] Dial. V, p. 131 (Gentile, *Op. ital.*, I, 259; Lagarde, *Op. ital.*, I, 285).

[22] "Argument," pp. 17-18 (Gentile, *Op. ital.*, I, 143-44; Lagarde, *Op. ital.*, I, 207-8).

c. *On the Infinite Universe and Worlds (De l'Infinito Universo et Mondi)*[23]

The third of Bruno's philosophical works in the vernacular is the longest. Bruno himself tells us that it sees the birth of ideas inseminated in the work *On Cause, Prime Origin and the One*. In fact, while almost every idea in this work is foreshadowed in the two previous volumes, we have here the impression of the attainment of that joy in philosophic contemplation of which the author tells us and which we pray may indeed have sustained him through the awful sufferings which were ahead of him.

The speakers are Philotheo once more, Elpino, Fracastoro, Burchio, and Albertino. We have already hazarded the guess that Elpino may be Thomas Hill.[24] Girolamo Fracastoro of Verona is a historical figure whom we have already considered.[25] Burchio is less easy to identify. This person, persistently and arrogantly sceptical of the new message, is perhaps Thomas Bourchier, an English Franciscan educated at Oxford who was in Paris during Bruno's first visit, and had published there in 1582 both a Franciscan Martyrology and a Prayer for the Paris Convent addressed to the Minister General of the Order. Burchio is parallel to Gervasio in *On Cause, Prime Origin and the One*. Albertino appears in Dialogue V as "a learned person of a happier talent who, howbeit educated in the contrary doctrine, nevertheless by his power of judgement of that which he hath heard and seen, can distinguish between two disciplines and can easily alter and correct his views." We have already given reasons for identifying Albertino with Alberico Gentilis, the distinguished Italian refugee who was established at Oxford.[26]

---

[23] An initial difficulty confronts us as to the title of this work. In the first edition seen through the press by Bruno, the title occurs in two forms—*De l'infinito, universo et mondi,* which we should render *On the Infinite, the Universe and Worlds;* and without the comma, *De l'infinito universo et mondi,* the form chosen here. The form chosen by us occurs on Bruno's first title-page and again at the end of the work. The comma is inserted in the Title on Fol. 1, where the work begins in *Dialogo primo*. Florio inserts the comma after *universo* when he lists this work among those he had read in order to compile his dictionary.

[24] Cf. p. 39. [25] Cf. pp. 68, 71, 105. [26] Cf. pp. 31, 43; also p. 140.

The months in London had not abated Bruno's love for Mauvissière,[27] which in the Dedication to this work finds perhaps its most attractive expression. The Dedication suggests that Bruno is already beset with anxieties. In all his works the reader, almost overwhelmed by exaggerated verbiage, is apt to find himself suddenly held by a terse expression of the loftiest thought. Here we read, "It is Unity that doth enchant me. By her power I am free though thrall, happy in sorrow, rich in poverty, and quick even in death." This exaltation sustained Bruno at his moments of greatest suffering, and has held his memory in the hearts of succeeding generations who have struggled for truth and freedom. This quality we may suspect was the link between Mauvissière and Bruno.

The Arguments incorporated by Bruno in the Dedication are much longer than in the previous works. The reader may find it convenient to have a full analysis of this work. We shall summarize Bruno's own Arguments, supplementing from the Dialogues themselves.

Bruno presents a highly symmetrical scheme in the Argument of the first Dialogue. To the reader who has studied the Dialogue itself, it is clear that he is attempting to present a logical framework for the result of a complex psychological process comprising ecstatic vision and also aesthetic joy in the use of the mind. The first Dialogue, for example, is in fact not set forth in two parts and in numbered themes as in the Argument. Here is the content of Bruno's Argument to the first Dialogue:

DIALOGUE I, PART i [28]

Theme 1. Sense-perception must be interpreted by reason.

Theme 2. The universe is infinite. There is no proof of a boundary.

Theme 3. The universe is infinite because a finite world could not be self-contained and could not be imagined without position.

Theme 4. Quotes Lucretius: "If the universe is finite, what is beyond?"

Theme 5. The difficulty of defining position of a finite world in infinite space.

Theme 6. A finite universe requires the conception of a Void.

---

[27] Cf. pp. 26-7.

[28] For convenience of reference, we will, in citing the Themes, give always the Dialogue number (with Part number, if any) as well as the Theme number.

Theme 7. The space containing our universe would be void but for it. Therefore the space beyond is as our space; and in both is eternal action.

Theme 8. Sense-perception suggests rather than denies infinity (quoting Lucretius); so does reason.

Theme 9. Infinite space is the only possible conception to our minds, and can only be denied verbally, not with our thought.

Theme 10. "It is well" that this world exists—therefore also that an infinity of other worlds exists.

Theme 11. The virtue [*Bonta*] of this world cannot be communicated to another world.

Theme 12. Since we accept individual all-embracing infinity [i.e., God], no reason and no sense-perception will fail to admit also corporeal and extended infinity.

Theme 13. Our little surrounding space is as nothing to infinity and can have no relation to it; but as "it is well" that our space exists, so also is it for countless others.

Theme 14. Infinite power must act on the infinite, on infinite corporeal being.

Theme 15. Only an infinite universe can comprehend all perfection.

Theme 16 [partially repeating Theme 14]. Infinite Efficient Cause must produce infinite Effect.

Theme 17. An infinite universe is satisfying to our mind and the contrary brings difficulties and inconveniences—and we repeat Themes 2 and 3.

Theme 18. If our universe be spherical, then the space beyond it which adjoins it must also be spherical.

Theme 19. Elaborates the discussion of Theme 2.

Theme 20. Elaborates the discussion of Theme 10.

The passive power of the universe having been discussed in Part i of the first Dialogue, Part ii turns to the active power of the Efficient Cause.

DIALOGUE I, PART ii

Theme 1. Divine power should not be otiose—and a finite Effect would be no less otiose than none.

Theme 2. To assert that divinity has not created the infinite is to deny divine goodness and greatness, while the contrary view is in no way contrary to theology.

Theme 3. The converse of I, i, 12 [since there is an infinite Cause, there must be an infinite corporeal Effect]: distinction between the infinite whole [world] and the Completely Infinite [God].

Theme 4. Aristotelians, in supposing a finite world, are really accusing Omnipotence of lack of will and of lack of power.

Theme 5. If Omnipotence does not create the universe infinite, then it cannot do so: and if it cannot create it infinite, then also it cannot preserve the universe to eternity. For if finite in one respect [Space], the universe must be finite in every other respect [Time]. For in it, every mode is an object; and every object and mode are one and the same.

Theme 6. The converse of I, i, 10 [if "it is well" that the world exists, then "it is well" that an infinity of other worlds exist]. Shows why theologians defend the contrary view [because of the people's limited understanding and wrong use of knowledge]. The friendship between learned theologians and learned philosophers.

Theme 7. Distinguishes active power from individual actions; and expounds infinite power "better than theologians have ever done."

Theme 8. The motion of the infinite worlds is not by constraint but according to the inner nature of each; and yet an infinite motor force exists.

Theme 9. Infinite motion can be verified in each world. And, because each world moves itself and is moved at the same time, therefore each world can be seen in every point of the circle that it describes around its own centre—and this difficulty we will solve later in more detail.

We now turn to the Dialogue itself. In the opening lines of the first Part, each speaker displays his dramatic function. Philotheo propounds the new doctrine; Elpino is the enquirer, incredulous but not pertinacious in error; Fracastoro is the man of judgement who will give attention and appraise the speakers; while Burchio is merely frivolous in his ignorance. Albertino, the second enlightened convert, does not appear until the fifth and last Dialogue.

The first Part of the first Dialogue leads at once to the heart of the subject. The universe is infinite, the worlds therein are innumerable, the infinite First Cause is both transcendent and immanent; the infinite universe and all its parts move in conformity with their own nature, which is the creation of the Omnipotent First Cause, and thus are reconciled both Free Will and Necessity. I, i, Theme 1 culminates:

Wherefore truth is in but very small degree derived from the senses as from a frail origin, and doth by no means reside in the senses . . . but in the sensible object as in a mirror; in reason, by process of Argument and discussion; in the intellect, either through origin or by conclusion; in the mind, in its proper and vital form.

Philotheo proceeds to refute Aristotelian arguments. I, i, Themes 3, 4 and 5 are taken together. There follow I, i, Themes 6 and 7, and the Aristotelian view is stigmatized as "mere words and excuses." We pass to I, i, Themes 8 and 9 and we are reminded, "Divinity hath not as aim to fill space, nor therefore doth it by any means appertain to the nature of divinity that it should be the boundary of a body (cf. I, ii, Themes 2, 4, etc.) and "that which containeth is eternally different from that which is contained." I, i, Theme 10 is introduced by a consideration of the "aptness" of single infinite space to receive an infinity of worlds. Fracastoro points out that the existence of Void beyond our universe is inconceivable by us, so that we are forced to accept an infinite Plenum. Fracastoro's acceptance of these views signalizes also the beginning of Elpino's conversion, and in the succeeding discussions Elpino finds himself reluctantly accepting more and more of the new view.

I, i, Themes 12-17 are set forth by Philotheo and are fully accepted by both Fracastoro and Elpino. This latter expands several of the themes already discussed, emphasizes I, i, Theme 17 and expounds I, i, 18-20. He is complimented by Fracastoro and then introduces Part ii of the first Dialogue by a question concerning the relation between infinite Cause and infinite Effect. The theme has been adumbrated by Bruno in the work *On Cause, Prime Origin and the One*. Once more Philotheo expounds his vision of infinite action and infinite passion, recapitulating the earlier themes, emphasizing I, ii, 1-2. He passes to I, ii, Theme 3, the distinction between the "explicit though not the all-comprehensive totality of the infinite universe" and the "whole comprehension and complete totality of the Creator," using arguments reminiscent of Cusanus.[29] I, ii, Theme 1 is next expanded in I, ii, Themes 4-5. Fracastoro avers that

[29] Cf. Trans., p. 262, n. 27.

the coexistence of infinite active power and infinite passive power provides the clue whereby "we perceive the complete identity of Liberty, Free Will and Necessity, and moreover recognize that Action and Will, Potentiality and Being are but one." The second part of I, ii, 5, as given in the Argument, is hardly explicit in the text, but we are told, "He who denieth infinite result denieth also infinite power."

Passing to I, ii, Theme 6, Fracastoro declares that there is no real difference between theologians and philosophers. Philotheo expounds I, ii, Theme 7, answering Elpino's faint surviving difficulties, and passes to a magnificent declaration of faith in the view presented by I, ii, Theme 8. This is denied by Elpino, who prefers "the glorious and presupposed foundation that the Best and Greatest doth move the whole. Nevertheless," he continues, avowing agreement as he presents the very marrow of Bruno's philosophy, "as regards that which you are wont to say concerning the soul of the world and concerning the divine essence which is all in all, filleth all, and is more intrinsically pervasive of things than is their very own essence, because it is the essence of essences, the life of lives, the soul of souls"; yet Elpino is still worried because "it doth none the less appear to me that we may say that 'He moveth all things rather than that He bestoweth on all things the power to move themselves.' " So in I, ii, Theme 9, Philotheo again expounds his synthesis of Necessity and Free Will, of Transcendent and Immanent Divinity, and shows them all exemplified in the complex motions of our earth (for which he uses a geometric figure already given in *The Ash Wednesday Supper*). Elpino accepts the statement and asks for further instruction at another meeting on which the speakers agree.

The second Dialogue is again concerned with the relationship between infinite first cause and the infinite created universe. Certain of Aristotle's general views of matter and space, incompatible with the infinite universe, are considered and confuted. Elpino presents the Aristotelian view mainly from the fourth and eighth books of the *Physica*.[30]

The following is the gist of Bruno's Argument to the second Dialogue:

---

[30] We give in the Translation references to the relevant passages of these works.

DIALOGUE II

Theme 1, (i). All attributes of divinity are together as each one singly.

(ii). Our imagination should not be able to aspire Beyond Divine Action.

(iii). Indifference of the distinction between Divine-Intellect and Divine Action.

(iv). If the corporeal quality perceptible to our sense is endowed with infinite active power, then what will be the absolute totality of active and passive power inherent in the totality of all things?

Theme 2. A corporeal object cannot be terminated by an incorporeal object, but either by a Void or by a Plenum.

In either case, beyond the world is space, which is as matter and has the same passive power. Refutation of Aristotle's view of the incompatibility of dimensions [i.e., Aristotle's denial of the identity of matter and space].

Theme 3. Distinction between the world [or finite universe as imagined by the Aristotelians] and the single infinite or comprehensive universe.

Theme 4. Elpino brings forward Aristotle's views *seriatim* and they are confuted by Philotheo. They concern both simple and compound bodies.

The vanity is shewn of six arguments concerning "motion which cannot be infinite" and other similar propositions. The reasons are shewn for change and termination of motion and for strong and weak impulses: It is demonstrated that an infinite body can be neither heavy nor light, and Aristotle's arguments in *De coelo et mundo* and from the third book of the *Physica* are each in turn confuted.

Thus the second Dialogue opens with further consideration of the infinite first cause.

II, Theme 2 leads to a consideration of the nature of position, space and the void.

After expounding II, Theme 3, Philotheo invites Elpino to put forward the opinions of Aristotle on these matters in turn (II, Theme 4). Elpino follows very closely the reasoning in *De coelo*. He presents a program of arguments: Can there be a simple body of infinite size? This is impossible for either (i) bodies of circular or (ii-vi) bodies of any other shape. Clearly, therefore, there can also be no composite body of infinite size. II, Theme 4, i is a geometrical argument based on the motion of a radius of an infinite circle. Philotheo replies that "never has one been found so barbarous and so ignorant as to have posited the infinite world, and to have attributed motion to it." Elpino agrees that all Aristotle's six arguments depend on the false assumption that his adversaries attribute motion to an infinite universe. The five last reasons suppose motion in a straight line and are based on the qualities of lightness and heaviness. Philotheo proceeds to enunciate, in phrases that might be from Cusanus (who is, however, not mentioned), the attributes of an infinite universe.[31]

Bruno gives a modification of the doctrine of the elements:

> No infinite body is either heavy or light. For these qualities belong to parts in so far as they tend toward their own whole. . . . Thus on our earth the particles of fire seeking to escape and mount toward the sun, carry ever with them some particles both of earth and of water with which they are conjoined; and these becoming increased do thus by their own natural impulse return to their own place . . . wherefore the earth in her own space is no heavier than the sun in his space or than Saturn or the North star in their own.

Aristotle's arguments concerning the parts of an infinite body are analyzed and refuted with some repetition of former matter and with a fine exposition of cosmic metabolism.

Philotheo resolves the difficulty of finite parts within a single infinity and discusses the arguments in the *De coelo* concerning motion of the parts and of the whole. To the Aristotelian arguments that the infinite cannot be agent or patient in regard to the finite, nor can an infinite body act on another infinite body, Philotheo replies that while he agrees with these theses, they do not affect the issue, since there can be no numerical relation between the parts and the infinite whole, nor between finite time and eternity. Moreover, whatever arguments to the contrary Aristotle may adduce, "this inference is not physically valid though logically it may be correct."

Philotheo's views are illustrated by geometrical demonstration and lead to the conclusion that "if two infinite contraries be opposed, either a finite change or none at all will come to pass" and that when two contraries are opposed, there ensues finite action and finite alteration.

---

[31] Cf. also Epitome of Dial. III.

We have now recapitulation. Philotheo again expresses his exalted vision of infinity. He derides the assumptions of the Aristotelian cosmology and affirms the relativity of all sense-perceptions. Elpino shows the completeness of his conversion by repeating the views of Philotheo and the rejection of the Aristotelian opinions.

The following is the gist of Bruno's Argument to the third Dialogue:

DIALOGUE III

Theme 1. Aristotle's heaven and spheres are again denied, since heaven is a single general space embracing infinite worlds. The Aristotelian view is an illusion created by sense-perceptions.

Theme 2. The motions of the heavenly bodies are also illusory sense-percepts.

Theme 3. All celestial bodies have motion. The suns, in which fire predominates, have different motion to that of the earth, in which water predominates. Thus too some stars shine by themselves like suns, some by reflection like earths.

Theme 4. Stars at vast distances may yet be heated by our sun, and distance explains the presence or absence of scintillation.

Theme 5. Cusanus is cited concerning the material and habitability of other worlds and concerning the cause of light.

Theme 6. No body appears light when viewed from itself.

Theme 7. "Quintessences" and the Aristotelian series of spheres are denied.

Theme 8. Distinction between the four elements is accepted, but not the Aristotelian order of the elements. The worlds are heterogeneous bodies, animate globes in which earth is no heavier than the other elements.

The movement of particles within each globe is likened to the movement of the fluids in the animal body.

The earth herself is without weight. Moreover the unifying body is not earth but water.

Theme 9. Concerns the nature of the animate globes and their inhabitants.

Theme 10. A gibe against the opponents of the new views.

The third Dialogue opens with a lyrical speech by Philotheo unfolding a view of the whole universe as One. "Immense and infinite is the complex of this space and of all the bodies contained therein." Later Philotheo bursts into a charming little sonnet on the endless motion of the earth and of all other bodies. The theory is propounded that stars more distant from the sun can nevertheless be heated by it as a result of their larger orbit and slower revolution, combined with a more rapid spin.

The Dialogue is very largely a recapitulation of the earlier two, and is well epitomized by Bruno's Argument. Elpino's conversion being now achieved, his questions are merely links between the speeches of the others, or occasionally he is himself the mouthpiece of a reiteration of Philotheo's views. The obstinacy in error of Burchio introduces occasional comic relief. After the end of this Dialogue, Burchio fades from the scene.

Bruno's Argument to the fourth Dialogue gives the main contents of the Dialogue under numbered headings which again are not in the text itself:

DIALOGUE IV

Theme 1. Recapitulation concerning the form of the universe with its infinity of worlds.

Theme 2. Recapitulation refuting arguments against the infinite bulk or size of the universe (discussed in the first Dialogue). Aristotle's arguments against an infinite multitude of worlds are refuted:

(i). on general principles;

(ii). by consideration as to the nature of heaviness and lightness with special regard to the hindrances to motion of heterogeneous parts from one to another earth.

Theme 3. Why celestial bodies are not close to one another nor can be close to a void.

Theme 4. Considerations of local space and of the behaviour to be expected of a stone equidistant between two worlds.

Theme 5. Aristotle's error in supposing a force of heaviness or lightness [of elements] attracting one body to another. The true cause of the universal tendency to resist change, a tendency which "causeth flight and persecution."

Theme 6. Motion in a straight line appertains not to worlds but to parts thereof which, if not too distant, tend to approach one another.

Theme 7. The behaviour of comets shows the error of Aristotle in supposing that a heavy body necessarily suffers attraction by its natural containing body, however distant.

Theme 8. Simple bodies of identical nature in innumerable diverse worlds have similar motion. "Arithmetical diversity" causes difference of locality, each part having his own centre and a common centre which is not the centre of the universe.

Theme 9. Bodies have no determined upper or lower portion, but have a natural direction of their conversation.

Theme 10. Motion is infinite.

A moving body tends toward infinity and to the formation of innumerable compounds. But neither heaviness nor lightness nor infinite speed follow: and motion of adjacent parts, so far as they preserve their own nature, cannot be infinite. Attraction of parts to their own containing body happens only within their local space.

The fourth Dialogue gives further recapitulation in the form of question and answer by Elpino and Philotheo with occasional comment by Fracastoro. Elpino, though he voices the Aristotelian objections, shows himself now convinced and sometimes takes up the exposition of the new view. The discussion is again based on the *De coelo* of Aristotle.

The discussion in the fourth Dialogue ranges over the themes of the single all-embracing infinite universe, the infinity of worlds and the behaviour of the diverse matter and the particles that build up our world and all other worlds—with a fine presentation of cosmic metabolism and of the eternal process of decay and regeneration. Philotheo observes, "Throughout the ethereal field, heat and cold, diffused from the bodies wherein they predominate, gradually mingle and modify one another to varied extent, so as to become the approximate origin of the innumerable forms and species of being." It is in this Dialogue that Philotheo mentions the plastic surgery which was arousing such interest in Italy during Bruno's boyhood.[32] Theme 4 is illustrated vividly by observation of the behaviour of a spreading fire. At the close of the Dialogue, Elpino promises that at their next meeting the Aristotelian views shall be well represented by Albertino.

The fifth and last Dialogue introduces Albertino, brought up in the old views but able to appraise and accept the new. Albertino brings forward twelve reasons against the opinions of Philotheo. Each in turn is

[32] Cf. p. 90, n. 121.

confuted to his ultimate satisfaction. Bruno's argument is somewhat discursive and the best survey of the fifth Dialogue is obtained by giving (not from the Argument, but from the Dialogue itself) each of Albertino's twelve (or rather thirteen)[33] theses with the reply to each. They are as follows:

DIALOGUE V

Thesis 1. Beyond our universe neither time nor space exists.

Answer 1. Beyond the imagined convex circumferences of the universe is time.

Thesis 2. There is one *primum mobile;* therefore there is one world.

Answer 2. Truly there is One—for all reduce to a single utterly simple and indivisible principle which is truth and being.

Thesis 3. We may deduce only one world from the positions occupied by bodies in motion.

Answer 3. There is no "natural position" and no innate heaviness or lightness. The same argument is enlarged in a diversion as to the similarity of our earth and the other celestial bodies.

Thesis 4. If there be many worlds, the centre of one will be nearer to its [elementally contrary] circumference than to the [elementally] kindred centre of another sphere.

Answer 4. Particles are not necessarily related to any centre except that of their own globe. Moreover, contraries are not necessarily at the furthest distance apart, since one may influence the other. Further, the four elements are intimately mixed in the various particles—and water is mixed with every part of our earth. And if the elements are to be arranged by qualities, water [instead of earth which is heaviest] must occupy the central position, if fire, which is lightest, is at the circumference: since water, which is cold and moist, is in both those qualities most opposed to fire.

Thesis 5. Similar to 4. If six circles are ranged round a seventh, the heavy element in the centre of one circle is nearer to the circumference of another than to the centre of that other.

Thesis 6. Similar argument to Thesis 5, as regards the interspheric triangles in the figure of Thesis 5.

Answer to 5 and 6. All these petty difficulties disappear when we realize that the universe is ONE.

[33] Cf. p. 114, nn. 34-7.

Thesis 7. If there are other worlds they must either (i) be infinite, which is for many reasons impossible, or (ii) be finite, in which case there must be a definite number. If so, why just this number? Why not a single one?

Answer 7. There is but one universe with innumerable worlds. Quotation from Lucretius, *De rer. nat.*, II, 1040-51.

Thesis 8.[34] Nature shuns superfluity [*sic!*]. She encloses herself in the smallest compass.

Answer 8. Against this thesis Philotheo quotes Lucretius, *De rer. nat.*, II, 1052-57, 1064-66, that seeds unnumbered on every side and with everlasting motion are driven in all directions. Therefore there must be a plurality of worlds.

Thesis 9.[35] It does not necessarily follow that because God *can* create more worlds, therefore they necessarily exist. There may not be the passive power to *be* created.

Answer 9. The argument that active power is limited in action by the limitation of passive power is a contradiction in terms. Lucretius is again quoted as to the certainty of a plurality of worlds and as to the behaviour of the seeds of things (*De rer. nat.*, II, 1067-76).

Thesis 10.[36] A plurality of worlds would be unreasonable, for civil intercourse between them would be impossible, and this would be a reflection on the gods who created them.

Answer 10. Such civil intercourse would be unnecessary and harmful. It is much better that living creatures should be dispersed. Quotation from Seneca, *Medea* (vv. 335-39) as to the harmful result of uniting lands by seafaring.

Thesis 10. *bis.*[37] Plurality of worlds is a thoroughly unpractical plan. The spheres would hinder one another's motion.

Answer 10. *bis.* In fact they do not collide but pursue their courses in comfort.

---

[34] Bruno accidentally numbers this again as the seventh.

[35] Continuing the error, this thesis is numbered as the eighth but in the answer it is called the ninth.

[36] Continuing the error, this thesis is numbered as the tenth but it is answered as "your next."

[37] Continuing the error, this thesis is called the tenth by Albertino. We number it 10 *bis.* as it is answered as the tenth. The numberings of these theses and of the answers are thus brought to correspond again.

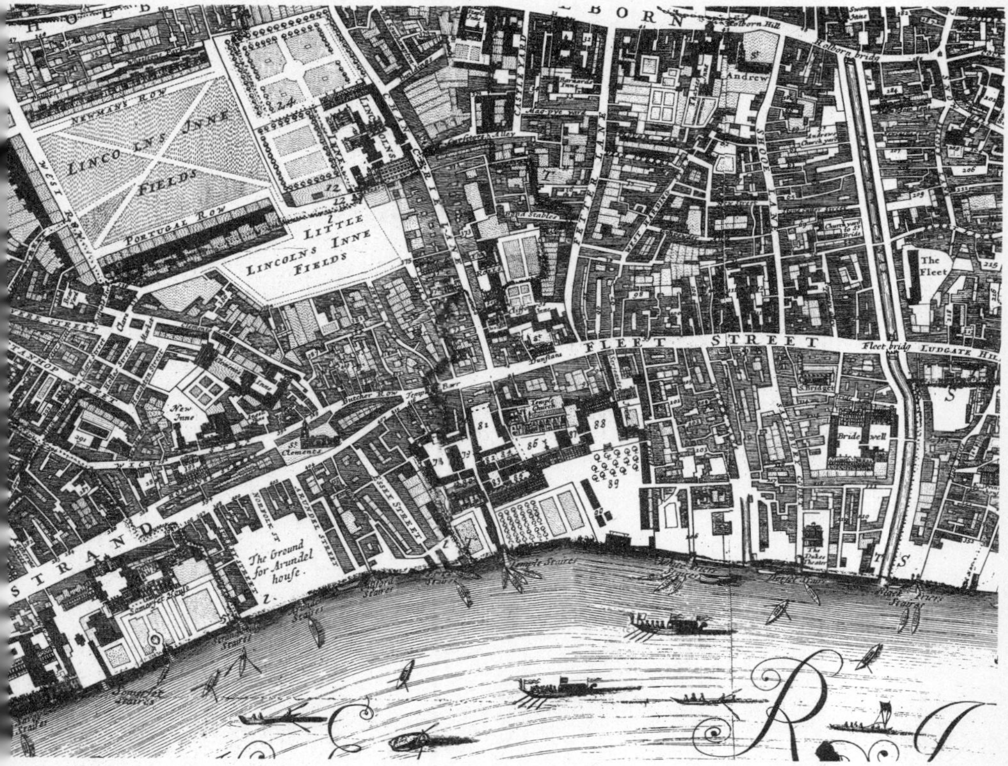

Fig. 11. Portion of a map of London, showing position of Butcher Row. From J. Ogilby, *London* (London, 1682), Part II, p. 58.

Fig. 12. Sir Philip Sydney, an unsigned portrait in the National Portrait Gallery.

Thesis 11. All multiplication is by division or generation. So how can worlds multiply?

Answer 11. Multiplication is by mere vigour of nature.

Thesis 12. The world is perfect. Therefore there is nothing to be added to it.

Answer 12. Plurality is not needed for the perfection of any of the single worlds, but for the perfection of the universe.

All the answers are given by Philotheo (except for one little shot from Elpino). Then Albertino bursts into a paean of admiration and praise for Philotheo, prophesies his future vindication and begs him to continue expounding the glorious truths concerning the infinite universe.

CHAPTER FIVE

THE ITALIAN ETHICAL WORKS[1]

a. The Expulsion of the Triumphant Beast (Spaccio de la Bestia Trionfante)[2]

WE NOW turn to the ethical works of Bruno, all bearing a false imprint of Paris, but all the product of his fruitful years in London.

The full title of the first of these may be rendered *Expulsion of the Triumphant Beast, Proposed by Jove, Effected by the Council, Revealed by Mercury, Reported by Wisdom, Overheard by Saulino and Registered by the Nolan. Dedicated to the Most Illustrious and Excellent Knight Sir Philip Sidney.*

There are three Dialogues. The symbolical setting is given at once by the names of the speakers, Sofia (Wisdom), Saulino, and Mercury (messenger of the gods). Saulino, who appears again in the next work, is named from a small district of Bruno's native Nola. The Dialogues are thronged by mythological figures whose words are quoted by the three

---

[1] See App. I, 10-12.

[2] There is an English version of *The Expulsion of the Triumphant Beast* by W. Morehead, published by J. Toland (1713). Morehead was a brother-in-law of Toland. Toland also published a brief "Account of Jordan's Book of the Infinite Universe and Innumerable Worlds" in *A Collection of Several Pieces* (1726), pp. 316-69. But this is merely a translation of part of the Dedication. The eighteenth century also saw an anonymous French translation of part of the *Spaccio* published in 1750, stated by Salvestrini (*loc. cit.*) to be the work of l'Abbé Louis Valentin de Vougny, *conseilleur de grand-chambre* and Canon of Notre-Dame. One of the best and briefer accounts of Bruno's Italian ethical works is by J. Roger Charbonnel, *L'Éthique de Giordano Bruno et le deuxième dialogue du Spaccio* (Paris, 1919).

already mentioned. Most prominent are Jove and Momus, the latter equated with *Sinderesi* or Conscience, "a certain light which resides in the watch-tower, cage or poop of our soul." [3]

A general idea of the Nolan's thought is given us in the "Explanatory Epistle" to Sidney (Fig. 12). Bruno is as usual lavish in praise and gratitude for kindness shewn and for appreciation of his thought. Sidney's qualities, he declares, were shewn to him from the moment of his arrival in Britain. Before leaving that land he would express his love and gratitude both to him and to that "noble and gentle spirit Sir Fulke Greville." (Fig. 10)[4] He disclaims either exaltation of vice or dispraise of virtue, "neither having nor desiring in thought, word or gesture aught but sincerity, simplicity and truth."

Bruno calls himself here GIORDANO in a passage in which he speaks of the pleasure of using correct and unfeigned names.

He will present to Sidney the numbered and ordered seeds of his moral philosophy—not that they may be admired, known and heard as something new (an accusation which we find refuted also in *The Infinite Universe and Worlds*) but that they may be examined, considered and judged. For from the world at large Bruno expects always only misunderstanding and abuse. He will treat of moral philosophy by virtue of the illumination afforded him by the divine sun of the intellect. But first (and not without need) he provides certain preliminary interpretation.

Jove, he announces, rules in heaven over forty-eight beasts or vices, as reflected "in the forty-eight famous pictures," [5] i.e., the constellations. These beasts or vices he would banish from heaven to certain terrestrial

[3] "Epistola esplicatoria," p. 18 (Gentile, *Op. ital.*, II, 13; Lagarde, *Op. ital.*, II, 412).

[4] Cf. *La cena de le ceneri*. Bruno adds, however, to this passage in the Dedication to Sidney that envious strife-makers had intervened between Greville and himself.

[5] The literary use of mythological, and especially of astrological, figures to symbolize human qualities has of course a long history. Cf. Cicero, *On the Nature of the Gods* and Lucian's *Parliament of the Gods* (2nd century). It would be interesting could we learn whether Bruno had seen the volume of Nicholas Berauld (1473-1550), the friend of Erasmus and teacher of Admiral de Coligny. Berauld's *Syderalis abyssus*, published at Paris in 1514, gives an illustrated figure to symbolize every human quality.

regions, and replace them by virtues which have been driven out and scattered. There will be, he says, many adventures and vicissitudes, for "each taketh what fruit he can, suited to his own containing form. For there is naught so vile but it can be utilized to an exalted purpose, and naught so worthy that it cannot become matter for scandal and for ignoble use." This is the implication of his view of what we have called cosmic metabolism. The basis of the whole universe is One, and the component atoms are never destroyed, but pass from one containing form to another. This applies even to Jove himself, who is not eternally the same, but is ever receiving and ever giving out particles of the cosmic infinity. Though the composition of eternal corporeal substance will change (as in Jove), itself is indestructible. Moreover:

> Spiritual substance, though it hath familiar intercourse with material bodies, is never completely blended with them;—but is rather the efficient and informative principle [6] within the body from, through and by means whereof the composition takes place; as the mariner to the boat, the father to the family, the architect to the building. And yet not without but within the fabric . . . for it is the efficient power, which holds the opposed elements together and effects the composition of the animal.

It embraces the whole and every part thereof, and yet, when the time comes, it goes forth by the same door whereby it once entered. Thus the soul never dies. Indeed, Bruno is much fascinated by the doctrine of metempsychosis "which many philosophers have held to be true." Jove, he tells us elsewhere, "is not to be taken as too legitimate or true a representative of the primal and universal origin," but himself exemplifies the principle of eternal change. Again Jove represents every one of us. With the expulsion of the triumphant beast, that is, of the vices wont to overcast the divine, "the soul will purify itself from error, will deck itself with virtues through love of the beauty in goodness and natural justice, through seeking for the fruits thereof, and through hatred and fear of the grief and deformity that appertain to the misshapen contrary thereof." [7]

---

[6] "Principio."

[7] "Epistola dedicatoria," p. 19 (Gentile, *Op. ital.*, II, 14; Lagarde, *Op. ital.*, II, 412).

Bruno passes to a detailed exposition of the mythology of his Heaven. Supreme is Truth,[8] occupying the site of the Great Bear constellation, for she is the first as well as the central and the last thing, occupying the most exalted position in Heaven, filling the span of Being, Necessity, Goodness, Origin, Medium, End, Perfection. Bruno's very human impatience and troubles are revealed in the names of some of the expelled Vices, such as loquacity and "senile and bestial fables with foolish Metaphor, vain Analogy." The names of expelled Vices and of the Virtues established in their place fill several pages. Ambition and Cruelty are among the fallen; Tolerance, Kindness, Patience and Courage are among those established. On the altar are Religion, Piety and Faith. From the eastern corner there fall down Credulity, Superstition and Triviality; from the western corner Impiety and insane Atheism plunge violently down. On high is the prize of Honour, Glory and all Delight, the fruits of industrious virtues and study, true Repose and Happiness.

These themes, propounded in the "Explanatory Letter" to Sidney, are expounded in the three Dialogues of the work. The mythological form gives scope to Bruno's fantasy, and exuberant discursions are numerous. For example, Pallas suggests that

> The Cardinal of Cusa shall be entrusted with the triangle . . . if haply he may thereby liberate the much-cumbered geometers from that weary search for the squaring of the circle . . . but I would bestow on them that infinitely greater and more precious gift for which the Nolan should offer me not one but a hundred hecatombs. For to him it was first revealed and by his hand it has been passed to the multitude. For by contemplation of the equality between maximum and minimum, between outer and inner, between origin and end, there was spread before him a life more fruitful, richer, more open and more secure, whereby was demonstrated to him not only how the square may be made equal to the circle, but the same, suddenly, of every triangle, every pentagon, hexagon or whatsoever polygonal figure you will; and also of line to line, surface to surface, field to field and content to content of solid figures.[9]

[8] "Epistola esplicatoria" and Dials. I and II, pp. 20, 49, 74-75 (Gentile, *Op. ital.*, II, 14, 62, 89; Lagarde, *Op. ital.*, II, 412, 444, 457-58).

[9] "Corpo a corpo nelle solide figure." Dial. III, ii, 4, 188-90 (Gentile, *Op. ital.*, II, 170-71; Lagarde, *Op. ital.*, II, 518-19).

The allusions are fully explained so that the reader may be aware what vice the Nolan is castigating, what foible he is deriding and then suddenly what quality he is presenting for our aspiration. Patience, tolerance, long-suffering and generosity are virtues "most necessary to the world." [10] Animals and plants, Jove explains to Momus, are the living effects of Nature, and Nature is no other than God revealed.[11]

The work ends in the third Dialogue with an extravagant paean of praise of King Henry III, who, it will be remembered, undeterred by Bruno's talent for embroilment, had sent him to Mauvissière and to his happy sojourn in London.

b. Cabal of the Cheval Pegasus with Appendix on the Cillenican Ass, Described by the Nolan (Cabala del Cavallo Pegaseo con l'aggiunta dell' Asino Cillenico,[12] Descritta dal Nolano)

Bruno was peculiarly ingenious and whimsical in inventing names for his works. The first word above is a pun and perhaps a double pun. The word "Cabala," Mystery or Revelation (Cabbala), is chosen because the word also suggests a horse. Moreover, it was the name of an exotic, miraculous creature that was much discussed at the time. The doctrine of the coincidence of contraries equates this miraculous Cabal, comparable to Pegasus, the steed of the Muses, with the Cillenican ass, that is none other than winged Mercury, who was born in a grotto on Mount Cillene.

The volume with this strange title has a strange dedication to "the most Reverend Don Sapatino, Abbot of San Quintino and Bishop of Casa Marciano." There was no such Abbey and no such Bishopric. The researches of Spampanato have established [13] that a certain Sabatino

---

[10] *Ibid.*, p. 196 (Gentile, *Op. ital.*, II, 177; Lagarde, *Op. ital.*, II, 522).

[11] *Ibid.*, p. 209 (Gentile, *Op. ital.*, II, 186; Lagarde, *Op. ital.*, II, 529).

[12] The same theme is adumbrated in one of the last of Bruno's works, *On the Composition of Images, Symbols and Ideas* (*Op. lat.*, II, iii, 237-38). Cf. App. I, 24. For the history and popularity of the theme of *the Ass,* see Spampanato, *Giordano Bruno e la letteratura dell' asino* (Portici, 1904).

[13] From the *Notamento de tutti li inguidati e sposati*, p. 62, and the *Sacra visita* (1585), p. 216. Cf. Spampanato, *Vita di Giordano Bruno,* I, 61.

Savalino was in fact priest of *Santa prima,* close to Nola, from 1576 (the date when Bruno left the monastery). The Abbacy and Bishopric attributed to him by Bruno are entirely apocryphal. The Savolino family were relatives of the Nolan, and one of the speakers in both the *Spaccio* and the *Cabala* is named from their village, Saulino.

After satirically enumerating the hypothetical persons who have refused the gift of this work, Bruno apostrophizes Don Sapatino, saying that, of course, if the production is declined, it may be passed on to another, but that the Nolan trusts it will be accepted as no less worthy than *The Ark of Noah,* which he had dedicated to Pope Pius V; [14] *The Shadows of Ideas* dedicated to King Henry III of France; *The Thirty Seals,*[15] dedicated to his legate Mauvissière; and *The Triumphant Beast,* a gift to Sir Philip Sidney. So this donkey is an excellent beast to mould custom, institute doctrines, reform religions. Why should we not give him even academic rank?

After a sonnet on Asininity comes a long-winded "Declamation to the studious, devoted and pious Reader devoted mainly to the ass and his asininity." "The ideal and cabalistic ass of the sacred writings" is no other than "the horse Pegasus treated figuratively in poetic writings." In the First Mind, the ideal ass, the origin of the asinine species, is one with the idea of human species and of the species of earth, moon and sun and also those of intelligences, demons, gods, worlds and the universe. It is also that species from which depend not only asses but also men, stars, worlds and all mundane animals—in which there is no difference of form or subject, of one from another, for it is utterly simple and One." [16]

The fools of the world have been those who have established religions, ceremonies, laws, faith, rule of life. The greatest asses of the world are those who, lacking all understanding and instruction, and void of all civil life and custom, rot in perpetual pedantry; those who by the grace of heaven would reform obscure and corrupted faith, salve the cruelties [17] of perverted religion and remove abuse of superstitions, mending the rents in their vesture.

[14] This work of Bruno has not come down to us. See App. I, i.

[15] Cf. App. I, 1 (a) and 5 (b).

[16] p. 16 (Gentile, *Op. ital.,* II, 243-44; Lagarde, *Op. ital.,* II, 566).

[17] *Medicano le ferite.* Florio gives *ferita,* wildnesse, beastlinesse, fiercenesse, cruelty, monstrousnesse, inhumanity.

It is not they who indulge impious curiosity or who are ever seeking the secrets of nature, and reckoning the courses of the stars. Observe whether they have been busy with the secret causes of things,[18] or if they have condoned the destruction of kingdoms, the dispersion of peoples, fires, blood, ruin or extermination; whether they seek the destruction of the whole world that it may belong to them: in order that the poor soul may be saved, that an edifice may be raised in heaven, that treasure may be laid up in that blessed land, caring naught for fame, profit or glory in this frail and uncertain life, but only for that other most certain and eternal life.

Bruno hastens to add that the ancients have recounted these things in their myths of the gods:

Pray, O pray to God, dear friends, if you are not already asses—that he will cause you to become asses. . . . There is none who praiseth not the golden age when men were asses: they knew not how to work the land. One knew not how to dominate another, one understood no more than another; caves and caverns were their refuge; they were not so well covered nor so jealous nor were they confections of lust and of greed. Everything was held in common.[19]

A second ribald sonnet is followed by the three Dialogues of the *Cabal of the Cheval Pegasus*. The speakers are Saulino, Sebasto and Coribante.

The work is at once connected with the *Spaccio* and we are told of the place of asininity in the reformed Heaven. Bruno's range of citation includes the Cabbalistic writings while his mocking invention is even more far-reaching. In the midst of buffoonery he suddenly passes to an altogether different plane. Following the Areopagite, following Augustine,[20] he would turn us from intellectual pride to humble ignorance. "Asininity" or ignorance may be the surest guide to salvation. There is a purposeful confusion between the Ass and Pegasus, noblest of horses.

---

[18] i.e., been occupied with illicit magic.

[19] "Declamation to the Studious, Devoted and Pious Reader," pp. 21-2, 24, 25-26 (Gentile, *Op. ital.*, II, 247, 249, 250; Lagarde, *Op. ital.*, II, 568-9, 570, 571).

[20] Dial. I, p. 51 (Gentile, *Op. ital.*, II, 269; Lagarde, *Op. ital.*, II, 583). Cf. Pseudo-Dionysius, *Opera* (Antwerp, 1684), II, 62, and Augustine, *Opera omnia* (Lyons [haered. Guinta], 1561), IX, 958.

In the second Dialogue, the Ass appears as Onorio, who relates how, after he had broken his neck by falling from a precipice, his owner sold his body to feed the ravens. His soul, released from its mortal prison house, was free to wander at will, and he suddenly realized that his spiritual substance differed in no wise from that of all the other spirits similarly released and "transmigrating," whether from human or from asinine bodies. He took his way to Parnassus where he was acclaimed as either a flying ass or the veritable horse Pegasus. The point is brought out that acceptance of metempsychosis forces belief in this essential unity of the "substance" of all souls, of man and beast, of fly and fish, and indeed of the plants if we allow that they too have a kind of life and soul. Thus it may happen that more of reason and of talent may reside in an animal than in a man, though the animal lacks the instruments of expression. The ass is brought to express the Nolan's conviction that efficient intelligence is One and universal; and every individual is moved and illumined by reason which pervades all, even as a flame extends to compass all combustible fuel. Thus there is a supreme agent that by sense-impression stimulates all living things [21] to action; and a supreme intelligence that rouses all through their understanding to a reasoned activity. Moreover, every individual is endowed with sense-perception and with potential intelligence, the variety of which is no less than the number of varieties of corporeal forms and dispositions.[22]

To the objection that reason is not in the lower animals, Onorio replies that if that be so, they must have *some* cognitive power other than either sense-perception or reason. It is immaterial whether we name this power instinct or reason, or whether we adopt the terms of Averroes, but above all we must recognize that even as a homogeneous piece of wax can take diverse and contrary forms, so a single primal corporeal substance is the substratum of all bodies and a single primal spiritual substance appertains to all souls. This doctrine is received with horror, yet Onorio constrains his audience to recognize that it was proclaimed by many of the wisest rabbis, implied in the Biblical story of Nebuchad-

---

21 "Animali."

22 Bruno uses the Aristotelian term *complexions.*

nezzar, and exemplified in the Gospel account of the reincarnation of Elias as St. John the Baptist.[23]

In the second part of the Dialogue, the Ass Onorio explains that he is known as the Horse Pegasus on his periodic visits to Parnassus in the intervals between his mortal incarnations, of which one was in the body of Aristotle. He describes the unfortunate fate of Aristotle who wrote on "physical matters" of which he understood naught, and his books were solemnly commented.[24]

The third Part of the second Dialogue again sets out to show that next to truth there is no virtue so exalted as ignorance and asininity. For if the human mind has some access to truth, it can only be either by science and knowledge or by ignorance and asininity. There is in the rational mind no point intermediate between ignorance and knowledge—and this is illustrated by many examples of human foolishness.

The third Dialogue is merely a few lines to close the work.

There follows a sonnet to *The Cillenican Ass* which introduces the appended Dialogue with the same title. The Nolan gives expression to his contempt for the academic pedants; the Ass makes good his claim to academic honour.

The speakers are the Ass, the Pythagorean Micco (i.e., the Ape), and Mercury. The Ass implores Jove who has given him talent, to give him also speech. Micco expresses his horror, but the Ass declares that he desires to be a member of a college so that he may become a doctor, a grade for which he feels fully equipped. Micco admits that God might cause asses to speak, but cannot conceive that He would secure their admission to a Pythagorean school. "Be not so proud, O Micco," retorts the Ass, "remember that thy Pythagoras teaches that naught within the bosom of nature shall be despised. Moreover I who have now the form of an ass, may have been and may presently be in the form of a great man." They exchange quips on the subject and at length the Ass exclaims: "Tell me now, which is more worthy, that a man should become

---

23 Cf. Matthew XI, 14; Luke I, 17. Cf. Dial. II, i, 54-55, 56-59, 60-62 (Gentile, *Op. ital.*, II, 272-74, 275, 277-78, 279; Lagarde, *Op. ital.*, II, 584-85, 586-87, 588-89).

24 Several of the names given to these commentators have been identified with fellow monks of Bruno in the Convent of St. Benedict.

like to an ass or that an ass should become like to man? But here comes my Cillenican," and he appeals to Mercury, who now intervenes. Claiming to have bestowed many gifts and graces on the Ass, Mercury declares:

> I now with plenary authority ordain, constitute and confirm thee an academician, a general dogmatic, that thou mayest enter and dwell everywhere, that none may hold the door against thee or offer thee outrage or hindrance . . . nor do we desire that thou shouldst be bound by the Pythagorean rule of biennial silence. . . . Speak then to those who can hear, reflect and contemplate among mathematicians; discuss, enquire, teach, declare and determine among the natural philosophers,[25] mix with them all, fraternize, unite thyself and identify thyself with all things, rule all things, be all.

The work closes with Micco's dour reply to the triumphant enquiry of the Ass: "Hast thou heard?" "We are not deaf."

c. *On Heroic Frenzies*[26] *(De gl' Heroici Furori)*

This is perhaps the most discursive of the series of Italian works that deal with moral philosophy through Bruno's eccentric and ebullient symbolism. In complicated exposition, with quotations from the classics and from the Preacher, we learn of the surpassing vision of love, or wisdom, which resolves all conflicts, abolishes suffering and vain pursuit of glory, and leads to the perfect peace of the One ultimate godhead of whom all individuals and all kinds are a partial reflection. Many sonnets are interspersed in the work. Their symbolism is explained in the prose that follows them.[27] These verses are specifically mentioned in the Arguments but they are not the happiest products of Bruno's muse.

---

[25] "Fisici." (We give Florio's translation of the word.)

[26] *De gl' heroici furori,* 1585. (See App. I, 12.) *The Heroic Enthusiasts* in the translation of L. Williams of 1887. But *furore* is translated by Florio as "Fury, rage, bedlam, madness."

[27] Cf. Frances Yates, "The Emblematic Conceit in Giordano Bruno's *De gli eroici furori* and in the Elizabethan Sonnet Sequences," *Journal of Warburg and Courtauld Institutes,* VI (London, 1943), 101-21.

The characters are taken from the Nolan's childhood environment. One is the poet Tansillo, an eminent Nolan often quoted by Bruno, and perhaps known at least to his parents. Another is Mount Cicada itself.

The Heroic Frenzies is, like *The Expulsion of the Triumphant Beast,* dedicated to Sir Philip Sidney. In his Dedication, the Nolan boldly states that he would have liked to emulate King Solomon and to have entitled his work a *Canticle,* "since many mystic and cabalistic doctors interpret Solomon's work as similarly presenting divine and heroic frenzies under the appearance of loves and ordinary passions."

The Dedication opens with a rodomontade on the evils that ensue from allowing thoughts of love to usurp the whole of a man's mind. This passage, which is developed as an attack on the Petrarchists, was probably intended to reproach Sidney himself with too great a preoccupation with Stella. This view is none the less plausible even though Bruno, with tardy caution, concludes his Dedication with a lyrical burst of praise for some Englishwomen who must be included in any discussion of the female sex—"not female, not women, but nymphs in the similitude thereof, divine, of celestial substance, among whom is that unique Diana," i.e., Queen Elizabeth—a theme repeated in the sonnet, *The Nolan's Apology,* which is prefixed to the first Part.

The Dedication provides an Argument to each of the ten Dialogues that make up the two Parts of the work. We will give the main heads of each Argument as set forth by Bruno, supplementing occasionally from the Dialogues themselves.

Under metaphorical figures, Bruno explains, are manifested immanent causes and primal motives whereby the soul is pervaded by God, toward the one perfect and final end, which should eclipse all war and dispute. The Will is captain of the advance, and the four standard-bearers are Heroic Passion, the Power of Fate, the Appearance of the Good (as the object of Love) and Remorse of Jealous Passion, each with their varied and opposed cohorts of adherents, ministers and powers. We are then led to the contemplation of the unity of contraries through harmony and combination, the resolution of all strife in concord, of all diversity in unity.

The second Dialogue of the first Part has an analysis of the contraries whose opposition can thus be resolved. Virtue is the mean, and the further it passes toward an extreme the more will it lose its character as virtue, for virtue is the point of unity between contraries.

The third Dialogue analyses the force of will, manifested as love, and culminating in love of God that can bring to pass the happy resolution of contraries.

The final object of the soul is the divine:

Is then the body not the habitation of the soul? No, for the soul is in the body not as location but as intrinsic form, extrinsic formative influence. . . . The body is in the soul, soul in mind. Mind either is God or is in God, as said Plotinus; and since the mind as essence is in God which is the life thereof, similarly by the act of the mind, and by the consequent act of will, the mind turneth to his light and to his beatific object. Worthily then is the passion of heroic inspiration nourished on so exalted an enterprise. Nor is this because the object is infinite, in act most simple, and our intellect unable to apprehend the infinite save in a certain manner of thought, that is, as a potentiality, even as he who is at the edge of an immense wave pictureth to himself an end where no end is. For indeed there is no final end.[28]

Necessity, Fate, Nature, Council, Will, all are thus recognized as a single unity. Again we are reminded of the complete wheel of life wherein Jove himself passes through diverse forms, and each one of us may at last attain to the Divine.

The power of reason is the subject of the fourth Dialogue. Even as in the myth the hunter is converted into the hunted, so is the mind united with its quarry in accordance with the mode of rationality, and the will according to the mode of will; that is, with such reason as reposes therein. Tansillo recites the first of the three beautiful Italian sonnets which the Nolan had already printed, prefixed to *The Infinite Universe and Worlds*. But reason halts not after achieving unity with her object: she presses ever forward, prompted by her own light toward that which comprises all knowledge, all will, the fount of the whole ocean of truth and beauty. Thus a distinction is drawn between the soul of the universe, perfect, motionless, pervading infinity, and the souls of each part thereof

[28] Part I, Dial. III, pp. 77-78 (Gentile, *Op. ital.*, II, 367; Lagarde, *Op. ital.*, II, 647).

and of each of our worlds, subject to eternal circular motion and vicissitude.[29]

The fifteen sections of the fifth Dialogue of the first Part are overlaid with symbolism and with discursions. Many writers are cited and Bruno recalls passages in his own work. We are shewn how reason governs the conflicting thoughts and passions of those who are inspired, and pervades the whole world. We again have the distinction between lower intellect, "potential, the intellect of power and of passion, uncertain, multiform," and the higher intellect which appertains to man. Again we are led yet further to contemplate the Supreme Intelligence which pervades the whole universe.[30]

The first two Dialogues of the second Part take us again to the individual life of him who is inspired by heroic frenzy. We are reminded that the pleasure of generation is impossible without also the drawback of corruption, and where they are combined in a single subject, there too joy and sadness are together. We hear of the many vicissitudes around the wheel of fate, of resulting conflicts and how they can be resolved only by lofty contemplation.

The Nolan uses his favourite similes of light and fire, sun and moon, and we are told that to see the Divine is to be seen thereby, even as to see the sun is to be within sight thereof. But intellectual power can never be still; it must seek ever further toward truth still uncomprehended, even as Will must seek ever beyond finite apprehension. And the essence of the soul is referred to inferior things even as divinity itself is communicated infinitely throughout the infinite universe, or finitely, producing only this universe accessible to our eyes and common reason. Wherefore strife arises in the soul of him who is inspired since the soul is ever drawn downward toward low and hostile country while struggling toward its natural and exalted habitation. In such a condition, the Nolan tells us, he had been for six lustres before he could reach clarity of thought, before "he could make for himself a dwelling fit for all sorts of pilgrims,

---

29 Part I, Dial. IV, pp. 88, 89-90, 92-93 (Gentile, *Op. ital.*, II, 376, 377, 378-80; Lagarde, *Op. ital.*, II, 652, 653, 654-55).

30 Part I, Dial. V, pp. 114-21, 129-30, 149 (Gentile, *Op. ital.*, II, 396-99, 405-6, 418; Lagarde, *Op. ital.*, II, 666-70, 674, 684).

that could be offered freely and equally to all who beat on the gate of the mind." At length, he being now encamped in twofold holy rays of light, love, which had on diverse occasions assailed him in vain, could now reach him, revealing divine beauty by means of the ray of truth binding the intellect and the ray of goodness warming the passions. The language of the sonnet which follows suggests almost a sudden revelation after his thirtieth year. Again we are assured, love has dominion over all and transcends and fuses all things.[31]

This is further expounded in the second Dialogue. All the diversity of different individuals is needed for the comprehensive whole. It is remarkable to find Bruno, so intolerant of the ignorant and the stupid, yet forced to this logical conclusion of his own thought. We soon have an example of his intolerant mood of biting sarcasm:

> Who that is wise doth not see the advantage when Aristotle, master of Alexander in humane letters, raiseth his soul on high to resist and wage war on the Pythagorean doctrine and that of the natural philosophers . . . with his logic-chopping and fantasy . . . heedful of the faith of the multitude . . . founded on surface appearances rather than on truth which is hidden within and is the very substance of things.

Yet the nourishment of each individual must conform to his own nature, and for the human soul are needed contemplation and reasoning as instruments in the search for truth. For this truth is sought, though hidden and most hard to reach. Again we find ourselves in the pursuit of Diana on whom but few may hope to gaze; once more we are told of the hunter transformed to the nature of his quarry: "Look then on Amphitrite,[32] the source of all numbers, of all species and arguments,

---

[31] Part II, Dial. I, pp. 171, 181-85, 190-5, 200-1 (Gentile, *Op. ital.,* II, 436, 444-46, 450-53, 457; Lagarde, *Op. ital.,* II, 696, 702-4, 706-9, 712). Bruno was some thirty-seven years old when these words were published. Gentile refers the revelation to the thirtieth year of his life, and suggests that he may have been in Venice as late as 1578 and may have proclaimed his vision in the work published there, *On the Signs of the Times* (Gentile, *Op. ital.,* II, 453-54). Or the vision may perhaps have occurred in Toulouse in his thirty-first year.

[32] Amphitrite, wife of Poseidon and goddess of the sea. Perhaps here equated with Diana because this goddess loved to be near wells? Or rather, as suggested in the fifth Dialogue, the two goddesses represent the utter contrast of sea and desert and yet they are one and the same.

the monad, the true essence of all being, very Diana herself. And if you are not permitted to gaze on her veritable essence in the absolute light, yet you will see her offspring, her image similar to herself. For from the monad which is Divinity proceedeth the monad which is Nature, our universe, . . ." whereby as in a mirror, man may attain to reason.[33]

The same images reappear in the third Dialogue of the second Part. This Dialogue is still occupied with the coincidence of contraries though to each thing appertains its distinct function. Being is regarded as a mode of cognition and appetitive power. Will is conditioned by cognition, cognition by will. Can then reason or cognitive power or the cognitive act be greater than will or appetite or passion? But the act expressing the will to good is boundless, just as the act expressing knowledge of truth is infinite and without limit. Thus being, truth and good are but three words all signifying the same single force.

But we learn in the fourth Dialogue the weakness and failure of humanity in apprehending the Divine. Ninefold is the blindness of man. Mysterious divine judgement has bestowed on him the will to thought and investigation, but not the power to rise beyond the consciousness of his own blindness. But at least mankind should realize his own ignorance.[34]

The "Allegory of the Fifth Dialogue" of the second Part, most of which is, like the fourth, in verse, presents two women who, "as is the custom in my country," reject the male method of reaching truth by argument, apprehending rather by intuition and the power of prophecy the spirit which resides in matter. This which they have apprehended they leave to be expounded by the talent of the male.

The Nolan would show that only the blind invoke the instrumentality of external cause. Such is the vulgar imagination of the nine spheres as responsible for the infinite diversity which informs the ultimate unity of the universe. We have a discussion on the views of "Cabbalists,

---

[33] Part II, Dial. II, pp. 211-13, 218-20, 222-5 (Gentile, *Op. ital.,* II, 464-65, 469-70, 471-74; Lagarde, *Op. ital.,* II, 717-18, 721-22, 723-25).

[34] The fourth and fifth Dialogues echo the poem of Marco Antonio Epicuro, *Dialogo di tre ciechi* (Naples, 1535). In the fifth there are again echoes of Tansillo.

Chaldeans, Magicians, Platonists and Christian theologians." Only Origen among theologians has, like all great philosophers and the much blamed Sadducees, dared to express the universe as eternal change and motion. Indeed, says the Nolan, this doctrine I share and confirm when speaking with theologians and with those who make laws and institutions for the people. But the spreading of such views has justly brought reproof, since if the multitude is with difficulty restrained from vice and impelled to virtue by belief in eternal punishment, what would ensue if they were persuaded to a different view? But for the wise, endowed with heroic frenzy toward truth, Bruno expounds an elaborate myth of Circe, daughter of the Sun. Progress, we are told, is not direct from one to another form. Rather—by an image reminiscent of the writings of Raymond Lull—change may be likened to motion around a wheel, so that each in turn is illuminated by the object in which converge the trinity of perfections,—beauty, wisdom and truth; sprinkled by the waters which in the sacred books are termed waters of wisdom, rivers of water of eternal life. These are found not on our earth but on the bosom of Ocean, of the goddess Amphitrite, in whose realm is the miraculous stream that flows from Divinity, and those nymphs, those blessed and divine intelligences who minister to her sublime intelligence even as the nymphs of the desert to Diana. "Amphitrite alone by her triple virtue openeth every seal, looseth every knot, discovereth every secret." Thus is revealed to us the ultimate harmony of the whole, the true meaning of the nine spheres. We see that the beginning of one is the end of another. Beginning and end, light and darkness, infinite power, infinite action, all are One, as the Nolan has elsewhere demonstrated. Thus we contemplate eternal harmony of all spheres, intelligences, Muses and instruments.

> The heaven, the motion of worlds, the works of Nature, the operation of reason, contemplation of the mind, the decrees of divine providence, all together celebrate the exalted and magnificent periodic vicissitudes whereby lower waters become upper waters, night passeth into day, and day into night, so that divinity pervadeth the whole, even as the whole is thus able to contain the whole, and infinite goodness is communicated infinitely in accordance with the capacity of all things.

The Argument presents these themes more succinctly than the prose and verse of the Dialogues. In the text of the fifth Dialogue, elaborate praise of "the lovely and gracious nymphs of the Thames" is woven into the Circe myth. After ten years of wandering, sight is restored to nine blind youths by these nymphs. (Gentile interprets the period as the interval between Bruno leaving Naples in 1576 and the publication of the *Heroic Frenzies* in 1585.) This diversion in praise of Sidney's country-women is omitted from the Argument of "The allegory of the fifth Dialogue" which closes as "the Italian" presents his discourse to Sidney as to one who can truly hear and appreciate.

CHAPTER SIX

LAST WANDERINGS: THE GREAT LATIN POEMS AND OTHER LATIN WRITINGS

a. Bruno's Second Sojourn in Paris (1585–86)

THE recall of Mauvissière to Paris at the end of 1585 brought an abrupt end to Bruno's sojourn in London. It is not easy to follow why Mauvissière was recalled or why payments had ceased to reach him in London. His financial embarrassments were increased by the failure of Mary Queen of Scots to repay large sums of money which he had lent to her. Moreover, a letter from him has come down to us describing the disastrous robbery of all his personal possessions during the voyage back from England.[1] The last years of his life were saddened by the ill-health of his wife and then by her death in childbirth a year after they left England. After his return to Paris, Mauvissière was employed in com-

[1] Public Record Office, Hist. MSS Comm., Salisbury Papers, III, 1585-89 (1889), pp. 110, 112-3. The letter is dated from Paris, 1585 $\frac{\text{Oct. } 24}{\text{Nov. } 3}$ and is addressed to Archibald Douglas. This was presumably the parson of Glasgow, grandson of the second Earl of Morton. Douglas was involved in intrigues for Mary of Scots, and was accused of complicity in the murder both of Rizzio and of Darnley. He was acquitted of both charges, and is said to have won the favour of Elizabeth by disclosing to her his transactions with Mary. Elizabeth sent Douglas in 1586 on a diplomatic mission to the court of King James, and he returned from Scotland as the King's ambassador to Elizabeth, a post he held for only a year. In 1593 he was deposed from the parsonage of Glasgow for neglect of duty and he is stated to have resigned from the position in 1597!

mand of armies both under Henry III and Henry IV. He died in 1592, the year in which Bruno passed from the world to the eight years of his martyrdom.

On their arrival in Paris toward the close of the year 1585, Mauvissière was in no position to offer hospitality. But Bruno seldom failed to attract round him a group of cultured persons fascinated by his talk, and he stated to the Venice Tribunal that he lived in Paris "in the house of gentlemen of my acquaintance, but mostly at my own expense." It appears that he lodged near the College of Cambrai where he may have found congenial acquaintances.

Bruno during this period made a great effort toward reconciliation with the Church. He described at the Venice trial how he first approached the Bishop of Bergamo, the Papal Nuncio in Paris. Armed with an introduction from Mendoza, whom he had known as Spanish Ambassador in England, Bruno begged the Bishop to intercede for him with Pope Sixtus V. He also invoked a Jesuit Father, Alonso Spagnolo. But both the Bishop and Spagnolo refused to attempt to secure Bruno's absolution and admission to the Mass unless he would return to his Order, and this Bruno would not contemplate.[2]

Three volumes from Bruno's pen appeared in Paris in 1586, the year after his arrival from England, all from the same publisher. The first of these is entitled *A Figure of the Aristotelian Physical Teaching*. The first part illustrates the application of Bruno's mnemonic system and his use of figures, for it gives instructions for memorizing the contents of the eight books of the *Physica*. It is dedicated to the Abbot Pierre Dalbène of Belleville.[3] But to interpret these instructions requires an expert in the Art! There follow two paragraphs: "The Division of Universal Philosophy" (according to Aristotle); and Aristotle's "Division of Natural Philosophy." Eight works or groups of writings by

---

[2] *Doc. Ven.* XVII.

[3] Cf. App. I, 13. Pierre Dalbène, or Delbène, presumably belonged to the ancient and distinguished Florentine family. Nicholas Delbène migrated from Florence and settled at the end of the fourteenth century in France where he and his descendants held various posts of honour. The Augustine Abbey of Belleville in Beaujollais, in the diocese of Lyons, was a twelfth century foundation.

Aristotle on "Natural Philosophy" are enumerated.[4] The second half of the little volume gives an epitome of the eight books of the *Physica*. It shows signs of having been printed in haste and not fully completed.

Bruno's mind was also running on mathematics. He met in Paris Fabrizio Mordente of Salerno who wrote on Integration and had also invented the eight-pointed compass.[5] As though he had not enough

---

[4] Bruno's list is *Auscultatio physica; De coelo et mundo; De generatione et corruptione* ("in two books and a third which is without reason attached as Bk. 4 to the *Meteorologica*"); *Meteorologica; De mineralibus; De plantis;* "books on animals, *De generatione animalium* and *De animalibus*"; and "On the origin [*principio*] of generation, life, motion, of vegetative life, of sentience and of reasoning in *De anima* and in the *Parva naturalia.*" Bruno adds that he has not included the *Problemata* since it is itself a commentary on the others. He of course does not know that the *Problemata* is spurious.

[5] Mordente's first work *Il compasso et riga* was published at Antwerp in 1584 and reprinted in Paris in 1585. See P. Riccardi *Biblioteca Matematica Italiana* (2 Parts, Modena, 1873-6, 1893), Part I, Vol. i, Coll. 198-9; and Part I, Vol. ii, Col. 184. It appeared again in a volume bearing the names as joint authors of Fabrizio Mordente and his brother Gaspari who had served with Bruno's father in the Nola militia. The title of this volume is *La quadratura del cerchio, la scienza de' residui; il compasso et riga.* It was published in Antwerp in 1591 under the patronage of the Farnese. See Riccardi *loc. cit.*, Part I, *Corr. et. Agg.*, Ser. V, Coll. 110-11. (The earlier editions may well have borne also this longer title. No copies of them appear to be known.) Only one other work by Fabrizio Mordente is recorded. The Catalogue of the Magliabecchi Library (now incorporated in the *Biblioteca Nazionale* in Florence) cites a volume by him, now lost: *Le proposizione per sapere come da numero a numero la proporzione ch'è fra qualsivoglia due date specie di quantità d'un medesimo genere misurabili o pesabili, create o fabbricate dall' arte; per sapere per numeri le radici quadre de' numeri non quadrati* . . . (Rome, 1597). See Riccardi *loc. cit.*, Part I, *Corr. et Agg.*, Ser. III, Col. 180. Riccardi cites from Leonardo Nicodemo *Addizioni copiose alla biblioteca napoletana del D. Niccolo Toppi* . . . (Naples, 1683), another edition of this work, published in Rome in 1598. See Riccardi *loc cit.*, Part I, Vol. ii, Coll. 183-4. This is cited also by J. C. Brunet *Manuel du Libraire* (6 Vols., Paris, 1860-65), Vol. III, Col. 1892, from the Libri 1857 Catalogue (where it bears the number 1365). No copy of the work in either edition appears to be known now. Fabricius Mordente was in fact not without recognition, for when Bruno reached Prague in 1588, Mordente was Imperial Astronomer. In the title of the 1598 volume, he is described as Mathematician to the Emperor Rodolph II. Moreover, Michel Coignet, himself the inventor of a "pantometer or proportional compass," and Mathematician to Prince Albert Farnese, Duke of Parma, published in Antwerp in 1608 . . . *Della forma et parti del compasso di Fabritio Mordente Salernitano. Con gli usi di esso* . . . ; and in Paris

troubles of his own, Bruno found himself overwhelmed with indignation at the neglect of this mathematician's work and especially of his eight-pointed compass. Bruno now issued in Paris a volume *Concerning the Almost Divine Invention by Fabrizio Mordente of Salerno for the Perfect Practice of Cosmic Measurement.* After a paean of praise to the shamefully neglected Mordente, Bruno describes and figures the instrument in two Dialogues. He appends to the volume a "Dream" (Insomnium) in which he figures an astronomical device for ascertaining the position and the motion of heavenly bodies. Bruno declares that he cannot remember the face or the habit of the inventor of the method, who, however, described it in the "Dream" so that it has remained vividly in his mind.[6]

By a happy chance, one of those who met Bruno at this time in Paris has recorded his impressions. The diarist was Guillaume Cotin, librarian of the Abbey of St. Victor.[7] He first mentions Bruno as visiting his library on the 6th December, 1585. Bruno was back on the following day, and on the 12th December he brought his own works on the art of memory to show to the librarian. Two more visits are recorded in December—and then a final visit early in February. We may imagine that a friendship sprang up between the two men, as many details of Bruno's early life are recorded by Cotin, as well as notes on Bruno's published and unpublished works.

It is clear that the pious librarian of St. Victor was at first fascinated

---

in 1626 *La géométrie réduite en un facile et briefve praticque, par deux excellens instrumens, dont l'une est le pantometre ou compas de proportion de Michel Connette . . . L'autre est l'usage du compas a huict poinctes inuenté par Fabrice Mordente . . .* See Riccardi *loc. cit.,* Part I, *Corr. et Agg.,* Ser. IV, Col. 205; and Part I, Vol. ii, Col. 184.

[6] See App. I, 14a-b.

[7] This diary was discovered in the Bibliothèque Nationale (MS fr. 20309 ff. 354v *seqq.*) by L. Auvray, who published "Giordano Bruno à Paris d'après le témoignage d'un contemporain 1585-6" in *Mémoires de la societé de l'histoire de Paris et de l'Ile-de-France,* XXIV (Paris, 1900), 288-99. The paper has been reprinted frequently. The entries in Cotin's diary are given as *Documenti Parigini* in Spampanato, *Vita di Giordano Bruno* and in Spampanato, *Documenti della vita di Giordano Bruno.* Cf. also F. Yates, *The French Academies of the Sixteenth Century* (Warburg Institute, London, 1947), pp. 17-18, 229-30.

by his visitor. He refers to the inquisitors who threatened Bruno at Rome in 1576 as "ignorant and not understanding his philosophy." [8] He cites Bruno's views and speaks of his writings. We hear that "Jordanus told me that Fabricius Mordentius Salernitanus is in Paris, aged 60, a god among geometers . . . yet knowing no Latin. Jordanus will print a Latin account of his works." [9] Cotin quotes Bruno's opinions also of the scholars and preachers of the day. A certain Hebrew convert seems to have been alone among preachers in winning Bruno's admiration both for his learning and his eloquence. Another preacher, Bossulus, was praised only for eloquence and clear pronunciation.[10] Bruno was for the most part a biting critic. He expressed his contempt for Toletus[11] and the Jesuits who were preaching in Italy.

There ensued an estrangement between Bruno and the librarian. Though both remained in Paris for some four months longer, no further visits are recorded. Moreover, in March 1586, Cotin is listening to an unfriendly account of Bruno's humiliation at Geneva seven years pre-

---

[8] *Doc. Par.* II.

[9] *Doc. Par.* VII.

[10] *Doc. Par.* III. Matthaeus Bossulus had taught Rhetoric at the University of Valencia in Spain and was a famous orator. In 1583 he was Rector of the small College of Boncourt (founded at Paris in 1353). Since he won Bruno's praise, we are not surprised to hear that Bossulus was condemned for heresy, but he was later reinstated and established a reputation for eloquence.

[11] Francesco de Toledo (1532-1596) was a Spaniard of humble origin. He studied in Valencia and in Salamanca where he became professor. In 1558 he joined the Jesuits, and was sent by Francisco Borgia to Rome where he acquired fame as philosopher and theologian. He became Preacher in Ordinary to Pius V (1569) and to succeeding Popes. He was employed on several diplomatic journeys and he took part in the negotiations leading to the absolution of Henry IV of France. In 1593 he received the Cardinal's hat from Clement VIII. Francesco de Toledo wrote on Logic, and produced numerous Aristotelian commentaries besides sermons and theological works.

Cotin also records from these conversations Bruno's disapproval of Cujas and of Passerat. Jacques Cujas (1522-1590), renowned for his knowledge and exposition of Roman law, had held several Chairs and was at this date professor at Bourges where he was occupied on his great text and commentary of the *Corpus juris.* His pupil, Jean Passerat (1534-1602), had abandoned the law and in 1572 had succeeded Ramus as Professor of Rhetoric and Poetry at the Collège de France. He was somewhat suspect as a partisan of the Huguenots but was a popular figure in Paris.

viously. In May he reports dryly and without comment the disastrous affair at the College of Cambrai which must now be recounted.

In Pentecost week of 1586, Bruno boldly challenged all and sundry to impugn the *One Hundred and Twenty Articles on Nature and the World* sustained against the Peripatetics by his pupil John Hennequin.[12] It seemed that his challenge would be left unanswered. But at the last moment there arose to reply a young advocate, Raoul Callier. This young man was a close relative of Nicolas Rapin of Fontenay in Poitou, notorious for his harsh treatment of Huguenots. At his death-bed confession, strangely reported in full by the priestly Father who officiated, Rapin declared that "The only good thing that he remembered to have done since his youth was that he prevented the public teaching of atheism . . . in Paris."[13] Had Rapin assisted Callier or intervened against Bruno during or after the disputation? We cannot tell, but we may well believe that with such affiliations, Callier applied himself to his task with zest. He spoke with such effect that the students, ignoring Hennequin, set upon Bruno and demanded that he should either reply or retract his calumnies against Aristotle. Bruno undertook to reply on the following day, when, however, the proceedings again opened with an oration by the brilliant young Callier. "Hennequin could reply only to the first argument," records Cotin. Bruno was then called to speak, but he declared, so runs the diarist's report, that the hour was too late. Nor would he appear on the following day, "saying that he was already vanquished." The *One Hundred and Twenty Articles* were, however, published while Bruno was still in Paris. The copy in the British Museum is believed to be the sole survivor of the edition. The volume bears a dedicatory inscription to King Henry III, and one to Jean Filesac,

---

12 App. I, 15. It would be pleasant to trace the further fate of John Hennequin who so doughtily but unsuccessfully stood for his teacher's doctrine. He is presumably the young Doctor of Law (perhaps of the noble family descended from the Artois), who wrote *Notae ad accursum et glossae,* published with Peter Brosseus *Thesaurus accursianus* (Lyons, 1589, and Vienna, 1606), and also wrote *Le guidon général des finances* (Paris, 1605). Perhaps it was he who became "Intendant of France"? (Zedler, *Universal Lexicon,* XII, 1406).

13 Claude Pierre Goujet, *Bibliothèque française ou histoire de la littérature française* (Paris, 1752), XIV, 119-35.

Rector of Paris University.[14] But this was the end of Bruno's second visit to Paris. Once more he resumed his wanderings. "Because of the tumults," he stated to the Inquisitors at Venice, "I left Paris and went to Germany." [15]

b. Marburg and Wittenberg (1586–88)

Taking up his wanderings once more, Bruno passed through Mainz and Wiesbaden where, as he related to the Venice Tribunal, he could find no livelihood. He came to Marburg, and on 25th July, 1586, he matriculated in the university there. After his name on the matriculation roll, "Iordanus Nolanus Neapolitanus, theologiae doctor romanensis," the newly elected Rector has recorded the events which brought Bruno's sojourn to a precipitate close:

> When the right publicly to teach philosophy was denied him by me for good cause and with the assent of the philosophical Faculty, he burnt with rage, and impudently reviled me in my own house as though I had acted in defiance of the law of nations, against the custom of all German universities and contrary to all schools of the humanities. Wherefore he declared that he had no wish to remain a member of the Academy. So his fee was readily returned to him, and he was discharged from the register of the university.

The Rector's action appears nevertheless not to have been unanimously supported by his colleagues: Spampanato, who viewed the Register, points out that, whereas the original inscription of Bruno's name was crossed through by the Rector, the letters remained legible, but that the words, "with the accord of the Faculty," had been completely obliterated by a later hand.[16]

But Bruno resumed his wanderings, and at length he reached a tem-

---

[14] The dedication to Filesac is reproduced by C. E. de Boulay, *Historia universitatis Parisiensis* (Paris, 1673), VI, 786. Jean Filesac (1550?-1638) was himself a voluminous writer on theological subjects.

[15] *Doc. Ven.* IX.

[16] Quoted as *Documento Tedescho* I by Spampanato, from the manuscript *Jahrbücher* of the University of Marburg. The name of the irate Rector was Petrus Nigidius, Doctor of Law and Professor of Moral Philosophy.

porary haven at Wittenberg in Saxony, where he found his compatriot, the jurist Alberico Gentilis, of whom we have already had a glimpse in Oxford.[17] Gentilis, he relates, obtained an invitation for him to lecture on the *Organon,* which resulted in his being engaged to lecture for the next two years. Three new works were published by Bruno during this breathing space: two volumes published in 1587, and his speech of 1588, expressing his thanks and farewell to the university.[18] In addition, an enlarged edition of the *One Hundred and Twenty Articles against Aristotle* appeared at Wittenberg under the cryptic title of *Camoeracensis acrotismus,* which we may perhaps render *The Abruptly Ended Discourse in the College of France.*[19] The volume bears, prefixed to the Dedications to Henry III and to Filesac, a new Dedication to the "Philosophers of Paris and to other philosophers in the generous realm of Gaul who are friends and defenders of the dogmas of a wiser philosophy."

The first of the Wittenberg volumes bears a cumbrous title which we may epitomize as: *On the Synthetic Lullian Lamp leading to infinite propositions . . . to the understanding of all things . . . the sole Key to all Lullian works and no less to Pythagorean and Cabbalistic mysteries.*[20] . . . Bruno was never niggard of gratitude and the long

---

[17] Cf. pp. 31, 43, 102 *seqq.,* 112-13.

[18] App. I, 16, 17, 19.

[19] App. I, 18.

[20] App. I, 16. Though printed in 1587, the work would seem to have been drafted at the end of 1586, for a volume now in the *Kreis und Stadt Bibliothek* of Augsburg contains, besides certain manuscript works of Bruno, a copy of this printed volume with marginal glosses and with the manuscript "title-page," *Lampas combinatoria lulliana tradita privatim in Academia Witebergense a Jordano Bruno Nolano,* CICIC XIVC. (See App. III, p. 220.) Another copy of this work (now in the former ducal library of Gotha) bears the following inscription in Bruno's hand: "Admodum generoso, nobili studiosissimoque D. Iacobo Cunoni Francofurtensi benevolentiae ergo et in sui memoriam dedicavit author" (Spampanato, *Vita,* II, 668, *Doc. Ted.* X). Sigwart observes that Cuno figures in the list of matriculants at the University of Frankfurt-on-the-Oder for the winter term 1569-70. He is described as "Jacob Cuno, son of Master Jacob Cuno the distinguished astronomer of the Elector of Brandenburg." This master Jacob Cuno published works on mathematics and astronomy, and at least one on astrology. (See Christopher Sigwart, *Kleine Schriften* [2 vols., Freiburg, 1889], I, 294-95.)

Preface to the Rector [21] and Senate of Wittenberg University expresses heartfelt thanks for the benevolence and hospitality extended to him,

> a person of no name, fame or value among you, supported by no prince's praise, distinguished by no outward trappings such as the vulgar are wont to admire, a fugitive from the Gallic tumults; nor was I examined or interrogated on your religious dogma, with that custom of harsh discipline of perfidious barbarians, violators of the laws of nations, to whom should be closed that heaven and earth which they either entirely deny as a common and social possession ordained by nature for all men, or concede them only with impious and deadly calculation.

As Bruno expatiates on the humanity of his hosts, their urbanity, true benignity, and devotion to the Muses, "whereby he recognizes truly a university," we catch the same accents with which he saluted his beloved friend Mauvissière who had similarly extended to him the priceless benefit of leisure and freedom for thought and study. He used his leisure, studying Eriugena, Cusanus, Paracelsus, his hero Raymond Lull, "already commented by Cornelius Agrippa," the humanists Lefèvre of Etaples and de Bovelles,[22] at whose works we have already glanced, and many other writers of East and West. Each of the faculty of that great university he mentions with affection and admiration, not omitting the Chancellor and the Rector. Once more we recognize the transparent honesty of Bruno's passion to learn and to know. The Lullian Art which he would set forth in honour of these men is no less than the whole Art of Thought expounded in the Lullian manner with the aid of geometric figures, concentric circles and tables.

The second Wittenberg volume treats *Of the Advance and Enlightening Hunt for Logic* and is in a somewhat similar vein, inspired by

---

[21] The Rector of Wittenberg was Petrus Albinus Nivemontius. Cf. extract from the *Album* of the University cited by Spampanato (*Vita,* II, 664, *Doc. Ted.* I). He was an historian whose ancestor Weisen, or Weiss, had been ennobled by the Emperor Maximilian in 1497. His birthplace, as indicated by the name, was Schneeberg in Meissen. He studied at Leipzig and Frankfurt and was Historiographer of Chur in Saxony and "State Secretary at Dresden" to the princes Augustus and Christian I of Chur, successively. These posts he held at the same time as his professorship at Wittenberg University.

[22] Cf. pp. 77-8.

Lullian methods. It is dedicated to George Mylius, Chancellor of Wittenberg University.[23]

A further work has come down to us from the sojourn at Wittenberg, though never published by Bruno. This is *The Art of Peroration Delivered by Jordano Bruno, the Italian of Nola, Communicated by Johann-Henricus Alstedius for the Benefit of Those Who Wish to Know the Force and Method of Eloquence,* which was published in 1612, long after his death, by the house of Antonius Hummius in Frankfurt.[24] In the Dedication to "his most noble and learned patron" Count Abraham Wrsotzky Gorni of Poland, Alstedt recalls the talk they had both enjoyed with Count Vladislaus ab Ostrorog, and records his admiration and love for Count Wrsotzky Gorni. He states that the book has been in his hands for two years and that he has edited and corrected any suspected errors, taking care to change the work of Bruno as little as possible:

> For no one will seek here for elegance of style or mere entertainment, since neither of these was the author's purpose. Had I wished to make from this a new treatise, verily it would have emerged more elegant. But I preferred to communicate to the studious the doctrine delivered in his own style by the author, a man indeed not without erudition, rather than to concoct a new treatise . . . I have striven to produce the same form as in the "Canonical Triads" which, Sir Count, I dedicated to you, that these two books may unite to testify to the philosophy and the Christianity that was with the three of us.

Alstedt dates his Dedication from Herborn in Nassau, May, 1612. The sub-title of the volume is *Introduction to the work on Rhetoric of Jordano Bruno the Nolan from Italy*. In an *Introduction to the Reader,*

---

[23] App. I, 17. George Mylius was a Lutheran theologian. Born at Augsburg in 1544 he studied at Tübingen, Marburg and Strasbourg. He held several church appointments and in 1579 became Rector of the Evangelical Theological College at Augsburg. Difficulties ensued as he opposed the Gregorian Calendar, and he had to retire to Ulm. In 1584 he became Professor of Theology at Wittenberg. In 1589 (the year after Bruno's departure) Mylius became Professor of Theology at Jena, but in 1603 he was appointed again to Wittenberg where he remained until his death in 1607.

[24] App. I, xii.

Alstedt gives an epitome of the two Parts of the work. This Introduction ends with a Table of the logical method for oratory prescribed by Bruno. Part I is entitled: *Explanation of the Work on Rhetoric Sent by Aristotle to Alexander, Privately Dictated by Jordano Bruno the Italian of Nola at Wittenberg in 1587.* Part II is entitled *The Art of Rhetoric,* and gives elaborate schemes for the construction of an oration, with sundry alternatives, synonyms, etc., illustrated by elaborate diagrams.

There have come down to us in manuscript from this period two other works by Bruno on Lullian mnemonics and another commentary on the *Physics* of Aristotle. None of these reached publication under his own supervision.[25]

But once more the course of political events brought to an abrupt end Bruno's respite of quiet study and teaching. His exposition to the Venice Tribunal is somewhat confused, but it is apparent that the death of the aged Elector Augustus (Bruno calls him Duke) in February 1586, and the accession of Christian I, had brought disturbance and a shift of power from Lutherans to Calvinists.[26] The latter were not disposed to harbour Bruno, and ultimately he had to leave. His Valedictory Oration to the Rector, professors, and to his noble and learned audience at the university is full of praise for his hosts, though a less peaceful situation is perhaps indicated by the cloudy complexity of his mythological analogies.[27] We know that he was forced to salute and depart. Perhaps he had hardly expected an extension of peaceful life.

Two documents from the Wittenberg period bear witness to his saddened outlook. One is the Family Album of Hans von Warnsdorf of Wittenberg,[28] and the other is a print portraying the Siege of Nola by

25 App. I, xiii, xiv, and xv.

26 Or to the "Philippist" sect. See *Cambridge Modern History,* III, 711. In some respects, the rule of Christian I appears to have been more liberal than that of his predecessor.

27 App. I, 19.

28 A long notice in Zedler is devoted to the ancient and distinguished family of von Warnsdorf, early settled in the region, and ennobled by the Emperor Frederick I in 1190 for crusading service. The Album is now in the Public Library of Stuttgart. The verse is on fol. 117. On fol. 31 of the same volume occurs the signature of Michael Forgacz of Hungary. The Forgacz or Forgach family belonged to the Hungarian nobility and owned land at Ghymes (Gimes). Francis Forgacz was a

the troops of Hannibal.[29] On each are inscribed under the caption *Salomon et Pythagoras* these lines from Ecclesiastes, a work we have seen already haunting Bruno in his early days in Paris:

> Quid est quod est? Ipsum quod fuit.
> Quid est quod fuit? Ipsum quod est.
> Nihil sub sole novum.
> Iordanus Brunus Nolanus.

The date inscribed in the Warnsdorf Album is "Wittenberg, 18 Sept." It must have been written in 1587. The print bears the date 9th March, 1588.

c. Prague and Helmstedt (1588–90)

In 1588 the changeless rhythm of Bruno's life was renewed, and he passed to the imperial town of Prague to the Court of Rudolph II, where again he found a friend, the mathematician Fabricius Mordentius of Salerno.[30]

He immediately published a brief new work, *A Scrutiny of the Lullian Categories,* to which he appended a reprint of *The Synthetic Lullian Lamp,* published the year before at Wittenberg. The whole new volume[31] was dedicated under the date 10th June, 1588, to William San Clemente, Ambassador from the King of Spain to the Emperor. This statesman, we gather from the Dedication, had, like King Henry III of France, fallen under the spell of Bruno's expositions of Lull's methods of logical thought and of memory. The two works in the present volume will, the author promises, afford to his patron's talent a complete understanding of the Lullian Art. The latter work, he explains, is not so much to give the ordinary principles of medicine as to shew that the general

Cardinal in the sixteenth century. Cf. Alexius Horanyi, *Memoria hungarorum et provincialium scriptis editis notorum* (3 vols., Vienna, 1775-77), I, 682-98. The name of Michael Forgacz comes up again in connection with Bruno's return to Italy in 1592. Cf. p. 58, n. 4; and cf. Sigwart, *Kleine Schriften.*

[29] This was the property of M. Olschki of Florence and was published by F. Tocco, "Un nuovo autografo di G. Bruno," in *La bibliofilia* (Florence, 1906), IX, 342-45.

[30] Cf. pp. 135-7.

[31] App. I, 20 (a) and (b).

Lullian Art applies to all sciences and faculties whereby anyone may acquire knowledge of real medicine. A few pages, partly in Bruno's own hand containing a tract *On Lullian Medicine* are referred to this period. From Bruno's hand too we have a later version of a figure illustrating his Commentary on the *Physics of Aristotle* (p. 143) as well as some alchemical recipes, and perhaps also a Mnemonic table found with these.[32]

Soon Bruno presented to the Emperor himself a volume on the *Principles and Elements of Geometry.* It comprises *One hundred and sixty Articles against the Mathematicians and Philosophers of this age; one hundred and eighty Exercises, for the solution by a possible and easy method of one hundred and eighty Problems, some hard, some indeed impossible by any other method.*[33] In his Dedication he declares that he would be unworthy of the light vouchsafed to him if he did not try to illuminate also other men. While the form of the work borrows from Euclid's *Elements,* the very first axioms warn us that we are in a non-Euclidean universe. "The Universe is the maximum. . . . The individual is the minimum, neither perfect nor imperfect, the universal measure . . ." and we soon reach symbolism for Mind, Intellect, Love.

Such symbolism has many parallels in the literature of the period. In the ensuing pages are many elaborate figures, some using Hebrew script. We may not be surprised that the Emperor Rudolph II, rewarding the writer with three hundred *talari,*[34] issued no invitation for his

---

[32] App. I, xvi, xvii (a) and (b), xviii. The last is a loose leaf of parchment, and therefore cannot quite definitely be linked with the other parts of the manuscript volume in which it was found (cf. App. III). Tocco and Vitelli are inclined to ascribe it to the year 1589, but they suggest it may have been written in Frankfurt about 1590-91. Cf. *Op. lat.,* III, xxix, xx.

[33] App. I, 21.

[34] *Talari* is Bruno's word. We may recall that the word dollar in fact derives from a *Tal* or *valley* in Bohemia. The silver mines of the small settlement of Konradsgrün and Thal (later Joachimsthal or Jachymov) near Carlsbad were exploited at least as early as 1512. In 1518 the owner, Count Stepan Slik, established a mint in which were coined the first "Joachimsthaler Groschen." These coins came to be called *Slik's tallars,* whence the modern word *dollar.* Jachymov has in modern times become famous for its radium. Cf., F. Behounek and F. Ulrich, "Jachymov Radium" in *Selections from Czecho-Slovak Literature and Sciences* (The American Institute in Czecho-Slovakia, Prague, 1935).

further sojourn in Prague. So within six months of his arrival, Bruno fared forth, this time northward again, to the newly founded *Julia Academy* of Helmstedt in Brunswick, where he was able to live for a year on the Emperor's gift.

His only publication in 1589 was the *Consolatory Oration* which he was honoured to make to the university on the 1st July on the death of the Founder, the beloved Duke Julius, which had taken place in the previous May.[35]

The oration is a somewhat extraordinary document. For Bruno not only expresses his customary gratitude for a quiet haven of study, but in describing the disturbances and woes of the rest of Europe, permits himself the bitterest strictures on his own land. "Spain and Italy," he declares, "are crushed by the feet of the vile priests." He contrasts the free pursuit of study at Helmstedt with the tyranny and greed that pervaded his own land. Yet, at Helmstedt we know that Bruno's path was not entirely smooth. For there has survived a document dated 6th October, 1589, bearing Bruno's signature and addressed to the Pro-Rector of the University of Helmstedt:[36]

Jordanus Brunus the Nolan, excommunicated in public assembly but without a hearing by the Chief Pastor and Superintendent of the Church in Helmstedt—who acted both as judge and executioner—appeals to the Pro-Rector and . . . Senate, humbly protesting against the public execution of this private and most unjust sentence: he pleads to be heard so that should judgement fall upon his rank and good name, he shall at least know that it has fallen justly. . . .

The matter is somewhat obscure, since it is fairly certain that Bruno never formally joined the Protestants, and therefore could not have been excommunicated by them. Moreover, no record survives of the result of

---

35 App. I, 22.

36 This is numbered *360 novorum fol.* among the Archives of Helmstedt University now in the library of Wolfenbüttel. Cf. *Doc. Ted.* VI. See App. I, xix (*Op. lat.*, III, xii, xiii). The Pro-Rector was Daniel Hofmann, no friend to strange beliefs. The Chief Pastor was Boethius, who himself came later under ecclesiastical censure. Cf. E. L. T. Henke, *Die Universität Helmstadt in 16ten Jahrhundert* (Halle, 1833), p. 69.

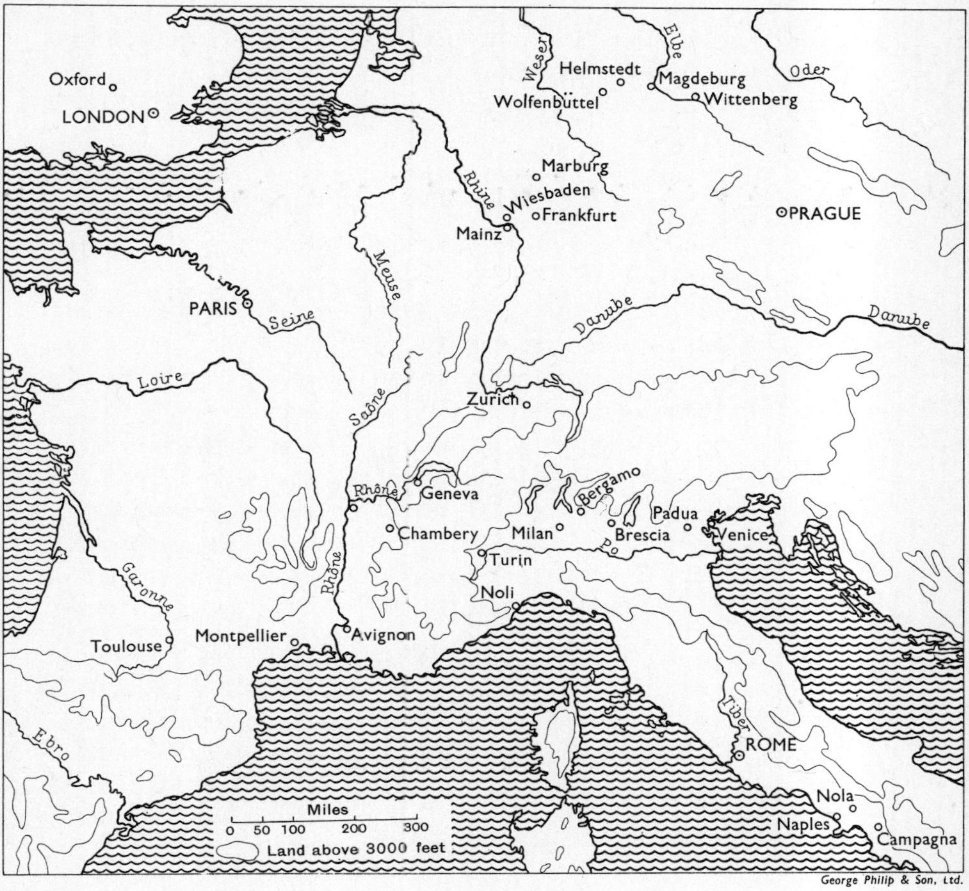

Fig. 13. Map of Bruno's wanderings.

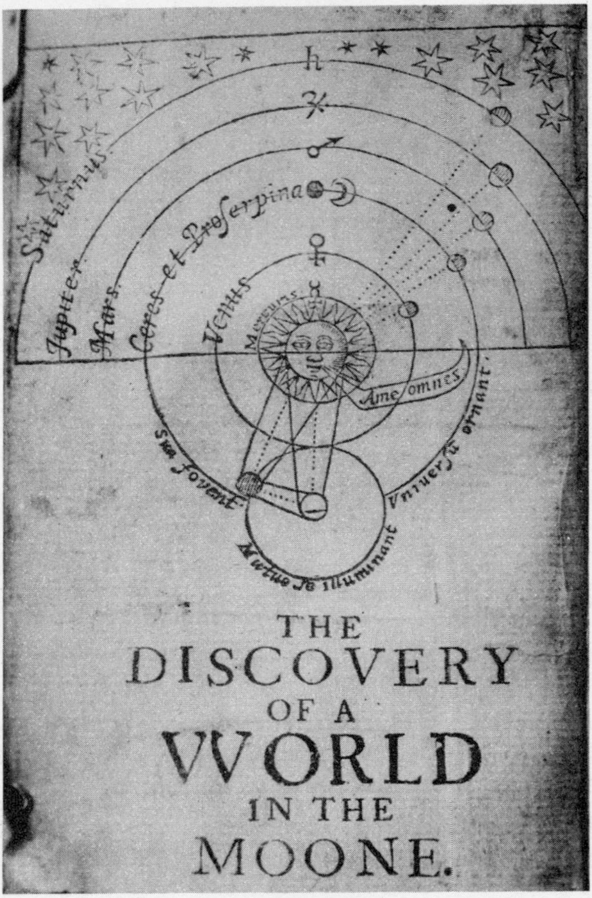

Fig. 14. John Wilkins' representation of the universe. From his *The Discovery of a World in the Moone . . .* (London, 1638).

his appeal. Perhaps this episode explains why none of his works except the almost official *Consolatory Oration* was published at Helmstedt. Possibly at this time Bruno made a brief visit to Frankfurt. For the Italian bookseller Brictanus, called to give evidence at Bruno's Venice trial in May 1592, stated that he had first met him "at Frankfurt some three years ago." But the winter 1589-90 must have been passed by Bruno at Helmstedt. He stated at the Venice trial that he left the town equipped with eighty scudi given to him by the young Duke as a reward for his oration, and he set forth for Frankfurt, the emporium of books, to arrange for the printing of his great Latin philosophical works, in combined verse and prose. These we shall examine presently.

Two letters from Jerome Besler of Nuremberg (1566-1632), a friend and secretary of Bruno, give an interesting glimpse of the last days of Bruno before starting for Frankfurt.[37] Besler had matriculated at Helmstedt in November 1589,[38] and Bruno had employed him as secretary during the winter 1589-90. He came of a family of some learning, his father having been the first Protestant pastor of Sprottau in Silesia. His name appears in the Venice trial as a pupil of Bruno who acted as his scribe again in the last months at Padua. Besler had meanwhile turned to the study of medicine, in which he graduated at Basle in 1592. He settled in his native town where he became a physician of some eminence, and among his pupils was his brother Basil the botanist (born in 1561) and his son Michael Robert (1607-1661), author of several medical works. But his long life brought Jerome no episode so important as his association with Bruno. The two letters from Helmstedt are dated respectively the 15th April and 22nd April, 1590, and are addressed to Besler's uncle, the physician Wolfgang Zeileisen. In the first letter Besler describes having gone with Bruno to Wolfenbüttel to claim fifty florins promised him by the Prince, "a thing marvellous and unexpected." A

---

[37] These letters are now in the library of Erlangen, MS. 1826 (Cf. *Doc. Ted.* VII and VIII).

[38] Sigwart (*Kleine Schriften,* Vol. I) found the record of Besler's matriculation. He also makes the interesting point that pp. 11-86 of the Moscow MS. in Besler's hand (cf. App. III) are on the same paper as Bruno's letter to the Rector of Helmstedt.

few days later Bruno had intervened in a disputation. He was working hard, and soon handed Besler a new tract on *The Inventive Art* (of Lull), then one *On Medicine,* and again one on *The Lullian Art.* If occasion should offer to print a work in Magdeburg and thus to give pleasure to the Prince, Bruno would stay in that town. A week later Besler writes again, explaining that they have been delayed by lack of carriages, but mentioning one which they propose to hire on the following day. Bruno was anxious to take counsel with Wolfgang Zeileisen.

Several works that survive in Besler's hand are believed to have been dictated by Bruno at this period, and are perhaps those to which Besler refers in the letters. The titles are: *On Magic; Theses on Magic; On the Origin, Elements and Causes of Things;* a longer but incomplete version of the *Lullian Medicine;* and *On Mathematical Magic.*[39]

Next to the Lullian studies that wasted Bruno's time and energy, the reader is most puzzled by his long work *On Magic.* We have already considered the problem.[40] It has to be remembered that the theme *natural magic,* that is to say, the medley of misunderstood and misrepresented devices—technical and other, which was covered by this title—took at the time and especially among those without technical knowledge, somewhat the place of what might now be called the "wonders of science." Many phenomena that we now explain on scientific grounds were then treated as "magic that worked according to rule." Of such was believed to be the nature of Bruno's marvellous memory for which exalted persons were always seeking "the rules." In the MS. *On Magic,* Bruno considers Lullian symbolism as the avenue to wisdom. He reviews the "magical" attempts of various peoples, defines *natural magic* as "the application of the passive and active properties of things as in medicine and chemistry," and points out that Aristotle used the term *magus* as a synonym for *wise.*[41] He includes in his survey "veneric or malevolent magic," but he is striving towards a synthetic philosophy based on most diverse sources. He enunciates a cosmic hierarchy[42] and cosmic metabolism;[43] he reiterates his conviction that every soul and spirit has a certain

[39] App. I, xx-xxiv.
[40] Cf. p. 18.
[41] *De magia* (*Op. lat.,* III, 400).
[42] *Op. lat.,* III, 402.
[43] *Ibid.,* III, 407-8, 415.

continuity with the spirit of the universe;[44] he is again considering the hypothesis of a Void.[45]

Bruno's unhappily named tract, *On Mathematical Magic,* is a philosophical work illustrated by mathematical forms. Thus the first sentence states: "God floweth into the angels, the angels into celestial bodies . . ." while the first section of the second paragraph runs: "Thus God or the emanation from God has descended through the world to the animal; and verily the animal has ascended through the world to God." It is a "scala naturae," partly Aristotelian and partly inspired by Bruno's reflections on Infinity.

On the Origins and Elements of Things, and on Their Causes is dated 16th March, 1590. It opens thus: "The efficient and moving causes of things are intellect and soul, above which is a single absolute origin, mind or truth, of which the essence and power are infinite, intensively and extensively." The Averroist conception of the continuity of the spirit Bruno re-enunciates as a theory of all things "linked in absolute mind or truth . . . a single infinite space."[46] He closes with an elaborate figure of "influences" from the sun, but remarks that none of these influences are conveyed from heaven to individuals below unless by some seed brought to the individual at an appropriate time and place, thus applying and limiting the general and universal quality.

No doubt Bruno profited by his leisure during this year 1589-90 to make substantial progress with the great Latin poems in which his developed philosophy is set forth.

d. Frankfurt, Zurich and Frankfurt Again (1590–91)

There is some obscurity in the movements of Bruno from the time of his departure with Jerome Besler from Helmstedt on 23rd April, 1590. Did they visit Besler's uncle at Magdeburg? In any event, he was soon on his way in the opposite direction travelling to Frankfurt on the Main, where he arrived probably at the beginning of July. At Frankfurt he

[44] *Ibid.,* III, 408. [45] *Ibid.,* III, 414. [46] *Ibid.,* III, 509-10.

devoted himself to the production of the great Latin works which had been in his mind and partly on paper from the period of his sojourn in London. As usual, a publisher was at once forthcoming, and indeed the Frankfurt firm of John Wechel and Peter Fischer smoothed his path in every way. The Wechels had been in contact with Sir Philip Sidney (who had died four years previously) and this may have led to Bruno's introduction to them. On 2nd July, 1590, Bruno petitioned the Senate for permission to lodge in Wechel's house, but this was refused.[47] Not to be beaten, the printer succeeded in obtaining permission for him to dwell in the Carmelite Monastery, and here he was established for six or eight months. Yet he did not see the first of his great poems completely through the press. The volume[48] appeared with no preface from Bruno, but with a Dedication to the Duke of Brunswick,[49] penned by the faithful John Wechel. The title is *Five Books on the Threefold Minimum and on Mensuration for the Foundation of the Three Speculative Sciences and Many Active Arts*. Wechel, expressing Bruno's desire to dedicate the volume in gratitude to Duke Henry Julius, describes how the author actually carved his own figures for printing, and corrected every detail of the book until, when he had reached the very last folio, he was suddenly "torn from us." At his request, the publishers therefore offered the volume to the Duke in his name and their own.[50] This Dedication is dated "The Ides of February 1591" so that Bruno had probably left Frankfurt about the end of January. The guess has been hazarded that the civic ban on Bruno's residence in Frankfurt was sud-

---

47 App. I, xxv. Spampanato (*Doc. Ted.* IX) prints the petition, in so far as it is legible. Reference to it occurs in the Protocol Book of the Council of Frankfurt (J. Lewis McIntyre, *Giordano Bruno* [London, 1903], p. 63). The Book of the Burgomaster under the same date records the refusal (Sigwart, *op. cit.*, p. 121).

48 App. I, 23.

49 He is described in this and the subsequent Dedications as Prince Henry Julius, Duke of Brunswick and Lüneburg and Bishop of Halberstadt. Henry Julius had held the Bishopric since childhood, when it was conferred on him as part of a settlement between Protestant and Catholic claims in the Empire. Cf. *Cambridge Modern History*, III, 153.

50 The indefatigable Wechel also obtained permission for printing and publication (Sigwart, *op. cit.*, pp. 121-22).

denly put into operation. All we know is that he journeyed to Zurich where he was among a congenial circle of friends.[51]

There survives, perhaps from the sojourn in Frankfurt at this period, or from the visit to Zurich, the first draft of a work expanded later during his last months of freedom at Padua, *On Links*.[52]

Among his Zurich friends was a young Swiss, John Henry Heinz, son of a learned and wealthy Swiss Protestant who had married a Bavarian lady and settled in Augsburg. The young John Henry had, however, aroused the wrath of the City Council, apparently because he took the wrong view of the New Calendar. After some adventures he and his brother bought the castle of Elgg in the canton of Zurich where they entertained scholars and pursued their studies, among which were alchemical investigations. Bruno wrote for this friend his work in three books, *On the Composition of Images, Signs, and Ideas for all sorts of Discoveries, Dispositions and Recollections,* which was published within a few months by Wechel.[53] The preface gives a glimpse of the answer to a question that must present itself to every student of Bruno. Why should this man, occupied with the formulation of a lofty philosophy, have turned aside and spent so much time on the idle elaborations of logic and mnemonics devised by Raymond Lull?

Idea [he tells us], imagination, analogy, figure, arrangement, notation—this is the universe of God, the work of nature and of reason, and is possessed also by the analogy thereof, so that nature may admirably reflect divine action, and human talent may thereupon rival the operation of nature and almost reach yet more exalted things. Who doth not see with how few elements nature maketh so many things? No one indeed is ignorant of how she doth variously place, order, compound, move, and apply the same Four [elements] and under various signatures she advances these forms and figures from the depth of potentiality to the sublimity of action. And, by immortal God what can be easier to man than the use of number? . . . The whole light thereof is more present, clear and understood by our intel-

---

51 The bookseller John Brictanus of Antwerp testified to having known Bruno, first at Frankfurt, then at Zurich, subsequently at Venice (*Doc. Ven.* VII).

52 App. I, xxvi (Cf. xxx).

53 App. I, 24. *Ad Joan. Hainricum Haincellium Elcouiae dominum.* In the title to the dedication we have: *Heinrico Eincellio.*

ligence than the light of the sun to our eyes . . . Why is that which is present to us even over the whole heaven yet believed by us to be remote? Because the eye seeth other things, but it seeth not itself. And what is this eye which thus seeth other things that it may see itself? That which seeth all things in itself, and which is all things at the same time. To such sublime reason should we be akin if we had power to understand the substance of our nature, so that our eye might perceive itself and our mind might embrace itself. Then would it be possible to understand all things, nor would it even be hard to accomplish all things.

He quotes Aristotle: "Our intelligence, that is the operation of our intellect, is either fantasy or not without fantasy," and again, "We understand naught unless we observe the images."

"This is to say" [explains Bruno]:

we comprehend not by any simplicity, mode or unity but through composition, collation and a plurality of terms, making use of discourse and reflection. And if our talent is thus, thus too should without doubt be the works thereof, that, by enquiry, motion, judgement, arrangement and memory, it may avoid wandering away from the mirror and may thus not be moved without images. And if a polished and smooth mirror be placed here by Nature, and if by art, the light of the reckoning of the Canons doth prosper and glow on the horizon, immediately by reason of the faculty bestowed on us by the clear images of things coming into view, we are directed toward that supreme joy in the composite nature of action which indeed most beseemeth man when most he is man. . . . In the first Book are generalities which deal with the diverse kinds of meaning; the various conditions are explained in which subjects are visible and are disposed, images are impressed and inscribed. We then teach how to build various sorts of halls and spaces, and when at length they are built we shew in them [*lit.*, and we shew them when built; in them at length are] all things which can be uttered, known or imagined; all arts, languages, works, signs. In the second Book are twelve figures of princes . . .

with their symbolic implications; while in the third Book the author reverts to the figures of the Thirty Seals.[54] Among the devices in this work to assist the memory is some mere doggerel verse.

---

[54] *Op. lat.*, II, iii, 89-93.

Another of Bruno's works may be traced to his visit to Zurich. For he met there his pupil Raffaele Eglin (Raffaele Eglinus Iconius).[55] Eglin gives a vivid description of Bruno "standing on one leg, going as fast as the pen could follow, at once dictating and reflecting; so rapidly did his talent work, so great was the power of his mind." From the notes thus taken, Eglin published a work at Zurich in 1595, when the prison doors had already closed on Bruno. The ponderous title of the volume is *Survey of Metaphysical Terms for the Understanding of Logic and the Study of Philosophy excerpted from the manuscript of Jordanus Brunus the Nolan, on the Scale of Being*.[56] The arrangement is suggested by the fifth Book of the *Metaphysics* of Aristotle, being a series of brief paragraphs discussing each term. Characteristically, Bruno chooses as his first two terms *Substance* and *Truth*. Eglin's Dedication is inscribed "To the noble youth Frederick à Sales, son of the most generous John." Eglin addresses Frederick à Sales almost as Bruno might have done, "not because thou art in need of his words, but because alone and best of all thou dost understand and dost love." He refers to their

---

[55] Raffaele Eglinus or Eglinus Iconius (1559-1628) had himself a somewhat chequered career. Born at Goetz in Switzerland, he studied at various centres in that country, spending two years under Beza at Geneva. Before he met Bruno, he had successively held the posts of *Pedagogus alumnorum* at Bâle, and of Dean and Professor of the New Testament at the School of Zurich Cathedral. Soon after his appointment to the latter position, we find him under various pseudonyms, publishing works on alchemy. Perhaps his interest in this art was not unconnected with the debts which, we are told, forced him to leave Zurich in 1601. He was also accused of having embraced Catholicism, which he denied. His correspondence with the Church authorities in Zurich suggests that it was his alchemical preoccupations that led to his dismissal from his professorship at the Cathedral. Quite in the manner of Bruno, he was given 25 guilders travelling expenses for his departure. He was fortunate, however, in gaining the patronage of the Landgraf Maurice of Hesse who (again supplying travelling expenses and admonishing him to relinquish alchemy) appointed him Professor of Theology at Marburg where he remained for the rest of his life. His theological works included a genealogy of Jesus. See J. J. Simmler, *Sammlung alter und neuer Urkunden zur Beleuchtung der Kirchengeschichte des Schweizerlands* (Zurich, 1767), II, 803, 816. The name Iconius is an adaptation of "from Goetz," as explained by Raffaele's father in a letter written from Chur on 21st September, 1571, to Bullinger (cf. Simmler, II, 803).

[56] App. I, xxviii.

discussion concerning Jordanus at the house of Frederick's father the previous autumn. Eglin's pious care for Bruno's writings was not exhausted by the publication of this small volume, for in 1609 when he had become Professor of Theology at Marburg, he republished the work with a second Part, also from manuscript, entitled *Scale of Practice or the Application of Being.*[57]

Probably Bruno spent at least some weeks at Zurich, returning to Frankfurt perhaps in the spring of 1591 to supervise the printing of the volume dedicated to Heinz,[58] and the production at last of the second and final volume of his great trilogy of Latin philosophical works in verse and prose. We can but marvel as to how he raised means to cover the hundreds of miles involved in each of these journeys. Perhaps to those free of all possessions, travel was almost as cheap as residence in a fixed spot! Bruno himself in his evidence at Venice stated that he had spent six months in Frankfurt. After examining all other hypotheses, our two best authorities, Tocco and Spampanato, both conclude that this must refer only to his second sojourn, which may have extended from March to September 1591. Perhaps his silence concerning the first months in Frankfurt was due to reluctance to account for his sudden departure to Zurich or to mention the Zurich visit.

Bruno's last months in Frankfurt were occupied with the proofs of the second volume of his Latin masterpieces in verse and prose. It contains two works: *On the Monad, on Number and Form in One Book, being a Sequel to the Five Books on the Great Minimum and on Measurement;* and the finest of all the Latin works, *On the Innumerable, the Immense, the Formless; On the Universe and Worlds,* in eight Books.[59] The volume is prefaced by a Dedication, this time from Bruno's own hand, to Duke Henry Julius of Brunswick. It is entitled *Dedicatory*

---

[57] App. I, xxix (a) and (b). Only three copies of the 1609 volume are known to exist. Bound up with the volume is an extract from the pseudo-Athanasian Definitions edited by Rodolphus Goclinius Senior, of which, however, the style and language have nothing in common with the writings of Bruno. Rudolph Goeckel, Senior (1547-1628), was professor of philosophy at Marburg and was a poet. He wrote much on logic as well as on philosophy and ethics.

[58] App. I, 24.

[59] App. I, 25, 26.

Letter and Key and deals with the previous poem of the great series as well as with the two works to which it is attached:

In the first volume we studiously desired [*sic*], in the second we sought in uncertainty, in the third we arrived most clearly. In the first, sense-perception is most important; in the second, words; in the third, the thing itself. The first concerns what is within us; the second, things heard; the third, that which is discovered. In the first, the method is mathematical; in the second, divine [i.e., theological]; but in the third it is natural.

The first deals with simple objects, the second with abstract, the third with composite. In the first, wisdom pervadeth the body; in the second, the shadow; in the third, the soul. The elements of the first are limit, minimum, size; the subjects are the line, the angle, the triangle; learned doctors, the temple of Apollo, of Minerva and of Venus, which are [*sic*] constructed in circles which are in apposition, interpenetrating and containing one another; in which figures, numbers and measurements are all implicit, sought out, explicit by means of definitions, axioms, theorems. In the second work the monad is the substance of the matter; number is the internal quality or specific difference; form is the external accident and signature. We contemplate the monad in the circle; number in the triplex triad of the other archetypes; and form in the individual we contemplate according to the element thereof, in the totality however according to the effect thereof. Viewed according to the monad all things are in harmony; viewed by number they mostly differ one from another; but viewed according to form they are in complete opposition. For the monad is the individual substance of a thing, number is an unfolding of the substance, but form is indeed the orderly flowing forth from the [original] site of the unfolded origins. The monad is that which is absolutely true; number is goodness in its own nature; form is beauty in a certain relation. For truth is different in different situations; the good is different to different persons and in different places; beauty is different to different persons, in different places and at different times. The monad teacheth him who is happy to remain so; him who is unhappy the monad teaches to change his place; number teacheth to change his name; form his condition.

In the third work, entrance from darkness to light is given by means of colour. The distinction is drawn between the boundary, the finite and the infinite. And again between the efficient cause, the element and the effect. Furthermore, between motion, quiet and immobility. It is shewn that the principal elements in the universe are water, light and air; the principal substances are sun, our earth, and the Heaven (under one Being, lord of all things, unconditioned by any form). So that the hindrance to natural knowledge and the main foundation of ignorance is the failure to perceive in things the harmony between substances, motions and qualities. For the perfection of the universe proceedeth from unity, truth and goodness, by the virtue of active force, by the disposition of passive force and by the worthiness of results. This true perfection can exist only in an innumerable multitude, in immense size and in the evident beauty of order. Thus by a certain circle of learning (*encyclopedia*), all things are brought forth, directed and applied. They are distinguished in a threefold order in succession on a single ladder, so that ease may exist with brevity, truth with ease, and certitude with truth. Furthermore seemliness is considered in the matter, order in the diversity of the propositions, sufficiency in the paucity of the undetermined (*mediorum*) whereby nature hath meaning, reason is regarded, God worketh all things in all things. It is these things, many of which when seen from afar may be deemed odious and absurd, but if observed more nearly they will be found beautiful and true, and when known very closely they will be wholly approved, most lovely and certain withal. In their light will undoubtedly be dispersed those gloomy fabrications which by the compulsion of custom are thought to be true and beautiful, though in the even balance of reason they are discovered to be uncertain and infelicitous. At length by the light of that nature which shineth forth by means of our sense-perceptions and demonstrations, they are recognized as most vile and impossible.

The reader will be no less grateful than is the present writer that Bruno has given us his sketch of what he regarded as the most important features of these volumes. We will not attempt to give in a few pages even a sketch of their whole content. A word may be added as to the form of these works. Bruno is perhaps most eloquent in the Lucretian Latin verse which he has chosen as the vehicle of his thought in these volumes. It is true that scholars will at times be startled by his Latinity, and Bruno boldly defends his coinage of new words. But the lines roll forth with sweeping vigour. Certain passages, especially in the *De immenso et innumerabilibus* carry the reader with irresistible force into the realm of Bruno's thought. But as though he suspected that this would be his last effort to deliver his message, Bruno has appended to each canto or "chapter" a prose exposition or commentary. These are among the most lucid passages of his writings.

The shades were gathering. His nostalgia for Italy was reinforced by his eager acceptance of new adventure, perhaps too by his never-quenched hope for reconciliation with the Church. To Italy he went and we turn to the sombre tragedy of his last years.

CHAPTER SEVEN

MARTYRDOM (1591-1600)

a. Padua and Venice (1591–92)

AMONG those of exalted rank who hoped to obtain from Bruno the hidden secrets not only of knowledge but of power, one has earned unenviable fame. This is Zuane[1] Mocenigo, a Venetian of noble birth. Bruno received in Frankfurt two letters from Mocenigo, inviting him to Venice to teach him "the art of memory and invention." Bruno gave to the Venice Inquisition in May 1592 an account of the events which followed.[2] He accepted Mocenigo's invitation and came to Venice in September or October 1591,[3] staying first in rooms.[4] He was soon again

[1] The name Zuane is a form of Giovanni.

[2] *Doc. Ven.* VIII. See *supra,* p. 4, n. 2.

[3] The bookseller Ciotti, testifying before the Venice Inquisition in May 1592, stated that he first met Bruno in Frankfurt "two years ago come next September," that is, in September 1590. He then describes how subsequently Mocenigo gave him a letter of invitation to take to Bruno "who appeared here seven or eight months ago," i.e., in September or October 1591 (*Doc. Ven.* VI). Bruno himself also testified in May 1592 that he had come to Italy "seven or eight months ago" (*Doc. Ven.* VIII).

Since Ciotti states that Mocenigo first approached him on the matter *after the appearance* of *De minimo* (*Doc. Ven.* VI, f. iv), the first letter cannot have been conveyed before the spring of 1591. But Ciotti also asserts (*Doc. Ven.* VI, 12v) that, after the arrival of Bruno, Mocenigo approached him, asking him, during his visit to Frankfurt at *Easter 1592,* to make enquiries about Bruno's character.

[4] In Venice and subsequently in Padua. Cf. pp. 161-2, Ciotti's evidence. Bruno's action in coming to Italy appeared incredibly rash to his contemporaries as it does indeed to the observer today. For there have survived two letters written from Bologna by Valens Havekenthal (Acidalius) to Forgacz (cf. p. 144, n. 28) who

discoursing to a group of gentlemen and Besler was acting as his secretary. There survive from this period several fragments of a work, *On Links in General,*[5] of which the first section was probably drafted in Frankfurt or Zurich. Though prolix and obscure, these fragments reiterate Bruno's faith which he so gloriously vindicated in the supreme victory of the spirit. The earlier section bears the title, "Concerning the Link of the Spirit, Natural, Animal and Divine." "Without these," Bruno declares,

> there is no physician, no soothsayer, no operator, no lover, no philosopher. By virtue of these all persons are all things. Nothing is absolutely beautiful so that it binds, but is beautiful in relation to something else. . . . Similarly nothing which attracts is absolutely good, but since all things or the universe and being is composed of contraries, so good is also composed of contraries. . . .[6]

The argument is continued that love binds all and is the urge to all good. The Paduan fragments, *On Links in General,* open with the statement: "For him who needs to bind, it is necessary to have in some sort the universal Reason[7] of things, that he may be strong to bind man

was then in Padua. On 21st January, 1592, Acidalius is writing to Forgacz of the report that their mutual friend Lipsius had received an invitation from the great Duke of Etruria to come to Pisa under splendid conditions. "It is incredible, but I am assured by Mercurialis that it is true that he is to have complete liberty of religion and freedom to believe whatever he in fact believes [quidquid sentiat, sentire]." He continues: "I would enquire concerning a certain Jordanus Brunus the Nolan, the same whom thou knewest in Wittenberg, who is said now to be living among you and lecturing. Is it indeed so? And what sort of a man is this who ventures into Italy whence, as he himself was wont to tell us, he had been exiled? I am amazed and hitherto I have not credited the rumour even though I heard it from those most trustworthy sources. Thou, however, wilt definitely inform me whether it be true or false."

On 3rd March he writes again marvelling at such incredible news. Cf. Christianus Acidalius frater Valentis Acidali, *Epistolarum Centuria* (Hanover, printed by Wechel, 1606), Epist. 2, p. 10.

Valens Acidalius (1567-1595) was a humanist writer. Born at Weistock in Brandenburg, he studied successively at Rostock and Helmstedt and then spent three years in Italy. After his return to Germany he settled at Breslau and adopted the Catholic faith.

[5] App. I, xxx. Cf. App. I, xxvi. [6] *Op. lat.,* III, 637.

[7] *Rationem,* perhaps better rendered "principle."

(who is as it were the Epilogue of all things)."[8] This gives the key to the consideration of "Links" in this curious work.

Presently Bruno moved to Mocenigo's own house. When, however, he informed Mocenigo of his desire to return to Frankfurt to get certain of his works printed, Mocenigo expressed jealous fear that Bruno's real intention was to impart his precious knowledge to others. To deter Bruno from leaving him, Mocenigo threatened the unfrocked monk several times with the Holy Office. This Mocenigo could do with the more confidence since he had himself held high office, perhaps attached to the Venice Inquisition.[9] Bruno hardly took the threats seriously, but Mocenigo protested angrily that he had still not been initiated according to promise into the secret of Bruno's memory system, and he threatened that if his victim persisted in his intention to depart, he would "find means to keep him." On the next night, Bruno having persisted with preparations for departure, threats were translated to action. Bruno was roused from his bed by Mocenigo, accompanied by a stalwart band who seized and imprisoned him,[10] Mocenigo still protesting that he de-

[8] *Op. lat,* III, 653.

[9] Domenico Berti (*Vita di Giordano Bruno del Nola* [Florence, Turin and Milan, 1868], App. II), was the first to identify the persecutor of Bruno with Giovanni Mocenigo, the correspondent of the literary courtier, G. Battista Leoni, whose *Lettere familiari* were published by Ciotti himself in 1592 (and a further volume in the following year). In September 1583, Leoni was congratulating Mocenigo *del Saviato*, and hoping that this would be but the beginning of further honours. He writes of Mocenigo's "first entry into the *Collegio*." In 1594 he refers to his labours "among the *Pregadi*" and to his responsibility as a Senator to lead a virtuous life. Spampanato (*Vita di Giordano Bruno,* II, 459) states that Mocenigo was elected in 1583 a *Savio agli ordini,* citing Leoni's letter of 24 September, 1583, *"cominciar facilioribus."* For the grades of the members of the *Collegio,* cf. S. Romanin, *Storia documentata di Venezia* (18 books in 10 vols., Venice, 1853-60), VIII, 331-32. J. Lewis McIntyre, (*op. cit.,* p. 68) and William Boulting (*Giordano Bruno, His Life, Thought and Martyrdom* [London, 1916], pp. 225-26) both suggest that Mocenigo was a *Savio all'eresia.*

[10] At this first stage of the proceedings there appears the ominous co-operation of State and Church, since Mocenigo employed for both the arrest and the consignment of Bruno to the prison of the Holy Office one Mattheo de Avantio, captain in the service of the Council of Ten (*Doc. Ven.* V). For the establishment and function of the Venice Inquisition, see Marco Ferro, *Dizionario del diritto comune e Veneto* (2 vols., Venice, 1847); and Paolo Servita (i.e., Sarpi), *Historia della sacra inquisizione* (Serravalle, 1638), pp. 19 *seqq.*

manded only to be taught Bruno's secrets of memory and of geometry. After twenty-four hours, the prisoner was removed to another dungeon. That evening he was conducted to the jail of the Holy Office. This was on Saturday, 23rd May, 1592.[11]

The wretched Mocenigo in his own account states that he acted "by the constraint of his conscience and by the order of his confessor." Was it his desire from the first to lure the philosopher to express dangerous views? Or what black deeds had he hoped that he would be enabled to perpetrate by means of Bruno's mysterious powers?

Mocenigo stated that Bruno had been accused of throwing into the Tiber his accusers at Rome "or those whom he thought to have accused him to the Inquisition." In denouncing Bruno, Mocenigo felt it necessary to explain that when he wished to learn from this criminal he was unaware of his true views. But when he heard these during the two months that Bruno passed in his house, he determined to incarcerate and at the same time to denounce him.[12]

Mocenigo invoked as witnesses two booksellers of Venice, Ciotti[13] and Britano.[14] Both these men, and especially Ciotti, when summoned to give evidence, made on the whole a courageous effort for Bruno.

---

[11] *Docc. Ven.* V and VIII.

[12] *Ibid.*, I-IV. Mocenigo's letters of accusation against Bruno are addressed to the Father Inquisitor of Venice, J. Gabriele of Saluzzo. The Tribunal that proceeded to investigation consisted of the Father Inquisitor; the Papal Nuncio Ludovico Taberna—sometimes represented by his "auditor" Livio Passero; and Laurentio Priolo, the Patriarch of Venice, on one occasion represented by his Vicar. Aloysio Foscari, who was of a noble family, was present at many of the sittings and on two occasions also "the illustrious Sebastiano Barbadico." One session is described in the record as *cum licentia* of this Sebastian Barbadico (*Doc. Ven.* XIV). The Barbadico or Barbarigo were one of the most powerful of the Venice noble families, tracing their descent from a certain Arrigo, an Istrian who had repelled the Saracens from Trieste with great valour in the year 880. Two of the family had occupied the Doge's seat in Venice in the fifteenth century. Giovanni Superanti joins Thomas Morosini on one occasion in attending the Tribunal (*Doc. Ven.* XVII. See also below, n. 17).

[13] "Joannes Baptistus Ciottus senensis [i.e., of Sienna], bookseller, at the sign of Minerva, living in Venice" (*Docc. Ven.* VI, VII and XVI).

[14] "Jacobus Brictanus de Antwerpia, living in Venice" (*Doc. Ven.* VII). Spampanato calls the booksellers Ciotti and Britano (*Vita*, II, 451); McIntyre calls Brictanus "Bertano" (*op. cit.*, p. 69).

Ciotti stated that he had first seen him when he went to the Frankfurt Book Fair in September 1590, and lodged according to his custom in the Carmelite convent.[15] He had spoken and argued with Bruno several times during his sojourn of a fortnight, recognized him as a much-lettered man who had read many books. And Bruno had subsequently come several times to his shop in Venice to buy books. Ciotti testified that Sir Zuane Mocenigo had bought from him Bruno's book *De minimo magno et mensura* and had at the same time (i.e., in 1591) asked Ciotti whether he knew Bruno and could tell Mocenigo where he was, saying that he wished to send for Bruno to teach him "his secrets of memory and the other things that he teaches as may be seen in that book." He described how Mocenigo entrusted him with a letter summoning Bruno "who appeared here seven or eight months ago" (i.e., in September or October 1591) and afterwards moved to Padua, where he stayed for some three months, moving freely between the cities. Ultimately he moved to Mocenigo's house, "where I think he is now." Ciotti was interrogated as to Bruno's past life and other works—on which he made general statements that were no doubt well known to the Tribunal. He testified that he had never heard anything from Bruno that would throw doubt on his being a Catholic and good Christian. Then he bore witness that recently when he was going to Frankfurt for the Easter Fair, Mocenigo had employed him to make enquiries in Frankfurt concerning Bruno, since he was dissatisfied with his teaching. But the bookseller, though he "spoke with various scholars who had attended his lectures there," could not learn that Bruno had done anything with the marvellous memory "and he was regarded in Frankfurt as a man with no religion." Ciotti adds that when he reported to Mocenigo, the latter replied that certainly he had his doubts about Bruno, but that he was anxious to salve what he could of knowledge in return for his outlay on the fellow, after which he would denounce him to the Holy Office.[16]

[15] He described Bruno as small and lean with small black beard, about 40 years old. Bruno, however, is officially described at the Venice trial (*Doc. Ven.* VIII) as of average stature and with a *chestnut* beard.

[16] *Doc. Ven.* VI.

A later witness, Andrea Morosini,[17] testified that Ciotti had actually arranged that Bruno should lecture to him and to other gentlemen in Padua.[18] Among them no doubt was Michael Forgacz, whom he had known in Wittenberg.[19] The witness maintained that Bruno had never given cause to believe he held any opinion contrary to the Faith. Morosini had not considered the lecturer to be other than a Catholic. Had he entertained the slightest suspicion of him, continued this cautious witness, Bruno would never have been permitted to enter his house. It is noteworthy that Thomas Morosini was present at the Tribunal when Andrea was under interrogation.[20] Thomas was no doubt another member of the same prominent family.[21]

Jacob Britano, called to the witness box, stated that he had known Bruno in Frankfurt three years previously,[22] and later at Zurich and again recently in Venice. He admitted that, having read some of his works, he had been curious to know Bruno, and had taken advantage of the chance of meeting him in the street and walked home with him. Evidently he too had fallen under the spell. In reply to interrogation he stated:

---

[17] Andrea Morosini (the Latin form of the name was Mauroceno) (1557-1618) belonged to a noble family that had migrated at least as early as the tenth century from Moresini in Hungary to Venice, and had already produced three Doges. His father Jacob was a senator of Venice. Andrea was an eager student of the New Learning. He held office at various times both at Padua (the University of Venice) and as ambassador from the Republic. In 1598 he became Official Historiographer, in 1600 Senator and in 1605 member of the *Collegio dei Savii* or Cabinet of Ministers.

[18] *Doc. Ven.* XV.

[19] Cf. *supra*, pp. 158-9, n. 4.

[20] *Doc. Ven.* XV.

[21] See above, notes 12, 17, and 20, and below, p. 167, n. 38. Thomas Morosini was present again at the September meetings of the Tribunal when Cardinal Santaseverina's letters were considered, and he accompanied the deputation conveying the demand of the Papal Tribunal to the Venice Council Chamber of the *Rogati* for consent to the consignment of Bruno to Rome (*Docc. Ven.* XVIII, XIX). On that occasion he is described as "uno dei signori assistenti al santo Tribunale dell' Inquisizione."

[22] *Doc. Ven.* VII. For this date of 1589, when Bruno was at Helmstedt, cf. *supra*, p. 158, n. 3.

The Prior of the Convent in Frankfurt told me that Bruno was mainly occupied in writing and in devising foolishness and astrology [23] and seeking new things. The Prior said he had a fine talent as man of letters, was a "universal" man. The Prior believed that he had no religion, for the said Giordano declares that he knows more than the Apostles knew and that he would have dared, had he so desired, to bring about that the whole world should be of one religion.[24]

Britano himself had heard nothing from Bruno contradicting Christianity. He says that Giordano lectured to heretical doctors in Frankfurt, since everyone in that town is a heretic: "and he told me that he lectured in Zurich to certain doctors." Thus we learn that in these last stages of his wanderings Bruno was again lecturing to a small but fascinated band just as we have seen him at Noli, at Toulouse, in Paris and in London, as well as to the young Duke at Helmstedt.

These gatherings were evidently a source of Mocenigo's jealousy. Probably he expected to end them when Bruno came to live under his roof, and we may conjecture that Bruno's Padua audience may still have tried to get into touch with him. Probably it was not entirely pleasant for the booksellers or for Signor Andrea Morosini to find themselves involved as witnesses in the case.

Bruno first appeared before his judges on 26th May, 1592.[25] The hearings were protracted through long weeks. Bruno was required to give an account of his whole life. The accuracy and consistency of his story themselves testify to his amazing memory. Few whose lives have run in quieter places for a life course of forty-four years could give so connected and consistent a story. Only concerning his most recent movements is there a certain ambiguity for which it is easy to guess reasons.

In his earliest works Bruno had shewn how little relevance or importance attached in his eyes to the religious controversies of the day.[26] From the first, he had sought reconciliation with the Church so long as he might escape the convent life that held such horrible mem-

---

23 "Chimerizando e strologando cose nove" (*Doc. Ven.* VII).

24 "Gli bastava l'animo de far, se avesse voluto, che tutto il mondo sarebbe d'una religione" (*Doc. Ven.* VII).

25 *Doc. Ven.* VIII.

26 *Doc. Par.* II.

ories for him, scars of his early life from which his mind would never quite be freed.

May passes into June. He is cross-examined concerning his writings. He mentions that a former German pupil, Herman Besler of Nuremberg, has been acting as copyist for him for the last two months in Padua.[27]

The prisoner admits that his books with the imprint of Venice were in fact printed in England, and states that this is true also of nearly all his other books, though bearing the name of Paris or other places.[28] "The printers preferred to print the name of Venice which facilitated the sales."

Examined at tremendous length on points of doctrine and especially on the Three Persons of the Trinity, he pleaded that he wrote as a philosopher and believed "in the Pythagorean manner," and he quoted in support of his views the *Wisdom of Solomon,* St. Thomas Aquinas and the *Aeneid* of Virgil.[29] He acknowledged that he did not regard the Second and Third Persons as entirely distinct from the First, "but in fact, I never wrote or taught this, but merely doubted. And I believed and believe all the teaching of Mother Church concerning the First Person." "And I thought the Arian doctrine less pernicious than was believed" because it had been misunderstood. And again he pleaded that the heretical passages in his works were not in defiance of the Catholic Faith but were philosophic expressions when not merely recitations of beliefs of heretics. Successive points of dogma were raised, and Giordano was required to state his belief concerning them.[30]

He was cross-examined also as to his relationship with heretic monarchs, and especially as to the extravagant praise of Queen Elizabeth in his Italian writings. This he explained was a convention but acknowledged his error.[31]

---

[27] *Doc. Ven.* XI. Cf. pp. 147-8 *seqq.,* and App. III.

[28] *Doc. Ven.* XI. While many of the Paris imprints, like all those of Venice, were false, no surviving books bearing the imprint of other towns can be attributed to England. *None* of Bruno's books bears the imprint of an English town or printer.

[29] *Doc. Ven.* XI.

[30] *Docc. Ven.* XI-XIV.

[31] *Doc. Ven.* XIII, Spampanato (1933), pp. 115, 121-2.

It is clear that Bruno, always the most unpractical of men, actually cherished at first a wild hope that he could convey to the Inquisitors themselves the message of his philosophy. "In this sense, I understood that divinity was added to the humanity of Christ. For I deemed it unworthy to constrain Infinity within finite number."[32]

But by the end of the first day of his theological cross-examination Bruno was making a desperate effort to placate the judges. He confessed to having transgressed the laws prescribing days for abstention from meat. At the end of a long session on the 3rd June,[33] held within the prison itself, he is asked, does he renounce and detest his errors? "All the errors which I have committed until today," he declares with a sad cynicism which is lost on his judges,

in regard to Catholic life and the profession of a Regular [religious] such as myself and all heresies which I have believed, and the doubts I have entertained concerning the Catholic Faith and in matters determined by Holy Church, I now detest and abhor them all and I repent having done, held, said or believed or doubted concerning anything non-Catholic. And I beseech the Holy Tribunal, knowing my infirmity, to embrace me to the breast of Mother Church, providing me with remedies suitable for my welfare and using me with mercy.

He describes how innocently he first fell under suspicion. He reiterated his never-relinquished desire for absolution.[34] Ever he cherished the strange hope which was, so far as we can see, wholly devoid of foundation, that if only he could get to the Fount of authority at Rome, he would be not only understood but honoured, and his writings accepted. That this extraordinary belief was honestly held by him is confirmed by the evidence at Venice of one of the many Church dignitaries whom he had consulted.[35]

---

[32] *Ibid.*, p. 117.

[33] *Ibid.*, pp. 123-24.

[34] *Doc. Ven.* IX (1933), p. 87; X, p. 89; XVII, pp. 132-34.

[35] On the 31st May the Inquisitors summoned Fra Domenico da Nocera, Friar Preacher of the Province of the Kingdom (of Naples) and Regent of the Stadium of St. Dominic at Naples. He testified that the Inquisitor of Venice had brought him from the convent of St. John and St. Paul, and ordered him to write down whether he had spoken to Fra Jordano di Nola in Venice and what Jordano had said. He described how he had been accosted as he left the sacristy of the church,

Bruno endures an ominous pause of two months. Not until 30th July is he recalled, and again he maintains the substance of his former statements. The position is becoming desperate. Bruno confesses that he has given grave cause for suspicion. Again he protests his repentance, and pleads his efforts at reconciliation with the Church. Does he wish to say any more? No more.[36] Silence for another two months.

Then in September Cardinal Santaseverina, the Supreme Inquisitor of Rome, addressed letters to the Venice Holy Office demanding that Bruno be consigned forthwith to Ancona to be conveyed to Rome to stand his trial before the Holy Tribunal of the Inquisition there. On 17th September it was decided to comply with this demand.[37] But action was not immediately taken. The matter was not quite simple. Venice had always claimed independence of Papal authority and especially the power to deal independently with her own delinquents.

The scene now changes to the *Collegio dei Savii* or Cabinet meeting of the Republic.[38] On the 28th September, 1592, appeared a deputation consisting of the Vicar of the Patriarch of Venice and the Father Inquisitor, accompanied by the sinister figure of Thomas Morosini. They brought from the Patriarch information of the arrest and imprisonment of Bruno and the accusations against him. The Patriarch through the Vicar pointed out that Bruno was accused not merely of heresy, but that as a *Heresiarch* he had composed various books in which he praised

---

and had realized that his interlocutor was Jordano Bruno, one of the brothers of his province and a literary man (literato). Jordano led him to a secluded corner of the church, told him his history and that he was comfortably off in Venice, and hoping to compose and write a book which he had in mind, and that he proposed to present it to his Holiness personally and to implore permission to dwell in Rome as a Scholar and thus to shew his merit and perhaps to give some lectures (*Doc. Ven.* X).

36 *Doc. Ven.* XVII.

37 *Ibid.*, XVIII.

38 Spampanato (*Vita di Giordano Bruno*, II, 531) gives the names of these 16 *Savii del collegio*, noting that one was a brother of Mocenigo. For the function of the various governmental bodies in Venice, see S. Romanin, *op. cit.*, VIII, 323-50. See also Donato Ciannotti, *Libro de la republica de Venitiani* (Rome, 1592) and G. Contarino, *Conciliorum magis illustrium summa, et de magistratibus et republica Venetorum* (Paris, 1543). Cf. also *Cambridge Modern History*, I, 271-76.

the Queen of England and other heretical persons, and had written in a fashion unseemly, even though philosophically intended, concerning their religion. Moreover he had dwelt in many lands and he had been under these accusations in Naples and elsewhere; wherefore the Supreme Inquisitor Cardinal Santaseverina demanded that the Venice Inquisitor should dispatch Bruno forthwith for trial in Rome. Moreover the Vicar read the passage in Santaseverina's letter prescribing that Bruno should be consigned to the Governor of Ancona who would send him on to Rome. But the Patriarch wished first to inform his Serenity (the Doge) and the *Collegio* and to request their authorization to take advantage at once of a convenient opportunity that presented itself for the safe dispatch of the prisoner. The *Savii* retired to consider this demand from Rome. The Father Inquisitor, it seems, returned the same afternoon, reiterating his demand, and pointed out that a vessel was ready to convey Bruno. But the *Savii* refused to be hurried. They pointed out that the matter was important; that the occupations of State were numerous and grave; that they had not yet reached a decision; and they suggested that the vessel should for the present be dismissed.[39] On 3rd October the record was read to the *Rogati* (or *Pregadi*, the Senate, which dealt with foreign affairs).

The Senate *(in Pregadi)* forthwith decided to resist the Papal demands. On the same day, instructions were formulated by them,[40] submitted to the *Collegio* and dispatched to Donato, the Venetian Ambassador Extraordinary in Rome. He was informed of the circumstances and of the reply given to the Father Inquisitor that the consignment to Rome of prisoners of the Venice Holy Tribunal would gravely detract from the

---

[39] *Doc. Ven.* XIX. It was in 1844 that Ranke published from the Venice Archives the letter of Cardinal Santaseverina to the Venice Inquisition demanding the surrender of Bruno to Rome, and the deliberations of the *Collegio* when asked for authorization for this procedure. Gradually the other documents regarding this episode were discovered and published. The story is told by Spampanato (*Vita di Giordano Bruno,* II, 669) in introducing the documents, which have been printed several times. The records of the Venetian Inquisition were found in 1849 among the Papal Archives.

[40] The record of votes bears the numbers + 117; —2; —6. Perhaps the last six abstained.

authority of the Venice Tribunal and would be a bad precedent.[41] A week later these instructions were acknowledged. Donato had passed on the matter to the Ambassador in Ordinary.[42]

On 22nd December, the Papal Nuncio, Taverna, himself appeared before the *Collegio* and again pressed for authorization for the Venice Holy Inquisition to consign Bruno to the Holy Inquisition in Rome. He cited the express request made by the Pope to the Venetian Ambassador in Rome. Donato reported to the *Collegio* that, having been instructed by the Senate, he had spoken on the matter to His Holiness, pointing out that the Venice Holy Tribunal had always administered justice independently, by the authority of the Pope himself. He thought that His Holiness had accepted these representations although he had raised the matter again before the ambassador's departure from Rome. The Nuncio replied that Bruno was a Neapolitan, not a Venetian, and that proceedings against him had been started in Naples, and continued in Rome. He alleged that in more than two dozen special cases like the present, the accused had been consigned to the Holy Tribunal in Rome which was superior to all the others. He again emphasized that Bruno's was no ordinary case.

Whereupon the reply was finally given to the Nuncio that the *Collegio* unanimously desired always to give every possible satisfaction to His Holiness. Bruno's fate was thus sealed.[43] On the same day, the Papal Nuncio was reporting his success.[44]

The Doge then commanded that the *Collegio* should summon Federico Contarini, Procurator (Magistrate), and should expound him the circumstances concerning Bruno. Thereafter, on 7th January, 1593, Contarini submitted to the Doge a written opinion. He repeated the points raised by the Nuncio, and remarked that Bruno, a foreigner to the city, had been received in the house of a gentleman here in Venice who had denounced him "for the discharge of his Christian conscience." Quite without evidence as it seems, he accused Bruno of breaking prison, and even alleged that he had done so twice. The Nuncio himself had

---

41 *Doc. Ven.* XX. 42 *Ibid.*, XXI. 43 *Ibid.*, XXII.

44 In a letter to the Pope's nephew, Monsignor Cinzio Aldobrandini (*Doc. Ven.* XXIIb).

brought no such accusation. "The crimes of this person," Contarini declared, to be "most serious as regards heresy, although he is otherwise one of the most excellent and rare talents that can be desired, and of exquisite doctrine and knowledge." While submitting to the prudent decision of his Serenity (the Doge), the magistrate opined "that it would be convenient to satisfy the desire of His Holiness" as had been done in other similar cases. He then related that he had informed the accused of the opinion that he was about to pronounce. Bruno, it seems, had yet again expressed his fatal confidence and desire to present his last work to the Pope, and he had declared that he would rejoice to be remitted to the justice of Rome. Contarini recommended that this surprising reaction of Bruno should be kept profoundly secret.[45]

On the same day the Senate (*in Pregadi*) together with the Doge's Council, by 142 out of 172 votes, passed their Resolution[46] which was read to the *Collegio*. The Resolution repeated the accusation of prison-breaking as well as of heresy. The Nuncio was to be informed on the following day that Bruno would be handed over to him that he might be consigned to the Pope, for trial by the Inquisition at Rome, it being expedient—especially in so exceptional a case—to gratify His Holiness. Moreover, the Republic Ambassador in Rome was to be informed of the decision that he might report it to His Holiness as a sign of the continued readiness of the Republic to give him pleasure.[47]

Finally, there is the dispatch dated 16th January from Paolo Paruta, statesman scholar of the type of Andrea Morosini, whom he preceded as Historiographer of the Republic. Paruta had just been appointed Venetian Ambassador to the Papal Court. He recounts how he had impressed on the Pope that the surrender of Bruno was a demonstration of the desire of the Doge to gratify His Holiness, and had received corresponding courteous assurances of the Papal desire for co-operation with the Republic.[48]

---

45 *Doc. Ven.* XXIII.

46 The votes recorded for the momentous decision were + 142; −10; −20. Again we conjecture that 20 may have abstained from this act of appeasement of the Papal power.

47 *Docc. Ven.* XXIV and XXV.

48 *Ibid.*, XXVI.

So on 27th February, 1593, Bruno passed through to the dungeons of the Inquisitors of Rome.[49]

b. Years of Endurance[50] *The End*

Almost two years have passed. In December 1593, in congregation of the Roman Inquisitors, there is brought before the assembled illustrious Cardinals and General Inquisitors "Brother Jordanus, son of the late John Bruni of Nola, apostate from the Order of friars preachers, priest, imprisoned in the prisons of the Holy Office." He is cross-examined on his heresies and other matters. His judges also visit him in prison. They

---

[49] *Docc. Rom.* XX, XX[3].

[50] The record of Bruno's remaining years remained buried in the Vatican until 1849, when the Archives of the Vatican were examined on the proclamation of the cessation of the temporal power of the Papacy. There came a time when representatives of the Vatican were at pains to deny the judicial burning of Giordano Bruno. The discovery and publication of the relevant documents from the Archives of Venice and of the Vatican and of other contemporary evidence has finally established the record of Bruno's trials both in Venice and in Rome.

The *Archivi dei savii sopra eresia* were first discovered in 1844-48, and most of the remaining Vatican documents concerning Bruno were published in 1864. Many of the records of the Inquisition in Rome concerning Bruno, including the final sentence on him, were first discovered in 1849 when the Archives of the Vatican were thrown open by the Republic under Mazzini; the remainder of these records have gradually been brought to light. See Spampanato, *Vita,* II, 581-86, 765 *seqq.*, 769; Salvestrini, *loc. cit.*, no. 432, p. 209; Boulting, *loc. cit.*, 293; McIntyre, *loc. cit.*, 93-5, 301-4, etc.; as well as the *Documenti.*

In quite recent times, a further document has been published by the Vatican under the title *Sommario del processo di Giordano Bruno, Docc. Rom.* XX, XX[3], ed. by Angelo Mercati in *Studii e testi,* No. 101 (Citta del Vaticano, 1940). The editor furnishes a long introduction. He gives certain Vatican records of the events of 1810, 1815-17 and 1849 and states his opinion that the full record of the trial has disappeared. He describes his discovery of the *Sommario* as follows: In 1925 when he became Prefect of the Secret Vatican Archives, he learned of the discovery in 1887 of the document concerning Giordano, and also that Pope Leo X had then ordered that it should be sent immediately to himself and should be revealed to none ("che non vole assolutamente che detto Processo sia dato al alcuno"). Mercati accordingly instituted a search which lasted until November 1940, when he discovered the document in the personal Archives of Pope Pius IX. Mercati expresses the opinion that the document was compiled not earlier than the spring

graciously hear him concerning his necessities and it is commanded that he be provided with a cloak and a pillow and with the *Summa* of St. Thomas.[51] What had been his condition during those two years?

Months pass. In April 1594 Bruno is again "visited and heard." It is determined to proceed with his trial, and the order is given for the preparation of the documents.[52] The order is repeated on 31st May, and in September the Inquisitors again enact that the proceedings against Bruno shall be pursued.[53]

In December 1594 Jordanus is yet again "visited and heard." He presents "pages of writings" rebutting the accusations against him.[54] It is January 1595 before the accusations are again considered at two meetings of the Inquisition. In the following month the case is read once more before the Holy Congregation.[55] In March 1595 there is again the ominous record: "Brother Jordanus . . . was brought before the Lord Cardinals and was visited and interrogated by them and *heard concerning his necessities*."[56]

The visits and the appearance in Court as well as the consideration of his necessities were repeated in April 1596. In September his propositions in defence of himself were censured. In December the process was repeated and he was heard "concerning the merit of his cause and concerning food." It was decided that he should be examined concerning the propositions extracted from his writings and concerning the censures

---

of 1597. The document itself as printed gives no dates and no account of the composition of the Court. It opens abruptly: "Quod frater Jordanus male sentit de sancta fide catholica contra quam et eius ministros obloquutus est." There follows evidence given by Mocenigo and the booksellers. The account as here published comprises 34 articles of accusation of heresy, and is in sections numbered from 1 to 261. Part of the ground covered in the Collection of Documents published by Spampanato and others is covered here also. There are more detailed doctrinal accusations from attestations by Mocenigo and by Bruno's fellow-prisoners. This use of his fellow-prisoners by the Court and the report of theological discussions and accusations comprise the only new facts that emerge from the record. The editor gives a running picture of the course of the interrogations, based on the *Documenti* already known and on the new *Sommario*. He concludes: "The Church could intervene, was bound to intervene and did intervene," an elegant phrase for the years of imprisonment and final burning of Bruno.

[51] *Doc. Rom.* I. [52] *Ibid.*, II. [53] *Ibid.*, III, IV.
[54] *Ibid.*, V. [55] *Ibid.*, VI, VII, VIII. [56] *Ibid.*, IX.

on him.[57] In March 1597 Bruno was again brought before the august Congregation and they visited him yet again. Again that terrible implication, *"they heard him concerning his necessities."* Then he was admonished that he should relinquish the vanities concerning diverse worlds and it was commanded that he be strictly cross-examined. Thereafter judgement should be delivered.[58]

In December 1597 the ghastly process is repeated.[59] After another three months it is decided that his cause cannot be determined before the departure of His Holiness.[60] In December 1598 it is commanded that Brother Jordanus be given writing paper and *advice how to use it* with the Breviarium as used by the Friars Preachers.[61]

Something more must be done. The long months and years have drifted to 14th January, 1599. Eight heretical propositions extracted from his works are read to the prisoner. Will he recant?[62] On 18th January he is given six days to make his decision; On 25th January he declares his readiness to accept the personal decision of His Holiness, but still insists on defending his views.[63] On 4th February it is decreed by the Pope in full Congregation, "after mature and diligent consideration" of the charges against Brother Giordano Bruno, that there shall be pointed out to him by the Theological Fathers, namely by the General of his Order, by Cardinal Bellarmini and by the Father Commissar,[64] all those propositions (from his works) that not only are heretical but have been declared so by the earliest Fathers, by the Church and by the Apostolic See. If he will recognize these propositions as heretical, then, well and good. If not, he shall be condemned after 40 days for repentance to the treatment usual for impenitent and pertinacious persons

57 *Docc. Rom.*, X, XI, XII.
58 *Ibid.*, XIII.
59 *Ibid.*, XIV.
60 *Ibid.*, XV.
61 *Ibid.*, XVI.
62 *Ibid.*, XVII and XVII². The formulation of these propositions is among the Vatican documents that have not yet come to light.
63 Of these events on 18th and 25th January, the record is in the final recapitulation of the case in *Doc. Rom.* XXVI, and an allusion in *Doc. Rom.* XVIII² to Bruno's written defence.
64 R.P.D. fr. Albertus Tragagliolus Episcopus Thermolensis Commissarius Generalis Sancti Officii (*Doc. Rom.* XXIV²).

in that fashion or any better one which can and should be applied to them.[65]

On 18th February, 1599, the propositions are duly read to the prisoner.[66] Then darkness descends again. It is April before the next visit by the Inquisitors is recorded; Bruno shews something written in his hand.[67] His name figures in two lists of prisoners of the Holy Office apparently drawn up in the same month.[68] In August he is given pens, paper, ink and a pencil "but no knife or compasses (*circinnus*)" and is commanded to retract two heretical propositions shewn the previous April.[69] In September and again in November, his case is under consideration.[70] On 21st December he is visited but declares that he neither should nor will retract, nor has he aught to retract.[71] On the same day

he was brought forth into the presence of the most Illustrious, the members of the Congregation by whom also he was visited; and he was heard concerning his universal pretensions and concerning the merits of his cause and concerning his necessities for food and other things; and afterwards, he having been withdrawn from the Hall of the Congregation, it was decreed by the illustrious Lord Cardinals there present that the Reverend Father Hippolytus Maria the General, and the Reverend Father Paul, Vicar of the aforesaid Order [of Friars Preachers] [72] should act on Brother Jordanus and should shew him the propositions to be adjured, that he might acknowledge his errors, reform, and dispose himself to recantation, and that they should gain him over (ipsumque lucri faciant) so that he might be liberated.[73]

On 20th January, 1600, Bruno's Memorial to the Pope is "opened but not read." It is reported to the Holy Office by their reverend emissaries that Brother Jordanus de Nola

---

[65] *Docc. Rom.* XVIII and XVIII².

[66] *Ibid.*, XIX.

[67] *Ibid.*, XX².

[68] *Ibid.*, XX, XX³.

[69] *Ibid.*, XXI.

[70] *Ibid.*, XXII, XXIII. According to *Doc. Rom.* XXVI, his condemnation was determined on 10th September, 1599 (Spampanato, *Documenti della vita di Giordano Bruno* [1933], (p. 191).

[71] *Doc. Rom.* XXIV.

[72] Called, in *Docc. Rom.* XXV and XXV², "a Procurator General of the Order."

[73] *Docc. Rom.* XXIV² and XXIV³.

refused to consent, declaring that he had proffered no heretical propositions but that they had been unadroitly excerpted [from their context] by the Ministers of the Holy Office. Wherefore he was ready to give an account of all his writings and sayings and to defend them against any theologians: but he would not abide by the decision of the theologians, but only by the decision of the Apostolic See concerning things said or written by him, if any such decision were given; or by the sacred canons, if it should be proved that there was in his writings or sayings anything contrary to them.

"Notwithstanding," reported the angry dignitaries, "that he had already been informed by the Holy Office and that judgement would be given, that manifest heresies were contained in his writings and theses." Whereupon "the most holy Lord, Pope Clement VIII, decreed and commanded that the cause should be carried to extreme measures, *servatus servandis* [i.e., with all due formalities] sentence should be pronounced and the said Brother Jordanus be committed to the secular court." [74]

The months and years of suffering reached their dreadful close. Bruno is now fifty-two. On the 8th February, 1600, the Inquisitors once more summoned their prisoner and the long indictment was read. The accused was reminded (as though there were need) that "already some eight years ago" he had been accused of naming as blasphemy belief in transubstantiation of the holy bread; that on 18th January of the previous year he had been given six days to recant. The agony of that month was rehearsed. On the 25th January the prisoner had declared that if the Apostolic See and His Holiness definitely declared those eight propositions to be heretical, if His Holiness knew them to be such or by the Holy Spirit declared them so to be, then he was disposed to retract. But immediately he had presented a long written defence, addressed to His Holiness and to the Inquisitors.

On the 4th February, 1599, a year ago it was determined that the eight heretical propositions should once more be presented to thee, and this was done on the 15th; [75] that, shouldst thou recognize them as heretical and abjure them, then thou wouldst be received for penitence; but, if not, then shouldst thou be condemned on the fortieth day from then for repentance; and thou

---

[74] *Ibid.*, XXV, XXV².

[75] Or on the 18th February, according to *Doc. Rom.* XIX.

didst declare thyself ready to recognize these eight propositions as heretical and to detest and abjure them in such place and time as might please the Holy Office, and not only these eight propositions, but thou didst declare thyself ready to make thine obedience concerning the others which were shewn to thee. But then, since thou didst present further writings to the Holy Office addressed to His Holiness and to Us, whereby it was manifest that thou didst pertinaciously adhere to thine aforesaid errors; and information having been received that at the Holy Office of Vercelli thou hadst been denounced because in England thou wast esteemed an atheist and didst compose a work about a *Triumphant Beast,* therefore on the 10th September, 1599, thou wast given forty days in which to repent, and it was determined that at the end of these days proceedings should be taken against thee as is ordained and commanded by the holy Canon law: and since thou didst nevertheless remain obstinate and impenitent in thine aforesaid errors and heresies, there were sent unto thee the Reverend Father Hippolytus Maria Beccaria, General of thine Order and Father Paul Isaresio della Mirandola, Procurator of the Order, that they might admonish and persuade thee to recognize thy most grave errors and heresies. But thou hast ever persisted with obstinate pertinacity in these thine erroneous and heretical opinions. Wherefore the accusation brought against thee has been examined and considered with the confessions of thy pertinacious and obstinate errors and heresies, even while thou didst deny them to be such, and all else was observed and considered; thy case was brought before our General Congregation held in the presence of His Holiness on 20th January last, and after voting and resolution we decided on the following sentence.

Having invoked the name of Our Lord Jesus Christ and of his most Glorious Mother Mary ever Virgin in the cause and aforesaid causes brought before this Holy Office between on the one hand the Reverend Giulio Monterenzii, doctor of laws, Procurator Fiscal of the said Holy Office, and on the other hand thyself, the aforesaid Giordano Bruno, the accused, examined, brought to trial and found guilty, impenitent, obstinate and pertinacious; in this our final sentence determined by the counsel and opinion of our advisers the Reverend Fathers, Masters in Sacred Theology and Doctors in both Laws, our advisers: We hereby, in these documents, publish, announce, pronounce, sentence and declare thee the aforesaid Brother Giordano Bruno to be an impenitent and pertinacious heretic, and therefore to have incurred all the ecclesiastical censures and pains of the Holy Canon, the laws and the constitutions, both general and particular, imposed on such confessed impenitent pertinacious and obstinate heretics. Wherefore as such we verbally degrade thee and declare that thou must be degraded, and we hereby ordain and command that thou shalt be actually degraded [76] from all thine ecclesiastical orders both major and minor in which thou hast been ordained, according to the Sacred Canon Law: and that thou must be driven forth, and we do drive thee forth from our ecclesiastical forum and from our holy and immaculate Church of whose mercy thou art become unworthy. And we ordain and command that thou must be delivered to the Secular Court—wherefore we hereby deliver thee to the Court of You [*sic*] the Governor of Rome here present—that thou mayest be punished with the punishment deserved, though we earnestly pray that he will mitigate the rigour of the laws concerning the pains of thy person, that thou mayest not be in danger of death or of mutilation of thy members. Furthermore, we condemn, we reprobate and we prohibit all thine aforesaid and thy other books and writings as heretical and erroneous, containing many heresies and errors, and we ordain that all of them which have come or may in future come into the hands of the Holy Office shall be publicly destroyed and burned in the square of St. Peter before the steps and that they shall be placed upon the Index of Forbidden Books, and as we have commanded, so shall it be done. And thus we say, pronounce, sentence, declare, degrade, command and ordain, we chase forth and we deliver and we pray in this and in every other better method and form that we reasonably can and should.

Thus pronounce we, the undermentioned Cardinal General Inquisitors:

LUDOVICUS CARDINALIS MADRUTIUS.
JUL. ANT. CARDINALIS SANTA SEVERINA.
P. CARDINALIS DEZA.
D. CARDINALIS PINELLUS.
F. HIERONYMUS CARDINALIS ASCULANUS.
L. CARDINALIS SAXUS.
C. CARDINALIS BURGHESIUS.
P. CARDINALIS ARIGONIUS.
ROB. CARDINALIS BELLARMINUS.

---

[76] There has survived the account of the payment duly made by the Inquisition of two scudi to the Bishop of Sidonia for the service of "actual degradation" of Giordano Bruno the heretic. The Bishop was rewarded on the same day by a further two scudi for the "degradation" of a second prisoner (*Doc. Rom.* XXXIII).

The above sentence made and given by the aforesaid most Illustrious and Reverend Lord Cardinals, General Inquisitors, sitting in Rome as a tribunal in the general Congregation of the Holy Roman and Universal Inquisition in the presence of the aforesaid Illustrious and Reverend Cardinal Madrutius in the Church of St. Agnes in Agony, in the year of the Nativity of our Lord Jesus Christ 1600, on the 8th day of February, having been recited yesterday to the aforementioned Giordano Bruno who was brought by one of the police of His Holiness our Lord the Pope in order to hear the aforewritten sentence.

On the same day after it had been signed, the aforesaid Brother Jordanus having been summoned by the aforesaid most illustrious and Reverend Lord Cardinals of the General Inquisition and having been brought forth from the said prisons of the Holy Inquisition and removed to the palace which is the usual residence of the aforesaid most Illustrious and Reverend Cardinal Madrutius and having been brought into the Hall of the aforesaid Congregation into the presence of the said most Illustrious and Reverend Cardinals, then in his presence and while he did listen, the said sentence was by their order promulgated and read by me the notary hereaftermentioned, in a loud and clear voice, the doors of the hall of the said Congregation being open, there being present the most Reverend Father Benedictus Manninus, Bishop of Caserta, the most Reverend Father Petras Millinus of Rome I.U.D. and Referendario of each of the Signatures of His Holiness Our Lord the Pope and the Reverend Father Franciscus Petrasancta de Ripalta of the Order of the Friars Preachers, prelates and counsellors of the said Holy Inquisition, several other persons being present as witnesses.[77]

Yet one more document in the Roman Archives records the transference of the prisoner to the Secular Arm on the 8th February.[78]

The day appointed for the martyrdom was 12th February. Yet again there was postponement. Finally, on Saturday 19th February, 1600, the judicial burning took place in the great Square of Flowers at Rome.

The intense interest and public excitement concerning Bruno is reflected in a copy of three paragraphs from the contemporary manuscript *Avvisi e ricordi,* the earliest form of news-sheet. One of these records

---

[77] *Doc. Rom.* XXVI.
[78] *Doc. Rom.* XXVII.

that Bruno declared that he died a willing martyr and that his soul would rise with the smoke to paradise.[79]

A gloating account of the whole ritual is given in a letter written on the very day by a youth named Gaspar Schopp of Breslau, a recent convert to Catholicism to whom Pope Clement VIII had shewn great favour, creating him Knight of St. Peter and Count of the Sacred Palace. Schopp was addressing Conrad Rittershausen. He recounts that because of his heresy Bruno had been publicly burned that day in the Square of Flowers in front of the Theatre of Pompey. He makes merry over the belief of the Italians that every heretic is a Lutheran. It is evident that he had been present at the interrogations, for he relates in detail the life of Bruno and the works and doctrines for which he had been arraigned, and he gives a vivid account of Bruno's final appearance before his judges on 8th February. To Schopp we owe the knowledge of Bruno's bearing under judgement. When the verdict had been declared, records Schopp, Bruno with a threatening gesture addressed his judges: "Perchance you who pronounce my sentence are in greater fear than I who receive it." Thus he was dismissed to the prison, gloats the convert, "and was given eight days to recant, but in vain. So today he was led to the funeral pyre. When the image of our Saviour was shown to him before his death he angrily rejected it with averted face. . . . Thus my dear Rittershausen is it our custom to proceed against such men or rather indeed such monsters." [80]

---

[79] We read that on Saturday 12th February the public expected to be entertained by the judicial burning (*Doc. Rom.* XXVIII). On 19th February the martyrdom is recorded with horrible detail: "His tongue imprisoned on account of his wicked words." The transcript is in the Vatican MS. Urbane 1068 (*Docc. Rom.* XXXI and XXXII).

[80] *Doc. Rom.* XXX. This letter was first published in a version not quite complete, in 1621, in a volume entitled *Macchiavellizatio, qua unitorum animos dissociare nitentibus respondetur; in gratiam Dn. Archiepiscopi castissimae vitae: petri Pazman succincte excerpta . . . addita est epostola Casp. Scioppii, in qua hereticus jure infelicibus lignis cremari concludid . . .* (Saragossae Excudebat Didacus Iba ra. MDCXXI). Salvestrini states that the volume was printed at Ingolstadt, and not at Saragossa. The authenticity of this letter was hotly contested prior to the publication of the Documents concerning Bruno from the Archives of the Venetian Republic and of the Vatican. The procedure related with

A yet more minute description was discovered in the Records of the Company of St. John the Beheaded,[81] called also the Company of Mercy and Pity, whose duty it was to follow condemned heretics to the stake. It is recorded that information was sent to them at two o'clock in the morning, wherefore at six they betook themselves to the Nona Tower where Bruno was now held. He was handed over to them and they "exhorted him in all charity," reciting his errors, in which occupation they were accompanied by two Holy Fathers from the Dominicans, two from the Jesuits, "two from the new Church" and "one from St. Jerome."

Through the early hours of Thursday, the 16th February, their solicitations were continued. At length the prisoner, nude, bound to a stake, accompanied by the mocking solemnity and chanted prayers of his tormentors and held to a terrible silence,[82] was brought forth to the Square of the Flowers in Rome. His body was consigned to the flames. His Message has re-echoed down the years.

---

such odious unction by Schopp was then undoubtedly confirmed. Moreover the original letter was found in the Communal Library of Breslau and was published in full by B. G. Struve in the *Acta litteraria* (Jena, 1707), V, 67-74. The letter has been published many times in several languages. It was translated into English by M. de La Roche, *Memoirs of Literature* (London, 1722), II, 244, and by J. Toland, *A Collection of Several Pieces* (London, 1726), I, 307. Schopp again took occasion to gloat over Bruno's martyrdom in a volume, *Serenissimi D. Jacobi magnae Britanniae regis oppositus* (Hartbergae, 1611) (*Doc. Rom.* XXX). Salvestrini states that this volume was printed at Meitingen, and not at Harterberg as stated on the frontispiece.

[81] XVI, 87. Cf. *Doc. Rom.* XXIX. The document has been published elsewhere and is printed "by command of the Royal Ministry" in the Introduction to the final volume of the National Edition of Bruno's Latin works (*Op. lat.*, III, xi-xii).

[82] See above, n. 79.

CHAPTER EIGHT

INFLUENCE OF BRUNO

a. More Links with England: Plurality of Worlds

THE end—the fruitless end. So it must have appeared to Bruno on that February morning. We have gleaned from the Inquisition Archives some notion of the physical privation and suffering during those eight long years. We stand abashed before the mental and moral strength, the amazing courage that could still attempt to convey to the arraigning judges the beauty and the exaltation of his message. But they stubbornly refused the message. As he passed to his dreadful death, he must have thought himself and his message doomed to utter and complete oblivion.

Yet perhaps not one of the intervening years between then and now has gone without Bruno's name passing men's lips, without his message bringing its rousing summons to great thought and great deeds. Many volumes have been written on different aspects of Bruno's thought, on the development of his philosophy and the influence derived from him by many of the great minds of Europe. In the few pages that follow, only the briefest outline can be given of the influence traceable to him in the three centuries following his death.

Certain developments from his sojourn in England must first be considered. Attention has already been drawn to Bruno's connection both with the "School of Night" and with Hariot and other astronomers in England.[1] His contacts with Raleigh, with Sidney and with others of the English Court have been traced.[2]

[1] See pp. 30, n. 9; 37, n. 28; 62-70 (for Hariot, pp. 37, 67-8). Grant McColley traces the history of the conception of other inhabited worlds and gives numerous seventeenth century examples in *Annals of Science,* I, iii (Oxford, 1936), 385-430.

[2] See pp. 36-7 *seqq.* Cf. also pp. 116, 125, 150.

Francis Bacon (1561-1626), too, just mentions Bruno. In the Introduction to the *Historia naturalis et experimentalis* (1622), citing philosophers who seek for knowledge through imagination instead of through experiment, he remarks: "Patrizzi, Telesio, Bruno, Severin of Denmark, Gilbert of England, Campanella, have tried the stage, acted new plays which were neither marked by applauding favour of the public nor by brilliancy of plot." [3]

Perhaps the idea that most caught the fancy of Bruno's English audience was that of inhabitants of other worlds, derived by Bruno from Nicolaus of Cusa.

The idea is found in the Introduction to Book Two of Spenser's *Faerie Queene* (1590):

> Right well I wote, most mighty Soueraine,
> That all this famous antique history,

[3] *Opera,* ed. by Ellis and Spedding, II, 13. Cf. McIntyre, *op. cit.,* p. 326. McIntyre notes that Bacon may nevertheless be indebted to Bruno for certain mythological stories, while the suggestion of spiral instead of circular motion of the heavenly bodies (*Novum organum* [1620], 1 Aph. 45) might also have arisen in Bacon's mind after reading Bruno's writings. Gentile points out phrases in the *Novum organum* (Lib. I, Cap. 48) very close to phrases in *The Ash Wednesday Supper.* It may be recalled that Bacon himself was not innocent of faith in foolproof intellectual methods! Gentile notes also passages in Galileo very similar to passages in the same work. Cf. Gentile, "Veritas filia temporis: Postilla Bruniana" in *Scritti varii di erudizione e di critica in onore di R. Renier* (Turin, 1912), and Gentile, *Op. ital.,* I, 88. Cf. also Spampanato, *Quattro filosofi Napolitani nel carteggio di Galileo,* I, 11-35, and Berti, "Storia dei MSS Galileani della bibl. naz. di Firenze" in *Atti dei Lincei* (1875-76), S. 2a, Vol. III, Part 3, Mem. sc., p. 102.

Campanella (1568-1639), in his desire to reconcile the Church with the new philosophy based on physical experience, denied that Bruno's scientific views were the reason for his being burnt (cf. H. Höffding, *History of Modern Philosophy* [Eng. edition], I, 159, and Amabile, *Fra Tommaso Campanella ne' castelli di Napoli, in Roma e in Parigi,* II, 85, Doc. 197). Campanella cites Cusanus and the Nolan as authorities for the existence of "both other suns and other planets travelling around the stellar firmament" (*Apologia pro Galileo* [Frankfurt, 1622]). Many years later from his haven in France, he cites Tycho on the subject and repudiates the doctrines of Copernicus and of the Nolan (T. Campanella, *Disputationes . . . suae philosophiae* [Paris, 1637], pp. 103, 106). The following year he is again considering the views of Cusanus and of the Nolan (Campanella, *Universatis philosophiae seu metaphysica . . . rum rerum . . .* [Paris, 1638], Pars. III, Lib. 11, pp. 52, 54; Lib. 15, p. 105).

Of some, th' aboundance of an idle braine
Will iudged be, and painted forgery
Rather than matter of iust memory;
Sith none that breatheth liuing aire does knowe,
Where is that Land of Faery,
Which I so much doe vaunt, yet no where showe
But vouch antiquities, which no body can knowe.
But let that man with better sense advise
That of the world least part to us is read:
And daily how through hardy enterprise
Many great Regions are discouered,
. . .
Why then should witlesse man so much misweene
That nothing is, but that which he hath seene?
What if within the Moone's fair shining spheare,
What if in every other starre unseene
Of other worlds he happily should heare?
He wonder would much more: yet suche to some appeare.

Ben Jonson, on the other hand, in a Masque performed at Court on Twelfth Night, 1620, and entitled *News from the New World Discovered in the Moon,* ridiculed the idea of the moon's being inhabited.[4]

Bruno's most remarkable, though unavowed, disciple was acquired in his Oxford adventure.[5] When Bruno was in Oxford in 1583 there was a young graduate at Christ Church named Francis Godwin[6] just about to take his Master's Degree. Godwin heard the discourse of Bruno, this uncouth foreigner who produced such a scandal in the university. Promptly the young man wrote a skit on the whole affair entitled *The Man in the Moone or a Discourse of a Voyage Hither, by Domingo Gonsales, the Speedy Messenger*. Bruno becomes a Spaniard; he is represented as a wanderer who had got into sundry embroilments like Bruno himself. Having killed a man in a duel, he decides that he must quit this earth, and he trains a team of geese to fly up and convey him to the moon. A digression assures us that this proceeding is in con-

[4] Ben Jonson, *Works* (ed. W. Gifford, London, 1875), VII, 333.
[5] Cf. pp. 27-35.
[6] 1562-1633.

formity with all religion, and we then hear an account of his adventures. True to the ideas of Bruno, Gonsales tells us how the earth soon came to look like the moon. After eleven or twelve days, free of that lodestone the earth (the phrase becomes familiar to us in Gilbert), Gonsales reaches the moon and many are his adventures there, until at length, having acquired a new sort of lodestone, an antidote to the attraction of the earth, he is able to float himself safely down again, landing in China.

Godwin himself never published this work. He was destined to become a distinguished historian and a pillar of the Church of England as Bishop first of Llandaff and later of Chester. His best-known work, which earned him his preferment, was a Catalogue of the Bishops of England, dedicated to that Lord Buckhurst whose name figures in Bruno's *Ash Wednesday Supper*. *The Man in the Moone* was, however, published after his death, and one *E.M.* of Christ Church contributed an interesting "Epistle to the Reader." The work reached at least three editions [7] and was translated into French, inspired the *Voyage to the Moon* of Cyrano de Bergerac, which in turn gave hints to Dean Swift for his *Gulliver's Travels* (1726). Bishop Godwin had, however, written another work in light vein, perhaps also in his student days. This was called *The Inanimate Messenger from Utopia.* It is in Latin and describes methods of comunication by beacon lights. A translation of the Latin work by one Dr. T. Smith of Magdalen College, Oxford, was published posthumously as *Mysterious Messenger Unlocking the Secret of Men's Hearts,* together with the second edition of *The Man in the Moone.*[8]

The combined work attracted the attention of another young divine, John Wilkins (1614-1672), who also became a bishop. Wilkins began life as a Parliamentarian. He accepted the Restoration, and his kindliness and moderation helped the religious adjustments of the period. In 1638, soon after taking his Oxford M.A., Wilkins published anony-

[7] 1638, 1657 and 1768. For the second edition, see below, n. 8.

[8] See preceding note. This volume appeared in 1657 so we do not hazard the identification of "Dr. S. Smith of Magdalen College" with the Smith of *The Ash Wednesday Supper* (cf. p. 37).

mously his *Discovery of a World in the Moon tending to prove that 'tis probable that there may be another habitable world in that Planet.* The work was, we are told, well known to be from the hand of Wilkins. It soon reached a second and again a third edition with sundry additions each time. The third (of 1640) has also a "Discourse concerning the Possibility of a Passage thither." It too was translated into French.[9] His next work, *Mercury or the Secret Messenger,* not only bears his name, but is frankly inspired by Godwin. Both Godwin's *Mysterious Messenger* and also the adventures of Don Gonsales himself are cited by Wilkins.

Now Bishop Wilkins, when he resided in London, had been an eager member of that *Invisible College* which met for the exhibition and discussion of scientific matters. When in 1648 he became warden of Wadham College, Oxford, the meetings of the scientists forming the *Invisible College* were transferred to Wadham. At this time Sir Christopher Wren was among his pupils at Wadham. Later on Wilkins presided at a meeting in London which resulted in the foundation of the Royal Society of which he was the first secretary.

Thus from Wilkins, one of the founders of the Royal Society, we trace back the line of ideas through Godwin with his character of Don Gonsales and with his cosmology based on that of Bruno, yet further back beyond Bruno to the great mind, at once exalted and constructive, of Nicolaus of Cusa, and beyond Nicolaus to the philosophers of Islamic Spain, who themselves formed part of the wave of Islamic thought which during the centuries had swept from Persia and Asia Minor westward to the frontier of France.

But there resulted from the new metaphysical conceptions a subtler and yet more important change in the conception of the physical uni-

---

[9] By Sieur de la Montagne as *Le monde dans la lune* (Rome, 1655). The first and second editions of Wilkins' work (both of 1638) are discussed by Grant McColley, "The Second Edition of *The Discovery of a World in the Moon*," *Annals of Science,* I, 3 (London, July, 1936), pp. 330-34. An excellent survey of the whole subject is given by McColley in "The Seventeenth Century Doctrine of a Plurality of Worlds," *Annals of Science,* I, 4 (London, Oct., 1936), pp. 385-430. McColley traces the history of the conception of other inhabited worlds, and gives a number of seventeenth century examples.

verse. We have seen that the earth no longer formed the summit of a hierarchy. The universe itself came to be regarded as a continuum rather than as a hierarchy. Thus mutual interaction of the parts of the universe assumed new meaning, and the way was prepared for Newton's great message of universal interaction through universally acting law.

The mention of Newton brings to mind that charming French writer of the turn of the seventeenth century, le Bovier de Fontenelle. De Fontenelle does not mention Bruno by name but his *Entretiens sur la pluralité des mondes*[10] is in the succession of the works we have been considering. De Fontenelle too cites astronomers: "Ask Flamstead about the interior of the moon." He reminds us of an author also cited by Bruno in a different context. "Here," says de Fontenelle, "is Ariosto's talk about Astolfo who was carried to the moon by St. John." He thinks the inhabitants of these other worlds must be quite different from man, but that communication with them will one day be possible. To the sun he does not ascribe inhabitants very different from man. He forecasts the human art of flying, but feels obliged to explain hastily that this suggestion was his joke, an insuperable difficulty lying in the differences in the atmosphere at different heights. In 1695 this work was translated into English by John Glanville (1664-1735). Another English translation which purports to have been revised by Fontenelle himself was published in 1783 and contains also a translation from the Latin of an *Oration in Defence of the New Philosophy spoken in the theatre at Oxford, July 7th, 1693 by Mr. Addison*. This latter gives a brief but very spirited defence of the new cosmology which it ascribes to Descartes; microscopes and the objects seen through them are cited, as well as Boyle's air pumps. Monsieur de Fontenelle was a nephew of Corneille. He was Secretary to the Académie des Sciences. It is recorded that he refused to vote either for the admission or the exclusion of a candidate for the Academy whose qualification was the friendship of the Duc d' Orléans. It appears that he was the only member who refused to admit political grounds for exclusion of a candidate. De Fontenelle was the friend of Voltaire, and he discovered and introduced to Paris society

---

[10] Paris, 1686.

Mademoiselle Cordier de Launay who became Madame de Staël. He became famous for his preface to the Marquis de l'Hôpital's *Des infiniment petits* and it was he who delivered the official obituary oration on the death of Newton. He lived almost to his hundredth birthday.

We may quote also the astronomer Edmund Halley (1656-1742) to whom we owe not only the observation of the famous comet, but also the publication of Newton's great work (to which the chief obstacle was the author's own reluctance to publication). "It is now taken for granted that the Earth is one of the Planets and they are all with reason suppos'd habitable, though we are not able to define by what sort of Animals." [11]

Finally we may recall the posthumous work *Cosmotheoros* of the Dutch astronomer Christian Huygens (1629-1695). Huygens accepts the view that the stars are suns vastly further from us than our own sun. With an engaging combination of sound astronomy, fantasy and piety, he expounds his view that the planets of our sun and of the other stars must have living inhabitants. He notes that Plutarch and "later Authors such as Cardinal Cusanus, Brunus, Kepler (and if we may believe him Tycho was of that opinion too) have furnish'd the Planets with Inhabitants" and he cites the "ingenious French author" (De Fontenelle). But he does not follow Cusanus and Bruno in having "allow'd the Sun and fixed Stars theirs too." The suns Huygens believes to be too hot for living inhabitants, but rather by their light and heat to enable their planets to support life. Except as regards the habitation of the moon, which he accepts after some doubt, he rejects the views of Kepler's *Mysterium cosmographicum* as "nothing but an idle Dream taken from *Pythagoras* or Plato's Philosophy." He sets forth on a sound astronomical basis his view of a vast universe and of the immensely numerous and distant stars, so that to reckon them "requires an immense Treasury not of twenty or thirty figures only, in our decuple Progression, but of as many as there are Grains of Sand upon the shore. And yet who can say, that even this number exceeds that of the Fixed Stars? Some of the Ancients and *Jordanus Brunus* carry'd it further, in declaring the Num-

[11] Second paper on "The Cause of Change of the Variation of the Magnetical Needle" in *Miscellanea curiosa* (London, 1705), p. 56.

ber infinite." Huygens considers that Bruno's arguments for infinity are not conclusive, though he is inclined to accept his views. "Indeed it seems to me certain that the Universe is infinitely extended; but what God has bin pleas'd to place beyond the Region of the Stars, is as much above our knowledge as it is our Habitation." [12]

b. Bruno's Younger Contemporaries: The Seventeenth Century

It may well be believed that former pupils of Bruno when they met together in safe seclusion, were wont to recall the man and his works. To four of them, Eglin, Alstedt, Nostitz and Besler, we owe a special tribute for their pious faithfulness. Raffaele Eglin dared to publish in 1595 the gist of a course of lectures that the Master had given in Zurich; and a further volume was issued from the majesty of Eglin's Chair of Theology at Prague in 1603.[13] Mention has been made of the slight work from Bruno's words published by his pupil Alstedt in 1612.[14] Before another three years had passed, the Hungarian pupil Nostitz had published the gist of lectures delivered thirty-three years earlier in Paris.[15]

Besler, the pupil who was working with him as his scribe up to his imprisonment, published no works of Bruno. It is not hard to understand that wisdom did not suggest a wider advertisement of their connection. But the manuscript from Besler's hand furnishes the only copy of some of Bruno's works.[16]

Above all, the debt of our modern world is to the publisher in England of the six brief Italian works and to the devoted task of Wechel and

[12] We quote from a charming little English translation that appeared in the same year as the Dutch original. *The Celestial Worlds Discover'd; or, Conjectures concerning the Inhabitants, Plants and Productions of the Worlds in the Planets written in London by Christianus Huygens, and inscrib'd to his Brother, Constantine Huygens, late Secretary to His Majesty K. William* (printed for Timothy Childs, London, 1698).

[13] Cf. pp. 153-4.

[14] Cf. pp. 142-3.

[15] Cf. pp. 19-20.

[16] See pp. 147-8 and App. III, M.

Fischer in publishing the great Latin poems.[17] While we are considering the seventeenth century, it may be recalled that a second edition of the poems *De monade* and *De innumerabilibus* was published by Fischer in 1614.

The names of William Gilbert and of Bruno are often mentioned together by the astronomers of the earlier seventeenth century. Galileo (1564-1642) may have first heard of Bruno through reading the *De magnete.* In a passage commenting on the pusillanimity of men of talent who neglect Gilbert's work, he attributes his own possession of *De magnete* to "a famed peripatetic philosopher who presented it to me, I think in order to purge his own library of the contagion thereof." [18] But Johannes Kepler (1571-1630) is reported as reproaching Galileo for omitting to mention his own debt. For Martin Hasdale (1571-1630), a member of the Emperor Rudolph's court and a great purveyor of gossip as well as a devoted admirer of Galileo, writes to him as follows from Prague on 15th April, 1610:

I had this morning occasion for friendly dispute with Kepler when we were both lunching with the Ambassador of Saxony. . . . He said concerning your book [the *Sidereus nuncius*] that truly it has revealed the divinity of your talent, but that you had given cause of complaint not only to the German nation but also to your own, since you make no mention of those writers who gave the signal and the occasion for your discovery, naming among them Giordano Bruno as an Italian, Copernicus and himself.[19]

Kepler himself in his published works as early as 1606 cited both "infelix ille Jordanus Brunus" and Gilbert. He set forth their view of an infinite universe which he rejected, and of infinitely numerous worlds which he accepted.[20] In the following year he is writing to Brengger that not only

---

[17] See App. I, 7-12 (England), and 23, 25 (a) and (b).

[18] *Dialogo sopra i due massimi sistemi del mondo* (1632), Giornata terza (Galileo, *Edizione nazionale,* VII, 426).

[19] Galileo, *Ed. naz.,* X, 315. Hasdale or Hastal was a German who had studied in Italy. In 1603 Edmond Brutius or Bruce (see below, n. 23) was writing to Kepler that Galileo described Kepler's discoveries as his own (see *Ed. naz.,* X, 335).

[20] J. Kepler, *De stella nova serpentaria qui sub ejus exortum de novo iniit trigono igneo* (Prague, 1606), Cap. XXI, 104-10.

Bruno but following him Tycho Brahe (1581-1627) accepted the plurality of inhabited worlds.[21]

In 1610, writing to Galileo and discussing Galileo's discovery of the satellites of Jupiter, and the possibility of another planet, Kepler cites the comment on Galileo's discovery of their friend Wacker[22] who had said, if there are four more "planets" why not an infinity of planets? Then, writes Kepler, "either the world is infinite as Melissus and Gilbert the Englishman thought or, as Democritus, Leucippus, Bruno and our friend Brutus[23] believed, there are innumerable other worlds similar to ours."[24]

In the reprint of Kepler's letter published in the same year with his commentary on Galileo's *Sidereus nuncius,* there is interpolated before this passage a definite statement that Wacker had no doubt that such new planets circulate around some of the fixed stars "which," remarks Kepler, "has for a long time been in my mind through the speculations of Cusanus and Bruno."[25] Moreover, in drawing a distinction between the views of Gilbert and of Bruno, Kepler now notes that Bruno gave the name of *earths* to the infinitely numerous celestial bodies. There are repeated references to Bruno throughout the letter. For example, "What

---

[21] Kepler's correspondence with Brengger concerning *De stella serpentaria* is published in the *Opera omnia,* II, 591-96. They incidentally discuss Bruno's fate. Johann Georg Brengger was a physician of Bâle and later of Kaufburin in Bavaria (Galileo, *Ed. naz.,* XX, indice biografico).

[22] John Matthias Wacker (1550-1619) studied law in Strasbourg, Geneva and Padua. Later he settled at Breslau. In 1592 he renounced the reformed faith for Catholicism. Soon after, he was ennobled as Wacker of Wachenfels, and in 1597 he was nominated a member of the Emperor's Council in Prague. In 1616 he was created Count Palatine.

[23] Edmondio Brutius was a correspondent of Kepler in 1602 and 1603 (see above, n. 19). The learned editors of the *Edizione nazionale* of Galileo failed to trace any particulars of him, except in Paolo Gualdo's Latin *Vita G. B. Pinelli* [1535-1601] (Augsburg, 1607; London, 1704), where Edmond Bruce is described as "a noble Englishman knowing much of the mathematical disciplines, of military matters and of herbaria." The letters to Kepler are from Florence and Padua respectively.

[24] Galileo, *Ed. naz.,* X, 320-1 (cf. III, 106). This letter is incorporated in Kepler, *Dissertatio cum nuncio siderio nuper ad mortales misso a Galilaeo* (Prague, 1610); published also in Galileo, *Ed. naz.,* III, 97-145.

[25] Galileo, *Ed. naz.,* III, 106, § 3.

else then O Galileo may we infer than that fixed stars send forth their light from within to impinge on planets, that is, if I may use Bruno's words, these as suns and those as moons or earths?" [26]

Kepler accepts Bruno's views of the existence of innumerable worlds but rejoices that he considers that Galileo's work on the satellites of Jupiter rebuts the conception both of Bruno and of Edmund Bruce that there are planets revolving around the fixed stars.[27] In spite of the phrase contrasting Bruno's views with those of Gilbert, Kepler calls Bruno "the defender of infinity." [28] Kepler of course has the mystic conception: "after the sun, no globe is nobler or more apt for Man than our Earth . . . the Sun, the inciter of the motion of all the others, the true Apollo as Bruno repeatedly names him." [29] In 1611 he is again referring to the views of "Cardinal Cusanus, Bruno and others" as to an infinity of "planets" circulating around an infinity of fixed stars.[30]

In 1690 J. J. Zimmermann (1644-1693) dedicated to Duke Rudolph of Brunswick a work in defence of Copernicus, Kepler and Bruno, and begged the Duke to command a new edition of the *De immenso,* recalling that this work had been dedicated to the Duke's ancestor.[31]

But it was on the philosophers of subsequent centuries rather than on the astronomers that Bruno exerted most lasting influence. Though Bruno is nowhere directly cited by Spinoza (1632-1677), the infinite and all-embracing Unity of Spinoza's thought, especially in the *Short Treatise of God and Man and His Well-being* is very reminiscent of Bruno. The connection between the teaching of the two men has been noted by many

---

[26] *Ibid.,* III, 118, § 2; X, 333, § 4.

[27] *Ibid.,* X, 334, 335 and III, 119, 120.

[28] *Ibid.,* X, 338 and III, 123.

[29] *Ibid.,* X, 339 and III, 124.

[30] Kepler, *Narratio de observatis a se quatuor Iouis satelitibus erronibus* (Frankfurt, 1611), Galileo, *Ed. naz.,* III, 183.

[31] Johann Jacob Zimmermann, *Scriptura S. Copernizans seu potius astronomia Copernico-Scripturaria bipartita* (Hamburg and Altona, 1690). J. J. Zimmermann of Wayhingen was a distinguished mathematician. He held minor clerical posts, but his unorthodox theology led him to project emigration to Pennsylvania, for which purpose he received from a follower of Penn a grant of money, and from Penn himself a grant of land in the colony. Zimmermann, however, died in Rotterdam when on the point of embarkation.

of Spinoza's biographers from Nicéron [32] and F. H. Jacobi (p. 195) to those of the nineteenth and the present century.[33] Nor can we leave the seventeenth century without recalling that Spampanato traced Candelaio as a source for scenes and characters in no fewer than ten of the plays of Molière (1622-73).

c. The Eighteenth Century: The Romantic Movement

With the eighteenth century began the translations of Bruno's works. They had already been heralded by *Boniface et le pédant, comédie en prose imitée de l'Italien de Bruno Nolano,* Paris, 1633. In London, 1713, we have *Spaccio della bestia trionfante or the Expulsion of the Triumphant Beast. Translated from the Italian of Jordano Bruno.*[34] It is notable that this first translation from the corpus of Bruno's philosophy appeared in England. It was followed in 1750 by a French translation of the same work: *Le ciel réformé, essai de traduction de partie du livre Italien "Spaccio della bestia trionfante": demus alienis obiectationibus veniam, dum nostris impetremus, Plin.*[35] The *Spaccio* appears to have been espe-

[32] Jean-Pierre Nicéron, *Mémoires pour servir à l'histoire des hommes illustres dans la république des lettres* (Paris, 1732), XII, 201-20. For Bruno's influence on Molière, cf. Spampanato, *Vita,* II, 325; also Louis Moland, *Molière et la Comèdie Italienne,* 2nd ed. (Paris, 1867), pp. 105-11.

[33] Cf. Sigwart, *Kleine Schriften.* Cf. also Arthur O. Lovejoy, "The Dialectic of Bruno and Spinoza," University of California Publications, *Philosophy,* I (November 1904), 141-74.

[34] Perhaps by John Toland (1670-1722), the deist and prolific writer on matters political, literary and religious. Toland was a warm defender of Bruno. In his posthumous *Collection of Several Pieces* (London, 1726), I, 307-15, is an article entitled "De genere loco et tempore mortis Jordani Bruni Nolani," giving the letter of Scioppius (cf. pp. 179-80). There follows (pp. 316-49) a rather inadequate "Account of Jordano's Book On the Infinite Universe and Innumerable Worlds" with a translation of the Dedicatory Epistle. The translation of the *Spaccio,* which is anonymous, may however be by a brother-in-law of Toland, William Morehead.

[35] This translation is attributed to the Abbé de Vougny in Brunet, *Manuel du libraire,* I, 1298. Jean Marie Quérard describes him as *l'abbé Louis Valentin de Vougny, conseiller clerc en la grand chambre de parlement et chanoine de l'église de Paris* (i.e. Notre-Dame), and mentions besides the 1750 edition of *Le ciel réformé* another of 1754, the year of de Vougny's death. (Cf. *La France littéraire*

cially regarded in England. In the *Spectator* of 1712 is a notice of the sale of a copy of this work with an epitome and the remark, "the author is a professed atheist." [36] This term atheist had also been unjustly used of Bruno by Mersenne.[37] The accusation against Bruno of atheism was renewed and disputed by several writers during the eighteenth century.

One of the most ardent admirers of Bruno was the philosopher C. A. Heumann (1681-1746) who became professor of theology at Göttingen. He wrote an analysis of the three great Latin poems and of the *Oratio valedictoria,* prefacing to the latter a defence of Bruno from the accusation of atheism [38] and thus starting a considerable controversy. He wrote a further contribution on the metaphysics of Bruno.[39] Heumann was cited by the Swiss writer J. J. Zimmermann who published in Zurich a Dissertation defending Bruno from the charge of atheism.[40]

It has been said that the philosophical third Earl of Shaftesbury (1671-1713) was much influenced by Bruno's conviction of interrelationship of all things throughout the universe, and that Bruno's writings led him to his view of the living whole as a harmonious organism. Johann George Hamann of Königsberg (1730-1788), in reaction against Kant's *Critique of Pure Reason,* adopted from Bruno the conception of the coincidence of contraries.

[Paris, 1838], IX, 459.) Salvestrini in his bibliography mentions (No. 94) only the 1750 edition which he attributes to de Vougny, giving him the same titles as in Quérard.

[36] Vol. V, No. 389, pp. 301-5 (London, 1712).

[37] *L'impiété des déistes et des plus subtils libertins découverte et refutée* (2 vols., Paris, 1624).

[38] *Acta philosophorum* (Halle, 1715, 1716, 1718 and 1720). Other contributors to this controversy were Johann Franz Buddée, Mathurin Veyssière de Lacroze and Johann Benedict Carpzow. Their writings on the subject are listed in Salvestrini, *loc. cit.*

[39] *Acta philosophorum* (Halle, 1724).

[40] In *Museum helveticum,* V, Fasc. XX, pp. 577-601 and VI, Fasc. XXI, pp. 1-34. The study was reprinted in his *Opera* (Zurich, 1751-57), II, ii, 1128 *seqq.* This writer is not to be confused with Zimmermann of Wayhingen. J. J. Zimmermann of Zurich held a succession of theological Chairs. The volumes of the *Museum helveticum* show him as a Pythagorean, concerned to defend from the charge of atheism many philosophers from Plato onwards.

Daniel Morhof of Weimar (1639-1691), historian and scholar, wrote a charming appreciation of Bruno.[41] Goethe (1749-1832) read this in his youth and read also Gottfried Arnold's account of Bruno.[42] A recent writer has remarked "the rapturous delight . . . roused in Goethe's mind . . . by any fulfilment of his desire to resolve the antithesis between the Many and the One—a desire which is the keynote to the whole of his biological work," and gives a translation of the prose-poem *Die Natur* of Goethe or possibly by his friend Tobler.

Discussing the poem, the translator continues: "His solution, however, was not truly synthetic, since it led him to stress the One, and to absorb the Many into it." These words might have been written of Bruno, who might almost have penned such passages in the poem as:

"She is perfectly whole, and yet always incomplete. Thus, as she now works, she can work for ever.

"To each man she appears as befits him alone. She cloaks herself under a thousand names and terms, and is always the same." [43] Goethe refers in *Faust* to the martyrdom of Bruno. But in the *Annalen,* published in 1812, he remarks that the works of Bruno are indeed characterized by the exaltation of his outlook, but that to extract the solid gold and silver from the mass of such unequally precious lodes is almost beyond human strength.[44]

Leibnitz (1646-1716), Lessing (1729-1781) and Herder (1744-1803)

---

[41] In the *Polyhistor* (4th ed., Lübeck, 1747).

[42] *Dichtung und Wahrheit,* VI and VIII (*Sämtliche Werke* [Stuttgart, 1851], XIII, 216 and 315-16).

[43] A. Arber, "Goethe's Botany" in *Chronica Botanica,* X, No. 2 (Waltham, Mass., 1946), 63-126.

[44] *Sämtliche Werke* (Jubilaeum Edition, Stuttgart, 1940), XXXI, 269. For relationship of Goethe and Schiller with Bruno, cf. L. Kuhlenbeck, *Giordano Bruno's Einfluss auf Goethe und Schiller* (Leipzig, 1907; Vortrag in der Richard Wagner Gesellschaft zu Berlin, am 25.x.1906) and Werner Sänger, *Goethe und Giordano Bruno* (Berlin, 1930). Cf. also H. Brunnhofer, "Giordano Bruno's Einfluss auf Goethe" in *Goethe-Jahrbuch,* VIII (Frankfurt, 1886), 241-50; and B. Croce, "G. Bruno e Volfgango Goethe" in *Juvenilia 1883-1887* (Bari, 1914), pp. 69-72. See also Walter van der Bleek, *Giordano Bruno, Goethe und der Christus Problem, Naturwissenschaft und Bibel* (Berlin, 1911). Other works on the subject are listed by Salvestrini.

have been described as disciples of Bruno.[45] Herder corresponded with Hamann concerning him.[46] J. F. Abel (1751-1829) is said to have first directed the attention of Schiller (1759-1805) to Bruno's writings. Schelling (1775-1854) wrote a Dialogue entitled *Bruno, or the Divine and the Natural Principles of Things*.[47]

F. H. Jacobi (1743-1819) had yet earlier drawn attention to Bruno. In his *Letters to Moses Mendelssohn on the Thought of Spinoza* he remarks that he cannot understand why the philosophy of Bruno has been called obscure. He considers that there is hardly a purer or more beautiful exposition of pantheism to be found, and he regards Bruno's work as essential for the understanding both of this doctrine and of its relationship to other philosophies. He gives the gist of some extracts from *De la causa, principio et uno* together with some of the original Italian "lest you should think me inaccurate." [48]

Hegel (1770-1831) did not accept Jacobi's high estimate of Bruno. He was revolted by the Italian's exuberance and he criticized both Jacobi and Schelling for their advocacy of Bruno. Nevertheless, the thought of Hegel can perhaps trace surprising ancestry in the doctrine of the coincidence of contraries.[49]

---

[45] The relationship has been perhaps most tersely and clearly traced in H. Brunnhofer, *Bruno's Lehre von Kleinsten als die Quelle der Prästabilirten Harmonie von Leibnitz* (Leipzig, 1890); and in the same author's *Giordano Bruno's Weltanschauung und Verhängnis* (Leipzig, 1882), part of which appeared in an anonymous English translation privately printed by Trübner, London, 1883.

[46] Cf. Walter van der Bleek, *op. cit.* (Cf. note 44).

[47] F. W. J. von Schelling, *Bruno, oder über das göttliche und natürliche Principium der Dinge* (Berlin, 1802).

[48] *Uber die Lehre des Spinoza in Briefen an Herrn Moses Mendelssohn* (in the second edition only, Breslau, 1789). Jacobi gives an account of Bruno in the Preface to this second edition, and the translations in an Appendix. See also above, p. 192. Jacobi is also believed to be the author of the German translations from Bruno in Rixner and Siber, *Leben und Lehrmeinungen berühmter Physiker am Ende des XVI und am Anfang des XVII Jahrhunderts* (Sulzbach, 1824), Vol. V. These comprise the main part of the 10 Dialogues of the *De la causa, principio et uno* and of the *De l'infinito universo et mondi* (without the Dedicatory Epistles and Arguments), and some translations of extracts from the Latin works. Some German translations in the same volume of sonnets from these two Italian works and from the *Spaccio* are attributed to M. Waldhausen.

[49] Cf. p. 86.

The romantic movement found plenty of inspiration from Bruno. Coleridge (1772-1834) was profoundly impressed by him. Both in manuscripts and in his published works, Coleridge refers to Bruno many times and gives quotations and translations from his works, especially from *De monade* and *De innumerabilibus.* The copy of the latter work in the Bodleian Library contains manuscript notes by Coleridge. In a letter to W. Sotheby of 13th July, 1802, he quotes from the final lines of the poem.[50] In the composite volume *Omniana,* the references to Bruno are clearly from Coleridge's pen. Thus in the essay on *Egotism* we have:

> Paracelsus was a braggart and a quack: so was Cardan: but it was their merits and not their follies which drew upon them that torrent of detraction and calumny which compelled them so frequently to think and write concerning themselves that at length it became a habit to do so . . . and the same holds good of the founder of the Brunonian system[51] and of his namesake Giordano Bruno.[52]

In the essay on the *Circulation of the Blood* is an even more interesting product of Coleridge's erudition; he writes:

> The ancients attributed to the blood the same motion of ascent and descent which really takes place in the sap of trees. Servetus discovered the minor circulation from the heart to the lungs. Do not the following passages of Giordano Bruno (published 1591), seem to imply more? We put the question, pauperis forma, with unfeigned diffidence.
>
> "*De Immenso et Innumerabili,* lib. vi, cap. 8:
> "Ut in nostro corpore sanguis per totum *circumcursat*
> et recursat, sic in toto mundo, astro, tellure."

---

[50] Ernest Hartley Coleridge, *Letters of S. T. Coleridge* (2 vols., London, 1895), I, 371. William Sotheby (1757-1833) was a minor poet and playwright. He was a nephew of Sir Hans Sloane and prominent in the circle of Coleridge, Wordsworth and Samuel Rogers. Among his friends also were Sir Walter Scott, Maria Edgeworth and Mrs. Siddons. The latter, with Kemble, performed in 1800 Sotheby's play *Julian and Agnes.* Sotheby started life in the army, but soon retired. In 1794 he became both F.S.A. and F.R.S. He made no contribution to the *Phil. Trans.*

[51] John Brown (1735-1788), founder of the "Brunonian" system of medicine, once the subject of acute controversy.

[52] *Omniana or Horae otiosores* (2 vols., London, 1812), I, 216-17, Essay 110.

"Quare non aliter quam nostro in corpore sanguis
Hinc meat, hinc remeat, neque ad inferiora fluit vi
Majore, ad supera e pedibus quam deinde recedat"

and still more plainly, in the ninth chapter of the same book:

"Quid esse
Quodam ni gyro Naturae cuncta redirent
Ortus ad proprios rursam; si sorbeat omnes
Pontus aquas, totum non restituatque perenni
Ordine: qua possit rerum consistere vita?
Tanquam si totus concurrat sanguis in unam,
In qua consistat, partem, nec prima revisat
Ordia, et antiquos cursus non inde resumat." [53]

We must, however, reject this claim of Coleridge for Bruno. The passages quoted are but examples of Bruno's doctrine of cosmic metabolism and this is clearly shewn by the complete heading to Book VI, Chapter 8, of which Coleridge quotes only a part.[54]

In the essay on *Magnanimity,* seven verses are quoted out of the eight prefixed by Bruno to *De monade.*[55] Coleridge in his notes introducing the verses remarks:

If the human mind be, as it assuredly is, the sublimest object which nature affords to our contemplation, these lines which pourtray the human mind under the action of its most elevated affections, have a fair claim to the praise of sublimity.

After quoting the verses he observes:

The conclusion alludes to a charge of impenetrable obscurity in which Bruno shares one and the same fate with Plato, Aristotle, Kant, and in truth with every great discoverer and benefactor of the human race; excepting only when the discoveries have been capable of being rendered palpable to the

---

[53] *Ibid.,* I, 234-37, Essay 122. Coleridge then cites the claims of the sixteenth century Spanish veterinary writer Francisco de la Reyna to have anticipated the discovery of the circulation of the blood.

[54] Cf. Dorothea Waley Singer, "Coleridge Suggests Two Anticipations of the Circulation of the Blood," in *Archeion* (Santa Fé, 1943).

[55] *Op. lat.,* I, ii, 321-22.

outward senses, and have therefore come under the cognizance of our "sober judicious critics"; the men of "sound common sense," i.e., of those snails in intellect who wear their eyes at the tips of their feelers, and cannot even see unless they at the same time *touch*. When these finger-philosophers affirm that Plato, Bruno, etc., must have been *"out of their senses,"* the just and proper retort is "Gentlemen! it is still worse with you! you have *lost your reason."*

By the bye, Addison in the *Spectator* has grossly misrepresented the design and tendency of Bruno's *Bestia Trionfante;* the object of which was to show of all the theologies and theogonies which have been conceived for the mere purpose of solving problems in the material universe, that as they originate in the fancy, so they all end in delusion, and act to the hindrance or prevention of sound knowledge and actual discovery. But the principal and more important truth taught in this allegory, is, that in the concerns of morality, all pretended knowledge of the will of heaven, which is not revealed to man through his conscience; that all commands, which do not consist in the unconditional obedience of the will to the pure reason, without tampering with consequences (which are in God's power and not in ours); in short, that all motives of hope and fear from invisible powers, which are not immediately derived from, and absolutely coincident with, the reverence due to the supreme reason of the universe, are all alike dangerous superstitions. The worship founded on them, whether offered by the Catholic to St. Francis or by the poor African to his Fetish, differ in form only, not in substance. Herein Bruno speaks not only as a philosopher but as an enlightened Christian; the evangelists and apostles everywhere representing their moral precepts, not as doctrines then first revealed, but as truths implanted in the hearts of men, which their vices only could have obscured.[56]

In 1814, writing under his own name, Coleridge quotes from the *De umbris idearum*.[57]

In 1817 he writes: "The *De immenso et innumerabilibus* and the *De la causa, principio et uno* of the philosopher of Nola, who could

[56] *Omniana or Horae Otiosores,* I, 240-45, Essay 129. Cf. Bruno, *Op. lat.,* I, ii, 321-22.

[57] Felix Farley's *Bristol Journal,* 6th August, 1814, opening a series of "Essays on the Fine Arts" by Coleridge; we have not seen the Essay, which is cited by Joseph Cottle, *Early Recollections Chiefly Relating to the Late S. T. Coleridge* (2 vols., London, 1837), II, 202, Appendix.

boast of a Sir Philip Sidney and Fulke Greville among his patrons and whom the idolaters of Rome burnt as an atheist in the year 1660" [*sic*] and again, "We [i.e., himself and Schelling] had both equal obligations to the polar logic and dynamic philosophy of Giordano Bruno." [58]

An essay in *The Friend* suggests to the modern reader that the doctrine of the coincidence of contraries (which, it will be recalled, goes back through Bruno and Cusanus to Pseudo-Dionysius the Areopagite) contributed also towards the development of the doctrine of dialectic materialism. Coleridge writes:

> As far as human practice can realise the sharp limits and exclusive proprieties of science, law and religion should be kept distinct. There is in strictness no proper opposition but between the two polar forces of one and the same power.

Coleridge continues in a note:

> Every power in nature and in spirit must evolve an opposite, as the sole means and condition of its manifestation: *and all opposition is a tendency to re-union.* This is the universal law of polarity or essential dualism, first promulgated by Heraclitus, two thousand years afterwards republished and made the foundation both of Logic, of Physics, and of Metaphysics by Giordano Bruno. The principle may be thus expressed. The *identity* of *thesis* and *antithesis* is the substance of all being; their opposition the condition of all existence, or being manifested; and every thing or *phaenomenon* is the exponent of a *synthesis* as long as the opposite energies are retained in that *synthesis.* Thus water is neither oxygen nor hydrogen, nor yet is it a commixture of both: but the *synthesis* or indifference of the two.[59]

In the same volume Coleridge quotes and translates from the first chapter of *De immenso et innumerabilibus* a long passage with the challenging phrase, "Anima sapiens non timet mortem." He adds:

> In the last volume of this work . . . I purpose to give an account of the life of Giordano Bruno, the friend of Sir Philip Sidney who was burnt under

[58] *Biographia Literaria* (London, 1817), I, 138, 150.

[59] *The Friend* (3rd ed.; ed. Coleridge, London, 1818), I, 149, Essay XIII; and I, 193-97, Essay XVI. Cf. Bruno, *Op. lat.*, I, 265-66. Other references to Bruno are in the *Literary Remains of S. T. Coleridge* (London, 1839), IV, 141, 422.

pretence of Atheism, at Rome, in the year 1600 and of his works which are perhaps the scarcest books ever printed. They are singularly interesting as portraits of a vigorous mind struggling after truth, amid many prejudices, which from the state of the Roman Church, in which he was born, have a claim to much indulgence. One of them (entitled Ember Week) is curious for its lively accounts of the rude state of London, at that time, both as to the street and the manners of the citizen. The most industrious historians of speculative philosophy have not been able to procure more than a few of his works . . . out of eleven, the titles of which are preserved to us I have had an opportunity of perusing six. I was told, when in Germany, that there is a complete collection of them in the Royal Library at Copenhagen. If so, it is unique.[60]

d. Later Times

It is a mark of Bruno's genius that later thinkers find ever fresh implications in his thought. We have seen how he himself derived from thinkers so opposed as Cusanus and Lucretius. Similarly, elements in his own philosophy may have contributed to the birth of views very different from his.[61] The liberation movements of the nineteenth century shew Bruno as an almost legendary figure stimulating youth, inspiring alike *Risorgimento* in Italy and *Aufklärung* in Germany. The formidable industry of his Italian bibliographer enumerates in the nineteenth century alone no less than 634 publications in which Bruno figures. A good example is the enthusiastic study of David Levi, *Giordano Bruno e la religione del pensiero: l'uomo, l'apostolo e il martiro,*[62] published just before the erection of the statue on the site of his martyrdom.

To the present generation it is no surprise to learn that the denial of the spirit is a crime that may infect those who act in the very name thereof. Victims of the savage ideology that afflicted the land where

---

60 *The Friend*, I, 149, Essay XVI.

61 At least two very diverse works of the twentieth century may be cited in illustration. These are Joseph Needham *Time and the Refreshing River* (London, 1943) and Lance Whyte, *The Next Development in Man* (London, 1944).

62 Turin, 1887.

Bruno found sanctuary in his last years, may derive solace and hope from the knowledge that on the very site of his humiliation and martyrdom there gathered to do him honour after 289 years, representatives from almost every land. His compatriots with a just perception linked his name on that occasion with that of the great Italian interpreter of the Catholic faith. At the dedication of his statue in the *Piazza dei Fiori* on this occasion, speeches swelled with the noble sentiments so much easier to arouse for past than for future action. "Farewell ye ashes. Yet in these ashes is the seed which reneweth the whole world." Of the monument, Bruno's biographer Berti wrote in 1889:

> Monuments are our great instructors: I would that from this statue of Bruno our youth should learn the quality and the amount of sacrifice which is the price of loyalty to our own conscience. It behoveth us all to see that the grand records be not lost and that every noble nation pay regard to them.[63]

We have tried to get some insight into the thought of Bruno, a spirit so noble and soaring, so humanly frail, so vividly inspiring to those who followed him in the great struggle of the human race upward to the light of reason. We will close our study, echoing his own words, which we may believe gave him courage for his ordeal even as they give courage to those who carry on his effort for the emancipation of the human spirit:

> The wise soul feareth not death; rather she sometimes striveth for death, she goeth beyond to meet her. Yet eternity maintaineth her substance throughout time, immensity throughout space, universal form throughout motion.[64]

---

[63] D. Berti, *Vita di Giordano Bruno* (Turin, 1868 and 1889). From Preface to the edition of 1889.

[64] *De immenso,* Lib. I, Cap. 1 (*Op. lat.,* I, i, 205).

APPENDIX I

LIST OF BRUNO'S WRITINGS

AN EXCELLENT comprehensive bibliography of Bruno's works and of references to him by other writers was published by Virgilio Salvestrini at Pisa in 1926. This volume is provided with a good index and is very well arranged. It gives also facsimile reproductions of the title-page of the first edition of each of Bruno's works that was published before the nineteenth century.

The table that follows includes lost works. Chronologically arranged, it provides a bird's-eye view of Bruno's literary career. There is, however, room for difference of opinion as to the order of composition of the items bearing Roman numerals, that is, the group of works the publication of which he did not supervise.

CHRONOLOGICAL LIST OF THE WRITINGS OF GIORDANO BRUNO

Date published; if unpublished by Bruno, propable date of composition [a]	Place published and printer; if unpublished by Bruno, probable place of composition	Title and subject matter [b]	References to collected editions	Manuscript sources [c]
(i) Not later than 1572. LOST. [176]	Naples?	*De arca Noe.* Probably symbolic exposition of moral philosophy in style of *Cabala del cavallo Pegaseo.*	——	——
(ii) Not later than 1582. LOST. [177]	?	Poem, expounding that contraries are changed into one another; 8 lines from it are cited in Act 1, Scene 2 of *Candelaio.*	——	——
(iii) 1576–81. LOST. [178]	?	*De sfera.* Lectures to a group at Noli in 1576 and at Toulouse in 1581.	——	——
(iv) 1576. LOST. [179]	Venice	*De' segni de' tempi.* Perhaps philosophy. According to Bruno, publication was authorized by the Dominican humanist, Remigio Nannini.	——	——
(v) 1579. LOST. [180]	Geneva	Broadsheet, attacking errors in De la Faye's lectures.	——	——
(vi) 1579–81 LOST. [181]	Toulouse	*De anima.* Lectures on Aristotle.	——	——
(vii) Before 1582. LOST. [182]	Toulouse or Paris?	*Clavis magna.* Mnemonics.	——	——

(viii) 1581. LOST. [183]	Paris	*De' predicamenti di Dio.* 30 lectures "to make himself known."	——	——
(1) 1582 [17]	Paris, Aegidius Gorbinus	(a) *De umbris idearum.* (b) *Ars memoriae.* A volume on artificial memory.	*Op. lat.*, II, i, 1-55, 56-177	——
(2) 1582 [22]	Paris, Aegidius Gillius	*Cantus circaeus.* Mnemonics.	*Op. lat.*, II, i, 179-257	——
(3) 1582 [25]	Paris, Aegidius Gorbinus	*De compendiosa architectura et complemento artis Lullii.* On artificial memory.	*Op. lat.*, II, ii, 1-65	——
(4) 1582 [28]	Paris, Guglelmo Giuliano	*Candelaio.* A comedy.	Gentile, *Op. ital.*, III, 1-219; Lagarde, *Op. ital.*, I, 3-112	——
(5) 1583 [44]	London, J. Charlewood	(a) *Recens et completa ars reminiscendi et in phantastico campo exorandi, ad plurimas in triginta sigillis inquirendi disponendi atque retinendi implicitas nouas rationes et artes introductoria. Intentio authoris de arte . . . Ars brevior et expeditior ad verborum memoriam . . . Aenigmatis interpretatio.* Mnemonics, with many figures.	*Op. lat.*, II, ii, 69, 73-119. Prelims. and notes, 68, 70-72[1]	——

[a] Roman numerals in parenthesis, publication not supervised by Bruno; Arabic numerals in parentheses, publication supervised by Bruno; Arabic numerals in brackets, number given to the work in Salvestrini's *Bibliografia Bruniana* (Pisa, 1926)

[b] Titles marked (a), (b), (c), etc., are distinct works, though they appear together in a single volume.

[c] See App. III.

[1] Not all copies containing (a), (b), and (c) also contain (d); nor is the order of the texts the same in every copy of the volume.

Date published; if unpublished by Bruno, probable date of composition [a]	Place published and printer; if unpublished by Bruno, probable place of composition	Title and subject matter [b]	References to collected editions	Manuscript sources [c]
		(b) *Explicatio triginta sigillorum ad omnium scientiarum et artium inventionem dispositionem et memoriam.* Mnemonics.	*Op. lat.*, II, ii, 121-60	——
		(c) *Sigillus sigillorum ad omnes animi operationes comparandas et earundem rationes habendas maxime conducens.* Mnemonics.	*Op. lat.*, II, ii, 161-217	——
		(d) *Epistola ad excellentissimum Oxoniensis academiae Procancellarium, clarissimos doctores atque celeberrimos magistros.* Bombastic expression of Bruno's claim to be heard.	*Op. lat.*, II, ii, 76-8	——
(ix) Not later than 1583. LOST. [184]	?	*Purgatorio de l'inferno.* Philosophy.	——	——
(x) 1584? LOST. [191]	London?	*Mnemosine*, or *Templum mnemosine.*[2] Mnemonics.	——	——

(6) 1584 [47]	London, J. Charlewood	Slightly variant issue of (7).	Gentile, *Op. ital.*, I, 1-132, 421-4	——
(7) 1584 [47]	London, J. Charlewood ("in Venetia")	*La cena de le ceneri.* Cosmology and philosophy.	Gentile, *Op. ital.*, I, 1-132; Lagarde, *Op. ital.*, I, 113-97	——
(8) 1584 [53]	London, J. Charlewood ("in Venetia")	*De la causa, principio et uno.* Philosophy and cosmology	Gentile, *Op. ital.*, I, 133-266; Lagarde, *Op. ital.*, I, 199-290	——
(9) 1584 [69]	London, J. Charlewood ("in Venetia")	*De l'infinito universo et mondi.* Cosmology and philosophy.	Gentile, *Op. ital.*, I, 267-418; Lagarde, *Op. ital.*, I, 291-400	——
(10) 1584 [79]	London, J. Charlewood ("Stampato in Parigi")	*Spaccio de la bestia trionfante.* Ethics.	Gentile, *Op. ital.*, II, 1-350; Lagarde, *Op. ital.*, II, 403-57	——
(11) 1585 [99]	London, J. Charlewood ("Antonio Baio, Parigi")	(a) *Cabala del cavallo Pegaseo con* (b) *L'aggiunta dell' asino cillenico.* Ethics.	Gentile, *Op. ital.*, II, 231-96, 297-305; Lagarde, *Op. ital.*, II, 559-600, 600-6	——
(12) 1585 [107]	London, J. Charlewood ("Antonio Baio, Parigi")	*De gl' heroici furori.* Ethics.	Gentile, *Op. ital.*, II, 307-519; Lagarde, *Op. ital.*, II, 607-754	——

NOTE: For footnotes [a], [b], and [c], see page 205.

[2] Cited several times in Bruno's works. Cf. "E tu Mnemosine mia ascosa sotto trenta sigilli, e rinchiusa nel libro carcere dell' ombre de le idee, intonami un poco ne l'orecchio." *La cena de le ceneri,* Dial, I, p. 5; Gentile, *Op. ital.*, I, 21; Lagarde, *Op. ital.*, I, 5. This sentence, however, does not appear in the text here numbered 7.

CHRONOLOGICAL LIST OF THE WRITINGS OF GIORDANO BRUNO—*Continued*

Date published; if unpublished by Bruno, probable date of composition [a]	Place published and printer; if unpublished by Bruno, probable place of composition	Title and subject matter [b]	References to collected editions	Manuscript sources [c]
(xi) Not later than 1585. LOST. [185]	?	*Arbor philosophorum.*	——	——
(13) 1586 [118]	Paris, Pierre Chevillot	*Figuratio Aristotelici physici auditus.* Commentary.	*Op. lat.* I, iv, 129-221	
(14) 1586 [120]	Paris, Pierre Chevillot	(a) *Dialogi duo de Fabricii Mordentis Salerntani prope divina ad inventione ad perfectam cosmimetriae praxim.* On Mordente's mathematics.	*Op. lat.*, I, iv, 225-56	——
		(b) *Insomnium.* On a mathematical instrument.[3]	*Op. lat.*, I, iv, 256-7	
(15) 1586 [122]	Paris	*Centum et viginti articuli de natura et mundo, adversus peripateticos per Joh. Hennequinum propositi.* On cosmology and philosophy.	*Op. lat.*, I, i, 53-190; II, ii, 219-24	——
(16) 1587, perhaps drafted in 1586 [124]	Wittenberg, Zacharius Krafft?	*De lampade combinatoria Lulliana.* On artificial memory.	*Op. lat.*, II, ii, 227-327	Cf. title-page in Ms. A, f. 2 (App. III). Ms. A, ff. 6-57v has the printed edition with marginal glosses.

(17) 1587 [128]	Wittenberg, Zacharius Krafft?	*De progressu et lampade venatoria logicorum*. On the *Topica* of Aristotle.	*Op. lat.*, II, iii, 1-84	——
(xii) 1587 [165]	Wittenberg. Published posthumously, 1612, Frankfurt, Hammius	*Artificium perorandi traditum a Jordano Bruno*. Commentary on Pseudo-Aristotle, "Letter to Alexander on Rhetoric," with elaborate Method of Rhetoric, illus. by Tables. Communicated by Johann-Henricus Alstedius.	*Op. lat.*, II, iii, 323-404	
(xiii) 1587 [168]	Wittenberg	*Animadversiones circa lampadem Lullianam*. On Lullian mnemonics.	*Op. lat.*, II, ii, 357-66	Ms. A, ff. 58-62 (a fragment) is the only source.
(xiv) Probably 1587 [169]	Wittenberg	*Lampas triginta statuarum*. On Lullian mnemonics—logic.	*Op. lat.*, III, 1-258	Ms. A, ff. 98-103^{v}, 106-205^{v}.
(xv) Probably 1587 [170]	Wittenberg	*Libri physicorum Aristotelis explanati.*	*Op. lat.*, III, 259-393, and facsimile reproduction of Ms. B, f. 35, at end of the volume.	Ms. C, ff. 2-56^{v}, and partly from Ms. B, ff. 3-71^{v}.
(18) 1588 [137]	Wittenberg, Zacharius Krafft	*Camoeracensis acrotismus sue ratione articulorum physicorum adversus peripateticos*. Enlarged version of the *Centum et vigenti articuli*, with several Epistles added.	*Op. lat.*, I, i, 52-190	——

NOTE: For footnotes [a], [b], and [c], see page 205.

[3] "Revealed clearly by one of whom I cannot remember the visage or habit."

CHRONOLOGICAL LIST OF THE WRITINGS OF GIORDANO BRUNO—*Continued*

Date published; if unpublished by Bruno, probable date of composition [a]	Place published and printer; if unpublished by Bruno, probable place of composition	Title and subject matter [b]	References to collected editions	Manuscript sources [c]
(19) 1588 [132]	Wittenberg, Zacharius Krafft	*Oratio valedictoria ad . . . professores, atque auditores in Academia Witebergensi.* Valedictory address.	*Op. lat.*, I, i, 1-25	——
(20) 1588 [141]	Prague, Georgius Nigrinus	*De specierum scrutinio et lampade combinatoria Raymundi Lulli.* On artificial memory.	*Op. lat.*, II, ii, 225-356	——
(21) 1588 [145]	Prague, Georgius Daczicenus	*Articuli centum et sexaginta adversus huius tempestatis mathematicos atque philosophos.* On Mordente's mathematics.	*Op. lat.*, I, iii, 1-118	——
(xvi) 1588 or 1589; before Besler became secretary in November, 1589 [174]	?	*Medicina Lulliana.* Lullian medicine. A short but complete version in the hand of Bruno and of unknown secretary.	*Op. lat.*, III, 569-617	Ms. M, ff. 162-80^{v}.
(22) 1589 [147]	Helmstedt, printed by Jacobus Lucius	*Oratio consolatoria.* Funeral oration.	*Op. lat.*, I, i, 27-52	——
(xvii) 1589-1590	Frankfurt or Zurich	(a) Later version of figure as in xv.	*Op. lat.*, III, xix	Ms. M, f. 6.
		(b) Some chemical recipes in the margin of (a).	*Op. lat.*, III, xix	

(xviii) 1591	?	Mnemonic figure.	*Op. lat.*, III, xx	Ms. M, f. 161, loose parchment folio.[4]
(xix) 1589 (Oct. 6)	Helmstedt	Letter to Rector of Helmstedt University protesting against exclusion from Mass.	*Op. lat.*, III, 12-13	Wolfenbüttel Ms. 360 Novorum fol., in Bruno's hand.[5]
(xx) 1590 [171]	Helmstedt	*De magia*. Natural magic as a road to wisdom and philosophy.	*Op. lat.*, III, 393-454	Ms. M, ff. $7\text{-}27^{v}$; Ms. C, ff. $58\text{-}74^{v}$.
(xxi) 1590 [171]	Helmstedt	*Theses de magia*. Synthetic philosophy illustrated by mathematical forms.	*Op. lat.*, III, 455-91	Ms. M, ff. $28\text{-}38^{v}$; Ms. C, ff. 76-89.
(xxii) 1590 (Mar. 16). [173]	Helmstedt	*De rerum principiis et elementis et causis*. Cosmic philosophy.	*Op. lat.*, III, 507-67	Ms. M, ff. $39\text{-}54^{v}$.
(xxiii) 1590 (before Apr. 12). [174]	Helmstedt	*Medicina Lulliana*. Lullian medicine; a later and longer version of xvi, but incomplete.	*Op. lat.*, III, 569-633	Ms. M, ff. $55\text{-}69^{v}$.[6]
(xxiv) 1590 [172]	Helmstedt	*De magia mathematica*. Mostly extracts from Trithemius, Cornelius Agrippa, Ps.-Albertus, etc.	*Op. lat.*, III, 494-506	Ms. M, ff. $70\text{-}86^{v}$.
(xxv) *circa* June 1590	Frankfurt	Petition to the Senate of Frankfurt to reside there (fragment only).[7]	*Op. lat.*, III, xviii	Ms. M, f. 5^{v}.

NOTE: For footnotes [a], [b], and [c], see page 205.

[4] Tocco and Vitelli do not give a definite date to this sheet. They ascribe it "probably to Bruno's hand" (III, xxi), and think it should perhaps be grouped as early as the text here numbered xvi (III, xix) or xviib (III, xxii).

[5] Tocco and Vitelli believe the whole letter is written by Bruno, although they note that some think only the signature and date to be in his hand.

[6] Ms. M, f. 181 is a rough sketch for the figure on f. 57 of the same Ms., illustrating text here numbered xxiii. Tocco and Vitelli attribute the sketch to Bruno's own hand (*Op. ital*, III, xxi). They note that a "less imcomplete" version of the figure occurs on f. 166 of Ms. M, in the course of the text here numbered xvi. They reproduce the figure from f. 67 (Cf. *Op. ital.*, III, x and 577).

[7] The Senate of Frankfurt has a record of the request, dated 2 July 1590.

Date published; if unpublished by Bruno, probable date of composition [a]	Place published and printer; if unpublished by Bruno, probable place of composition	Title and subject matter [b]	References to collected editions	Manuscript sources [c]
(23) 1591 [150]	Frankfurt, J. Wechel and P. Fischer	*De triplici minimo et mensura ad trium speculativarum scientiarum et multarum activarum artium principie libri V*. With preface by Johann Wechel. Cosmology and philosophy.	*Op. lat.*, III, 119-361	——
(xxv) 1590 or 1591	Frankfurt or Zurich	*De vinculis in genere*, first draft. Synthetic philosophy.	*Op. lat.*, III, 635-52	Ms. M, ff. 1-5.
(xxvii) Not later than 1591. LOST. [190]	?	*De rerum imaginibus*. Philosophy; mentioned in *De monade*.	——	——
(xxviii) 1591, published 1595. [161]	Zurich, Joannes Wolphius	*Summa terminorum metaphysicorum ad capessandum logicae et philosophiae studium*. On metaphysical terms. The arrangement is based on Aristotle's *Metaphysica*, Book V.	*Op. lat.*, I, iv, 1-72	
(xxix) Published 1609 [162]	Marburg, Rudolphus Hecklerus	(a) Second edition of *Summa terminorum* . . . (xxviii).	*Op. lat.*, I, iv, 1-72	——
		(b) *Praxis descensus seu applicatio entis*.	*Op. lat.*, I, iv, 73-128	——

(24) 1591 [159]	Zurich or Frankfurt, J. Wechel and P. Fischer, Frankfurt	*De imaginum signorum et idearum compositione. Ad omnia inventionum dispositionum et memoriae genera libri tres.* Aids to memory, with philosophical discussion.	*Op. lat.*, II, iii, 85-322	——
(25)[8] 1591 [154]	Frankfurt, J. Wechel and P. Fischer. (Reprinted in 1614 by Jacob Fischer, Frankfurt)	*De monade, numero et figura liber consequens quinque de minimo magno et mensura.* Cosmology and philosophy. In one volume with the following work.	*Op. lat.*, I, ii, 319-484	——
(26)[9] 1591 [175]		*De innumerabilibus immenso et infigurabili; sue de universo et mundis libri octo.* Cosmology and philosophy. The last and greatest of Bruno's published works.	*Op. lat.*, I, i, 191-398; I, ii, 1-318	——
(xxx) 1591 [175]	Padua	*De vinculis in genere.* Synthetic philosophy. The first draft is here numbered xxvi.	*Op. lat.*, III, 653-700	Ms. M, ff. 87-98
(xxxi) 1591 [169]	Padua	*Lampas triginta statuarum.* Beautifully written clean copy of xiv.	*Op. lat.*, III, 3-238	Ms. M, ff. 99-160
(xxxii) 1592. UNFINISHED AND LOST. [188, 189]	Venice	*Delle sette arti liberali e sette altre arti inventive.*[10]		

NOTE: For footnotes [a], [b], and [c], see page 205.

[8] Numbers 25 and 26 are a single volume, prefixed by an "Epistola dedicatoris et clavis" to Duke Henry Julius of Brunswick, dedicating to him the *De triplici minimo* . . . (here numbered 23).

[9] Some parts were written in England and on subsequent travels.

[10] This was to be dedicated to the Pope, from Bruno's evidence (*Docc. Ven.*, IX, XVII), and the evidence of Ciotto (*Doc. Ven.*, XVI).

APPENDIX II

PRINTERS OF BRUNO

a. Early Wanderings

THE only printer whose name has come down to us from Bruno's earliest wanderings is that of Jean Bergeon who, having printed the "libellous" attack on Antoine de la Faye at Geneva in 1579, proceeded to disclaim all responsibility. This Bergeon may be identified with Jacques Berjon who had been admitted to citizenship in Geneva in 1576. We find him (or perhaps his son?) "Jean Berjon, from a French refugee family together with Jacques Stoer, of German origin" described as the principal workers of the well-established printer Pyramus de Candolle. In 1617 de Candolle moved to Yverdon. Then trouble arose because these two, "having learnt their craft from him," continued to print in Geneva, establishing a firm in their own name.[1] They appear to have successfully rivalled de Candolle in the book markets of France and Germany.[2]

---

[1] Æ. H. Gaullieur, *Études sur la typographie génevoise du xve au xixe siècles, et sur les origines de l'imprimerie en Suisse* (Geneva, 1855), pp. 193-96. Gaullieur cites the admission of Jacques Berjon to citizenship from the *Registres des admissions à la bourgeoisie de Genève*. In a list of Genevan printers from 1552 onward, Gaullieur (p. 178) mentions "Math. Berjon" as printing in 1597, but does not then mention Jean. Perhaps Bruno's broadsheet was Jean's first excursion into independent printing, and he may well have found it wise to retire at least temporarily into anonymity!

[2] F. C. Longchamp, *Manuel de la typographie génevoise* (Paris and Lausanne, 1922), p. 104. Longchamp also (p. 95) mentions "Matthieu et Jean Berjon" as undistinguished printers in Geneva *circ.* 1600.

b. France, First Sojourn

The confusion inseparable from all Bruno's life clings also to the identity of his printers. Three names appear on title-pages of Bruno's works with the imprint of Paris, dated during his first sojourn there in the year 1582. These are Aegidius Gorbinus,[3] Aegidius Gillius,[4] and Guglelmo Giuliano.[5] The first two appear to have been one and the same person, Gilles Gourbin or Gorbin. His career has been traced by Renouard[6] through apprenticeship, admission to "exercise" his craft in 1550 and as "libre-juré" in 1555. He died in 1590.

"Guglelmo Giuliano" was Guillaume Julian or Jullian, also a "libre-juré," who exercised his craft from 1553 until his death in 1589.

c. England

Though in England the great consorted freely with Bruno, his printer cautiously preferred the veil of anonymity. Of the seven volumes bearing his name that have come down to us from his sojourn in England, the one containing Latin works on mnemonics bears neither place nor date of publication.[7] But it may safely be ascribed to the English period both on typographical grounds and from the Dedicatory Epistle to Mauvissière. Some copies also contain an *Epistle* to the Vice-Chancellor, Doctors and Masters of Oxford University. The evidence, both typographical and internal, is no less conclusive for the remaining six volumes, all in Italian. The three cosmological works,[8] all dedicated to Mauvissière, bear the imprint "Venetia 1584" with no printer's name. The first of the three volumes of ethical works[9] is inscribed "Parigi 1584" and is again without a printer's name. The two succeeding volumes,[10]

---

[3] See App. I, 1a-b, 3. [4] See App. I, 2. [5] See App. I, 4.

[6] P. Renouard, *Imprimeurs parisiens, libraries, fondeurs de caractères et correcteurs d'imprimerie depuis l'introduction de l'imprimerie à Paris jusqu'à la fin du XVI siècle* (Paris, 1898).

[7] App. I, 5a-d. [8] App. I, 6-9. [9] App. I, 10. [10] App. I, 11a-12.

both dedicated to Sir Philip Sidney, are inscribed "Parigi appresso Antonio Baio Anno 1585." This name *Antonio Baio* is known on no other books and is believed to be fictitious. Not only can the type of all these volumes be recognized as of English origin, but Bruno admitted at his trial in Venice that they were printed in England, and averred that his printers had advised him that the imprints of Venice and of Paris would increase the sale of his books. The long arm of the Inquisition did not reach to England, so no enquiry is recorded as to who was the printer who gave this advice.

Three printers, John Wolfe, Thomas Vautrollier and John Charlewood have in turn been credited with having promulgated the seven London volumes from Bruno's pen.[11] The typographical evidence finally marshalled in detail by Mr. Sellers awards the honour to John Charlewood.[12] Charlewood was one of a group who produced Italian and Spanish works both in the original and in translation. John Wolfe and John Charlewood were jointly cited before the Privy Council for pirating certain works in 1583, the year before the Bruno publications. Thus Charlewood would have been ready for a semi-clandestine adventure. Both he and Wolfe ultimately became respected members of the guild of their craft, the Stationers' Company of London.

d. France, Second Sojourn

In spite of his fallen fortunes, Bruno found in Paris in 1586 a distinguished Paris printer willing openly to issue his works. This was Pierre Chevillot who exercised his craft in Paris from 1579-94 and then moved to Troyes when he was named Printer to the King. Chevillot printed an Aristotelian commentary by Bruno and also his volume on the mathematics of his friend Fabrizio Mordente with Bruno's own "Dream" or

---

[11] Cf. A. Gerber in *Modern Language Review*, XXII (Baltimore, 1907), 133, 202, etc. A good account of John Wolfe by Harry Hoppe will be found in *The Library*, XIV, No. 3 (Oxford, 1933), 241.

[12] "Italian Books Printed in England before 1640" in *Transactions* of the Bibliographical Society (London, 1924).

project of a mathematical instrument.[13] But no printer's name is attached to the last disastrous Paris publication of Bruno's cosmological and philosophical views, the *One Hundred and Twenty Articles* put forward with his support by his pupil Jean Hennequin at the session at the Collège de Cambrai.[14] The volume bears the sardonic inscription, "Printed at Paris by the Author's desire, 1586."

e. Central Europe

Every succeeding stage of Bruno's wanderings is marked by publication. His Wittenberg printer was perhaps Zacharius Krafft[15] who with his brother Hans was established there from 1549 and printed the first edition of Melancthon.

The Prague volumes were issued by George Nigrinus,[16] and George Daczicenus[17] (possibly one individual?). Of them we have not succeeded in tracing further information.

In Helmstedt, Bruno's funeral oration for Julius Duke of Brunswick and Lüneberg[18] was printed by Jacobus Lucius, who was involved in various embroilments that seem to fit but too well in Bruno's environment. Lucius, who was sometimes called Transilvanus, was born in Kronstadt, and exercised the trade of printing in Helmstedt from 1556 to 1564. He then became printer to the University of Rostock with which, however, he had a dispute, so in 1579 he returned to Helmstedt. In 1588 Lucius was called from Helmstedt to Brunswick by Duke Julius to print certain biblical texts on the walls of a printing establishment set up in the *Gertrud Kapelle*. But the burghers of Brunswick protested that these texts should not have been applied without their permission,

---

[13] App. I, 13-14b. [14] App. I, 15.

[15] App. I, 16 and 17, as suggested by Salvestrini, though they bear no printer's name. Zacharius Krafft (or Crato) issued in 1588 the reprint of Bruno's final Paris volume (see App. I, 18) as well as his *Valedictory Oration* to Wittenberg University (App. I, 19). For the brothers Hans and Zacharius Krafft see F. Kapp, *Geschichte des deutschen Buchhandels* (Leipzig, 1886), I, 172.

[16] App. I, 20. [17] App. I, 21. [18] App. I, 22.

and they indignantly drove the printers out of their town. Lucius died in Brunswick in 1579, and bequeathed his printing business to his son.[19]

The printer to whom Bruno's readers are most indebted is undoubtedly John Wechel, third of his line to exercise the craft in Frankfurt.[20] We have seen[21] that it was the firm of Wechel and Fischer who made it possible for Bruno to reside in Frankfurt and who nursed the great Latin poems to publication. Their successor Jacob Fischer brought out in 1614 a reprint of the volume containing *De monade, numero et figura* and *De innumerabilibus immenso et infigurabili*.[22]

Finally we may mention again the name of Johannes Wolf, this time not the Englishman but the successor of Christopher Froschauer of Zurich. This Johannes Wolf was employed by Eglinus to publish the Zurich volume of 1595.[23] But it would take too long to pursue here the printers of those works of Bruno that were not seen through the press by himself.

---

[19] L. Irmisch, *Kurze Geschichte der Buchdruckereien im Herzogtum Braunschwicz* under the year 1588; J. Kirchner and W. Olbrich, *Lexicon des gesammten Buchwesens* (3 vols., Leipzig, 1935), II, 374; and Brunet, *Manuel du libraire, Supplément* under *Athenae ad Elenum* (i.e., Helmstedt).

[20] Brunet, *op. cit., Supplément* under *Francofurtum ad Moenum.*

[21] See App. I, 23-26 and Chap. 6 *d.*

[22] Salvestrini, No. 155.

[23] See App. I, xxviii. Cf. P. Heitz, *Die Zürcher Büchermarken bis zum Anfang des 17 Jahrhunderts* (Zurich, 1895).

APPENDIX III

SURVIVING MANUSCRIPTS OF BRUNO'S WORKS

WHEN Bruno's life of wandering is recalled, it seems extraordinary that writings in his own hand should have survived, as well as works dictated to secretaries who might be expected to have destroyed such dangerous evidence.

Bruno's autograph is in the Rector's Book of Geneva University,[1] in a family album of his friends,[2] on a print of his native Nola, on the manuscript sheet at Wolfenbüttel, and in the copy of his *De lampade combinatoria lulliana* that he presented to Jacob Cuno. Perhaps manuscripts of unpublished works from his hand may yet emerge from the archives of the Vatican.

Four manuscripts were at the disposal of the learned editors of his Latin works: one in the Kreis und Stadtbibliothek of Augsburg (Ms. A); two in the library of Erlangen University (Mss. B and C); one privately owned in Moscow (Ms. M), which now reposes in the Rumianzow Museum in that city.[3]

---

[1] Inscribed on his matriculation, 20th May, 1579. This *Livre du Recteur* has been published (Geneva, 1860). Cf. Doc. Gin., VI, pp. 36, 227 (1933 ed.).

[2] Now in the Public Library of Stuttgart.

[3] The Augsburg and Erlangen manuscripts (Mss. A, B, C) are fully described by Remigio Stölzle in *Archiv für Geschichte der Philosophie* (Berlin, 1890), III, 389-93, 573-8; also by Tocco and Vitelli in the Introduction to *Op. lat.,* III. These three manuscripts were discovered by Stölzle. Ms. M was discovered in Paris by Abraham de Noroff in 1866, and acquired by the Library of the Rumianzow Museum at Moscow. De Noroff described the manuscript in *Notice bibliographique*

Ms. A contains 216 folios. Ff. 1, 2^{v}–5^{v}, 62^{v}–97^{v}, 104–105, 206–216 are blank.

f. 2 Lampas combinatoria lulliana tradita privatim in Academia Witebergensi â Jordano Bruno Nolano, CIC IC XIVC [i.e., 1586].

ff. 6–67^{v} Printed copy of the above work (Wittenberg, 1587), with manuscript marginal notes, but without Preface.

ff. 58–62 *Animadversiones in Lampadem Lullianam.* A unique copy of this fragment. It bears the date: 13 Martii 87.

ff. 98–103^{v}, 106–205^{v} *Lampas triginta statuarum.*

Mss. B and C (Mss. 1215 and 1279 of the Erlangen University library) may be referred to Bruno's stay in Helmstedt.

Ms. B has lost a number of leaves. It now comprises 71 folios, of which the first two are blank. Ff. 3–71^{v} contain, in a sixteenth century German hand, an imperfect copy of *Libri physicorum Aristotelis explanati*; f. 68^{v} ends in the middle of a word—"occu" (*Op. lat.,* III, 369, line 20); f. 69 resumes with "vel minore" (*Op. lat.,* III, 376, line 12). The missing passage is supplied by Ms. C, ff. 47^{v}–50. F. 70^{v} ends with the word "Elixabilia" (*Op. lat.,* III, 379, line 20); f. 71 resumes with a long heading *De numero et definitione . . .* (*Op. lat.,* III, 387, line 1). This missing passage is supplied by Ms. C, ff. 51^{v}–54^{v}. F. 71^{v} ends abruptly with the words "ut pilus" (*Op. lat.,* III, 388, line 16). The missing passage is supplied by Ms. C, ff. 55–56^{v}.

Ms. C is in the hand of Bruno's faithful secretary, Besler. It comprises 92 folios. Ff. 1, 1^{v}, 57, 57^{v}, 75, 75^{v}, and 89^{v}–92^{v} are blank. Ff. 2–56^{v} contain *Libri physicorum Aristotelis explanati*; ff. 58–74^{v}, *De magia*; and ff. 76–89, *Theses de magia.* Tocco and Vitelli [4] think that the first item of Ms. C was probably copied from Ms. B before the latter had lost pages, while the remaining two items were probably copied by Besler from Ms. M.

---

sur un manuscrit autographe des oeuvres inédits de Giordano Bruno . . . (St. Petersburg, 1868); the manuscript was again described by W. Lutoslawsky in *Archiv für Geschichte der Philosophie* (Berlin, 1889), II, 526-71. The manuscripts are all further described by Tocco and Vitelli in *Op. lat.,* III.

[4] *Op. lat.,* III, xxxviii-xlix.

Ms. M is the most extensive of the manuscripts. It would seem that several documents were collected together in one volume, perhaps by the piety of Besler. Of the 181 folios that now comprise the volume, ff. 1–6, 162–168^{v} line 4, f. 181, and perhaps f. 161 are in Bruno's hand; ff. 168^{v} line 5 to 180^{v} are in an otherwise unknown hand, conjectured to be that of a secretary who worked for Bruno before Besler reached Helmstedt (he was matriculated into the University of Helmstedt in November, 1589); ff. 7–160^{v} are in the hand of Besler. The conjectural dates of the various items will be found in Appendix I.

The contents of Ms. M are as follows: [5]

(a^{i})	ff. 1–5	*De vinculis in genere* (first draft).
(a^{ii})	f. 5^{v}	Petition to the Senate of Frankfurt.
(a^{iii})	f. 6	Later version of figure for *Libri physicorum Aristotelis explanati.*
(a^{iv})	f. 6	Some chemical recipes in the margin. Same paper as ff. 11–86^{v}.
(b)	ff. 7–27^{v}	*De magia.*
(c)	ff. 28–38^{v}	*Theses de magia.*
(d)	ff. 39–54^{v}	*De rerum principiis et elementis et causis.* Headed "Lunedi 16 Marzo 1590."
(e)	ff. 55–69^{v}	*Medicina Lulliana.* Presumably before 12 April 1590, when they were leaving Helmstedt.
(f)	ff. 70–86^{v}	*De magia mathematica.*
(g)	ff. 87–98^{v}	*De vinculis in genere.* Different paper from that of the preceding folios, and identical with that of ff. 99–160^{v} but differently sewed from these folios.
(h)	ff. 99–160^{v}	*Lampas triginta statuarum.* Expl.: "Anno 1591. Mensis Octob. die 22 Padua." Appears to be a clean copy, as though prepared for printer. Separate pagination.
(i)	f. 161	Mnemonic figure on a loose parchment sheet.

---

[5] For convenience of reference, the foliation of Tocco and Vitelli has been used. They point out that there was an older foliation also, which has not been used here.

(k) ff. 162–180^v *Medicina Lulliana* (f. 180^v is misnumbered 181). Ff. 162–168^v line 4 in Bruno's hand; ff. 168 line 5 to f. 180^v in hand of unknown scribe.

(l) f. 181 Incomplete version of the cosmological diagram on f. 57 illustrating (e). (F. 181 is misnumbered 182.)

APPENDIX IV

SELECT BIBLIOGRAPHY OF BRUNO'S PHILOSOPHY

WE HAVE already said that the books on Bruno run to many hundreds. Among the most interesting comments on his philosophy (besides that of Cassirer already quoted) we would note (passing beyond his contemporaries and the interesting letter from Tycho to Galileo) the following:

Atanassievitch, Xenia. *La doctrine métaphysique et géométrique de Bruno.* Belgrade, 1923.

Brunnhofer, Hermann. *Giordano Bruno's Weltanschauung und Verhängnis.* Leipzig, 1882.

——— *Bruno's Lehre vom Kleinsten als die Quelle der Prästabilirten Harmonie von Leibnitz.* Leipzig, 1890.

Carriere, Moriz. *Die philosophische Weltanschauung der Reformationszeit in ihren Beziehungen zur Gegenwart.* Stuttgart and Tübingen, 1847; 2nd ed., Leipzig, 1887.

Charbonnel, J. Roger. *L'Éthique de Giordano Bruno.* Paris, 1919.

——— *La pensée italienne au XVI siécle.* Paris, 1919.

Croce, Benedetto. *Ciò che è vivo, ciò che è morto della filosofia di Hegel.* Bari, 1906, pp. 40 *seqq.*

——— *Cultura e vita morale.* Bari, 1926. Chapter XI, pp. 80-87, deals with Bruno.

——— Numerous shorter articles, including "G. Bruno e Volfgango Goethe" in *Juvenilia 1883–1887.* Bari, 1914, pp. 69-72.

Fiorentino, Francesco. *Il panteismo di Giordano Bruno.* Naples, 1861. (And many other works.)

Gentile, Giovanni. *Giordano Bruno e il pensiero del rinascimento.* Florence, 1920 and 1925.

Limentani, Ludovico. *La morale di Giordano Bruno.* Florence, 1924.

Lovejoy, Arthur Oncken. "The Dialectic of Bruno and Spinoza," University of California Publications, *Philosophy,* I (November 1904), 141-74.

Mondolfo, Rodolfo. *La filosofia di Giordano Bruno e la interpretazione de Felice Tocco.* Florence, 1912.

Namer, Emil. *Les aspects de dieu dans la philosophie de Giordano Bruno.* Paris, 1926.

Orrei, Ernesto. *Giordano Bruno e la sua dottrina.* Milan, 1931.

Sensini, Tito. *Sul pensiero filosofio di Giordano Bruno.* Camerino, 1927.

Singer, Dorothea Waley. "The Cosmology of Giordano Bruno" in *Isis,* XXXIII (June 1941), 187-96.

Spaventa, Bertrando. *Dei principii della filosofia pratica di Giordano Bruno.* Genoa, 1851.

——— "Giordano Bruno" in *Saggi di critica filosofia politica e religiosa.* Naples, 1867, I, 139-267.

——— "La dottrina della conoscenza di Giordano Bruno" in *Atti del R. Accad. di scienze morali e politiche di Napoli.* Naples, 1865, II, 295.

——— (Also other less succinct works on aspects of Bruno's philosophy.)

Tocco, Felice. *Giordano Bruno.* Florence, 1886.

——— *Le opere latine di Giordano Bruno esposte e confrontate con le italiane.* Florence, 1889.

Troilo, Erminio. *La filosofia di Giordano Bruno.* Turin, 1907.

The biographies, of course, also deal with Bruno's philosophy. The fullest, with reprint of all the surviving documents concerning Bruno's life, is that of Vincenzo Spampanato, 2 vols., Messina, 1921.

The comprehensive *Bibliografia Bruniana* by Virgilio Salvestrini, Pisa, 1926, chronologically arranged and well indexed, is indispensable to the student of Bruno.

GIORDANO BRUNO

On the Infinite Universe and Worlds

(DE L'INFINITO UNIVERSO ET MONDI)

CONTENTS

GIORDANO BRUNO

THE NOLAN

On the Infinite Universe and Worlds

To the Most Illustrious Monsieur de Mauvissière

Printed in Venice
in the year 1584

INTRODUCTORY EPISTLE addressed to the most illustrious Monsieur Michel de Castelnau, Seigneur de Mauvissière, de Concressault and de Joinville, Chevalier of the Order of the most Christian King, Privy Councillor, Captain of 50 men at arms, and Ambassador to Her most Serene Majesty the Queen of England.

IF, O most illustrious Knight, I had driven a plough, pastured a herd, tended a garden, tailored a garment: none would regard me, few observe me, seldom a one reprove me; and I could easily satisfy all men. But since I would survey the field of Nature, care for the nourishment of the soul, foster the cultivation of talent, become expert as Daedalus concerning the ways of the intellect; lo, one doth threaten upon beholding me, another doth assail me at sight, another doth bite upon reaching me, yet another who hath caught me would devour me; not one, nor few, they are many, indeed almost all. If you would know why, it is because I hate the mob, I loathe the vulgar herd and in the multitude I find no joy. It is Unity that doth enchant me. By her power I am free though thrall, happy in sorrow, rich in poverty, and quick even in death. Through her virtue I envy not those who are bond though free, who grieve in the midst of pleasures, who endure poverty in their wealth, and a living death. They carry their chains within them; their spirit containeth her own hell that bringeth them low; within their soul is the disease that wasteth, and within their mind the lethargy that bringeth death. They are without the generosity that would enfranchise, the long suffering that exalteth, the splendour that doth illumine, knowledge that bestoweth life. Therefore I do not in weariness shun the arduous path, nor idly refrain my arm from the present task, nor retreat in despair from the enemy that confronteth me, nor do I turn my dazzled eyes from the divine end. Yet I am aware that I am mostly held to be a sophist, seeking rather to appear subtle than to reveal the truth; an ambitious fellow diligent rather to support a new and false sect than to establish the ancient and true; a snarer of birds who pursueth the splendour of fame, by spreading ahead the darkness of error; an unquiet spirit that would undermine the edifice of good discipline to establish the frame of perversity.

Wherefore, my lord, may the heavenly powers scatter before me all those who unjustly hate me; may my God be ever gracious unto me; may all the rulers of our world be favourable to me; may the stars yield me seed for the field and soil for the seed, that the harvest of my labour may appear to the world useful and glorious, that souls may be awakened and the understanding of those in darkness be illumined. For assuredly I do not feign; and if I err, I do so unwittingly; nor do I in speech or writing contend merely for victory, for I hold worldly repute and hollow success without truth to be hateful to God, most vile and dishonourable. But I thus exhaust, vex and torment myself for love of true wisdom and zeal for true contemplation. This I shall make manifest by conclusive arguments, dependent on lively reasonings derived from regulated sensation, instructed by true phenomena; for these as trustworthy ambassadors emerge from objects of Nature, rendering themselves present to those who seek them, obvious to those who gaze attentively on them, clear to those who apprehend, certain and sure to those who understand. Thus I present to you my contemplation concerning the infinite universe and innumerable worlds.[1]

ARGUMENT OF THE FIRST DIALOGUE

YOU learn from the first Dialogue FIRSTLY, that the inconstancy of sense-perception doth demonstrate that sense is no source of certainty,

[1] Bruno's most appealing dedication to Mauvissière is reserved for the conclusion of the Arguments.

but can attain thereto only through comparison and reference from one sensible percept to another, from one sense to another, so that truth may be inferred from diverse sources.

SECONDLY, the demonstration is begun of the infinity of the universe;[2] and the first argument is derived from the failure to limit the world by those whose fantasy would erect around it boundary walls.

THIRDLY, it will be shown that it is unfitting to name the world finite, and contained within itself, since this condition belongeth only to immensity, as shown by the second argument. Moreover, the third argument is based on the inconvenience and indeed impossibility of imagining the world to occupy no position. For inevitably it would follow that it was without being, since everything whether corporeal or incorporeal doth occupy corporeally or incorporeally some position.

The FOURTH argument is based on a demonstration or urgent question put by the Epicureans:

> Moreover, suppose now that all space were created finite; if one were to run on to the end, to its furthest coasts, and throw a flying dart, would you have it that the dart, hurled with might and main, goeth on whither it is sped, flying afar, or think you that something can check and bar its way? . . . For whether there be something to check it and bring about that it arriveth not whither it was sped, and planteth not itself in the goal, or whether it fareth forward, yet it set not forth from the end.[3]

---

[2] Bruno uses "universo" for the infinite universe. His word "mondo" is throughout translated "world." Bruno uses "mondo" not only for our terrestrial globe, but for the universe as apprehended by our senses, and as conceived by the Aristotelians. Thus he speaks of our world (*questo mondo*)—including the stars that we see—occupying our space, bounded by the vault of heaven. This, together with innumerable other worlds—i.e., other systems of heavenly bodies, each system occupying its own space—forms for Bruno the one infinite universe (*universo*). Cf. also p. 235, n. 8.

[3] Lucretius, *De rerum natura,* I, 968-73, 977-79. Bruno quotes the Latin text. The English translations of this and all other passages from Lucretius are based on Dr. C. Bailey, *Lucretius on the Nature of Things* (Clarendon Press, 1910). It will be noticed that Bruno does not here give the name of Lucretius. He has a few textual deviations from the received Latin text. These are noted by Gentile, *Op. ital.,* I, 271. Throughout his edition, Gentile cites parallel passages in the other works of Bruno.

FIFTHLY, Aristotle's definition of position[4] is unsuited to primal, vast, universal space[4] and it befitteth not to take the surface nearest and adjoining the content or other such foolishness which would regard space[4] as mathematical and not physical, not to mention that between the containing surface and the content which moveth therein, there is always and inevitably an intermediate space[5] which should rather be named position;[4] and if we wish only to take the surface of space,[5] we need to go seeking a finite position[4] in the infinite.

SIXTHLY, if we posit a finite world, it is impossible to escape acceptance of the void, if void is that which containeth naught.

SEVENTHLY, this space in which is our world would without it be indeed a void, since where the world is not, there we must infer a void. Beyond our world then, one space is as another; therefore the quality of one is also that of the other; wherefore too this quality cometh to action, for no quality is eternally without action, and indeed it is eternally linked to action or rather is itself action, for in eternity there is no distinction between being and potential being [nor therefore between action and potential action].

EIGHTHLY, none of our sense-perceptions is opposed to the acceptance of infinity, since we cannot deny infinity merely because we do not sensibly perceive it; but since sense in itself is included in infinity, and since reason doth confirm infinity, therefore needs must that we posit infinity. Moreover, if we consider well, sense doth present to us an infinite universe. For we perceive an endless series of objects, each one contained by another, nor do we ever perceive either with our external or our internal sense, an object which is not contained by another or similar object.

Lastly before our eyes one thing is seen to bound another; air is as a well between the hills, and mountains between tracts of air, land bounds the sea

---

[4, 5] For the words marked[4] Bruno uses *loco;* for those marked[5] *spacio.* The meaning seems to be that Aristotle wrongly reduces the Greek word χῶρα to signify a space which occupies a definite position where it should be used for the infinite immensity of physical space. Cf. *Physica,* IV (I. Bekker, 208a 28; 208b 1, 23, 34, etc.). Sir W. D. Ross (*Aristotle,* London, 1923, p. 87) points out that Aristotle in fact rarely uses the word χῶρα or space.

and again sea bounds all lands; yet in truth there is nothing outside to limit the universe . . . so far on every side spreads out huge room for things, free from limit in all directions everywhere.[6]

From the testimony of our sight then we should rather infer the infinite, since there is no object which doth not terminate in another, nor can we experience aught which terminateth in itself.

NINTHLY, only verbally is it possible to deny infinite space, as is done by pertinacious fellows. For the rest of space where the universe is not, which is called void, where indeed it is pretended that nothing doth exist, cannot be conceived as without the capacity to contain no less a magnitude than that which it doth contain.

TENTHLY, since it is well that this world doth exist, no less good is the existence of each one of the infinity of other worlds.

ELEVENTHLY, the virtue of this world is not communicable to any other world soever, just as my being cannot be communicated to the being of this or of that man.

TWELFTHLY, there is no reason or sense-perception which, since we accept an infinity undivided, utterly simple and all-embracing, will not permit also a corporeal and extended infinity.

THIRTEENTHLY, our own surrounding space which appeareth to us so immense is neither part nor whole in relation to the infinite; nor can it be patient of infinite activity; compared to such activity, indeed, that which can be comprehended by our imbecile minds is merely non-being. And to a certain objection it may be replied that we base our argument for infinity not on the dignity of space but on the dignity of the natures [of worlds], since for the same reason that our space doth exist, so also should exist every other possible world; and their power of being is not actuated by our world's being, just as Elpino's power of being is not actuated by the existence of Fracastoro.

FOURTEENTHLY, if infinite active power doth actuate corporeal and dimensional being, this being must necessarily be infinite; otherwise there would be derogation from the nature and dignity both of creator and of creation.

---

[6] Lucretius, *De rerum natura,* I, 984-88; 1006-1007. Quoted in Latin.

FIFTEENTHLY, the universe as vulgarly conceived cannot contain the perfection of all things, save in the sense that I contain the perfection of all my members, and every globe containeth its entire contents. It is as though we named everyone rich who lacketh naught which he possesseth.

SIXTEENTHLY, efficient infinity would be utterly incomplete without the [infinite] effect thereof, as we cannot conceive that such an effect [of infinity] should be the efficient infinity itself. Furthermore, if such were or could be the effect, this doth in no way detract from that which must appertain to every veritable effect, wherefore theologians name action *ad extra* or transitive in addition to imminent action, so that thus it is fitting that both one and the other be infinite.

SEVENTEENTHLY, to call the universe[7] boundless as we have done bringeth the mind to rest, while the contrary doth multiply innumerable difficulties and inconveniences. Furthermore, we repeat what was said under headings two and three.

EIGHTEENTHLY, if the world be spherical, it hath figure and boundary; and the boundary which is yet beyond this boundary and figure (though it may please thee to term it nullity) hath also figure, so that the concavity of the latter is joined to the convexity of the former, since the beginning of this thy nullity is a concavity completely indifferent to the convex surface of our world.

NINETEENTHLY, more is added to that which hath been said under the second heading.

TWENTIETHLY, that which hath been said under heading ten is repeated.

In the SECOND PART of this Dialogue, that which hath already been shewn concerning the passive power of the universe is demonstrated for the active power of the efficient cause, set forth with arguments of which the first deriveth from the fact that divine power should not be otiose; particularly positing the effect thereof outside the substance thereof (if

[7] Bruno here uses *mondo,* contrary to his usual convention. In the next argument and in the FIFTH of the SECOND PART *mondo* denotes the Aristotelian conception. Cf. above, p. 231, n. 2.

indeed aught can be outside it), and that it is no less otiose and invidious if it produce a finite effect than if it produce none.

The SECOND argument is practical, shewing that the contrary view would deny divine goodness and greatness. While from our view there followeth no inconvenience whatever against what laws you will, nor against the matter of theology.

The THIRD argument is the converse of the twelfth of Part I. And here is shewn the distinction between the infinite whole and the completely infinite.

The FOURTH argument sheweth that no less from lack of will than from lack of power, omnipotence cometh to be blamed [by the Aristotelians] for the creation of a finite world, the infinite agent acting on a finite subject.

The FIFTH argument doth demonstrate that if omnipotence maketh not the world infinite, it is impotent to do so; and if it hath not power to create it infinite, then it must lack vigour to preserve it to eternity. And if finite in one respect, it would be so in all, for every mode therein is an object, and every object and every mode are the same, the one as the other.

The SIXTH argument is the converse of the tenth of Part I, and sheweth the reason why theologians defend the contrary view, not without expedient argument, and discourseth of friendship between these learned divines and the learned philosophers.

The SEVENTH doth propound the reasons which distinguish active power from diverse actions, and dischargeth such argument. Further, it expoundeth infinite power intensively and extensively in more lofty fashion than hath ever been done by the whole body of theologians.

The EIGHTH doth demonstrate that the motion of the infinity of worlds [8] is not the result of external motive force, but of their own nature, and that despite this there existeth an infinite motor force.

The NINTH sheweth how infinite motion may be intensively verified in each of the worlds. To this we should add that since each moving body

[8] Here and subsequently, Bruno's *infiniti mondi* is best rendered by *an infinite number of worlds* or *an infinity of worlds*. Cf. also above, p. 231, n. 2.

at the same time moveth itself and is moved, needs must that it may be seen in every point of the circle that it describeth around its own centre. And this objection we discharge on other occasions when it will be permissible to present the more diffuse doctrine.

ARGUMENT OF THE SECOND DIALOGUE

THE second Dialogue reacheth the same conclusion. FIRSTLY, four arguments are brought forward. The first sheweth that all the attributes of divinity are together as each one singly. The second doth demonstrate that our imagination should not be able to aspire beyond divine action. The third doth postulate the indifference of the distinction between divine intellect and divine action, and doth demonstrate that divine intellect conceiveth the infinite no less than the finite. The fourth argument enquireth, if the corporeal quality perceptible to our senses is endowed with infinite active power, then what will be the absolute totality of active and passive power inherent in the totality of all things?

SECONDLY, it is demonstrated that a corporeal object cannot be terminated by an incorporeal object, but either by a Void or by a Plenum, and in either case, beyond the world is Space which is ultimately no other than Matter; this is indeed that same passive force whereby active force, neither grudging nor otiose, is roused to activity. And the vanity is shewn of Aristotle's argument concerning the incompatibility of dimensions.[9]

THIRDLY, the difference is taught between the world and the universe, because he who declareth the universe a single infinity necessarily distinguisheth between these two terms.

FOURTHLY, there are brought forward contrary arguments, that regard the universe as finite, wherein Elpino referreth to all the sentences of Aristotle, and Philotheo examineth them. Some are derived from the nature of simple, others from that of composite, bodies. And the vanity

[9] *Physica,* IV, 2 (I. Bekker, 209b *seqq.*). Aristotle here combats the argument in the *Timaeus* concerning the identity of Matter and Space (cf. *Timaeus,* 52).

is shewn of six arguments taken from the definition of motions which cannot be infinite, and from other similar propositions which are without meaning, purpose or plausibility, as will be seen. For our arguments shew forth more convincingly the reason for the differences and for the termination of motion. And so far as comporteth with the occasion and place, they demonstrate the true understanding of strong and of weak impulses. For we shall shew that an infinite body is in itself neither heavy nor light, and we shall demonstrate in what manner a finite body can or again cannot receive such variations. Thus will be made clear the vanity of Aristotle's arguments against those who posit an infinite world, when he supposeth a centre and circumference, maintaining that our earth doth attain to the centre whether of a finite or of an infinite. Finally there is no proposition, great or small, adduced by this philosopher in order to destroy the infinity of the world, either in the first book of his *De coelo et mundo,* or in the third book of his *Physica,* which is not adequately discussed.

ARGUMENT OF THE THIRD DIALOGUE

IN THE third Dialogue there is first denied that base illusion of the shape of the heavens, of their spheres and diversity. For the heaven is declared to be a single general space, embracing the infinity of worlds, though we do not deny that there are other infinite 'heavens' using that word in another sense. For just as this earth hath her own heaven (which is her own region), through which she moveth and hath her course, so the same may be said of each of the innumerable other worlds. The origin is shown of the illusion of so many moving bodies subordinated to each other[10] and so shaped as to have two external surfaces and one internal cavity,[11] and of other *nostrums* and medicines, which bring nausea and horror even to those who concoct and dispense them, not less than to the wretches who swallow them.

---

[10] *Mobili deferenti.*

[11] i.e., whose orbit depends on the circular path both of deferent and of epicycle and is itself circular.

SECONDLY, we expound how both general motion and that of the above-mentioned eccentrics, and as many as may be referred to the aforesaid firmament are all pure illusion, deriving from the motion of the centre of the earth along the ecliptic and from the four varieties of motion which the earth taketh around her own centre. Thus it is seen that the proper motion of each star resulteth from the difference in position, which may be verified subjectively within the star as a body moving alone spontaneously through the field of space. This consideration maketh it understood that all their arguments concerning the [*primum*] *mobile* and infinite motion are vain and based on ignorance of the motion of this our own globe.

THIRDLY, it will be propounded that every star hath motion even as hath our own and those others which are so near to us that we can sensibly perceive the differences in their orbits and in their motions: but those suns, bodies in which fire doth predominate, move differently to the earths in which water predominateth; thus may be understood whence is derived the light diffused by stars, of which some glow of themselves and others by reflection.

FOURTHLY, it is shewn how stars at vast distances from the sun can, no less than those near to it, participate in the sun's heat, and fresh proof is given of the opinion attributed to Epicurus, that one sun may suffice for an infinite universe.[12] Moreover, this explaineth the true difference between stars that do and stars that do not scintillate.

FIFTHLY, the opinion of the Cusan is examined concerning the material and the habitability of other worlds and concerning the cause of light.

SIXTHLY, it is shewn that although some bodies are luminous and hot of their own nature, yet it doth not follow that the sun illumineth the sun and the earth illumineth herself, or that water doth illumine itself. But light proceedeth always from the opposed star; just as, when looking down from lofty eminences such as mountains, we sensibly perceive the whole sea illuminated; but were we on the sea, and occupying the same plane thereof, we should see no illumination save over a small re-

12 Cf. *Letter to Pythokles* in Diogenes Laertius, X. The first Latin translation of Diogenes Laertius appeared in Paris, probably in 1510. But Bruno's inspiration was probably Lucretius, V.

gion where the light of the sun and the light of the moon were opposed to us.

SEVENTHLY, we discourse concerning the vain notion of quintessences; and we declare that all sensible bodies are no other, and composed of no different proximate or primal principles than those of our earth, nor have they other motion, either in straight lines or circles. All this is set forth with reasons attuned to the senses, while Fracastoro doth accommodate himself to the intelligence of Burchio. And it is shewn clearly that there is no accident here which may not be expected also on those other worlds; just as if we consider well we must recognize that naught there can be seen from here which cannot also be seen here from there. Consequently, that beautiful order and ladder of nature [13] is but a charming dream, an old wives' tale.

EIGHTHLY, though the distinction between the elements be just, yet their order as commonly accepted is by no means perceptible to the senses or intelligible. According to Aristotle, the four elements are equally parts or members of this globe—unless we would say that water is in excess, wherefore with good cause the stars are named now water, now fire, both by true natural philosophers, and by prophets, divines and poets, who in this respect are spinning no tales nor forging metaphors, but allow other wiseacres to spin their tales and to babble. These worlds must be understood as heterogeneous bodies, animals, great globes in which earth is no heavier than the other elements. In them all particles move, changing their position and respective arrangement, just as the blood and other humours, spirits and smallest parts which ebb and flow are absorbed and again exhaled by us and other minor animals. In this connection a comparison is adduced shewing that the earth is no heavier by virtue of the attraction of her mass toward her own centre than is any other simple body of similar composition; that moreover the earth in herself is neither heavy, nor doth she ascend or descend; and that it is water which unifieth, and maketh density, consistency and weight.

NINTHLY, since the famous order of the elements is seen to be vain, the

[13] Of Aristotle.

nature is deduced of these sensible compound bodies which as so many animals and worlds are in that spacious field which is the air or the heaven, or the void, in which are all those worlds which contain animals and inhabitants no less than can our own earth, since those worlds have no less virtue nor a nature different from that of our earth.

TENTHLY, after it hath been seen how the obstinate and the ignorant of evil disposition are accustomed to dispute, it will further be shewn how disputes are wont to conclude; although others are so wary that without losing their composure, but with a sneer, a smile, a certain discreet malice, that which they have not succeeded in proving by argument—nor indeed can it be understood by themselves—nevertheless by these tricks of courteous disdain they [pretend to have proven], endeavouring not only to conceal their own patently obvious ignorance but to cast it on to the back of their adversary. For they dispute not in order to find or even to seek Truth, but for victory, and to appear the more learned and strenuous upholders of a contrary opinion. Such persons should be avoided by all who have not a good breastplate of patience.

ARGUMENT OF THE FOURTH DIALOGUE

FIRSTLY in this Dialogue is repeated that which hath been said on other occasions concerning the infinity of worlds and how each one of them moveth, and what is the configuration thereof.

SECONDLY, as in the second Dialogue arguments against the infinite mass or size of the universe were refuted, after the vast effect of immense vigour and power had been demonstrated with many arguments in the first Dialogue; even so, the infinite multitude of worlds having been demonstrated in the third Dialogue, we now refute the numerous contrary arguments of Aristotle; though this word *world* hath indeed one meaning when used by Aristotle and quite another when used by Democritus, Epicurus and others.

Aristotle, in arguments based on natural and impressed motion and on the nature of each which he formulateth, holdeth that one Earth should move toward another. To refute these doctrines, FIRSTLY, principles are established of no little importance for the elucidation of the true foundations of natural philosophy; SECONDLY, it is shewn that however closely the surface of one Earth were contiguous with that of another, it would not happen that parts of the one, that is to say, heterogeneous or dissimilar parts—I speak not of atoms nor of simple bodies—could move to the other Earth. Thereby the need is recognized to consider more carefully the nature of heaviness and of lightness.

THIRDLY, wherefore have these great bodies been disposed by nature at so great a distance one from another, instead of being placed nearer so that it would have been possible to pass from one to another? Thence to a profounder vision it doth appear why worlds could not be placed as it were in the circumference of the ether; that is, they could not be adjoining unto a void which hath neither power, virtue nor force, for it would then be impossible from one side to derive either life or light.

FOURTHLY, we consider in what respect local space may or may not change the nature of a body. And why it is that if a stone be equidistant between two earths, it will either remain stably poised or if it do not so, why it will move rather toward one than toward the other.

FIFTHLY, we consider how mistaken was Aristotle in holding the belief that between bodies, however distant, there is a force of heaviness or lightness attracting from one toward the other,[14] whence proceedeth the universal tendency to resist change of state (however lowly), whence arise flight and persecutions.

SIXTHLY, it is shewn that movement in a straight line doth not appertain to the nature of our earth or of other principal bodies, but rather to the parts of these bodies which, if not at too great a distance, move toward one another from the most diverse positions.

SEVENTHLY, it is argued from the behaviour of comets that it is not true that a heavy body, however distant, suffereth attraction or motion toward the body which containeth it. This hypothesis indeed was based not on truly physical principles, but on Aristotle's purely philosophical suppositions, formulated by him from a consideration of those parts which are vapours and exhalations of our earth.[15]

---

[14] Cf. *Physica,* IV, 4, 212a 25; 212b 30, etc.
[15] Cf. *Physica,* IV, 208b 1 *seqq.*

EIGHTHLY, concerning another line of reasoning, it is shewn that simple bodies of identical nature in innumerable diverse worlds have similar motion, and that merely arithmetical diversity causeth a difference of locality, each part having his own centre and being also referred to the common centre which cannot be sought within the universe.

NINTHLY, it is demonstrated that bodies and their parts have no determined upper or lower portions, save in so far as the direction of their conservation may be toward this way or that.

TENTHLY, it is shewn that motion is infinite, and that a moving body tendeth toward infinity and to the formation of innumerable compounds; but that heaviness or lightness do not therefore follow, nor infinite speed; and indeed the motion of adjacent parts, inasmuch as they preserve their own nature, cannot be infinite. Moreover the attraction of parts to their own containing body can only take place within the local space thereof.

ARGUMENT OF THE FIFTH DIALOGUE

IN THE beginning of the fifth Dialogue is presented a learned person of a happier talent who, howbeit educated in the contrary doctrine, yet by power to judge what he hath heard and seen, can distinguish between two disciplines and can easily alter and correct his views. Those too are indicated to whom Aristotle doth appear a miracle of nature, who misinterpret him and, with little talent, have an exalted opinion concerning him. Wherefore we should pity them, and flee from disputation with them, since against them it is only possible to lose.

Here Albertino, a fresh interlocutor, introduceth twelve arguments which comprise every point against a plurality or multitude of worlds. The FIRST suggesteth that outside our own world we can appreciate neither position, time, nor space, neither simple nor composite body. The SECOND asserteth the unity of the single motor power. The THIRD is based on the positions of mobile bodies; the FOURTH, on the distance of the centre from the horizons. The FIFTH argueth from the contiguity of the orbs of the worlds; the SIXTH from the triangular spaces which are caused by their contact. The SEVENTH doth maintain infinity in action (which hath indeed no existence), and supposeth a determinate number [of worlds] which is indeed no more rationally probable than the other. From the same reasoning we can infer not merely as well but much more easily that the number of worlds is not determined but is infinite. The EIGHTH [Aristotelian argument of Albertino] is based on the determination of natural bodies, and on the passive force of bodies which doth not yield to divine influence and active power. But here we must consider that it is highly inconvenient to suppose the Supreme and Highest to be similar merely to a performer on the zither who cannot play in the absence of the instrument; thus would a Creator be unable to create because that which he is able to create cannot be created by him. This would lay down an obvious contradiction which cannot be overlooked save by the most ignorant. The NINTH argument is based on urbane courtesy which lieth in conversation. The TENTH doth aver that from the contiguity of one world with another must be deduced that the motion of one doth impede that of the other. The ELEVENTH maintaineth that if this world is complete and perfect, it is impossible that one or more others should be added to it.

These are the doubts and motives whose solution involveth only so much doctrine as will suffice to lay bare the intimate and radical errors of the current philosophy, and the weight and force of our own. Here is the reason wherefore we must not fear that any object may disappear, or any particle veritably melt away or dissolve in space or suffer dismemberment by annihilation. Here too is the reason of the constant change of all things, so that there existeth no evil beyond escape, nor good which is unattainable, since throughout infinite space and throughout endless change all substance remaineth one and the same. From these reflections, if we apply ourselves attentively, we shall see that no strange happening can be dismissed by grief or by fear, and that no good fortune can be advanced by pleasure or hope. Whereby we find the true path to true morality; we will be high minded, despising that which is esteemed by childish minds; and we shall certainly become greater than those whom the blind public doth adore, for we shall attain to true contemplation of the story of nature which is inscribed within ourselves, and we shall follow the divine laws which are engraved upon our hearts. We shall recognize that there is no distinction between flight from here to heaven and from heaven hither, nor between ascent from there hither and from here to there; nor yet is there descent between one and the other. We are not more circumferential to those others than they to us; they are not more central to us than we to them. Just as we do tread our star and are contained in our heaven, so also are they.

Behold us therefore beyond reach of jealousy, liberated from vain anxiety and from foolish concern to covet from afar that great good which we possess close by and at hand. Behold us moreover freed from panic lest others should fall upon us, rather than encouraged in the hope that we may fall upon them. Since the air which sustaineth our globe is as infinite as that which sustaineth theirs, and this animal [the earth] wandereth through her own space and reacheth her own destination as freely as do those others. When we have pondered and understood this, ah, how much further shall we be led to ponder and understand.

Thus by means of this science we shall certainly attain to that good which by other sciences is sought in vain.

For here is the philosophy which sharpeneth the senses, satisfieth the soul, enlargeth the intellect and leadeth man to that true bliss to which he may attain, which consisteth in a certain balance, for it liberateth him alike from the eager quest of pleasure and from the blind feeling of grief; it causeth him to rejoice in the present and neither to fear nor to hope for the future. For that Providence or Fate or Lot which determineth the vicissitudes of our individual life doth neither desire nor permit our knowledge of the one to exceed our ignorance of the other, so that at first sight we are dubious and perplexed. But when we consider more profoundly the being and substance of that universe in which we are immutably set, we shall discover that neither we ourselves nor any substance doth suffer death; for nothing is in fact diminished in its substance, but all things wandering through infinite space undergo change of aspect. And since we are all subject to a perfect Power, we should not believe, suppose or hope otherwise, than that even as all issueth from good, so too all is good, through good, toward good; from good, by good means, toward a good end. For a contrary view can be held only by one who considereth merely the present moment, even as the beauty of a building is not manifest to one who seeth but one small detail, as a stone, a cement affixed to it or half a partition wall, but is revealed to him who can view the whole and hath understanding to appraise the proportions. We do not fear that by the violence of some erring spirit or by the wrath of a thundering Jove, that which is accumulated in our world could become dispersed beyond this hollow sepulchre or cupola of the heavens, be shaken or scattered as dust beyond this starry mantle. In no other way could the nature of things be brought to naught as to its substance save in appearance, as when the air which was compressed within the concavity of a bubble seemeth to one's own eyes to go forth into the void. For in the world as known to us, object succeedeth ever to object, nor is there an ultimate depth from which as from the artificer's hand things flow to an inevitable nullity. There are no ends, boundaries, limits or walls which can defraud or deprive us of the infinite multitude of things. Therefore the earth and the ocean thereof are fecund; therefore the sun's blaze is everlasting, so that eternally fuel is provided for the voracious fires, and moisture replenisheth the attenuated seas. For from infinity is born an ever fresh abundance of matter.

Thus Democritus and Epicurus,[16] who maintained that everything throughout infinity suffereth renewal and restoration, understood these matters more truly than those who would at all costs maintain belief in the immutability of the universe, alleging a constant and unchanging number of particles of identical material that perpetually undergo transformation, one into another.

Make then your forecasts, my lords Astrologers, with your slavish physicians, by means of those astrolabes with which you seek to discern the fantastic nine moving spheres; in these you finally imprison your own minds, so that you appear to me but as parrots in a cage, while I watch you dancing up and down, turning and hopping within those circles. We know that the Supreme Ruler cannot have a seat so narrow, so miserable a throne, so straight a tribunal, so scanty a court, so small and feeble a simulacrum that a phantasm can bring to birth, a dream shatter, a delusion restore, a chimera disperse, a calamity diminish, a

16 Bruno's authority for the views of these philosophers is of course Lucretius.

misdeed abolish and a thought renew it again, so that indeed with a puff of air it were brimful and with a single gulp it were emptied. On the contrary we recognize a noble image, a marvellous conception, a supreme figure, an exalted shadow, an infinite representation of the represented infinity, a spectacle worthy of the excellence and supremacy of Him who transcendeth understanding, comprehension or grasp. Thus is the excellence of God magnified and the greatness of his kingdom made manifest; he is glorified not in one, but in countless suns; not in a single earth, a single world, but in a thousand thousand, I say in an infinity of worlds.

Thus not in vain is that power of the intellect which ever seeketh, yea, and achieveth the addition of space to space, mass to mass, unity to unity, number to number, by the science which dischargeth us from the fetters of a most narrow kingdom and promoteth us to the freedom of a truly august realm, which freeth us from an imagined poverty and straitness to the possession of the myriad riches of so vast a space, of so worthy a field, of so many most cultivated worlds. This science doth not permit that the arch of the horizon that our deluded vision imagineth over the earth and that by our fantasy is feigned in the spacious ether, shall imprison our spirit under the custody of a Pluto or at the mercy of a Jove. We are spared the thought of so wealthy an owner and subsequently of so miserly, sordid and avaricious a donor. Nor need we accept nourishment from a nature so fecund and pregnant, and then so wretched, mean and niggard in her fruit.

Very different are the worthy and honourable fruits which may be plucked from these trees, the precious and desirable harvests which may be reaped from the sowing of this seed. We will not recall these to mind that we may not excite the blind envy of our adversaries, but we leave them to the understanding and judgement of all who are able to comprehend and judge. These will easily build for themselves on the foundations we have given, the whole edifice of our philosophy whose parts indeed, if it shall please Him who governeth and ruleth us and if the undertaking begun be not interrupted, we will reduce to the desired perfection. Then that which is inseminated in the Dialogues concerning *Cause, Origin and Unity* and hath come to birth in these Dialogues on the *Infinite Universe and Worlds* shall germinate in yet others, and in others shall grow and ripen, in yet other works shall enrich us with a precious harvest and shall satisfy us exceedingly. Then (having cleared out the tares, the darnels and other accumulated weeds), we shall fill the stores of studious and talented men with the best wheat that the soil we cultivate can produce.

Meanwhile (though I am sure it is unnecessary to commend him to you),[17] I shall yet not omit as part of my duty truly to commend to you one whom you maintain among your court not as a man of whom you have need, but rather as a person who hath need of you for many reasons you perceive. For in having round you many who serve you, you differ in no wise from the common folk, bankers and merchants; but in maintaining one in some sort worthy to be advanced, defended and prospered, in this you have been (as you have indeed ever shewn yourself) the peer of generous princes, of heroes and gods. These indeed have chosen such as you for the defence of their friends. And I would remind you, though such reminder is I know unnecessary, that when the end cometh, you will be esteemed by the world and rewarded by God, not because you have won the love and respect of princes of the earth, however powerful, but rather for having loved, defended and cherished one man such as I have described. For those with fortune greater than yours can do nothing for you who exceed many among them in virtue, which will outlast all your trappings and tapestries. But your achievement for others may easily come to be inscribed in the book of eternity—either that which is seen on earth or that other which is believed to be in heaven. For that which you receive from others is a testimony to their virtue, but all that you do for others is the sign and clear indication of your own virtue. Farewell.

---

[17] This moving peroration is addressed of course to Mauvissière.

Passing alone to those realms
The object erst of thine exalted thought,
I would rise to infinity: then I would compass the skill
Of industries and arts equal to the objects.[18]
There would I be reborn: there on high I would foster for thee
Thy fair offspring, now that at length cruel
Destiny hath run her whole course
Against the enterprise whereby I was wont to withdraw to thee.
Fly not from me, for I yearn for a nobler refuge
That I may rejoice in thee. And I shall have as guide
A god called blind by the unseeing.
May Heaven deliver thee, and every emanation
Of the great Architect be ever gracious unto thee:
But turn thou not to me unless thou art mine.

Escaped from the narrow murky prison
Where for so many years error held me straitly,
Here I leave the chain that bound me
And the shadow of my fiercely malicious foe
Who can [19] force me no longer to the gloomy dusk of night.
For he who hath overcome the great Python [20]
With whose blood he hath dyed the waters of the sea
Hath put to flight the Fury that pursued me.[21]
To thee I turn, I soar, O my sustaining Voice;
I render thanks to thee, my Sun, my divine Light,
For thou hast summoned me from that horrible torture,[22]
Thou hast led me to a goodlier tabernacle; [23]
Thou hast brought healing to my bruised heart.

---

[18] Could this phrase have suggested the passage in Browning's *Paracelsus* beginning: "I would love infinitely and be loved. First I would cast in bronze. . . ."?

[19] *Lit.*, "Thou canst."

[20] Apollo was said to have journeyed, four days after his birth, to Mt. Parnassus, and there killed the dragon Python who had pursued his mother Leto during her wanderings before she found resting-place at Delos to give birth to him. Cf. Ovid, *Metamorphoses*, I, 443.

[21] Megaera, one of the serpent-garlanded Eumenides or Erinnyes (Latin *Furiae* or *Dirae*), who personified curses on a guilty criminal.

[22] *Lit.*, "grapple."

[23] *Lit.*, "Thou madest thyself my leader to a happier mansion."

Thou art my delight and the warmth of my heart; [24]
Thou makest me without fear of Fate or of Death;
Thou breakest the chains and bars
Whence few come forth free.
Seasons, years, months, days and hours—
The children and weapons of Time—and that Court
Where neither steel nor treasure [25] avail
Have secured me from the fury [of the foe].
Henceforth I spread confident wings to space;
I fear no barrier of crystal or of glass;
I cleave the heavens and soar to the infinite.
And while I rise from my own globe to others
And penetrate ever further through the eternal field,
That which others saw from afar, I leave far behind me.[26]

---

[24] *Lit.*, "[Thou] who adornest me with plumes and warmest my heart."

[25] *Lit.*, "diamond."

[26] Gentile draws attention to the repetition of this poem in the *De gl' heroici furori* and of its substance in the *De immenso.* He also observes that the same theme occurs in poems of Tansillo, of Telesio, and of Teofilo Folengo (1491-1544).

FIRST DIALOGUE

Speakers: ELPINO. PHILOTHEO (occasionally called THEOPHILO). FRACASTORO. BURCHIO.

ELP. How is it possible that the universe can be infinite?

PHIL. How is it possible that the universe can be finite?

ELP. Do you claim that you can demonstrate this infinitude?

PHIL. Do you claim that you can demonstrate this finitude?

ELP. What is this spreading forth?

PHIL. What is this limit?

FRAC. To the point, to the point, if you please. Too long you have kept us in suspense.

BUR. Come quickly to argument, Philotheo, for I shall be vastly amused to hear this fable or fantasy.

FRAC. More modestly, Burchio. What wilt thou say if truth doth ultimately convince thee?

BUR. Even if this be true I do not wish to believe it, for this INFINITE can neither be understood by my head nor brooked by my stomach. Although, to tell the truth, I could yet hope that Philotheo were right, so that if by ill luck I were to fall from this world I should always find myself on firm ground.

ELP. Certainly, O Theophilo, if we wish to judge by our senses, yielding suitable primacy to that which is the source of all our knowledge, perchance we shall not find it easier to reach the conclusion you expressed than to take the contrary view. Now be so kind as to begin my enlightenment.

PHIL. No corporeal sense can perceive the infinite. None of our senses could be expected to furnish this conclusion; for the infinite cannot be the object of sense-perception; therefore he who demandeth to obtain this knowledge through the senses is like unto one who would desire to see with his eyes both substance and essence. And he who would deny the existence of a thing merely because it cannot be apprehended by the senses, nor is visible, would presently be led to the denial of his own substance and being. Wherefore there must be some measure in the demand for evidence from our sense-perception, for this we can accept only in regard to sensible objects, and even there it is not above all suspicion unless it cometh before the court aided by good judgement. It is the part of the intellect to judge, yielding due weight to factors absent and separated by distance of time and by space intervals. And in this matter our sense-perception doth suffice us and doth yield us adequate testimony, since it is unable to gainsay us; moreover it advertiseth and confesseth his own feebleness and inadequacy by the impression it giveth us of a finite horizon, an impression moreover which is ever changing. Since then we have experience that sense-perception deceiveth us concerning the surface of this globe on which we live, much more should we hold suspect the impression it giveth us of a limit to the starry sphere.

ELP. Of what use then are the senses to us? Tell me that.

PHIL. Solely to stimulate our reason, to accuse, to indicate, to testify in part; not to testify completely, still less to judge or to condemn. For our senses, however perfect, are never without some perturbation. Wherefore truth is in but very small degree derived from the senses as from a frail origin, and doth by no means reside in the senses.

ELP. Where then?

PHIL. In the sensible object as in a mirror. In reason, by process of argument and discussion. In the intellect, either through origin or by conclusion. In the mind, in its proper and vital form.

ELP. On, then, and give your reasons.

PHIL. I will do so. If the world is finite and if nothing lieth beyond, I ask you WHERE is the world? WHERE is the universe? Aristotle replieth, it is in itself.[1] The convex surface of the primal heaven is universal space, which being the primal container is by naught contained. For position in space is no other than the surfaces and limit of the containing body,

---

[1] Cf. *Physica,* IV, 3, 210a 29; 5, 212b 13, etc.

so that he who hath no containing body hath no position in space.[2] What then dost thou mean, O Aristotle, by this phrase, that "space is within itself"? What will be thy conclusion concerning that which is beyond the world? If thou sayest, there is nothing, then the heaven[3] and the world will certainly not be anywhere.

FRAC. The world will then be nowhere. Everything will be nowhere.

PHIL. The world is something which is past finding out. If thou sayest (and it certainly appeareth to me that thou seekest to say something in order to escape Vacuum and Nullity), if thou sayest that beyond the world is a divine intellect, so that God doth become the position in space of all things, why then thou thyself wilt be much embarrassed to explain to us how that which is incorporeal [yet] intelligible, and without dimension can be the very position in space occupied by a dimensional body; and if thou sayest that this incorporeal space containeth as it were a form, as the soul containeth the body, then thou dost not reply to the question of that which lieth beyond, nor to the enquiry concerning that which is outside the universe. And if thou wouldst excuse thyself by asserting that where naught is, and nothing existeth, there can be no question of position in space nor of beyond or outside, yet I shall in no wise be satisfied. For these are mere words and excuses, which cannot form part of our thought. For it is wholly impossible that in any sense or fantasy (even though there may be various senses and various fantasies), it is I say impossible that I can with any true meaning assert that there existeth such a surface, boundary or limit, beyond which is neither body, nor empty space, even though God be there. For divinity hath not as aim to fill space, nor therefore doth it by any means appertain to the nature of divinity that it should be the boundary of a body. For aught which can be termed a limiting body must either be the exterior shape or else a containing body. And by no description of this quality canst thou render it compatible with the dignity of divine and universal nature.[4]

---

[2] Cf. *Physica,* IV, 4, 211b 4; 212a 5-6.

[3] *Cielo.*

[4] *Lit.,* "And however thou mightest attempt to say this, thou wouldst be considered to detract from the dignity . . ."

BUR. Certainly I think that one must reply to this fellow that if a person would stretch out his hand beyond the convex sphere of heaven, the hand would occupy no position in space nor any place, and in consequence would not exist.

PHIL. I would add that no mind can fail to perceive the contradiction implicit in this saying of the Peripatetic. Aristotle defined position occupied by a body not as the containing body itself, nor as a certain [part of] space,[5] but as a surface of the containing body. Then he affirmeth that the prime, principal and greatest space is that to which such a definition least and by no means conformeth, namely, the convex surface of the first [outermost] heaven. This is the surface of a body of a particular sort, a body which containeth only, and is not contained. Now for the surface to be a position in space, it need not appertain to a contained body but it must appertain to a containing body. And if it be the surface of a containing body and yet be not joined to and continuous with the contained body, then it is a space without position, since the first [outermost] heaven cannot be a space except in virtue of the concave surface thereof, which is in contact with the convex surface of the next heaven. Thus we recognize that this definition is vain, confused and self-destructive, the confusion being caused by that incongruity which maintaineth that naught existeth beyond the firmament.

ELP. The Peripatetics would say that the outermost heaven is a containing body in virtue of the concave and not of the convex surface thereof, and that in virtue of the concave surface it is a space.

FRAC. And I would add that therefore the surface of a containing body need not be a position in space.[6]

PHIL. In short then, to come straight to my proposition, it appeareth to me ridiculous to affirm that nothing is beyond the heaven, and that the heaven is contained in itself and is in place and hath position only by accident, that is, by means of the parts thereof. And however Aristotle's phrase *by accident* be interpreted, he cannot escape the difficulty that one cannot be transformed into two, for the container is eternally

[5] For the following argument, cf. *Physica,* IV, 5, 212a-212b.

[6] *Lit.,* "there existeth a surface of a containing body which surface is not a position in space."

different from the contained,[7] so different, indeed, that according to Aristotle himself, the container is incorporeal while the contained is corporeal; the container is motionless while the contained hath motion; the container is a mathematical conception while the contained hath physical existence.[8]

Thus let this surface be what it will, I must always put the question, what is beyond? If the reply is NOTHING, then I call that the VOID or emptiness. And such a Void or Emptiness hath no measure and no outer limit, though it hath an inner; and this is harder to imagine than is an infinite or immense universe. For if we insist on a finite universe, we cannot escape the void. And let us now see whether there can be such a space in which is naught. In this infinite space is placed our universe (whether by chance, by necessity or by providence I do not now consider). I ask now whether this space which indeed containeth the world is better fitted to do so than is another space beyond?

FRAC. It certainly appeareth to me, not so. For where there is nothing, there can be no differentiation; where there is no differentiation there is no distinction of quality and perhaps there is even less of quality where there is naught whatsoever.

ELP. Neither also can there be then any lack of quality, and this more surely than the previous proposition.

PHIL. You say truly. Therefore I say that as the Void or Emptiness, which according to the Peripatetic view is necessary, hath no aptness to receive [i.e., no power of attracting the world], still less can it repel the world. But of these two faculties we see one in action, while the other we cannot wholly see except with the eye of reason. As therefore this world (called by the Platonists MATTER), lieth in this space which doth equal in size the whole of our world, so another world can be in

---

[7] *Physica,* IV, 5, 212b 13-14. Hardie and Gaye translate, "But other things are in place indirectly through something conjoined with them, as the soul and the heaven" (Oxford *Aristotle,* ed. W. O. Ross, Vol. II). The Latin edition (Venice, 1482) gives *secundum accidens:* "Alia uero secundum accidens ut anima et celestes partes non in loco quodammodo omnes sunt."

[8] *Physica,* IV, 4, 212a 10-23

that other space, and [other worlds] in innumerable spaces beyond of similar kind.[9]

FRAC. Certainly we may judge more confidently by analogy with what we see and know than in opposition to what we see and know. Since then, on the evidence of our sight and experience, the universe hath no end nor is terminated in Void and Emptiness, about which indeed there is no information, therefore we should reasonably conclude as you do, since if all other reasonings were of equal weight, we should still see that our experience is opposed to a Void but not to a Plenum: therefore we shall always be justified in accepting the Plenum; but if we reject it, we shall not easily escape a thousand accusations and inconveniences. Continue, O Philotheo.

PHIL. As regards infinite space, we know for certain that this is apt for the reception of matter and we know naught else thereof; for me, however, it is enough that infinity is not repugnant to the reception of matter, if only because where there is naught, there at least is no outrage. It remaineth to see whether or not it is convenient that all space be filled? And here, if we consider no less what it may be than what it may do, we shall still find the Plenum not merely reasonable but inevitable. That this may be manifest I ask you whether it is well that this world[10] exist.

ELP. It is very well.

PHIL. Then it is well that this space equal in size to the world (I will call it Empty Space, like to and indistinguishable from the space which thou wouldst call the nullity beyond the convexity of the first heaven) that this space I say should similarly be filled.

ELP. Certainly.

PHIL. I ask thee further. Dost thou think that as in this our space there existeth this frame that we call the world, so the same could have existed or could exist in another space within this great Emptiness?

ELP. I will say yes, albeit I do not see how we can posit any distinction between one thing and another in mere nullity and empty space.

---

[9] *Equale a questo.* Cf. the same phrase with the same connotation, n. 16, below.

[10] *Questo mondo,* i.e., our perceptible universe.

FRAC. I am sure that thou dost see, but thou art not anxious to declare it, for thou dost perceive whither this will lead thee.

ELP. Declare it indeed without hesitation.[11] For it behoveth us to declare and understand that our world[12] lieth in a space which without our world would be indistinguishable from that which is beyond your *primum mobile.*

FRAC. Continue.

PHIL. So just as this space can contain and hath contained this universal body, and is necessarily completed thereby as thou didst say, so also all the rest of space can be and hath been no less completed in this manner.

ELP. I admit it. What may be deduced therefrom? A thing can be or can have: therefore is it or hath it?

PHIL. I will expound so that, if thou wishest to make a frank confession, then wilt thou say that it can be, that it should be, that it is. For just as it would be ill were this our space not filled, that is, were our world[12] not to exist, then, since the spaces are indistinguishable, it would be no less ill if the whole of space were not filled. Thus we see that the universe[13] is of infinite size and the worlds[14] therein without number.

ELP. Wherefore then must they be so numerous rather than a single one?

PHIL. Because if it were ill that our world[15] should not exist, or that this Plenum should not be, then the same holdeth good of our space or space of similar kind.[16]

ELP. I say that 'twere ill as regards that which is in this our space, which might equally exist in another space of the same kind.[16]

PHIL. This, if thou considereth well, cometh all to the same. For the goodness of this corporeal being which is our space, or could be in another space similar to ours[16] doth explain and concern that goodness, suitability and perfection which may be in a space like to and as great as our own or in another similar[16] to ours, but doth not concern that

---

[11] The beginning of Elpino's conversion.

[12] *Mondo.*

[13] *Universo.*

[14] *Mondi.*

[15] *Mondo.*

[16] *Equale a questo.* Cf. above, p. 255, n. 9.

goodness which may be in countless other spaces similar to our own.[17] This argument is the more cogent since, if it is reasonable to postulate a finite goodness, a bounded perfection, all the more reasonable is the conception of an infinite goodness. For whereas finite goodness appeareth to us reasonable and convenient, the infinite is an imperative necessity.

ELP. Infinite Good doth certainly exist, but is incorporeal.

PHIL. We are then at one concerning the incorporeal infinite; but what preventeth the similar acceptability of the good, corporeal and infinite being? And why should not that infinite which is implicit in the utterly simple and individual Prime Origin rather become explicit in his own infinite and boundless image able to contain innumerable worlds, than become explicit within such narrow bounds? So that it appeareth indeed shameful to refuse to credit that this world which seemeth to us so vast may not in the divine regard appear a mere point, even a nullity?

ELP. But since the greatness of God lieth not at all in corporeal size (not to mention that our world doth add nothing to him) so also we should not conceive the greatness of his image to consist in the greater or lesser extent of the size thereof.[18]

THEO. Well said. But you do not answer the pith of the argument. For I do not insist on infinite space, nor is Nature endowed with infinite space for the exaltation of size or of corporeal extent, but rather for the exaltation of corporeal natures and species, because infinite perfection is far better presented in innumerable individuals than in those which are numbered and finite. Needs must indeed that there should be an infinite image of the inaccessible divine countenance and that there should be in this image as infinite members thereof, innumerable worlds, namely, these others that I postulate. But since innumerable grades of perfection must, through corporeal mode, unfold the divine incorporeal perfection, therefore there must be innumerable individuals, those great animals, whereof one is our earth, the divine mother who hath given birth to us, doth nourish us and moreover will receive us back; [19] and to contain these innumerable bodies there is needed an infinite space.

---

[17] *Simili a questo.*   [18] *Mole de' dimensioni.*

[19] *Lit.,* "moreover will not receive us back"; *non* is probably a printer's error.

Nevertheless it is well that there should be since there can be innumerable worlds similar to our own, even as our world hath achieved and doth achieve existence and it is well that it should exist.

ELP. We shall say that this finite world [20] with the finite stars embraceth the perfection of all things.

THEO. You may say so, but you cannot prove it. For the world [20] of this our finite space embraceth indeed the perfection of all those finite objects contained within our space, but not of those infinite potentialities of innumerable other spaces.

FRAC. Pray let us stop here and not act like those sophists who dispute merely for victory, and while they strive for their laurels prevent both themselves and others from comprehending the truth. For I believe there is none so pertinacious in perfidy and in slander withal as to deny that since space may contain infinity and in view of the goodness both individual and collective of the infinite number of worlds [21] which may be contained therein, therefore each of them, no less than this world which we know, may rationally and conveniently have his being. For infinite space is endowed with infinite quality and therein is lauded the infinite act of existence, whereby the infinite First Cause is not considered deficient, nor is the infinite quality thereof in vain. Let us then, O Elpino, be content to hear further arguments from Philotheo if they should occur to him.

ELP. To tell the truth, I see well that to pronounce the world (as you name the universe) boundless, carrieth no inconvenience and indeed freeth us from many difficulties in which the contrary opinion doth envelope us. In particular I recognize that, if we follow the Peripatetics, we must often assert that which hath no basis in our thought. For example, having denied the existence of empty space either without or within the universe,[22] when we seek to reply to the question "Where is the

[20] *Mondo.* [21] *De infiniti mondi.* Cf. p. 235, n. 8.

[22] Cf. *Physica,* IV, 6-9. In *Metaphysica,* 6, 1048b 9-15, in the course of a discussion on potentiality, Aristotle groups the conceptions of the infinite and of the void: "The infinite and the void and all similar things are said to exist potentially and actually in a different sense from that in which many other things are said to exist . . . the infinite does not exist potentially in the sense that it will ever actually have separate existence."

universe?" we must needs declare the universe to be within the very parts thereof, for fear of asserting that it is in no place whatsoever. As though we were to say *Nullibi, nusquam*. But it cannot be denied that by such arguments 'twere needful to declare that the parts occupy some position while the universe occupieth no position and is not in space. And this (as all will recognize) is meaningless nonsense, and is clearly an obstinate flight in order to avoid confession of the truth, and to refuse admission either of the infinity of the world and of the universe, or of the infinity of space. From such attempts there followeth double confusion to whoever adopteth them. I therefore affirm that if the universe [23] be a single spherical body, and therefore hath form and limit, then it must terminate within infinite space. And if we would say that nothing is within infinite space, then we must admit a truly empty space, and if this exist, it is no less reasonable to conceive it of the whole than of this part which here we see capable of enclosing this world. But if vacant space doth not exist, then must [the whole of space] be a plenum, and consequently this universe must be infinite. And it were no less foolish to affirm that the world must have position after we have asserted that nothing lieth beyond it, or to maintain that it is within the very parts of itself, than if we were to say that Elpino must have position because his hand is on his arm, his eye on his face, his foot on his leg, his head on his body. But to come to a conclusion, not behaving like a sophist standing on manifest difficulties or spending my time in chatter, I declare that which I cannot deny, namely, that within infinite space either there may be an infinity of worlds similar to our own; or that this universe may have extended its capacity in order to contain many bodies such as those we name stars; or again that, whether these worlds be similar or dissimilar to one another, it may with no less reason be well that one than that another should exist. For the existence of one is no less reasonable than that of another; and the existence of many no less so than of one or of the other; and the existence of an infinity of them no less so than the existence of a large number. Wherefore, even as the abolition and non-existence of this world would be an evil, so would it be of innumerable others.

[23] *Il tutto.*

FRAC. You explain right well, and you shew that you understand argument and are not a mere sophist since you accept that which cannot be denied.

ELP. Yet I would hear the further argument concerning the primal and eternal efficient cause; whether such infinite effect beseemeth thereto and doth therefore in fact follow therefrom.[24]

PHIL. This is indeed what I had to add; for, having pronounced that the universe must itself be infinite because of the capacity and aptness of infinite space; on account also of the possibility and convenience of accepting the existence of innumerable worlds like to our own; it remaineth still to prove it. Now both from the circumstances of this efficient cause which must have produced the universe such as it is, or rather, must ever produce it such as it is, and also from the conditions of our mode of understanding, we may easily argue that infinite space is similar to this which we see, rather than argue that it is that which we do not see either by example or by similitude or by proportion, or indeed by any effort of imagination which doth not finally destroy itself. Now to begin. Why should we or could we imagine that divine power were otiose? Divine goodness can indeed be communicated to infinite things and can be infinitely diffused; why then should we wish to assert that it would choose to be scarce and to reduce itself to naught—for every finite thing is as naught in relation to the infinite? Why do you desire that centre of divinity which can (if one may so express it) extend infinitely to an infinite sphere, why do you desire that it should remain grudgingly sterile rather than extend itself, as a father, fecund, ornate and beautiful? Why should you prefer that it should be less or indeed by no means communicated, rather than that it should fulfil the scheme of its glorious power and being? Why should infinite amplitude be frustrated, the possibility of an infinity of worlds[25] be defrauded? Why should be preju-

---

[24] This question of the relation between the nature of the Efficient Cause and that of the Effects and the Creations deriving therefrom is discussed repeatedly by Bruno. Cf. *De la causa, principio et uno,* Dial. II, where Efficient Cause is explicitly identified with God. The argument as in our text is succinctly expounded in *De immenso,* I, 9 (*Op. lat.,* I, i, 235).

[25] *Infiniti mondi.* Cf. p. 235, n. 8.

diced the excellency of the divine image which ought rather to glow in an unrestricted mirror, infinite, immense, according to the law of its being? Why must we affirm this opinion which beareth with it so many inconveniences and penalties and, without in any way fostering law, religions, faith or morality, destroyeth so many philosophical principles? Why wouldst thou that God should in power, in act and in effect (which in him are identical) be determined as the limit of the convexity of a sphere, rather than that he should be as we may say the undetermined limit of the boundless? The limit I say, without limit, that I may differentiate the one infinity from the other. For He is the whole, comprehensive [26] and complete totality of the infinite, but the universe is the explicit though not the all-comprehensive totality (if indeed we may in any wise use the term totality where there is neither part nor boundary). Therefore the nature of the one doth comprehend boundaries; that of the other is bounded. And this is not the distinction between infinite and finite. The distinction is rather that the one is infinite, while the other doth limit according to the nature of the totality and of the whole being thereof. So that although it is entirely infinite, the infinity thereof is not completely comprehensive, for this would be repugnant to dimensional infinity.

ELP. I would like to understand this better; indeed you would give me pleasure if you would somewhat further expound that which you call the comprehensive and complete infinite totality and the completely infinite.

PHIL. I say that the universe is entirely infinite because it hath neither edge, limit, nor surfaces. But I say that the universe is not all-comprehensive infinity because each of the parts thereof that we can examine is finite and each of the innumerable worlds contained therein is finite. I declare God to be completely infinite because he can be associated with no boundary and his every attribute is one and infinite. And I say that God is all-comprehensive infinity because the whole of him pervadeth the whole world and every part thereof comprehensively and to infinity. That is unlike the infinity of the universe which is comprehensively in

[26] *Complicatamente,* i.e., "unfolded."

the whole but not comprehensively in those parts which we can distinguish within the whole (if indeed we can use the name parts, since they appertain to an infinite whole).[27]

ELP. I understand. Now continue your proposition.

THEO. Then, by virtue of all those arguments by which this world understood as finite is said to be expedient, good and necessary, so also should all the innumerable other worlds be named expedient and good; and to them by the same argument Omnipotence doth not grudge being; and without them, Omnipotence would be reproached for deficiency either of will or of power in thus permitting a void or (if thou likest not the term void) an infinite space, whence would result diminishment not only of infinite perfection of being, but also of the infinite majesty of the efficient cause acting on created or on dependent things, if eternal. What argument would persuade us that the Agent capable of creating infinite good should have created it finite? And if he hath created it finite, why should we believe that the Agent could have created it infinite, since power and action are in him but one? For he is immutable, there is no contingency in his action or in his power, but from his determined and assured power there immutably do follow determined and assured results. Wherefore he cannot be other than what he is, nor can he be that which he is not, nor achieve that for which he hath no power, otherwise than as he willeth, and he necessarily cannot do other than he doth, since power without action appertaineth only to those things which are mutable.

FRAC. Certainly that which never was nor is, nor shall be, can neither exist nor be patient of power. If indeed the Prime Efficient Cause is unable to will save as he doth will, then is he unable to do other than as he doth. Nor can I understand what some mean when they speak of infinite active power to which correspondeth no infinite passive power, and aver that that Power doth create finite unity which could create

---

[27] Cf. Cusanus, *De docta ignorantia,* II, 3: "Deus est omnia complicans in hoc quod omnia in eo: est omnia explicans in hoc quod ipse in omnibus." And II, 4: "Igitur quae in primo libro de absoluto maximo nobis nota facta sunt. . . . Deus est absoluta maximitas atque unitas absoluta . . ." (quoted in full by Gentile, *Op. ital.,* I, 298-99).

innumerable beings in infinite immensity; for his action is determined by necessity, since it doth proceed from that will supremely immutable, wherein immutability and necessity are thus but one and the same. Wherefore we perceive the complete identity of liberty, free will and necessity and, moreover, we recognize that action and will, potentiality and being are but one.

PHIL. You agree and you speak right well. We have then to admit one or other of the two following propositions. EITHER Efficient Cause, since from him there can follow an infinite result, must be recognized as the cause and origin of the infinite universe which containeth innumerable worlds, whence there ariseth no inconvenience but all is in convenient harmony with science, with the law and with Faith. OR on the Efficient Cause there dependeth a finite universe with a determined number of worlds, which are the stars, wherefore this Efficient Cause must be recognized as endowed with a finite and determined active power, conformable to finite and determined action, for the quality of the action followeth that of both will and power.

FRAC. I complete and set forth a pair of syllogisms as follows: Had the First Efficient Cause willed to do other than in fact he willeth, then he could have done other than he doth; but (in fact) he cannot will to do other than he doth will to do. Therefore he cannot do other than he doth. Therefore he who affirmeth a finite result affirmeth also a finite action and finite power. Moreover (though it amounteth to the same), the Prime Efficient Cause can do naught but what he willeth to do, he willeth but what he doth, therefore he can do naught but what he doth. Wherefore he who denieth infinite result denieth also infinite power.

PHIL. These syllogisms if not simple are demonstrable. Nevertheless I praise some worthy theologians who accept them not. For considering the matter carefully, they know that rude and ignorant folk come to be unable to conceive how, under this necessity, free will and dignity or the rewards of justice can survive. Wherefore, confident or desperate under an irrevocable fate, they become inevitably very wicked. Thus sometimes certain corrupters of laws, faith and religion, wishing to appear wise, have infected with their views many peoples, rendering them more barbarous and wicked than they were before, despising good works, doing and confirmed in every vice and ribaldry on account of the conclusions which they draw from such premises.[28] Albeit to express to the wise a contrary opinion is not so scandalous nor derogatory to the divine greatness and excellence; but rather that which is true is pernicious to civil conversation and contrary to the object of laws not because it is true but because it is ill understood, both by those who use it maliciously and by those who are not fitted to hear it without wreck of their good habits.

FRAC. True. There hath never been found a learned and worthy philosopher who, under any kind of pretext, hath wished to deduce from such a proposition the necessity of human action and thus to destroy free will. Thus, Plato and Aristotle among others, in postulating the necessity and immutability of God, posit no less the moral liberty and power of our free will, for they know well and understand how compatible are that necessity and that free will. Wherefore some true fathers and pastors of the people perhaps deny this and similar opinions, that they may not provide opportunity for sinners and seducers hostile to decency and to the general weal, to draw harmful conclusions, and to abuse the simplicity and ignorance of those who can grasp the truth but hardly, and are but too readily inclined to evil. And such fathers and pastors will readily condone in us the expression of true propositions from which we have no wish to deduce aught but the truth concerning Nature and the excellence of her Author, such propositions not being propounded by us to the ignorant but only to the wise who can penetrate the true meaning of our discourses. This is why theologians no less learned than religious have never opposed the liberty of philosophers, while the true philosophers of civil worth and of good custom have ever fostered religions. For both sides know that faith is required for the rule[29] of the rude populace who must be

[28] Gentile remarks that at the Venice trial Bruno declared: "I have always maintained the need of works as well as faith." See Gentile, *Op. ital.*, I, 301, for other writings on this point.

[29] *Institutione,* i.e., legal constitution (corresponding to Machiavelli's *ordine*).

governed, while demonstration is for the contemplative who know how to govern themselves and others.

ELP. Enough of this protestation; return now to the proposition.

THEO. To come then to the discovery of that which we seek. I say that if in the first efficient Cause there be infinite power, there is also action from which there resulteth a universe of infinite size and worlds infinite in number.

ELP. What you say is very persuasive if not true. But this I will declare to be true, since it appeareth to me most probable, if you can resolve for me one important argument which forced Aristotle to deny intensive infinite divine power, though he admitted it in extension. And the reason of his denial was that as in God power and action are the same, therefore if he could move infinitely, then he would move infinitely and with infinite vigour; and if this were true he would see the heaven moved instantaneously, for if a stronger force moveth with greater speed, then an immensely strong force would move with immense speed, and infinite force [must] move instantaneously. The reason on the other hand for Aristotle's consent [as to infinite divine power in extension] was that God moveth the *primum mobile* with eternal regularity according to that law and rhythm whereby it moveth.[30] Thou seest therefore that by this reasoning Aristotle doth attribute to God extensive infinity but not absolute intensive infinity withal, whence I would conclude that as his infinite motive power is constrained to motive action in conformity with finite speed, so also the same power of creating the immense and the innumerable is limited by his own will to the finite and numerable. Some theologians have argued almost in the same way, since besides admitting infinity in extension, whereby God conveyeth perpetual motion to the universe, they require also intensive infinity with which he can create and move innumerable worlds, and cause each of them and all at once to move instantaneously; nevertheless God hath thus limited by his will the number of the innumerable multitude of worlds, and also the quality of utterly intensive motion. And as this motion, which proceedeth indeed from infinite

[30] For this last thesis only, cf. *Metaphysica,* XII, 7, 1072a 22-25.

power (nothing interfering), is recognized as finite, so also the number of worlds may easily be believed to be determinate.

THEO. This argument indeed is more persuasive and plausible than the other, with regard to which enough hath been said, since it asserteth that the divine will doth regulate, moderate, and limit the divine power. Whence there follow innumerable inconveniences at least to the philosopher, leaving aside theological principles which, however, by no means admit that divine power exceedeth divine will and goodness, or generally that one attribute consorteth more than another with the nature of divinity.

ELP. Then why do they speak in this fashion if such is not their meaning?

THEO. Through inadequacy both in stating and in solving these problems.

ELP. You then, who have certain principles with which you affirm one point, namely, that the divine power is infinite both intensively and extensively; and that action cannot be distinguished from power; that therefore the universe is infinite and the worlds innumerable (nor do you deny the further point that each of the stars or orbs—as thou art pleased to say—is moved within time and not instantaneously), shew me, with what statements and reasonings you can achieve salvation for your own views or deny those of others, who judge in contrary fashion from yourself.

THEO. For the solution that you seek you must realize FIRSTLY, that since the universe is infinite and immobile, there is no need to seek the motive power thereof. SECONDLY, the worlds contained therein such as earths, fires and other species of body named stars are infinite in number, and all move by the internal principle which is their own soul, as we have shewn elsewhere;[31] wherefore it is vain to persist in seeking an extrinsic cause of their motion. THIRDLY, these worlds move in the ethereal regions and are not fixed or nailed down on to any body, any more than is our earth, which is one of them. And we prove that this earth doth from innate animal instinct, circle around her own centre in diverse

[31] *La cena de le ceneri,* Dial. III, 4th Proposition of Nundinio (Lagarde, *Op. ital.*, I, 163, l. 18; Gentile, *Op. ital.*, I, 82-83) and *infra.*

fashion and around the sun. These matters having been thus declared, we are not, according to our principles, obliged to demonstrate either active or passive motion arising from infinite intensive force, for the moving body, as also the motor power, is infinite; moving soul and moved body meet in a finite subject, that is, in each of the aforesaid stars which are worlds. So that the Prime Origin is not that which moveth; but itself still and immobile, it giveth the power to generate their own motion to an infinity of worlds,[32] great and small animals placed in the vast space of the universe, each with a pattern of mobility, of motion and of other accidents, conditioned by its own nature.

ELP. Your position is well fortified; nevertheless you have not overthrown the structure of contrary opinions which have all as their glorious and presupposed foundation that the Best and Greatest doth move the whole. Thou sayest that it accordeth the power of moving itself to the whole which moveth itself, wherefore motion taketh place according to the power of the nearest motive force. Certainly, this saying of thine appeareth to me most reasonable and more rather than less convenient than the usual opinion. Nevertheless, as regards that which you are wont to say concerning the soul of the world and concerning the divine essence which is all in all, filleth all, and is more intrinsically pervasive of things than is their very own essence, because it is the essence of essences, the life of lives, the soul of souls, it doth none the less appear to me that we may say that he moveth all things rather than that he bestoweth on all things the power to move themselves. Whence the doubt already introduced appeareth to be well founded.

THEO. And in this I can easily satisfy you. I declare that there are to be observed (if you will) within things two active principles of motion: the one finite according to the nature of the finite subject, and this moveth within time; the other infinite, according to the nature of the soul of the world or indeed of Divinity which is as the soul of the soul which is all in all, and it createth the soul, all in all, and this doth move instantaneously. The earth then hath two motions just as all bodies which move themselves have two principles of motion. Of these the infinite

---

[32] *Infiniti et innumerabili mondi*. Cf. p. 235, n. 8.

principle is that which simultaneously moveth and hath moved, whereof according to that reasoning the mobile body is no less utterly stable than utterly mobile. This is clear in the present figure wherein is represented the earth which doth experience instantaneous motion, inasmuch as she is impelled by innate motive power of infinite force. The earth moveth herself so that her centre is transferred from A to E and turneth again from E to A, this all in a single instant.[33]

[*Diagram I*]

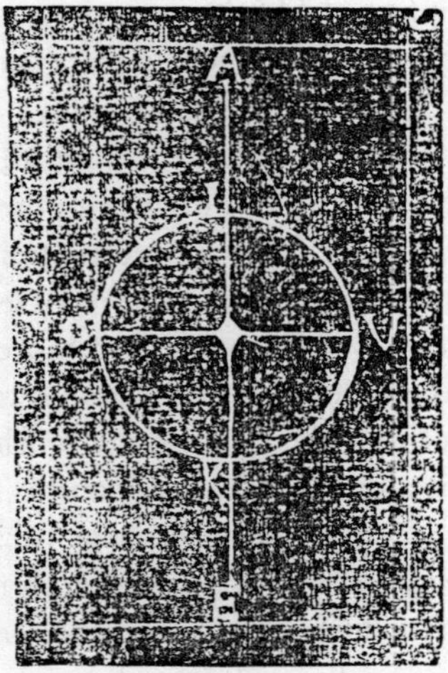

Thus at the very same moment the earth is in A and in E and in all the intermediate positions; moreover, at one and the same moment she hath

[33] The above diagram is used by Bruno also in *La cena de le ceneri,* Dial. V, p. 123 (Lagarde, *Op. ital.,* I, 195; Gentile, *Op. ital.,* I, 127), where he is describing how the four different sorts of terrestrial motion are fused into a single composite motion. This composite motion comprises, of course, the result of "the other active principle of motion . . . within time and in a certain succession." The reader must not be confused by the coincidence that the directions of the first two of Bruno's terrestrial motive impulses derived from an infinite cause (and therefore leading to instantaneous motion which is *indistinguishable from stillness*) exactly correspond with the first two of the four *recognizable* terrestrial motions whose source is intrinsic to the finite earth. The philosophic implications of the last sentence of Theophilus are discussed in Chap. 3 *e.*

departed and hath returned; and since this is always the case, it doth follow that the earth is always utterly stable. Similarly as regards the motion thereof around her centre, where the East thereof is at I, the South at V, the West at K and the North thereof at O. Each of these points revolveth by virtue of an infinite impulse, whereof each hath at the same moment started and returned; consequently each is for ever fixed and remaineth where it was. So that in conclusion, we see that for these bodies to be moved by infinite force amounteth to the same thing as though they were not moved, since instantaneous motion and stillness are one and the same thing. There remaineth then the other active principle of motion which is the result of intrinsic quality, and consequently is within time and in a certain succession. And this motion is distinct from immobility. Thus it is that we can say that God moveth all; and thus should we understand that He giveth the power of self-motion to all which moveth.

ELP. Now that thou hast in such exalted and efficacious manner removed and resolved for me this difficulty, I yield fully to your judgement. I hope moreover always to receive from you similar solutions, for though I have practised and attempted but little hitherto, I have yet received and understood a good deal. And I hope for great further benefit, for though I still do not fully see your meaning, from the ray which is diffused I apprehend that behind it is held either a sun or a yet greater luminary; and from to-day on it will be not with the hope of surpassing your ability, but with the object of affording occasion for your explanations that I will return to discourse with you, if you will deign to meet here at the same hour for as many days as may suffice for me to hear and understand as much as may fully quiet my mind.

PHIL. This I will do.

FRAC. I shall be very grateful and we shall be most attentive listeners to you.

BUR. And I, albeit understanding little, if I do not comprehend the ideas I shall hearken to the words; if I do not hearken to the words, I shall hear the voice. Farewell.

End of the First Dialogue.

SECOND DIALOGUE

PHIL. For as much as the Primal Origin is utterly simple, therefore if he were finite according to one attribute he would be finite according to all attributes. Or at least, if he were finite according to a certain intrinsic law of his nature and infinite according to another, we should inevitably regard him as composite. If then he is the active power of the universe, he certainly is infinite power, and produceth infinite effect; effect I say, inasmuch as all is dependent on him. Furthermore, as our imagination proceedeth easily to the infinite, and conceiveth dimensional size ever greater, and number beyond number according to a certain succession and "power" as it is called, so also we should understand that God actually conceiveth infinite dimension and infinite number; and from this conception there followeth the possibility and convenience and opportunity which we posit, namely that as [his] active power is infinite, so also as a necessary result, the subject thereof is infinite. For, as we have shewn on other occasions,[1] the power to create doth imply a power [that a subject] be created; that which may be measured implieth that which can be measured; the measurer implieth the measured. Moreover just as there do verily exist finite dimensional bodies, so also Prime Intellect conceiveth body and dimension; if he conceiveth this, he no less conceiveth it infinite; and if he conceiveth it infinite and conceiveth the body infinite, then such an infinite body must be intelligible, and being the product of the divine Intelligence it is most real; real indeed in such a sense that it hath a more necessary being than that which is actually sensible to our eyes. Whence it happeneth (if thou considerest well) that even as there is in truth one infinite and utterly simple individual entity, so also there is an immense dimensional infinite within that other, and within which is that other, in the same fashion as he is within all things and all things are within him. Moreover, if we perceive that a body hath corporeal quality whereby it hath power to increase itself to infinity, as

---

[1] Cf. *De la causa, principio e uno,* Dial. III (Gentile, *Op. ital.,* I, 218; Lagarde, *Op. ital.,* I, 247, l. 12; also 257, l. 24).

may be seen in a fire which, as everyone will agree, would increase infinitely if sufficient consumable material came within reach; what argument will then maintain that the fire which can be infinite and can exist (and therefore can be created infinite) cannot actually exist infinite? Certainly I know not how we can feign that there is in matter somewhat of passive power that doth not exist in the Efficient Cause as active power, consequently also as action, the very same action. Certainly the statement that infinity existeth potentially [2] and in certain [conceivable] succession, but not in action, inevitably implieth that active power can posit the infinite in successive action but not in completed action, because the infinite can never be completed; whence it would follow that the Prime Cause hath not a single simple active and absolute power, but hath one active power to which correspondeth infinite successive potentiality, and another to which correspondeth potentiality indistinguishable from action. I do not here emphasize that if we regard the world as bounded and since it is impossible to imagine a corporeal object whose circumference is bounded by an incorporeal object, this world would have the quality and power of self-destruction and self-annihilation: for, so far as we understand, all bodies are dissoluble. I say that I will not remind you that no argument would then deny that the empty infinite (even though we cannot conceive it as endowed with active power) would on occasion absorb this world into non-existence. Nor will I point out that Position, Space and the Void, if not identical with matter, have a resemblance thereto, as it would seem is sometimes maintained perhaps not without reason, by Plato [3] and by all those who define position as a certain space. Now if matter hath an appetite which should not exist in vain, since such appetite is according to nature and proceedeth from the order of primal nature, it followeth that Position, Space and the Void have also such an appetite. I leave aside the fact indicated above that none of those who aver that the world is bounded can, having affirmed the boundary thereof, invent any way how this may be; and at the same time some of

---

[2] *In potenza.* We have found it most convenient to translate *potenza* usually as "power"; *lo infinito é potenza* might be translated "the infinite hath power to exist." For "potentiality" Bruno uses generally *possibilita.*

[3] *Timaeus,* 52 A.

them while denying in their propositions and in words the void and empty, nevertheless as they proceed and in fact come inevitably to posit them. If there is an emptiness and a void, then it certainly hath containing power, and this can in no way be denied; since the same argument as maintaineth it to be impossible that in the space wherein is our world there is also at the same time contained another world, this same argument must maintain that in the space beyond our world or in that Nullity (for so Aristotle nameth that which he doth not wish to call the Void)[4] it is possible that such another world may be contained. The reason that he asserteth that two bodies cannot occupy the same space is the incompatibility of the dimensional volumes of the two bodies;[5] it followeth then, in so far as this argument doth require, that where the dimensional volume of the one is not, there the dimensional volume of the other can be. If there existeth this possibility, then space is in a certain sense matter; if it is matter it hath quality, if it hath quality, by what argument can we deny it action?

ELP. Very good. But prithee proceed further. Make clear to me wherein you distinguish between the world[6] and universe.

PHIL. The difference is well known except to the Peripatetic School. The Stoics distinguish between world and universe in that the world is all that which is filled and doth constitute a solid body; the universe is not merely the world but also the void, the empty space beyond the world; and therefore they call the world finite but the universe infinite. Epicurus similarly nameth the whole and the universe a mixture of bodies and of the void; and in this universe and in the capacity thereof to contain the void and the empty, and furthermore in the multitude of the bodies contained therein he maintaineth that the nature of the world,[7]

---

[4] *Physica,* IV, 8, 214b.

[5] *Incompossibilita delle dimensioni di uno et un' altro corpo,* i.e., the impossibility of the simultaneous occupation of an identical position by the separate volumes of the two bodies. Cf. *Physica,* 6, 213 b. This is in fact cited by Aristotle as part of an impartial survey of arguments for and against the Void. It is only after this survey that Aristotle determines against the existence of the Void.

[6] *Mondo.*

[7] World (*mondo*) here would seem a slip for universe.

which is infinite, doth exist.[8] We do not call aught Void as being mere nullity, but rather accept the view whereby that which is not corporeal nor doth offer sensible resistance is wont, if it hath dimension,[9] to be named Void, since we do not usually understand as corporeal that which hath not the property of offering resistance; whence they say that just as that is not flesh which is not vulnerable, so that which doth not offer resistance is not corporeal. In the same way we name infinite that which is an immense ethereal region in which are innumerable and infinite [numbers of] bodies such as the earth, the moon, and the sun, and these are called by us worlds, composed of Plenum and of Void: for this spirit, this air, this ether not only surroundeth these bodies but also penetrateth within them and becometh inherent in everything. Furthermore we speak of the Void according to the view with which we replied to his enquiry, where is the infinite ether and its worlds? [10] We replied, it is in an infinite space, a bosom in which the whole hath his being and is harmoniously conceived. Nor is it possible that the whole should exist or be conceived in any other space soever. Now Aristotle here confusedly giveth these two meanings to the Void, and a third one too he doth feign, which he himself is unable either to name or to define, while he seeketh in debate to deny the Void, and thinketh with this same line of argument to defeat completely all opinions concerning the Void, which, however, he no more doth than as if, having banished the name of a thing, anyone were to imagine the thing itself banished; for he destroyeth the Void if at all by destroying that argument which perhaps no one hath supported, since the ancients like ourselves regarded the Void as

---

[8] Epicurus, *Epistle to Herodotus* and Fragment 13 from *On Nature,* Book I, trans. C. Bailey in *Extant Remains of Epicurus* (Oxford, 1926); Ep. I, 40, p. 23, and Fragment 7, Bk. I, p. 125. Cf. also Lucretius, I, 420, etc. Dr. Bailey points out that the main source for the extant works of Epicurus is the *Life* in Diogenes Laertius, Bk. X. This work could have reached Bruno (the Latin translation appeared at Venice, 1475, and in numerous other editions); but his source is probably Lucretius.

[9] i.e., measurable volume. Cf. Lagarde, *Op. ital.,* I, 322, l. 18.

[10] Cf. p. 316, n. 15, and p. 372, n. 38. For a detailed discussion as to what and where is Space, cf. *Physica,* IV, 2 *seqq.,* 209a *seqq.;* similar arguments are then applied to the problem of the Void. Cf. also *Physica* IV, 8, 214b *seqq.*

that in which a body may have its being, that which hath containing power and doth contain atoms and bodies. Aristotle is alone in defining the Void as that which is nullity, within which is nullity and which can be naught save nullity. Giving to the Void a name and meaning accepted by none else, he raiseth castles in the air, and destroyeth his own Void, but not the Void discussed by all others who have used the term.

Nor doth this sophist act differently in discussing other propositions, such as those concerning motion, the infinite, matter, form, demonstration, being; for he buildeth always on the faith of his own definitions, and names used with a new meaning. Wherefore everyone not entirely bereft of judgment can easily convince himself how superficial is this man's consideration of the nature of things, how attached to his own suppositions which are neither accepted nor worthy of acceptance and are too vain in the domain of natural philosophy for them ever to succeed in feigning the realm of mathematics.

And you will see that Aristotle so gloried in his complacent vanity that even as regards the consideration of Nature, he aspired to be regarded as a ratiocinator or (as we may say) logician, and that by way of abuse he dubs as "natural philosophers"[11] those who have been most solicitous in the study of nature, reality and truth. Well, to pass to ourselves: since in his book on the Void[12] he sayeth naught which can justly mili-

[11] *Physici.* Florio gives *phisica* "art of natural philosophy"; *phisico* "understander or teacher of the causes of natural things, a physician." In several passages Aristotle points out the errors of the early natural philosophers, the φυσιολόγοι. Cf. *Metaphys.*, I, 5, 986b 14; I, 8, 989b 29; *De anima,* I, 2, 426a 20. Or perhaps Bruno's reference is to *Physica,* III, p, 203a 16: οἱ δὲ περὶ φύσεως ("those who study nature") or, as in Gaye and Hardie (*The Works of Aristotle* [Oxford, 1930] Vol. II): "The physicists, on the other hand, all of them, always regard the infinite as an attribute of a substance which is different from it and belongs to the class of the so-called elements—water or air or what is intermediate between them." Gaye and Hardie also render οἱ φυσιολόγοι by "physicists." In *De coelo,* I, 3, 271b Aristotle opens his discussion with the phrase: "Is there an infinite body as the majority of the ancient philosophers thought?" (ὥσπερ οἱ πλεῖστοι τῶν ἀρχαίων φιλοσόφων ᾠήθησαν). In *De part, animal.*, I, 1, 639a 39 *seqq.* he distinguishes the "mode of necessity and the mode of ratiocination" of natural science (τῆς φυσικῆς) from those in the theoretical sciences. It was not Aristotle but the mediaeval Aristotelians who envinced contempt for the study of nature.

[12] i.e., *Physica,* IV, 6-9.

tate either directly or indirectly against our belief, we will leave him where he is, returning to him perhaps on another more leisurely occasion. So, if it please thee, Elpino, do thou formulate and arrange those reasonings which persuade our adversaries against the infinite body; and after, bring forward the reasons which prevent their understanding that worlds are without number.

ELP. I will do so. I will relate the opinions of Aristotle in order, and you will express such comments as occur to you.[13] We have to consider, saith Aristotle, whether there existeth an infinite body as some ancient philosophers have averred, or whether this be impossible; further we have to consider whether there be one world or more. Most important is the resolution of these questions, for the acceptance of either of the opposed solutions is of such consequence as to give rise to one of two entirely opposed and contrary philosophies. Thus for example, we see that those who have posited discontinuous parts have by this fundamental error so barred their own progress that they have gone astray in a great part of mathematics.[14] We are therefore unravelling a subject most important for [the avoidance of] past, present and future difficulties, since, however small an error may be in origin, it becometh by ten thousand repetitions ever greater, just as the smallest error of direction in the beginning of a path, becometh greater and greater the further the distance we traverse, so that finally an exactly opposite goal is reached to that which was proposed. The reason is that beginnings are small in size though very great in influence. That is the reasoning for the solution of this doubt.

PHIL. All that he saith is most necessary and should be proclaimed no less by others. For even as he believeth that from a wrong under-

---

[13] The infinite is considered in the *Physica,* III, 4-8, 202b 30–208a 25. Aristotle accepts infinite divisibility and concludes that Time, movement and thinking are infinite, though "to rely on mere thinking is absurd, for then the excess or defect is not in the thing but in the thought": and "Magnitude is not infinite either in the way of reduction or of magnification in thought." In the following passages, however, to the end of Dial. II, Elpino's arguments are from *De coelo,* I, 5-7.

[14] *De coelo* I, 5, 271b 11. Aristotle says: "If you admit a minimum magnitude you will find that the minimum which you have introduced, small as it is, causes the greatest truths of mathematics to totter." Cf. p. 363, n. 27.

standing of this original point his adversaries have been led to great errors, so we on the contrary believe and see clearly that by the opposite opinion concerning this prime matter, he hath perverted all natural reason.

ELP. He goeth on: We must then enquire whether there can be a simple body of infinite size.[15] And firstly this must be shewn to be impossible in that prime body whose motion is circular. Afterwards the same must be shewn of other bodies; for every body being either simple or compound, this which is compound will follow the disposition of that which is simple. If then simple bodies are not infinite either in number or size, then it followeth necessarily that neither can a composite body have these properties.

PHIL. His argument promiseth well, for if he can prove that the body called the containing and prime body is indeed the containing first body and is finite, it becometh superfluous and vain to prove it afterwards of the contained bodies.

ELP. Now he proveth that a round body is not infinite.[16] For if a round body be infinite, the radii from the centre thereof will be infinite, and the distance will be infinite between one radius and another—the further they extend from the centre the greater will be the distance between them. For by the lengthening of the lines there necessarily resulteth a greater distance [between them], wherefore if the lines are infinite in length the distance between them will also be infinite. Now it is impossible that a body in motion can [completely] traverse infinite distance; and in circular motion one radius of the moving body must come in turn to occupy the position previously held by every other radius.[17]

PHIL. This reasoning is good but it answereth not his adversaries. For never hath one been found so barbarous and so ignorant[18] as to have posited the infinite world, infinite in size, and to have attributed motion to it. And he sheweth himself forgetful of that which he relateth

---

[15] *De coelo* I, 5 *seqq.*, 271b 7 *seqq.*

[16] *Ibid.*, I, 5 *seqq.*, 271b 26–272a 27.

[17] *Ibid.*, I, 5, 271b 28. The point is that this could never happen if the distance between radii were infinite.

[18] *Si rozzo e d'ingegno si grosso,* i.e., "of so coarse a grain" (*ingegno* can be either "nature" or "skill").

in his *Physica;*[19] that those who postulated a single being, one infinite origin, have similarly regarded it as immobile. Neither he nor any other person among his supporters can name a single philosopher or indeed any simple man who hath attributed motion to infinite size.

But like a sophist he taketh one part of his argument from the conclusion of his adversary; positing his own principle that the universe is mobile, also that it moveth and that it is of spherical form. Now observe whether, among the reasonings adduced by this beggar there is even one that doth militate against the belief of those who proclaim an infinite, motionless and formless immense universe, containing innumerable moving bodies which are the worlds, by some called stars, by others spheres. Just note in this and in other reasonings whether the premises that Aristotle adduced have been accepted by anyone.

ELP. Certainly, all the six arguments are based on that presupposition, namely that his adversary asserteth the universe to be infinite and that he himself attributeth motion to this infinite body. Certainly this is foolish and absurd, even if we did not desire to accept the identification of motion and infinite stillness, which thou didst prove to me yesterday of individual worlds.

PHIL. I do not assert this of the universe, to which by no reasoning should motion be attributed, for this is impossible; nor can, nor should motion appertain or be attributed to the infinite. Nor, as I have said before, hath anyone ever imagined such a thing. But this philosopher, as one who lacketh soil, raiseth his castles in the air.

---

19 "Melissus indeed infers from these considerations that the All is immovable" (*Physica,* IV, 6, 213b 12). "Even if it is really the case as certain persons assert that the existent is infinite and motionless, it certainly does not appear to be so if we follow sense-perception" (*Physica,* VIII, 3, 254a 25). Hardie and Gaye point out that this passage refers to Melissus. Again, "some of the ancient [philosophers] thought that *what is* must necessarily be one and immovable" (*De gen. et corr.,* I, 8, 325a). Several times in the *Physica* Aristotle himself expresses the view of a Supreme motionless motivator: "It is not possible for that which has no parts to be in motion or to change in any way" (*Physica,* VI, 10, 240b 30). Again, "It is reasonable, therefore, not to say necessary, to suppose the existence of the third term also, that which causes motion but is itself unmoved. So too Anaxagoras is right when he says that Mind is impressive and unmined, since he makes it the principle of Motion" (*Physica,* VIII, 5, 256b 24 *seqq.*).

ELP. Certainly I should desire a reason which would impugn what you say, for five other reasons adduced by this philosopher all take the same road and march in step. It therefore seemeth to me superfluous to repeat them. After he hath produced these which concern a circular motion of the world, he propoundeth reasons based on motion in a straight line; and he declareth it to be equally impossible that anything can be endowed with infinite motion toward the centre [of the world] or downward, and also upward from the centre; and his demonstration concerneth firstly the proper motion of such bodies, as well of those in an outer as of those in an intermediate position. Motion upward, he saith, and motion downward, are opposed; and the site of the one motion is opposed to that of the other.[20] Of these contraries, again, if one is determined, so must the other be, and the intermediate, which participateth in the properties of both determinates, must even be as they. For that which should pass beyond the centre must start not from anywhere you please but from a certain position, for the limits of the centre must be within two boundaries, a beginning and an end.[21] Since then the centre is determined, the extremes thereof must needs also be determined; and if the extremes are determined, so must be also the centre; and if these positions in space are determined, so must be the bodies that occupy them, for otherwise motion would be infinite.

And as for weight and lightness, the body which travelleth upward can reach the body which is situate there, for no natural motion is in vain. Now since in an infinite world (*mondo*) there is no space, neither is there within it position, nor an infinite body. Again, as regards weight: there is no infinite weight or lightness, therefore there is no infinite body. For if a heavy body be infinite, then the weight thereof would of necessity be infinite, and from this reasoning there is no escape. For if thou wouldst say that an infinite body hath infinite weight, three awkward consequences would ensue. FIRST, the weight or lightness of a finite body would be identical respectively with the weight or lightness of an infinite body. For I shall add to or subtract from a finite heavy body as

[20] *De coelo,* I, 5, 6, 271b 26–273a 22.

[21] *Lit.,* "for the limits of the centre must have a certain boundary where they begin and another where they end."

much as the difference of the weight thereof from that of the infinite body until the finite body hath attained the same quantity of weight or of lightness as the infinite body.

SECONDLY, the weight of a body of finite size might be greater than that of infinity.[22] For the same reasoning whereby the finite body may be equal in weight to the infinite sheweth also that the weight of the finite body may exceed that of the infinite by the addition to the finite body of as much as you please of weighty body; or [the proportion may be changed by] subtracting part from it, or if you please, by adding to it a piece of lighter body.

THIRDLY, the weight of a body of finite size and that of a body of infinite size would be identical [as shewn above]. And [furthermore] because the proportion of weight to weight is identical with the proportion of speed to speed, therefore it would follow similarly that speed or slowness of a finite body could be identical with speed or slowness respectively of an infinite body.

FOURTHLY, the speed of a finite body could be greater than that of the infinite.

FIFTHLY, the respective speeds could be equal. Or, indeed, even as weight may exceed weight, so speed would exceed speed: if the body have infinite weight, it will need to move through a certain space in less time than finite weight would take, or else it will move not at all, since speed and slowness depend on the size of the body. Wherefore, there being no proportion between finite and infinite, it will ultimately ensue that infinite weight will be immobile. For if it hath motion, it moveth not with a speed so great as to exceed that of any conceivable finite weight[23] traversing the same space.

PHIL. It would be impossible to find another person who in the name of philosophy could invent vainer suppositions and fabricate such foolish and contrary reasons to accommodate such levity as is discernible in his arguments. As for what he saith concerning the spaces occupied by bodies, and of the determinate upper, lower, and intermediate, I would

---

22 *De coelo,* I, 6, 273a 22–274a 18.

23 *Lit.,* "so great that there existeth not a finite weight which in the same time will achieve the same progress traversing the same space."

like to know against what opinion he is arguing. For all who posit a body of infinite size, ascribe to it neither centre nor boundary. For he who speaketh of emptiness, the void, or the infinite ether, ascribeth to it neither weight nor lightness, nor motion, nor upper, nor lower, nor intermediate regions; assuming moreover that there are in this space those countless bodies such as our earth and other earths, our sun and other suns, which all revolve within this infinite space, through finite and determined spaces or around their own centres. Thus we on earth say that the earth is in the centre; and all philosophers ancient and modern of whatever sect will proclaim without prejudice to their own principles that here is indeed the centre; just as we say that we are as it were at the centre of that [universally] equidistant circle which is the great horizon and the limit of our own encircling ethereal region, so without doubt those who inhabit the moon believe themselves to be at the centre [of a great horizon] that encircleth this earth, the sun and the other stars, and that is the boundary of the radii of their own horizon.[24] Thus the earth no more than any other world is at the centre; and no points constitute definite determined poles of space for our earth, just as she herself is not a definite and determined pole to any other point of the ether, or of the world space; and the same is true of all other bodies. From various points of view these may all be regarded either as centres, or as points on the circumference, as poles, or zeniths and so forth. Thus the earth is not in the centre of the universe; it is central only to our own surrounding space.

This disputant then hath proceeded by *petition principii,* first accepting that which he would prove. He beginneth, I say, by assuming the contrary of his opponent's views, assuming indeed a centre and a limit against those who, declaring the world (*mondo*) to be infinite, thereby necessarily deny limit and centre, and consequently deny motion either upward to the highest point or downward to the lowest depth.

The ancients indeed observed as we too observe that some things come to our earth, and some appear to depart from this earth or indeed from any place where we are; wherefore if we should wish to say that the

---

[24] This is derived from Cusanus.

motion of such things is upward or downward, it must be understood as applying only to a certain region from a certain viewpoint, so that if something receding from us proceedeth toward the moon, when we should say that it goeth upward, then the inhabitants of the moon, our own *anticephali,* would say that it is in descent. Motions then have no distinction of upward or downward, hither or thither in respect of the infinite universe; but only in respect of finite worlds which are within that universe, or according to the respective horizons of innumerable worlds, or to the number of innumerable stars. Hence it ensueth that the same thing, with the same motion, may be said to move upward and downward with respect to diverse bodies. Determinate bodies are therefore not endowed with infinite motion, but with motion finite and determined within their own limits. But the undetermined and infinite hath neither finite nor infinite motion, and knoweth no distinction of place or of time. Furthermore, as regards Aristotle's reasoning concerning heaviness and lightness, we will say [only] that this is one of the finest fruits produced by the tree of stolid ignorance. For weight, as we shall demonstrate in the appropriate place, is not situate throughout any whole body, or naturally disposed and concentrated therein; and therefore there is no distinction between the nature of one or other position in space nor of one or other species of motion. Furthermore we shall shew that heavy and light may be called the same thing directed by the same force and motion but in respect of diverse centres, just as in respect of diverse centres the same thing may be named high or low, in upward or in downward motion. And I say this in regard to individual bodies and individual worlds of which none is heavy or light; whose parts receding from them and dispersions are called light in weight, but returning to them are called heavy; just as particles of our earth and of terrestrial objects if directed toward the circumference of our ether are said to ascend and if toward the earth are said to descend.

But as for the universe and infinite body, who hath ever called it heavy or light? Or, indeed, who ever posited such premises or so raved that it was possible to infer from his statement that the infinite be heavy or light, could rise, ascend or soar? We shall demonstrate that no infinite body is either heavy or light. For these qualities belong to parts in so far as these tend toward their own whole, the place wherein they may best survive. Such qualities appertain not to the universe, but to the actual worlds wherein are contained the particles. Thus on our earth the particles of Fire seeking to escape and mount toward the sun, carry ever with them some particles both of Earth and of Water with which they are conjoined; and these becoming increased, do thus by their own natural impulse return to their own place. So it is the more certain that great bodies can by no possibility be heavy or light, the universe being infinite, nor can they have an affinity to be either distant from or close to either the circumference or the centre of the infinite universe. Wherefore the earth in her own space is no heavier than the sun in his space or than Saturn or the North Star in their own. We can, indeed, say that just as particles of the earth return to earth by the force of their weight (since we thus choose to describe the impulse of the parts toward the whole, of the wanderer toward his own place), such also is the action of the parts of other bodies; for there may be an infinite number of other earths or similar bodies, an infinite number of other suns or fires or similar bodies; and the parts of these all move from outer positions toward the bodies which contain them as toward a centre.

It would follow that there must be an infinite number of heavy bodies; nevertheless weight will not be infinite intensively in a single subject; but rather extensively in innumerable subjects. And this may be deduced from the sayings of all the ancients and ourselves; nor can our disputant produce any contrary argument. That which he asserteth of the impossibility of infinite weight, is so true and so patent that I am ashamed to mention it; and it contributeth no whit either to destroy his opponent's philosophy or to support his own. For all these arguments and words are thrown to the wind.

ELP. The vanity of the fellow's arguments is here more than obvious, so that not the whole art of persuasion would suffice to excuse it. Listen now to these arguments that he addeth to prove generally that there existeth no infinite body. "Now," saith Aristotle,[25] "it being clear to those

---

[25] *De coelo*, I, 7, 274a 30–274b 18.

who study individual cases that there is no infinite body, it remaineth to investigate whether such be a general possibility. For someone might aver that just as the world is disposed around us, so it were not impossible that there might be yet more heavens." But before we reach this problem, let us reason of the infinite universally.

Now every body must either be infinite [or finite] and if infinite it must be composed either of similar or dissimilar parts, which in turn must be either of finite or of infinite species. It is not possible that it be of infinite species if we accept our presuppositions aforesaid of other worlds similar to our own, since even as our world is disposed around us [i.e., around the Earth] so also it is disposed around other bodies; moreover there are other heavens. For if the primary motions around the centre are determined, then so also must be the secondary motions. And since we distinguish already five sorts of bodies, of which two are simply heavy or light, two moderately heavy or light, and one neither heavy nor light but active around the centre, so must there be also in the other worlds. Wherefore it is not possible that they be of infinite species. Nor yet can they comprise finite species. At the outset he proveth by FOUR arguments that they do not consist of Dissimilar Finite Species. FIRSTLY, each of these infinite parts must be Water or Fire, and must therefore be heavy or light, which hath been shewn to be impossible since heaviness or lightness cannot be infinite.

THEO. To this we have already replied adequately.

ELP. I know it: and he addeth the SECOND argument, saying that each of these species must be infinite, and must therefore occupy infinite space; it followeth that each must be endowed with infinite motion, which is impossible, for a descending body cannot fall infinitely low, as is manifest from what happeneth in all motion and transmutations. Similarly generation cannot seek to produce that which cannot be produced, nor doth local motion seek a position which can never be attained. That which cannot exist in Egypt cannot move toward Egypt, since Nature permiteth no vain process. It is therefore impossible that a body should move toward a goal that it cannot reach.

THEO. To this argument we have amply replied, and we declare that there are an infinity of earths, an infinity of suns, and an infinite ether—

or, as Democritus and Epicurus have it, an infinite Plenum and an infinite Vacuum, the one placed within the other.[26] There are, moreover, diverse finite species, one within another, and one related to another; and these diverse species concur as it were to form a single infinite universe. And again, they are as infinite parts of the infinite, inasmuch as from an infinity of earths similar to our own, there ariseth in fact *one* infinite earth, not as a single continuum but as a composite whole composed of their innumerable multitude. So also must it be understood of other species of bodies, whether four or two or three or what number you will, which I do not at present determine; since they are, in such fashion as we may use the phrase, parts of the infinite, therefore they must be infinite according to the dimension which resulteth from such multitude. Nor doth this require that the heavy body proceedeth infinitely downward. For as this heavy body seeketh the nearest or natural neighbour, so also doth that to the next, and it to the next again. This earth hath her parts which belong to her, another earth hath her own parts which belong to herself; so also the sun compriseth those parts which disperse away from him and then seek to return to him; and other bodies similarly reassemble naturally their own parts. Wherefore just as limits and distances from individual body to body are finite, so also are motions finite. And as no one setteth forth from Greece to journey to the infinite, but journeyeth rather to Italy or Egypt, so also when parts of this earth or of the sun are in motion, their goal is not infinity but is finite and determined. Nevertheless, the universe being infinite, and the bodies thereof transmutable, all are therefore constantly dispersed and constantly reassembled; they send forth their substance, and receive within themselves wandering substance. Nor doth it appear to me absurd or inconvenient, but on the contrary most fitting and natural that finite transmutations may occur to a subject; wherefore particles of [elemental] earth may wander through the ethereal region and may traverse vast space now to this body, now to that, just as we see the same particles change their position, their disposition and their form,

---

[26] Cf. *Physica,* IV, 6, 213a 12 for reference to this doctrine. In Theophilo's first sentence in this speech, we again render Bruno's adjective *infinito* by *an infinity of*. Cf. p. 235, n. 8.

even when they are yet close to us. Whence we deduce that if this earth be eternal, it is not so by virtue of the stability of any one part or individual, but through the vicissitudes of many parts, some being expelled therefrom, and their place taken by others. Thus soul and intelligence persist while the body is ever changing and renewed part by part.[27] This may be observed also in animals which survive only by absorption of nutriment and by evacuation of excrement. Whoever considereth well, will recognize that we have not in youth the same flesh as in childhood, nor in old age the same as in youth; for we suffer perpetual transmutation, whereby we receive a perpetual flow of fresh atoms, and those that we have received previously are ever leaving us. As atom joineth atom around the sperm by virtue of general intellect and soul (by means of the structure to which, as matter, they contribute), so the body attaineth form and growth when the influx of atoms exceedeth the efflux. Moreover this same body is of a certain consistency when the efflux equals the influx, and finally declineth when the efflux exceedeth the influx; but I do not speak of absolute efflux and influx, rather the efflux of what is convenient and native and the influx of what is foreign and inconvenient. This latter cannot be overcome by the original source which is weakened owing to the continuous efflux of vital as well as non-vital matter. Coming then to my point, I declare that on account of such vicissitudes, it is not inconvenient but on the contrary most reasonable to state that the parts and the atoms have an infinite course and infinite motion, owing to the infinite vicissitudes and transmutations both of form and of position. It would, indeed, be inconvenient if an object were found which tended to infinity as to a close prescribed limit of local motion or of change. This is impossible since a body is no sooner moved from one position than it findeth itself in another; no sooner is it deprived of one disposition than it hath acquired another, and no sooner hath it shed his being than it hath adopted another. This followeth necessarily from the change which is itself necessarily consequent upon local motion. So that a proximate and shaped subject cannot move except in

[27] *Lit.*, "In this way, to the same soul and intelligence, the body is ever part by part changing and being renewed."

a finite sense, for it easily changeth form if it changeth position. But the primal subject capable of form moveth infinitely through space and through an infinity of forms while the parts of the [composing] matter enter and go forth again, ever changing their position, their own parts and their containing whole. I understand perfectly.

ELP. He addeth for his THIRD argument,[28] that if the infinite were regarded as discrete and discontinuous, so that there were an infinity of separate fire particles, each of them finite, yet the fire which resulteth from all these individual particles would be infinite.

THEO. I have already admitted this and because it was known, he ought not to have opposed that which leadeth to no inconvenient conclusion. For if the body become separated and divided into distinctly located parts, of which one weigheth a hundred units, another a thousand, another ten, it will follow that the whole will weigh one thousand, one hundred and ten units. But this will be in virtue of several discrete weights and not in virtue of one continuous weight.

Now neither we nor the ancients have considered it an inconvenient hypothesis that discrete parts should meet in an infinite weight. For from these parts there resulteth logically, arithmetically or geometrically, a weight; but in truth and in nature they do not form a single infinite weight, even as they do not form a single infinite mass. But they form innumerable finite masses and finite weights. That this is stated, imagined and is the case is by no means the same as in the former hypothesis, but far different, for from this hypothesis there followeth not one infinite body of one species, but one species comprising an infinity of finite bodies. Nor, indeed, is one infinite weight made up of an infinity of finite weights, since this infinity [of finite weights] is not continuous, but is composed of discrete parts, which are in an infinite continuum which is the space, position and measurable form capable of containing the whole infinity of parts. Therefore it is by no means inconvenient that there should be this infinite number of discrete weights which do not constitute a single weight. Similarly an infinite number of drops of water do not form an infinite stretch of water, nor do an infinity of earth particles form an infinite earth, for there are bodies which, though

[28] *De coelo,* I, 7 *seqq.,* 274b 18–19.

infinite in number, yet do not physically form a single body of infinite size, and herein is the great difference; as may be seen in the same way in the hauling of a ship, which is achieved by [the co-operation of] ten persons united; nor will the ship ever be hauled even by a myriad of men not pulling together, or by each of them separately.

ELP. By this and other reasoning you have a thousand times resolved the problem posed in Aristotle's FOURTH argument, wherein is set forth that, if [the definition of] an infinite body is understood, it must necessarily be understood as infinite in every dimension, since on no side can there be aught beyond it. Wherefore it is impossible that within an infinite body there may be various dissimilar bodies, each infinite.[29]

THEO. All this is true and in no way contradicteth that which we have so many times stated, namely that there are many dissimilar finite bodies within a single infinity, and we have considered how this may be. Perhaps it may be expressed proportionately, as if one were to assert that many continuous parts form a unity, as for example in the case of a liquid mud, where throughout and in every part, water is continuous with water, earthy matter with earthy matter; wherefore, since the concourse of the atoms of earth, and the atoms of water, is beyond our sensible apprehension, these *minima* are called neither discrete nor continuous, but form a single continuum which is neither water nor earth, but is mud, while another person may as well please to state that water atom is not actually continuous with water atom, nor earth with earth, but that the water is continuous with the earth and so is the earth with the water; still a third may deny both these statements and may aver that mud only is continuous with mud. And according to these reasonings the infinite universe may be regarded as a single continuum in which discreteness is no more introduced by the interpolation of ether between the large celestial bodies than it can be within the mud by the interposition of air among the dry and the liquid particles, the difference being solely in the fineness and subtlety of the parts of the mud exceeding our sensible apprehension, as against the greatness, larger size and sensible qualities of the parts of the universe. And thus contrary and diverse mobile parts converge to constitute a

[29] *Ibid.*, I, 7 *seqq.*, 274b 19–22.

single continuous motionless body, wherein contraries converge to the constitution of a single whole, and pertain to a single order and finally form a single whole. It would certainly be both inconvenient and impossible to posit two infinites distinct from one another, since it would be impossible to conceive the dividing line between them, where the one infinity would end and the other begin; [30] wherefore each of the two would terminate within the other. Moreover it is most difficult to imagine [31] two bodies, each finite in one and infinite in the other boundary.

ELP. Aristotle giveth TWO FURTHER reasons against an infinite body composed of similar parts. THE FIRST [32] reason is that to such a body there must appertain one of these species of local motion; therefore it must either be of infinite weight or infinite lightness, or it must have an infinite circular movement; and the impossibility of all these we have already demonstrated.

THEO. And we have also made clear how vain are these discourses and arguments; and that the infinite whole moveth not, and that neither it nor, indeed, any other body occupying his own natural position is either heavy or light in itself, nor have the separate parts thereof these qualities when they have travelled a certain distance from their own regions. An infinite body then is according to our view neither potentially nor actually mobile; nor is it potentially or actually either heavy or light; so far is it from possessing infinite lightness or infinite weight in our view and in the view of others against whom the Peripatetic buildeth such fine castles.

ELP. The SECOND [33] argument is then equally vain, for from one who will never admit motion of the infinite, either potential or actual, it is vain to enquire whether the infinite moveth of its own innate nature or by impressed force.

---

[30] *Lit.*, "since there would be no way of imagining how the one would begin where the other would terminate."

[31] *Trovare.*

[32] To support the Fourth Argument. Cf. *De coelo*, I, 7 *seqq.*, 274b 22–29.

[33] Of the two arguments to support the Fourth. Cf. *De coelo*, I, 7 *seqq.* 274b 29–32.

He next proveth[34] that there is no infinite body, using arguments based on motion in general, after having reasoned from common motion. He declareth that an infinite body cannot act on a finite body, still less be patient of action by a finite body. And this he maintaineth with three arguments: FIRST[35] that the infinite cannot be patient of the finite; for all motion and consequently all impressed motion is within Time. For if it be so [i.e., if there can be action between an infinite and a finite body], and since it may happen that a smaller body may suffer action in proportion to his size; therefore it will follow that the proportion between the finite patient and the finite agent will be like to that of the finite patient to the infinite agent. This will be seen if we take the infinite body A, the finite body B, and, since all motion is within time, we will have time G, within which A either moveth or is moved [by B, Diagram II]. We will then take the smaller body B [i.e., smaller than infinity]; and the line D shall act on another body H, so that the action is completed in the same time G. Thus it will be observed that the proportion between D, the smaller [finite] agent, and B, the larger, is equal to the proportion between the finite patient H, and [some] finite part of A, viz., AZ. [D:B::H:AZ; Diagram II]. Now when we change the proportion between the first term, agent D, and the third term, patient H, so that this proportion shall equal that between the second term, agent B, and the fourth term, patient AZ, that is to say, the proportion will be the same between D and H as between B and AZ [D:H::B:AZ]—then B will in fact have taken the same time G to complete action on the finite and on the infinite, that is on AZ part of the infinite, and on A the infinite. This is IMPOSSIBLE. (See[37] p. 290.)

Therefore an infinite body cannot be either agent[36] or patient. For two equal patients will receive equal impress in the same time from the same agent; a lesser patient will receive equal impress from the same agent in less time, and a greater patient in a longer time. Moreover, when there are different agents during the same time, and their

---

[34] The Fifth Argument. Cf. *De coelo,* I, 7, 274b 33–275b 2.

[35] The First to support the Fifth.

[36] The argument concerning the Infinite as agent on a finite Patient is presented under SECONDLY and is illustrated in Diagram III.

action is completed, the proportion between agent and agent will be like to the proportion between patient and patient. Further, every agent acteth on the patient in finite Time (I speak of every agent which completeth action, not of the agent with continuous motion; and only the motion of translation can be completed); for finite action cannot take place in infinite time. Here then is the primary manifestation that the finite cannot achieve complete action on the infinite:

[*Diagram II*]

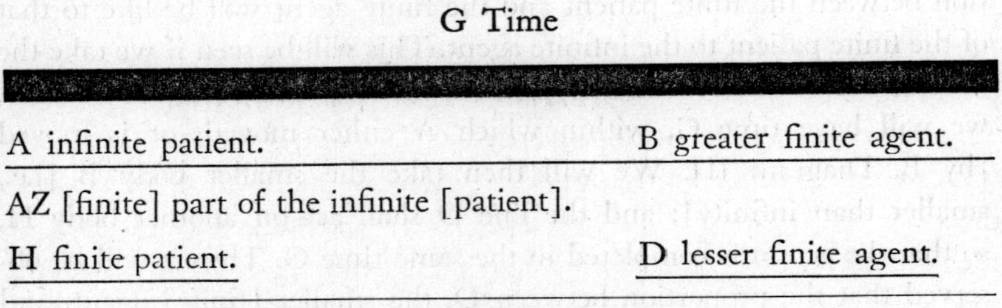

[37] The argument may be expressed thus (see Diagram II):

Given that A is moved by B in time G (I)

and that H is moved by D in time G (II)

and that $\frac{D}{B} = \frac{H}{AZ}$ (III)

From (III) therefore $\frac{D}{H} = \frac{B}{AZ}$

or D:H::B:AZ (IV)

Now from (II) H is moved by D in time G.

Therefore from (IV) AZ is moved by B in time G.

But from (I) A is moved by B in time G.

Therefore B completes action on the infinite A and on the finite part thereof AZ each in the same time G, which is IMPOSSIBLE.

The argument is illustrated by Diagram II.

Cf. *De coelo,* I, 7, 274b 33–275a 13.

In one respect, Bruno's Diagram is altered here. It is his convention to write the line AZ thus:

A . part of the infinite . Z.

To us, this is confusing and suggests that Z is an infinite. I have therefore followed the modern convention, and have given in the Diagram first the name AZ and then its description. The words in brackets are added to the Diagram to make the meaning clearer.

SECONDLY,[38] it is shewn in the same way that the infinite cannot act on the finite. For let there be an infinite agent A and a finite patient B and let A act on B, in finite time G; and let the finite body D act on BZ part of B, in the same time G. [And let H be a finite agent larger than D such that] the proportion between the patient BZ and the whole [finite] patient B is like to the proportion between the [finite] agent D and the other finite agent H [BZ:B::D:H; Diagram III]; and if the proportion between the agent D and the patient BZ be changed to correspond to the proportion between the agent H and the whole patient B [D:BZ::H:B], then B will be moved by H in the same time during which BZ hath been moved by D, that is in time G, within which time, however, B hath been moved by the infinite agent A. And this is IMPOSSIBLE.[39] This impossibility followeth from that which we have said—that if an infinite object act in finite time, the action cannot be in time, because there is no proportional relationship between finite and infinite. If then we take two diverse [finite] agents, which exert the same force on the same patient, the action of these two will necessarily occupy two different periods of time; and there will be between the times a relationship proportionate to that between the agents. But if we posit that two

[38] Secondly to support the Fifth Argument.

[39] The argument may be expressed thus:

Given that A moves B in time G (I)

and that D moves BZ in time G (II)

and that $\frac{BZ}{B} = \frac{D}{H}$ (III)

From (III), therefore $\frac{BZ}{D} = \frac{B}{H}$

or BZ:D::B:H (IV)

Now from (II), BZ is moved by D in time G.

From (IV), therefore B is moved by H in time G.

But from (I), B is moved by A in time G.

Therefore B is completely moved by the finite H and by the infinite A in the same time G.

Which is IMPOSSIBLE.

The argument is illustrated by Diagram III.

Cf. *De coelo*, I, 7, 275a 13–22.

In Diagram III again BZ is so named, though Bruno has:

B . part of the finite patient . Z.

agents, one infinite and one finite, have the same action on the same patient, then it must necessarily follow either that the action of the infinite taketh place in a [finite] instant, or that the action of the finite agent taketh place in infinite time. Either alternative is IMPOSSIBLE.

[*Diagram III*]

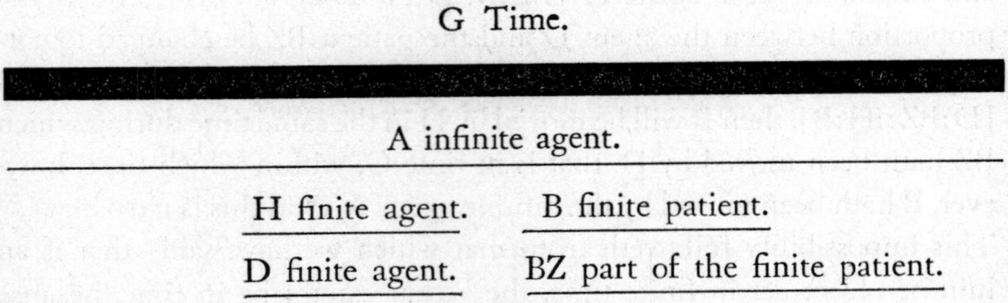

THIRDLY,[40] it is clear that an infinite body cannot act on another infinite body.[41] For, as is related in the *Physicae auditus,*[42] it is not possible that action or passion be endless; when, therefore, we have shewn that action of the infinite on the infinite can never be complete, it will have been proved that there can be no action between them. Let us then take two infinities, one B, patient of the other A in finite time G; for finite action is necessarily in finite time. We will, then, posit that part BD of the patient [B] suffereth the action of A; it will certainly be clear that the sufferance of the part BD will take place in a time Z shorter than G. The proportion then between time Z and time G will be like to that between BD part of the infinite patient [B], and BDH [some] greater part of the infinite patient B [Z:G::BD:BDH]; and BDH will be patient of A in [finite][43] time G. But the whole infinite B hath already suffered the action of A in the same time G. And this

[40] Thirdly to support the Fifth Argument. Cf. *De coelo,* I, 7, 275a 22–275b 2.

[41] But cf. p. 288, first par. and n. 30, where the conclusion is reached: "It would certainly be both inconvenient and impossible to posit two infinites distinct from one another."

[42] Cf. *Physica,* III, 8, 204b and *De coelo,* I, 7, 275a–275b.

[43] Bruno has here *infinite time G,* clearly a misprint for *finite time G.*

is false, for it is impossible that two patients [B and BDH], the one infinite, the other finite, should suffer the same action from the same agent, in the same time, whether the efficient cause be finite or, as we have posited, infinite.[44]

[*Diagram IV*]

Finite Time.

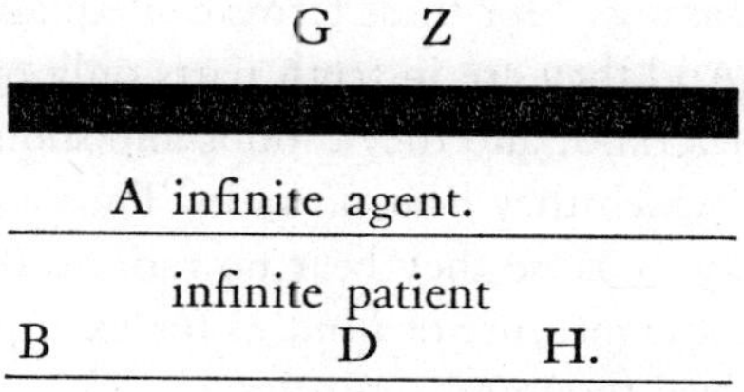

PHIL. All that is said by Aristotle I would deem well said if well applied, and when it concludeth cogently. But as we have already said, the method of no other philosopher who hath discoursed concerning the infinite can lead to such inconveniences as doth that of Aristotle. Nevertheless, not by way of reply, for [here] he differeth not from us, but solely to consider the importance of his opinions, let us examine his manner of reasoning.

FIRST then, he proceedeth on unnatural foundations, wishing to take this or that part of the infinite, though the infinite cannot have parts; unless, indeed, we would name the part infinite; and this implieth the

---

[44] The argument may be expressed thus:
Given that infinite A acts on infinite B in finite time G .... (I)
and that infinite A acts on BD (a smaller finite part of B) in finite time Z .... (II)
and that Z:G::BD:BDH (a larger finite part of B) .... (III)
From (III), $\frac{Z}{BD} = \frac{G}{BDH}$ .... (IV)
From (II), A acts on BD in time Z.
Therefore, from (IV), infinite A acts on finite BDH in time G.
But from (I) infinite A acts on infinite B in time G.
Therefore the infinite B and the finite BDH are patient of the same action in the same time G. Which is IMPOSSIBLE.
The Argument is illustrated by Diagram IV.
Cf. *De coelo*, I, 7, 275a 22–275b 2.

contradiction that there would be a greater part of the infinite and a lesser part, or a part which beareth a greater, and a part which beareth a lesser, proportion to the whole. But thou approachest no nearer to the infinite by hundreds than by threes, for infinite number compriseth infinite threes no less than infinite hundreds; infinite measure appertaineth to infinite feet no less than to infinite miles; therefore when we would speak of the parts of an infinity we do not say "a hundred miles," or "a thousand parasangs," for these terms can equally be used for parts of a finite whole. And they are in truth parts only of that finite whole, to which they bear a ratio; and they cannot and should not be regarded as parts of that to which they bear no ratio. Thus a thousand years are not parts of eternity, because they bear no ratio to the whole; but they are truly parts of some measure of time, as for example, of ten thousand years or of a hundred thousand centuries.

ELP. Expound then to me. What would you say are the parts that make up infinite duration?

PHIL. Parts of a time duration which bear a ratio to the duration and to time, but not to infinite duration or infinite time. For in infinite duration, the maximum time, that is, the greatest proportional part of a duration, becomes equivalent to the minimum, since infinite centuries have no greater duration than infinite hours. I say, indeed, that in infinite duration, which is eternity, there are not more hours than centuries. So that everything which can be described as a part of the infinite is in virtue thereof itself infinite, both in duration and in size. From this teaching, you may judge how careful is Aristotle in his hypotheses when he imagineth finite parts of the infinite; and you may estimate the force of the arguments of certain theologians who consider that the eternity of time involveth the inconvenience of as many infinites, one greater than another, as there are species of numbers. By my teaching I say you may escape from innumerable pitfalls.[45]

ELP. Particularly from that which resulteth from our intent of infinite feet and infinite miles, from which they would make a lesser infinite and another greater infinite within the immensity of the universe.

[45] *Lit.*, "labyrinths."

PHIL. SECONDLY, Aristotle doth not fortify his argument by demonstration. For since the universe is infinite and since there are in it an infinity of parts (I do not say they are parts thereof,[46] for it is different to speak of parts WITHIN and parts OF the infinite); and since all these parts experience both action and passion, and in consequence can be transmuted one into another; therefore Aristotle would infer either that the infinite doth experience action upon or passion from the finite, or that the infinite acteth upon the infinite and that this latter suffereth action and transformation from the former. We however maintain that this inference is not physically valid though logically it may be correct; since, however much, by computing with our intellect, we may discover infinite parts both active and passive; and these be regarded as contrary to those: yet, since the parts in nature are, as we see, not discrete or separate within distinct boundaries, they do not force or even incline us to say that the infinite is either agent or patient; but rather that within the infinite, innumerable finite parts exercise both action and passion. It may therefore be granted not that the infinite is mobile or alterable, but that there are therein innumerable mobile and alterable bodies; not that the finite suffereth action from the infinite, nor the infinite from the finite, nor the infinite from the infinite, in the natural and physical sense of infinity; but that just as from a logical and rational aggregation, within the infinite all weights are as one weight, though all weights do not make up one weight; so the infinite whole, resting ever immobile, unalterable, incorruptible, within it there can be and are motions and alterations, innumerable and infinite, perfect and complete. Moreover, add to what hath been said that, given two bodies which on the one hand are infinite and on the other hand are bounded each by the other, it doth not follow as Aristotle believed that the mutual action and passion would necessarily be infinite, for if one of the two bodies is acting on the other, the agent would not be exerting influence throughout his size and extent, since it is not throughout the whole of the latter or throughout all the parts thereof, neighbouring, near or joined and continuous with the other.

[46] i.e., parts of the substance thereof; the meaning is that these parts can leave their containing body.

We therefore posit the case in which two infinite bodies A and B are continuous and joined to one another along the line or surface FG [Diagram V]. Certainly neither will come to act on the other with his whole force: because not all the parts of the one are in propinquity to parts of the other, since mutual continuity is possible only along finite boundaries. And I say furthermore that even if we suppose the surface or line [F G] to be infinite, it will not follow that the bodies which are coterminous therein exert infinite action and [receive] infinite passion, since they are not intentive but extended,[47] and the parts also are extended. Whence it happeneth that in no part doth infinity exert his total force; but only part by part, extensively, discretely and separately.

[*Diagram V*] [48]

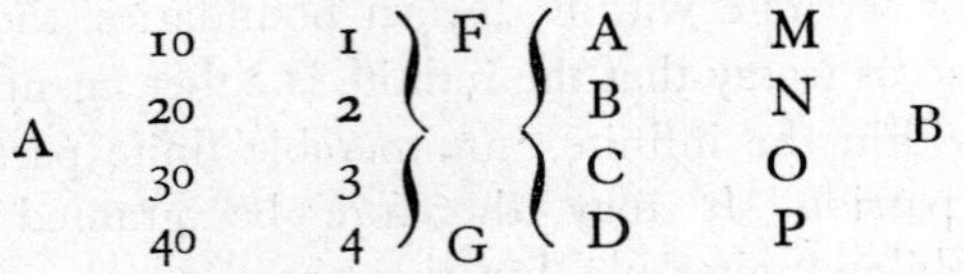

Supposing, for example, that the parts of two opposed bodies capable of action one on another are in propinquity as A to 1, B to 2, C to 3, D to 4 [Diagram V], and so on to infinity, thou wilt never be able to trace [49] infinite intensive action between them, for the parts of these two bodies can act on one another only within a certain and determined distance; [50] wherefore M and 10, N and 20, O and 30, P and 40 have not aptitude to act one on the other. Behold then the proof that, given two infinite bodies, infinite action between them would not follow. I say yet further that however much it may be supposed and conceded that these

---

[47] So Florio translates *intenso* and *estenso*.

[48] The numbers on the one hand and the letters on the other represent specimens of the innumerable particles of infinite A and infinite B respectively. The A, B, finite parts of the infinite B, must not be confused with either the infinite *A* or the infinite *B* shewn respectively on the left and on the right hand limits of this diagram. Unlike the other diagrams in this Dialogue, this figure precedes most of its text.

[49] *Lit.*, "verify."

[50] *Lit.*, "cannot act on one another beyond a certain and determined distance."

two infinite bodies can act intensively one on another with their whole force, nevertheless this doth not imply any effect of action or of passion, for the one is no less potent to oppose and resist than is the other to attack and insist, wherefore no change would ensue. Behold then the proof that if two infinite contraries be opposed, either a finite change or none at all will come to pass.

ELP. Then what will you say if we suppose one of the opposed bodies be finite and the other infinite? As, for example, if the earth were a cold body, and the heaven were fire and all the stars fires, supposing that the heaven were of infinite immensity and the stars innumerable? Do you consider that the result would be, as inferred by Aristotle, that the finite would be absorbed in the infinite?

PHIL. Certainly not, as can be deduced from what we have said. For if corporeal power were diffused throughout an infinite body, it would not thereby act on the finite body with infinite vigour and power, but it would be effective only with such force as it could diffuse from those finite parts within a certain limited distance; since it would be impossible that it should operate with the force of all the parts, but possible only with those nearest. This may be seen in our demonstration above [Diagram V] where we suppose A and B two infinite bodies which are not able to transmute one another except by means of those parts which are at the distance between [the group] 10, 20, 30, and 40 [on the one hand] and [the group] M, N, O, and P [on the other]; and however far B may move and grow toward infinity, naught will avail that the action [of B on A] be increased or gain in vigour—even though the body A remain finite.[51] Behold then the proof that when two contraries are opposed to one another, there ensueth always finite action and

---

[51] There is here a slight confusion. Diagram V which Theophilo invokes concerns the mutual influence of two infinite bodies the one on the other. But Elpino's last question concerns the influence of an infinite on a finite body. Theophilo therefore adds here the phrase, "even though the body A remain finite," to imply that the argument illustrated by Diagram V is no less conclusive if the patient body A be finite. (This of course is the problem illustrated by Elpino in Diagram III.) Theophilo goes on to a fresh formulation of his thesis covering both the case of action between two infinites and that of action between an infinite and a finite body.

finite alteration; and this is no less true if we suppose that one of the two be infinite and the other finite than if we suppose both to be infinite.

ELP. You have entirely satisfied me, so that it appeareth to me superfluous to marshal those further wild arguments whereby Aristotle seeketh to prove that there is no infinite body beyond the heaven. Such is the argument that every body occupying a position is perceptible to our senses, but beyond the heaven no body is accessible to our senses; therefore there is no such region.[52] Or the following: "Every body perceptible to us occupieth a place, but there is no place beyond the heaven; therefore no body is there. Still less is aught beyond;[53] because the word *beyond* implieth a difference of place, namely, of perceptible place, and cannot therefore be applied to a spiritual and intelligible body: Or as one might put it, that which is perceptible to our senses is finite." [54]

PHIL. I believe and understand that beyond this imagined edge of the heaven there is always a [further] ethereal region with worlds, stars, earths, suns, all perceptible one to another, that is each to those which are within or near; though owing to the extreme distance they are not perceptible to us. And in this matter, consider what foundation hath this man who maintaineth that because there are no bodies perceptible to us beyond our supposed circumference, therefore no such bodies exist. Wherefore he persuadeth himself that there is naught but the eighth sphere beyond which the astrologers of his time believed no heaven to exist.[55] And because they referred the apparent circular movement of the world around our earth always to one *primum mobile,* supreme above all others, therefore they established [a system with] such foundations that they continued even further, endlessly adding sphere to sphere, and they believed that some contained no stars, and therefore no perceptible bodies. Whilst the astrological suppositions and conceits have condemned this opinion, it is yet more completely condemned by those who understand better how the bodies said to belong to the eighth

---

52 Aristotle, *De coelo,* I, 7, 275b 7–9.

53 *Lit.,* "yet less is there a beyond."

54 Cf. *De coelo,* I, 7, 275b 9–11.

55 For the astronomical views put forward by Elpino in the remainder of this Dialogue, cf. above, Cap. 3 *d.*

sphere nevertheless differ from one another by their greater or smaller distance from our earth's surface no less than do the bodies in the other seven spheres, for the argument concerning their equidistance resteth only on the utterly false assumption of the fixity of our earth, against which all nature crieth aloud, all judgement and all reasoned opinion and informed mind must ever protest. Yet be this as it may, it is asserted against all reason, that the universe must terminate exactly at the limit of our perceptive power, because perceptibility is the cause of our inferring the existence of bodies. But invisibility may be caused by defect of our perceptive power and not by absence of the perceptible object, and it warranteth not the slightest suspicion that the bodies do not exist. For indeed if truth depended on such perceptive power on our part, bodies which appear close to one another or adjoining would be so in very fact. But we judge that a certain star that appeareth small in the heaven, and is named of the fourth or fifth magnitude, may be much larger than one named of the second or the first magnitude, because our perception falleth into error, being unable to recognize the effect [56] of the greater distance [of the apparently smaller star]. But, because we have recognized the motion of the earth, we know that those worlds are not equidistant from our own, and are not as it were in a deferent.[57]

ELP. You would deny that they are as it were embedded in a single cupola, a ridiculous notion which children might conceive, imagining perhaps that if they were not attached to the celestial tribune and surface by a good glue, or nailed with stoutest nails, they would fall on us like hail from the air immediately above us. But you consider that those innumerable other earths and vast bodies hold their positions and their proper distances in ethereal space just as doth our earth, which by her own revolution giveth an impression that they are all chained together and are revolving around her. You would say that there is no need to posit a spiritual body beyond the eighth or ninth sphere; but that just as this same air surroundeth and containeth earth, moon and sun, so

[56] *Raggione,* i.e., "reason" or "law of nature."

[57] Deferent: the path of regular uniform circular motion along which the centre of an epicycle moves. See above, pp. 47-8.

also it is extended infinitely to contain other infinitely numerous stars and great animals; and this air becometh thus the common and universal space, the infinitely spacious bosom which holdeth and embraceth the whole infinite universe, no less than that part which is perceptible to us owing to the innumerable lamps thereof.[58]

You would say that it is not this air, this enveloping body which moveth in a circle, sweeping[59] with itself the stars such as earth, moon and the others; but that these by their own impulse move within their own spaces, and have each their own motion, besides that mundane apparent motion which resulteth from the motion of our own earth, and besides the further movements which appear common to all stars, as though they were attached to a moving body, for they all have this appearance to us owing to the diverse motions of this star inhabited by ourselves, whose motion is quite imperceptible to us. You therefore would say that the air and the parts which inhabit the ethereal region have no motion save by way of restriction or amplification which must exist for the sake of the progress of these solid bodies through the ethereal region, while some circle around the others, and it is necessary that this spiritual body should fill the whole.

PHIL. Truly. Moreover I say that this infinite immensity is an animal though it have no determined form nor perception of exterior things; for it is imbued with all soul and embraceth all life and it is the whole of life. Moreover I declare that no inconvenience ariseth from this conception as doth happen from that of two infinities, for the universe being an animate body, it hath within it infinite motive power and infinite capacity to receive motion—in discrete manner as we have described. For the whole continuum is immobile both as regards spinning motion around his own centre and as regards motion in a straight line either toward or away from his own centre; for itself hath neither centre nor boundary. Moreover we say that it is not convenient to attribute the motions of heaviness and lightness either to an infinite body, or even to

58 *Lit.,* "this air becometh the common and universal space which embraceth the infinite spacious bosom, and containeth the whole infinite universe no less than that part which is perceptible to us, owing to the innumerable lamps thereof."

59 *Lit.,* "snatching."

any complete and perfect body within the infinite or to any part of these bodies, for each part occupieth his natural position and rejoiceth in his natural disposition. Once more I repeat that nothing is heavy or light absolutely, but only relatively to the position toward which the diffused and separated parts thereof retreat and congregate.

And now we have to-day sufficiently considered the infinite extent of the universe. To-morrow I will await you since you wish to understand concerning the infinite number of worlds within this infinite universe.

ELP. Though I believe that the teaching on the former matter hath enlightened me also concerning this further doctrine, nevertheless I will return in the hope of hearing further important details.

FRAC. And I shall come solely as audience.

BUR. And I too, since as I find myself little by little and more and more beginning to understand you, so by degrees I attain to holding as most likely or perhaps even as truth that which you pronounce.

END OF THE SECOND DIALOGUE

THIRD DIALOGUE

PHIL. [The whole universe] then is one, the heaven, the immensity of embosoming space, the universal envelope, the ethereal region through which the whole hath course and motion. Innumerable celestial bodies, stars, globes, suns and earths may be sensibly perceived therein by us and an infinite number of them may be inferred by our own reason. The universe, immense and infinite, is the complex of this [vast] space and of all the bodies contained therein.

ELP. So that there are no spheres with concave and convex surfaces nor deferent orbs; but all is one field, one universal envelope.

PHIL. So it is.

ELP. The opinion of diverse heavens hath then been caused by diverse motions of the stars and by the appearance of a sky filled with stars revolving around the earth; nor can these luminaries by any means be seen to recede one from another; but, maintaining always the same distance and relation one to another, and a certain course, they [appear to] revolve around the earth, even as a wheel on which are nailed innumerable mirrors revolveth around his own axis. Thus it is considered obvious from the evidence of our eyes that these luminaries have no motion of their own; nor can they wander as birds through the air; but they move only by the revolution of the orbs to which they are fixed, whose motion is effected by the divine pulse of some [supreme] intelligence.

THEO. Such is the common opinion. But once the motion is understood of our own mundane star which is fixed to no orb, but impelled by her own intrinsic principle, soul and nature, taketh her course around the sun through the vastness of universal space, and spinneth around her own centre, then this opinion will be dispelled. Then will be opened the gate of understanding of the true principles of nature, and we shall be enabled to advance with great strides along the path of truth which hath been hidden by the veil of sordid and bestial illusions and hath remained secret until to-day, through the injury of time and the vicissitudes of things, ever since there succeeded to the daylight of the ancient sages the murky night of the foolhardy sophists.

Naught standeth still, but all things swirl and whirl
As far as in heaven and beneath is seen.
All things move, now up, now down,
Whether on a long or a short course,
Whether heavy or light;
Perchance thou too goest the same path
And to a like goal.
For all things move till overtaken,
As the wave [1] swirleth through the water,
So that the same part
Moveth now from above downward
And now from below upward,
And the same hurly-burly
Imparteth to all the same successive fate.[2]

ELP. Indubitable that the whole fantasy of spheres bearing stars and fires, of the axes, the deferents, the functions of the epicycles, and other such chimeras, is based solely on the belief that this world occupieth as she seemeth to do the very centre of the universe, so that she alone being immobile and fixed, the whole universe revolveth around her.

PHIL. This is precisely what those see who dwell on the moon and on the other stars in this same space, whether they be earths or suns.

ELP. Suppose then for the moment that the motion of our earth causeth the appearance of daily world motion, and that by her own diverse motions the earth causeth all those motions which seem to appertain to the innumerable stars, we should still say that the moon, which is another earth, moveth by her own force through the air around the sun. Similarly, Venus, Mercury and the others which are all earths, pursue their courses around the same father of life.

PHIL. It is so.

ELP. The proper motions of each of these are those of their apparent motions which are not due to our so-called world motion; and the proper motions of the bodies known as fixed stars (though both their apparent fixity and the world motion should be referred to our earth)

---

[1] *Il buglo,* wave or bubble.
[2] i.e., involves all things in all possible movements.

are more diverse and more numerous than the celestial bodies themselves. For if we could observe the motion of each one of them, we should find that no two stars ever hold the same course at the same speed; it is but their great distance from us which preventeth us from detecting the variations. However much these stars circulate around the solar flame or spin round their own centres in order to participate in the vital heat [of a sun], it is impossible for us to detect their diverse approach toward and retreat from us.

PHIL. That is so.

ELP. There are then innumerable suns, and an infinite number of earths revolve around those suns, just as the seven we can observe revolve around this sun which is close to us.

PHIL. So it is.

ELP. Why then do we not see the other bright bodies which are earths circling around the bright bodies which are suns? For beyond these we can detect no motion whatever; and why do all other mundane bodies (except those known as comets) appear always in the same order and at the same distance?

PHIL. The reason is that we discern only the largest suns, immense bodies. But we do not discern the earths because, being much smaller, they are invisible to us. Similarly it is not impossible that other earths revolve around our sun and are invisible to us on account either of greater distance or of smaller size, or because they have but little watery surface, or because such watery surface is not turned toward us and opposed to the sun, whereby it would be made visible as a crystal mirror which receiveth luminous rays; whence we perceive that it is not marvellous or contrary to nature that often we hear that the sun hath been partially eclipsed though the moon hath not been interpolated between him and our sight. There may be innumerable watery luminous bodies—that is, earths consisting in part of water—circulating around the sun, besides those visible to us; but the difference in their orbits is indiscernible by us on account of their great distance, wherefore we perceive no difference in the very slow motion discernible of those visible above or beyond Saturn; still less doth there appear any order in the motion of all around the centre, whether we place our earth or our sun as that centre.

ELP. How then wouldst thou maintain that all of these bodies, however far from their centre, that is from the sun, can nevertheless participate in the vital heat thereof?

PHIL. Because the further they are from the sun, the larger is the circle of their orbit around it; and the greater their orbit, the more slowly they accomplish their journey round the sun; the more slowly they move, the more they resist the hot flaming rays of the sun.

ELP. You maintain then that though so distant from the sun, these bodies can derive therefrom all the heat that they need. Because, spinning at a greater rate around their own centre and revolving more slowly around the sun, they can derive not only as much heat but more still if it were needed; since by the more rapid spin around her own centre, such part of the convexity of the earth as hath not been sufficiently heated is the more quickly turned to a position to receive heat; while from the slower progress around the fiery central body, she stayeth to receive more firmly the impression therefrom, and thus she will receive fiercer flaming rays.

PHIL. That is so.

ELP. Therefore you consider that if the stars beyond Saturn are really motionless as they appear, then they are those innumerable suns or fires more or less visible to us around which travel their own neighbouring earths which are not discernible by us.

THEO. Yes, we should have to argue thus, since all earths merit the same amount of heat, and all suns merit the same amount.

ELP. Then you believe that all those are suns?

PHIL. Not so, for I do not know whether all or whether the majority are without motion, or whether some circle around others, since none hath observed them. Moreover they are not easy to observe, for it is not easy to detect the motion and progress of a remote object, since at a great distance change of position cannot easily be detected, as happeneth when we would observe ships in a high sea. But however that may be, the universe being infinite, there must ultimately be other suns. For it is impossible that heat and light from one single body should be diffused throughout immensity, as was supposed by Epicurus if we may credit what others relate of him.[3] Therefore it followeth that there must be innumerable suns, of which many appear to us as small bodies; but that star will appear smaller which is in fact much larger than that which appeareth much greater.

ELP. All this must be deemed at least possible and expedient.

PHIL. Around these bodies there may revolve earths both larger and smaller than our own.

ELP. How shall I know the difference? How, I say, shall I distinguish fiery bodies from earths?

PHIL. Because fiery bodies are fixed and earths are in motion; because fiery bodies scintillate and earths do not; of which indications, the second is more easily perceptible than the first.

ELP. They say that the appearance of scintillation is caused by the great distance from us.

PHIL. If that were so, the sun would not scintillate more than all the others; and the small stars which are more remote would scintillate more than the larger which are nearer to us.

ELP. Do you believe that fiery worlds are inhabited even as are watery bodies?

PHIL. Neither more nor less.

ELP. But what animals could live in fire?

PHIL. You must not regard these worlds as compounded of identical parts, for then they would be not worlds but empty masses, vain and sterile. Therefore it is convenient and natural to assume that their parts are diverse just as our own and other earths comprise diverse parts, though some celestial bodies have the appearance of illumined water as others of shining flames.

ELP. You believe then that the prime matter of the sun differeth not in consistency and solidity from that of the earth? (For I know that you do not doubt that a single prime matter is the basis of all things.)

PHIL. This indeed is certain; it was understood by Timaeus, and confirmed by Plato.[4] All true philosophers have recognized it, few have ex-

---

[3] Perhaps suggested by Lucretius, *De rerum natura,* V, 597-601.

[4] Cf. in *Timaeus,* 36, the division of all creation, "the unchangeable and indivisible and also the divisible and corporeal" between the heavenly bodies.

plained it, no one in our time hath understood it, so that many have confused understanding in a thousand ways, through corruption of fashion and defect of principles.

ELP. The *Instructed Ignorance* of the Cusan seems to have approached, if not reached, this interpretation when, speaking of the conditions of our earth, he saith:

> Think not that from her darkness and black colour we can argue that the earthly body is vile and more ignoble than others; for if we inhabited the sun, we should not see it so brilliant as we do from our circumferential position. Moreover even now if we fix our eye well on the sun, we discover that toward his centre he hath almost an earth or certainly as it were a watery and cloudy body which diffuseth bright and shining light as from a circumferential zone, whence we deduce that the sun no less than the earth is composed of his own elements.[5]

PHIL. So far the Cusan speaketh divinely. But continue and relate that which followeth.

ELP. From what followeth might be inferred that this earth is another sun and all the stars similarly suns. The Cusan speaketh thus: If some person were situated beyond the fiery zone of [elemental] fire, our earth would appear to him by means of the fire as a bright star on his horizon;[6] just as to us, who are within the horizon of the solar region, the sun appeareth very bright, and the moon appeareth not similarly bright, perhaps because in relation to her horizon we have a more median position or, as saith the Cusan, we are nearer the centre, that is, within the moon's humid and watery region; so though she may have her own light, nevertheless it doth not appear to us, and we see only the light reflected from the sun on the moon's watery surface.

PHIL. This honest Cusan hath known and understood much; he is indeed one of the most remarkably talented men who hath lived in our world. As to the apprehension of truth, however, he is a swimmer in the tempestuous waves cast now upward, now downward, for he did not see the light continuously, openly and clearly, and he swam not in calm

---

[5] Cf. Cusanus, *De docta ignorantia,* II, 12, etc.

[6] *Lit.,* "on the circumference of his own region," i.e., his horizon.

and quiet, but with interruptions and at certain intervals; the reason being that he did not discard all those false principles imbibed with the usual doctrine from which he had parted, so that perhaps by dint of industry the title came to fit him well of his own book concerning *Instructed Ignorance* or on *Uninstructed Doctrine*.

ELP. What is the principle which he should have discarded?

PHIL. That the element of fire is, like air, subject to attrition owing to the motion of the heaven, and that fire is an extremely subtle body; this is contrary to that reality and truth which is manifest to us, as we will consider in dealing with other subjects and in discourses on this very subject, where we conclude that there is necessarily one corporeal principle, solid and consistent, of a hot no less than of a cold body,[7] and that the ethereal region can be neither fire nor made of fire, but is enflamed and kindled by the neighbouring solid and dense body which is the sun. So that, when we can speak according to nature, there is no need to have recourse to mathematical fantasies. We see that no part of the earth shineth by her own brightness, but that some parts shine by reflection from elsewhere, as for example her watery region and her vaporous atmosphere which receive heat and light from the sun and can transfer both to the surrounding regions. Therefore there must be a primary body which must be of itself both bright and hot and consequently also unchanging, solid and dense; for a rare and tenuous body cannot hold either light or heat, as we shew elsewhere more than once under the appropriate headings. Finally the bases of the two opposed primal active qualities[8] must similarly be enduring; and the sun by virtue of those parts which are bright and hot must be like a stone, or

---

[7] The government of the world by two opposed forces, Heat and Cold, was the view of Bernardino Telesio of Cosenza. The first part of his *De rerum natura* was published in Rome in 1565, the second part not till 1587. "The most judicious" Telesio is praised by Gervasio for having waged "honourable war against Aristotle" in *De la causa, principio et uno,* Dial. III (Lagarde, *Op. ital.*, I., 236 l. 19; Gentile, *Op. ital.*, I, 202), where he is contrasted with de la Ramée and Patrizzi (though in fact the controversies of Patrizzi and Telesio were a friendly search for truth).

[8] *Prime qualitadi attive,* called by Telesio *nature agenti.*

a most solid incandescent metal;[9] not a fusible metal as lead, bronze, gold or silver, but an infusible; not indeed a glowing iron but that iron which is itself a flame; so that even as this star on which we dwell is cold in herself and dark, not participating in heat or light except insofar as she is heated by the sun, so the sun is in itself hot and bright, and participateth not at all in cold and darkness except as he is chilled by the surrounding bodies and containeth particles of water, even as our earth containeth particles of fire. Therefore, as in this most frigid body primarily cold and dark, there dwell animals which live by the heat and light of the sun, so in that most torrid and shining body there are beings which can vegetate by aid of the chill from surrounding cold bodies; and as our earth hath a certain participation in heat in her dissimilar parts, so also hath the sun a certain participation in cold throughout his parts.

ELP. But what of light?

PHIL. I say that the sun shineth not on the sun nor the earth on the earth, nor any body on itself, but that every shining body doth illumine the space around itself. Indeed, though the earth be bright owing to the rays of the sun striking her crystalline surface, yet her light cannot be perceived by us, or by anyone on this surface, but only by those who are opposite thereto. Moreover though the whole surface of the sea be illumined at night by the splendour of the moon, yet to those traversing the sea, this effect is not apparent except in a certain region opposite to the moon. But if they could rise further above the sea, then the extent of the illuminated surface would appear to them to increase; and the further they rose, the greater illuminated space they would see. It can thus easily be inferred that the inhabitants of bright or even of illumined stars do not perceive the light of their own but only that of the surrounding stars, just as within a single area, one particular part will be illumined from another.

ELP. Thus you would say that solar creatures derive daylight not from the sun but from another neighbouring star?

PHIL. Even so. Do you not understand this?

ELP. Who would not? Moreover, contemplating this matter I come

[9] Cf. the view of Anaxagoras (in Diogenes Laertius, *Lives of the Philosophers,* II, iii, 8 and 12).

somewhat to understand others which follow therefrom. There are then two sorts of bright bodies, fiery bodies which give their own primary light, and aqueous or crystalline bodies which give reflected or secondary light.

PHIL. That is so.

ELP. Then the cause of our light should be referred to no other source than these two?

PHIL. How can it be otherwise since we know of no other source of light? Why should we trust to vain fantasies when experience herself doth teach us?

ELP. It is true that we cannot imagine those bodies to have light merely by reason of intermittent accident, such as putrefaction of wood, scales and viscous incrustation of fish, or that most fragile back of a glow-worm concerning the cause of whose light we will speak on other occasions.

PHIL. As you like.

ELP. They therefore err who describe the outer surrounding bright bodies as certain *fifth essences,* certain divine corporeal substances of a nature contrary from that of the bright bodies which are near to us; herein they err no less than would those who would describe thus a candle or a bright crystal seen from afar.

PHIL. Certainly.

FRAC. This indeed conformeth with our every perception, our reason and mind.

BUR. Not however with mine, which would easily judge this your demonstration to be a gentle exercise in Sophistry.

PHIL. Fracastoro, do thou reply to him, for Elpino and I who have spoken much will listen to thee.

FRAC. My dear Burchio, for my part I will regard thee as Aristotle, and I will take the part of an idiot and a rustic who doth confess to complete ignorance. It must be supposed that I have understood naught of the words or meanings either of Philotheo, or of Aristotle and the rest of the world. I believe the verdict of the multitude, I believe in the fame and majesty of the supreme Peripatetic authority; I join an innumerable multitude in adoring the divinity of this veritable portent of nature, and for that reason I have come to thee to teach me the truth and to free me from the persuasive pressure of him whom thou hast called a sophist. Well, I ask you,[10] why have you said that there is very much, or much, or what you will, of difference between those distant celestial bodies and these which are close to us?

BUR. Those are divine, these compound of matter.

FRAC. How can you make me see and believe that those are more divine?

BUR. Because they are changeless, unalterable, incorruptible, and eternal, while these near us have the contrary qualities; those move with a perfect circular motion, these in straight lines.

FRAC. I would like to know whether, after careful consideration, thou wouldst affirm on oath that this body alone (which thou regardest as three or four bodies and not as members of a single complex) is not mobile as the other stars are mobile, it being accepted that the motion of those stars is imperceptible because we are removed beyond a certain distance from them. And their motion, if it doth occur, cannot be perceived by us, because, as hath been observed both by the ancients and by the moderns who have truly contemplated nature, and as experience manifesteth in a thousand ways to our perception, we cannot apprehend motion except by a certain comparison and relation with some fixed body. Wherefore if we suppose a person within a moving ship in the midst of waters, who knoweth not that the water is in motion, nor seeth the shores, he would be unaware of the motion of the ship. For this reason I might fall into doubt and hesitation as to this quiet and fixity [of our earth]; and I am able to believe that if I were on the sun, the moon or any other star, I should always imagine myself to be at the centre of a motionless world around which would seem to revolve the whole surrounding universe, though in truth the containing body on which I found myself would be spinning around its own centre. Thus I can feel no certitude of the distinction between a moving and a stable body. As to what thou sayest concerning motion in a straight line, we certainly cannot see our own body moving thus along a straight line, nor

[10] Professor Foligno suggests that the change here from "thou" to "you" is perhaps intended to group Burchio with all Aristotelians.

can we see others do so. If the earth moveth, she must have circular motion like that of other stars as is said by Hegesias,[11] Plato and all learned men, and as Aristotle and everyone else should admit; and that part of the earth which we see ascending and descending is not the whole globe but certain particles thereof which do not recede beyond that region which is reckoned as a part of this globe. For as in an animal, so in this our world there is an influx and efflux of the particles, a certain vicissitude, a certain change and renewal. And if all this happeneth likewise in other stars, it followeth not that the process must be perceptible to us. For rising of vapours and exhalations, successions of winds, rains, snows, thunder, sterility, fertility, inundations, birth, death—if these take place in the other stars, they similarly are not perceptible to us; only the stars themselves are perceptible to us owing to the continuous splendour which from a surface either of fire, of water or of cloud they send forth into wide space. Similarly our own star is perceptible to inhabitants of other stars by reason of the splendour which she diffuseth from the surface of the seas—and sometimes also from the revolution of nebulous bodies, as the opaque portions of the moon appear for the same reason less opaque. The aspect of these surfaces is changed only at vast intervals of eras and centuries, in the course of which seas are changed to continents, continents to seas.[12] Therefore our globe as well as those others are perceptible on account of the light they diffuse. The light which our earth diffuseth to other stars is neither more nor less eternal and changeless than that from other similar stars. And just as the motion in a straight line and alteration of their particles is imperceptible to us, so every other motion and every change which may happen to our world is imperceptible from those other worlds. Now just as from our earth (itself a moon) the diverse parts of the moon appear

[11] Hegesias, leading Cyrenaic philosopher, perhaps contemporary of Plato. Cicero narrates that Hegesias taught that Death frees man from evil but not from aught good and that "King Ptolemy" (perhaps of Macedon) forbade him to discourse on this subject. The same tale is in Valerius Maximus, *Factorum dictorumque memorabilum,* Lib. VIII, Cap. 9, ext. 3. Cf. for Hegesias, Diogenes Laertius, II, iii, 86, and 93-96.

[12] Cf. Fracastoro, *Homocentrica,* I, 12, for secular changes of earth to sea and sea to land—quoting Aristotle though only for changes in the heavens.

some more and some less bright—so from the moon (itself another earth) can the diverse parts of this earth be distinguished by the variety and difference of the portions of her surface. Moreover just as, if the moon were at a greater distance from us, then the diameter of the opaque parts would fail, while the bright parts would tend to unite for us and shrink in our view, giving us the impression of a smaller body of uniform brightness, similar also would be the appearance of our earth as seen from the moon if the distance between them were greater. Wherefore we may suppose that of the innumerable stars some are moons, some terrestrial globes, some worlds like our own, and around them our earth appeareth in their eyes to revolve just as they appear to us to revolve and to take their course around the earth. Why then should we affirm a difference between our own and those other heavenly bodies if we find every similarity between them [*lit.,* every convenience (in recognizing their similarity)]? And why should we deny that there is a similarity [*lit.,* this convenience] when neither reason nor sense-perception should lead us to doubt it?

BUR. So you consider it proven that these bodies do not differ from our own earth?

FRAC. Full well. For that which can be seen from them of our own world can be seen of them from here, and that which can be seen of them from here can be seen of our world by them. Namely, this appeareth a small body even as do those, each appearing bright in parts from a shorter distance, each appearing uniformly bright and smaller from a greater distance.

BUR. Where then is that beautiful order, that lovely scale of nature rising from the denser and grosser body which is our earth, to the less dense [sphere] which is water and on to the subtle [sphere] which is vapour, to the yet subtler which is pure air, on to the subtlest which is fire and finally to the divine which is the celestial body? From the obscure to the less obscure, to the brighter and finally to the brightest? From the dark to the most brilliant, from the alterable and corruptible to liberation from all change and corruption? From the heaviest to the heavy, thence to the light, on to the lightest and finally to that which is without weight or lightness? From that which moveth toward the centre to that which moveth from the centre and then to that which moveth around the centre?

FRAC. You would like to know where is this order? In the realm of dreams, fantasies, chimeras, delusions. For, as to motion, everything endowed with natural motion revolveth in a circle around either his own or some other centre. I speak of revolution, not having regard simply to the geometrical circle and circular motion, but according to that law which we observe to govern the physical changes in the position of natural bodies. Motion in a straight line is neither innate nor natural to any prime body, for it is never seen except in those particles which are either as excrement flowing from mundane bodies or else entering from outside into kindred spheres and containing bodies; even as we see waters which becoming subtilized through heat rise upward as vapour, and then condensed by the cold return downward in their original form. We shall speak of this process in the appropriate place when we consider motion. As for the disposition of the four bodies which they name earth, water, air, fire, I would know what nature, what art, what perception maketh it, verifieth and showeth it?

BUR. Then you deny the famous distinction of the elements?

FRAC. I deny not the distinction of the elements, for I leave everyone at liberty to distinguish as he pleaseth concerning natural things. But I deny this order, this disposition that the earth is surrounded and contained by water, water by air, air by fire, fire by the heaven. Because I say there is but one single container that comprehendeth all bodies and those great frames which appear to us as scattered and sparse in this vast field, wherein every one of those bodies, stars, worlds and eternal lights is composed of that which is named earth, water, air and fire. Those in the substance of whose composition fire doth predominate, will be called sun, bright in itself; if water doth predominate, we give the name tellurid body, moon or such like which shineth by borrowed light, as hath been said. In these stars then or worlds as we will call them, these dissimilar parts must be understood to be disposed according to their various and diverse complexions of rocks, pools, streams, springs, seas, sands, metals, caverns, mountains, plains and other similar sorts of composite bodies, sites and shapes; in the same fashion among animals the parts are named heterogeneous according to the diverse and varied complexions of bones, intestines, veins, arteries, flesh, nerves, lungs, members of one or another shape presenting their excrescences, hollows, caves, waters, spirits, fires, with the accidents corresponding to all meteoric impressions, such as catarrhs, inflammations, stones, vertigoes, fevers and innumerable other dispositions and qualities corresponding to mists, rains, snows, heats, lightnings, thunderbolts, thunders, earthquakes and winds, tempests, torrid or that toss sea-weed.

If then the earth and other worlds are animals not such as these creatures are commonly esteemed, then indeed they are animals with greater and more excellent mind than belongs usually to these creatures. How then can Aristotle or another prove the air to be rather around than within our earth, if there is no part of the earth in which the air doth not lurk and penetrate in the manner which perhaps the ancients meant by saying that the Void embraceth all from without and moreover doth interpenetrate the whole Plenum? How then can you imagine the earth to have thickness, density and consistency without water which linketh and uniteth the parts? How can you interpret the earth's being heavier toward its centre except by believing that the parts there are closer and denser, such density being impossible without water which alone can join part to part?

Who doth not see that over the whole earth there emerge islands and mountains above the water, and not only above the water but also above the misty and tempestuous airs which are shut in among high mountains and considered as parts of the earth that go to make up her perfect sphericity? So it is evident that waters exist within the earth's viscera even as within us are humors and blood.[13] Who doth not know that the chief accumulations of water are deep caverns and concavities of the earth? And if thou sayest that the earth is sodden on her shores, I reply that these are not the higher portions of the earth, for all that which formeth part of even her highest mountains is understood to be also

[13] The ready combination of moisture and dry matter is discussed by Fracastoro in the *De sympathia et antipathia* (Venice, 1546 [with *De contagionibus*]), Cap. 10. On water as a solidifying agent cf. Aristotle, *Meteorologica,* IV, 6, 382b, 31-33; 385b 1-2.

within her concavity. Moreover the same may be observed of drops covered with dust but hanging unbroken over a surface. For the intimate soul which both embraceth and interfuseth all things first performeth this operation, namely that, in so far as possible and according to the capacity of each subject, she uniteth the parts [14] thereof. Nor is this because water either is or can be of its nature above or around the earth, any more than the moisture of our human substance is above or around our body.

I leave aside the fact that from every part of the shore and from all great stretches of water, the surface of the water is observed to be higher in the centre: and if the parts of the dry land could thus unite, they would undoubtedly do the same, as indeed they clearly do assume the form of spherical globes when, by the aid of water, they are united, for all cohesion and viscosity of parts in the air is due to moisture. Since then waters exist within the bowels of the earth, and since every part of that earth which is cohesive and endowed with viscosity containeth more of moisture than of dry matter (for indeed, where is most viscosity there is most intermixture and domination by water which hath the quality of cohesion of the parts), who then will not declare rather that water is the basis of earth than earth of water? Rather that earth is founded on water than water on earth?

I leave aside the fact that the depth of water above the surface of our earth, namely the sea, cannot be and is not of so great a volume as even to compare with the volume of the whole sphere: it is in fact not around, as fools believe, but is within the earth as indeed Aristotle confessed in the first book of his *Meteorologica,* being compelled by truth or indeed by the customary belief among ancient philosophers; for he admitted that the two lower regions of turbulent and unquiet air are intercepted and contained by high mountains, and are as parts and members of the earth; [15] and the whole is surrounded and contained by air which is ever tranquil, serene and clear when seen from the stars, so that when they

---

[14] Cf. Fracastoro, *De sympathia et antipathia,* Cap. 3.

[15] *Meteorologica,* I, 3, 339b 13-16, noted also in *La cena de le ceneri* Dial. III, p. 74; (Gentile, *Op. ital.,* I, 85; Lagarde, *Op. ital.,* I, 165). Cf. p. 372, n. 38.

[in the stars] lower their eyes [to the earth] they perceive all the winds, clouds, mists, tempests, the ebb and the flow, which proceed from the life and breath of this great animal, this divinity that we call the Earth, which hath been named Ceres, figured as Isis, entitled Proserpine and Diana, and is the same which is called Lucina in the heaven; all these being understood as of one and the same nature with the Earth. Behold, too, how far is the good Homer, when he noddeth not,[16] from affirming the natural site of water to be above or around the earth where there are no winds nor rains nor foggy influences. And if he [Aristotle] had considered and pondered a little further, he would have perceived that even at the centre of our earth (if that is indeed the centre of gravity) there occurreth more of water than of dry earth. For the particles of the earth are only heavy when mixed with much water; without water they have no aptness through their own impulse and weight to descend from the air to the sphere to which they belong. What disciplined sense, what truth of nature distinguisheth and marshaleth these particles in such a manner as is imagined by the blind and foul vulgar folk, approved by those who speak without reflection, preached by those who talk much and think little? Moreover, who will deny the truth of Plato's opinion as recorded in the *Timaeus* and by Pythagoras and others—though if propounded by a man of no standing, it would be deemed laughable; if by a person of some renown and proved ability, it would be regarded as a mystery or parable and interpreted metaphorically; if by a man of more sense and intellect than authority it would be reckoned among the occult paradoxes. For the opinion is that we inhabit the dark concavity of the earth, and that our nature appeareth to the living beings above the earth as doth that of the fish to us; [17] that as the fish live in a

---

[16] For this phrase cf. Horace, *De arte poetica,* 359.

[17] The same thought is attributed to Plato in *La cena de le ceneri,* Dial. III (p. 73; Gentile, *Op. ital.,* I, 86, Lagarde, *Op. ital.,* I, 165). The reference is perhaps to the *Phaedo,* 109c. We have not found it in the *Timaeus* unless we cite the four species of created animal (*Timaeus,* 39-40) and again, "having given all these laws to his creatures that he might be guileless of future evil in any of them, the creator sowed some of them in the earth and some in the moon, and some in the other instruments of time" (*Timaeus,* 42). In neither passage, however, is there any mention of other Pythagoreans.

humid element denser and crasser than our own, so we live in a more foggy air than do those in the purer and more tranquil region; and as Ocean is mere water compared even to impure air, so is our dark air to that which is truly pure. From all this I would argue as follows: that the sea, springs, rivers, mountains, rocks and the air contained within them and held by them as far as their medial region [18] (as it is said) are no other than dissimilar members and parts of a single body, a single mass, comparable and proportionate to the parts and members with which we are all familiar in the composition of living bodies; the limits, convexity and outer surfaces of this body [which is our earth] are terminated by the edges of mountains, and by tempestuous air, so that the Ocean and streams remain in the depths of the earth, just as the liver which is believed to be the ultimate spring of the blood, and the branching veins are contained and distended by the several parts [of the animal body].

BUR. Then the earth is not the heaviest body and therefore in the centre? Nor is the next in weight and position the water which surroundeth it, and is heavier than air?

FRAC. If thou judgest weight by a greater aptness to interpenetrate parts and to reach to the midst, and from the central position, I will say that air is both the heaviest and also the lightest of all the so-called elements. For as every particle of earth, given the space, descendeth to the centre, so also the particles of air rush to the centre even more swiftly than the particles of any other body whatsoever; for it pertaineth to air to be first to occupy space and to prevent and fill a void; the particles of earth do not change their position with such speed, for they do not usually move except if penetrated by air; since for penetration by air, there is needed neither earth, water nor fire; neither do any of these forestall or vanquish air, nor exceed it in disposition or speed to fill every corner of the containing body. Moreover, if earth, which is a solid body, is removed, 'tis air that will fill the place thereof; but earth is not so apt to occupy space vacated by air. Since therefore it is the property of air to rush to penetrate every site and every remote corner, there is no body lighter than air, nor is any body heavier than air.

---

18 i.e., pervading their whole texture. See Fracastoro's next speech.

BUR. What then willst thou say of water?

FRAC. I have said and I repeat that water is heavier than earth. For we observe that moisture is more powerfully disposed to descend and to penetrate to the very centre of dry earth than is the dry earth to penetrate water. Moreover, dry earth, if entirely unmixed with water, will float on the surface of water without any aptness to penetrate within; nor will it descend until imbued with water and condensed thereby into a cohesive mass; only by dint of this cohesion and density can it penetrate within and below the water; while water, on the contrary, never descendeth by the assistance of earth but because itself doth aggregate, condense and multiply the number of its particles so that it may be sucked up and may thus gather together the dry earth. For we observe that a vase filled with really dry ashes holdeth more water than doth an empty vase of the same size. The dry particles as such float on the surface of water.

BUR. Describe this further to me.

FRAC. I repeat: if all water were to be removed from the earth so as to leave it completely dry, the result would be a body of no endurance, fine, friable, and easily dispersed throughout the air as innumerable discrete bodies. For whereas air formeth [of itself] a continuum, it is water that formeth [another body into] a continuum by means of cohesion, and the substance of this continuous body may be what you will, but will be cohesive and solid, sometimes of one matter, sometimes of another, sometimes a mixture. Since then weight resulteth solely from cohesion and density of particles, and since the particles of earth do not cohere to one another save by the aid of water, whose particles like those of air do spontaneously cohere; and since water hath, more than aught else if not in unique fashion, the power of endowing with cohesion the particles of other bodies—it therefore followeth that water is pre-eminently heavy as compared to other bodies which derive their weight from it. Wherefore those who affirm that the earth is established on the waters should by no means be regarded as fools but rather as most wise.

BUR. We, however, maintain that the earth should always be regarded as central, as hath been believed by so many highly learned personages.

FRAC. And hath been confirmed by fools.

BUR. What do you say of fools?

FRAC. I say that this opinion hath not been confirmed either by sense or reason.

BUR. Do we not see the ebb and flow of the seas, and the course of rivers over the surface of the earth?

FRAC. But the springs which give origin to the rivers, and form lakes and seas, do we not see them emerge from the bowels of the earth and yet not issue beyond the bowels of the earth—if indeed thou hast rightly understood what I have repeatedly said a short time back?

BUR. We see that the waters first descend from the air, and that springs are formed from these waters.

FRAC. We know that water, if indeed it descendeth from another atmosphere than that which appertaineth to the members of the earth, yet is primarily, originally, principally and totally within the earth, and only later, derivatively, secondarily and partially in the air.

BUR. I know that thou standest on this principle that the true estimate of the ultimate convex surface of the earth should be based not on the ocean surface but on the atmosphere level with the highest mountains.

FRAC. So indeed your leader Aristotle both stated and confirmed.

BUR. Our leader is indeed without comparison more celebrated, worthy and famed than yours who is yet to be known and seen. Wherefore, rejoice as you will in yours. I, however, am content with mine.

FRAC. Even though he leaveth you to die of hunger and cold, though he feedeth you with wind and sendeth you forth naked and barefoot.

PHIL. Pray do not dally with such useless and idle propositions.

FRAC. So be it. Burchio, what then do you say to all that you have heard?

BUR. I say that everyone, whoever he be, must ultimately see what is in the midst of this mass—thy star, thine animal. For if it be indeed pure earth, then the order in which these philosophers have ranged the elements is no vain imagination.

FRAC. I have stated and demonstrated that the midst is far more probably air or water than dry earth—and indeed such dry earth cannot reach thereto without considerable admixture of waters which ultimately become its foundation; for we see that the particles of water penetrate the earth with far more vigour than do particles of earth penetrate water. It is then more probable and indeed inevitable that there should be water in the bowels of the earth rather than earth in the depths of water.

BUR. What dost thou say of the waters which float and wander over the earth?

FRAC. None can fail to observe that this process taketh place by virtue of the same water, which having thickened and given cohesion to the earth, pressing together the parts thereof, thereby preventeth the further absorption of the waters, which would otherwise penetrate to the depth of the arid substance, as we see by universal experience. Water then must be at the centre of the earth to give to it that firmness which must depend not on primordial earth, but on water; for water uniteth and joineth the earth's particles; it followeth therefore that water causeth the density of the earth rather than the contrary, that earth giveth cohesion and density to the particles of water. But if thou wilt not accept that the central part of the earth is a mixture of earth and water, then it is more probable and conformable to all reason and experience that it should be water rather than earth. And if a dense body, it is more reasonable to conclude that water rather than dry earth predominateth; for water endoweth the particles of the earth with cohesion, for otherwise the earth would dissolve on account of the heat (not that I would postulate thus of the density of primordial fire which can be dissolved by its contrary). For the more dense and heavy is earthy matter, the more assuredly is it mixed with water. Wherefore the densest of those things which we know, we deem not merely to be those most mixed with water, but to be of the very substance of water, as is shewn when the heaviest and densest of all bodies, namely liquefiable metals, become molten. And indeed in every solid body whose particles cohere, we must presume the water which doth unite and join the parts, even the *minima naturae;* so that dry earth completely free from water is naught but wandering and scattered atoms. The particles of water are indeed more cohesive if unmixed with earth, since the earth particles have no cohesion without the aid of water. If then the central position is reserved for that which seeketh it with the strongest and swiftest impulse, it appertaineth first to air which filleth all, then to water, and only thirdly to earth; if it belongeth to that which is most heavy, dense and thick, then it appertaineth first to water, secondly to air and thirdly to dry earth. If we consider dry earth mixed with water, the central position appertaineth first to earth, second to water and third to air. So that according to various diverse arguments, the central position is variously assigned; according to truth and nature, no element is found without another, and there is no member of this great animal the earth in which are not all four, or at least three elements.

BUR. Quickly, your conclusion!

FRAC. I would conclude as follows. The famous and received order of the elements and of the heavenly bodies is a dream and vainest fantasy, since it can neither be verified by observation of nature nor proved by reason or argued, nor is it either convenient or possible to conceive that it exist in such fashion. But we know that there is an infinite field, a containing space which doth embrace and interpenetrate the whole. In it is an infinity of bodies similar to our own. No one of these more than another is in the centre of the universe, for the universe is infinite and therefore without centre or limit, though these appertain to each of the worlds within the universe in the way I have explained on other occasions, especially when we demonstrated that there are certain determined definite centres, namely, the suns, fiery bodies around which revolve all planets, earths and waters, even as we see the seven wandering planets take their course around our sun. Similarly we shewed that each of these stars or worlds, spinning around his own centre, hath the appearance of a solid and continuous world which taketh by force all visible things which can become stars and whirleth them around himself as the centre of their universe. Thus there is not merely one world, one earth, one sun, but as many worlds as we see bright lights around us, which are neither more nor less in one heaven, one space, one containing sphere than is this our world in one containing universe, one space or one heaven. So that the heaven, the infinitely extending air, though part of the infinite universe, is not therefore a world or part of worlds; but is the womb, the receptacle and field within which they all move and live, grow and render effective the several acts of their vicissitudes; produce, nourish and maintain their inhabitants and animals; and by certain dispositions and orders they minister to higher nature, changing the face of single being through countless subjects. Thus each of these worlds is a centre toward which convergeth every one of his own parts; toward it every kindred thing doth tend just as the parts of this our star, even though at a certain distance, are yet brought back to their own field from all sides of the surrounding region. Therefore, since no part which floweth thus outward from the great Body faileth ultimately to return thereto; it happeneth that every such world is eternal though dissoluble; albeit if I mistake not, the inevitability of such eternity dependeth on an external maintaining and provident Being and not on intrinsic power and self-sufficiency. But I will explain you this matter with special arguments on other occasions.

BUR. Then the other worlds are inhabited like our own?

FRAC. If not exactly as our own, and if not more nobly, at least no less inhabited and no less nobly. For it is impossible that a rational being fairly vigilant, can imagine that these innumerable worlds, manifest as like to our own or yet more magnificent, should be destitute of similar and even superior inhabitants; for all are either themselves suns or the sun doth diffuse to them no less than to us those most divine and fertilizing rays, which convince us of the joy that reigneth at their source and origin and bring fortune to those stationed around who thus participate in the diffused quality. The innumerable prime members of the universe are then infinite [in number], and all have similar aspect, countenance, prerogative, quality and power.

BUR. You will not admit any difference between them?

FRAC. [On the contrary]. You have heard more than once that some, in whose composition fire doth predominate, are by their own quality bright and hot. Others shine by reflection, being themselves cold and dark, for water doth predominate in their composition. On this diversity and opposition depend order, symmetry, complexion,[19] peace, concord,

[19] Of course in the Aristotelian sense.

composition and life. So that the worlds are composed of contraries of which some, such as earth and water, live and grow by help of their contraries,[20] such as the fiery suns. This I think was the meaning of the sage who declared that God createth harmony out of sublime contraries; [21] and of that other who believed this whole universe to owe existence to the strife of the concordant and the love of the opposed.[22]

BUR. In this way, you would put the world upside down.

FRAC. Wouldst thou consider him to do ill who would upset a world which was upside down?

BUR. Would you then render vain all efforts, study and labours on such work as *De physico auditu* and *De coelo et mondo* wherein so many great commentators, paraphrasers, glossers, compilers, epitomizers, scholiasts, translators, questioners and logicians have puzzled their brains? Whereon profound doctors, subtle, golden, exalted, inexpugnable, irrefragable, angelic, seraphic, cherubic and divine, have established their foundation?

FRAC. Add the stonebreakers, the rocksplitters, horn-footed highkickers.[23] Add also the deep seers, know-alls,[24] the Olympians, the firmamenticians, celestial empirics, loud thunderers.

BUR. Should we cast them all at your suggestion into a cesspool? The world will indeed be ruled well if the speculations of so many and such worthy philosophers are to be cast aside and despised.

FRAC. It were not well that we should deprive the asses of their fodder, and wish them to adopt our own taste. Talent and intellect vary no less than temperaments and stomachs.

BUR. You maintain that Plato is an ignorant fellow, Aristotle an ass and their followers insensate, stupid and fanatical?

---

[20] Cf. especially the closing passages of Fracastoro's unfinished work, *Fracastorius sive de anima.*

[21] This may refer either to Nicolaus Cusanus or to Pseudo-Dionysius the Areopagite.

[22] This view is attributed to Heraclitus by Aristotle in the *Nicomachean Ethics,* VIII, 2, 1155b 5-6.

[23] i.e., donkeys.

[24] *Palladii.* Florio gives *palladio professore,* one that professeth to know of Minerva's cunning.

FRAC. My son, I do not say these are foals and those asses, these little monkeys and those great baboons, as you would have me do. As I told you from the first, I regard them as earth's heroes. But I do not wish to believe them without cause, nor to accept those propositions whose antitheses (as you must have understood if you are not both blind and deaf) are so compellingly true.

BUR. Who then shall be judge?

FRAC. Every well-regulated mind and alert judgement. Every discreet person who is not obstinate when he recognizeth himself convinced and unable either to defend their arguments or to resist ours.

BUR. When I can no longer defend them, it will be the fault of my inadequacy, not of their doctrine; when you are able while attacking their doctrine to clinch your own, it will not be by the truth of your doctrine but by your importunate sophistries.

FRAC. If I knew myself ignorant of the principles, I should abstain from pronouncing judgement. If I felt so deeply as you on the matter, I should regard mself as instructed by faith, not by knowledge.

BUR. If thou wert better endowed, thou wouldst recognize thyself to be a presumptuous ass, a sophist, a disturber of good letters, a murderer of talent, a lover of novelty, an enemy of truth, suspect of heresy.

PHIL. So far that fellow hath shown himself poorly instructed. Now he will demonstrate that he is dowered with but little discretion and no manners.

ELP. He hath a loud voice and could not dispute more hardily if he were of the clog-shod brotherhood.[25] Burchio, my dear fellow, warmly do I praise the constancy of thy faith. From the very beginning thou hast said that even though true, thou wouldst not believe it.

BUR. It is so. I would prefer ignorance in the great company of the illustrious and the learned rather than knowledge with a few sophists, as I must deem these friends.

FRAC. Thou hast little skill to distinguish between the learned and sophists, if we must believe what thou hast said. The ignorant are not illustrious and learned, nor are those who know to be called sophists.

---

[25] A monk wearing clogs: applied to Franciscans.

BUR. I know that you understand what I would say.

ELP. It would be a great deal could we understand what you say. For you yourself have hard work to understand what you would say.

BUR. Go to, go to, ye who are more learned than Aristotle. Depart, ye who are more divine than Plato, more profound than Averroes, more judicious than so many philosophers and theologians of all ages and all nations who have commented, admired and raised him to heaven. Away with you. I know not who ye are, nor whence ye come, but ye would presume to set yourselves in opposition to the overwhelming opinion of so many great doctors.

FRAC. If that were an argument, it would be the best of all you have brought forward.

BUR. Thou wouldst be more learned than Aristotle wert thou not a beast, destitute, a beggar, miserable, fed on millet bread, dead with hunger, born of a tailor and a washerwoman, nephew of Neddy[26] the cobbler, son of Momus, postilion of whores, brother of Lazarus who shoes the asses. Remain a hundred devils, you who are not much better than he.

ELP. I pray you, magnificent Sir, do not trouble yourself to return to us, but await our coming to you.

FRAC. To demonstrate truth with further arguments to such fellows, 'twould be as though repeatedly to wash with varied soaps and sodas the head of an ass, which profiteth no more to be washed a hundred times than once, in a thousand fashions than in one, since washed or unwashed, he is unchanged.

PHIL. Moreover such a head will always appear more foul after a washing than before, for by adding more and more water and perfumes, the fumes within that head become at the end more and more agitated, and that noisome stench becometh noticeable which hitherto passed unnoticed, for it will be the more repulsive, the more it is revealed in contrast to aromatic liquors. We have spoken much to-day. I rejoice greatly in the intelligence of Fracastoro and in your mature judgement, O Elpino. Now that we have discoursed concerning the existence, the number

[26] *Cecco.* Florio notes that this word (an abbreviation of the name Francesco) is used as a nickname for a tame donkey.

and quality of the infinite worlds, it is well that to-morrow we see whether and of what sort may be the contrary arguments.

ELP. So be it.

FRAC. Farewell.

END OF THE THIRD DIALOGUE.

FOURTH DIALOGUE

PHIL. The infinity of worlds is not then as the imagined complex of this earth surrounded by numerous spheres, some containing one star, some, innumerable stars. For space is such that innumerable stars can wander through it; moreover each one of these stars can by its own inner power and quality move toward communication with convenient things. Each is so large and comprehensive as to be worthy to be considered a world in itself; not one lacketh the efficient principle and power to preserve and maintain perpetual generation and life to innumerable and excellent individuals. As soon as we have recognized that the apparent world-motion is caused by the real diurnal motion of our earth (which happeneth similarly to other similar stars), no argument will constrain us to accept the vulgar opinion that the stars are equidistant from us, that they are as though nailed and fixed in an eighth sphere; and no persuasion will hinder us from knowing that the differences are innumerable in the distances from us [1] of these innumerable stars. We shall understand that the orbs and spheres of the universe are not disposed one beyond another, each smaller unit being contained within a greater—as, for example, the infoldings of an onion. But throughout the ethereal field, heat and cold, diffused from the bodies wherein they predominate, gradually mingle and temper one another to varied degree, so as to become the proximate origin of the innumerable forms and species of being.

ELP. Prithee, come speedily to the refutation of the contrary arguments and especially those of Aristotle, the most famed of all, which are regarded by the foolish crowd as perfect demonstrations. That naught may appear forgotten, I will enumerate all the arguments and phrases of that poor sophist and you shall consider them one by one.

PHIL. So let it be.

ELP. It is to be discovered (saith he, in the first book of his *De coelo et mondo*) whether beyond this world there lieth another.[2]

---

[1] *Lit.,* "in the length of the radii of the distances from us." Bruno is thus conceiving the universe as an infinite sphere.

[2] See below, pp. 329-30, for the passage quoted *seriatim.*

PHIL. Concerning this question, you know that his interpretation of the word *world* is different from ours. For we join world to world and star to star in this vast ethereal bosom, as is seemly and hath been understood by all those wise men who have believed in innumerable and infinite worlds. But he applieth the name *world* to an aggregate of all those ranged elements and fantastic spheres reaching to the convex surface of that *primum mobile,* the perfect sphere which draweth the whole revolving with it at immense speeds around the centre near which we are placed. Therefore it would be a vain and childish entertainment if we were to consider such a conceit, argument by argument. But it will be well and expedient to overthrow his arguments in so far as they conflict with our judgement, and to ignore those which do not so conflict.

FRAC. What then shall we say to those who might upbraid us for equivocal disputation?

PHIL. We will say two things: firstly, that the fault is on the part of him who hath wrongly understood the world, fashioning for himself an imaginary corporeal universe; secondly, that our arguments are no less valid if we assume the significance of the world to be in accord with the imagination of our adversaries rather than with truth. For the points they suppose to be on the ultimate circumference of the world whose centre is our earth may be conceived as points on innumerable other earths beyond that imagined circumference. Thus they exist indeed, though not in accord with the imagination of those whose conception, whatever it be, doth not support or refute aught suggested concerning the size of the universe and the number of worlds.

FRAC. Well said; let Elpino now continue.

ELP. All bodies, saith he [Aristotle] [3] either move or are stationary; their motion or stationary condition is either natural or constrained. Moreover in every case, if a body remaineth in a certain position not by constraint but of his own nature, thither also it moveth not by constraint but of his own nature; and in that place whither the body is impelled without constraint, there it naturally resideth. So that everything which

[3] Cf. *De coelo,* I, 8, 276a 22 *seqq.*

is forced upward by constraint, is naturally impelled downward and *vice versa*. Thence it followeth that there are no more worlds than our own [4] when we reflect that if earth which is beyond our world moveth to the centre of our world by constraint; then earth within our world will of its own nature move to the centre of another world; and if the motion of earth from the centre of this world to the centre of another is by constraint, then the motion thereof from the centre of another world to our own will be natural. The reason of this is that if there be other earths, the power of one must be similar to the power of another, as also the power of fire will be similar in one and the other world; otherwise the parts of those worlds would be similar to the parts of ours in name only, and not in being; consequently such another world would not be a world like to ours except in name. Moreover, all bodies which have the same nature and belong to but one species, have the same motion—for every body is endowed with some natural motion. If, then, there exist on the other worlds earths like unto our own, and of the same species as our earth, then they will certainly have the same motion. So also, on the other hand, where the motion is the same, the elements performing it must be the same. This being so, earth in that world will necessarily approach earth in our own, and the fire of that other will approach ours, whence it followeth moreover that earth will move upward no less naturally than downward; and fire will move downward no less naturally than upward. Since these things are impossible, there can be but one earth, one centre, one mid-point, one horizon, one world.[5]

PHIL. To this we reply that in the very manner that our earth revolveth around our region in this infinite universal space and occupieth this part thereof, so also the other stars occupy their parts of space and revolve around their own regions in the immense field. And as our earth

---

[4] *Mondo.* The meaning is, of course, universe in the limited Aristotelian sense to which Bruno will not apply the term *universo.*

[5] Cf. *De coelo,* I, 8, 276a 22–276b 21, partly reproduced and partly paraphrased here. The word *earth* in this speech, of course, denotes the element earth. The gist of the argument is that an element (such as earth) that seeks always a central position would have to recede from the centre and seek the circumference of one world in order to reach the centre of another world. Therefore there cannot be more than one world.

is constituted by her own members, undergoeth changes, with flux and reflux of her parts as we have seen happeneth to animals, whose humours and parts suffer continual alteration and motion; so also the other stars are constituted by their members which are similarly affected. Again, even as our earth, moving naturally in accord with the whole universal frame, hath none but circular-like motion, whereby she doth spin around her own centre, and revolveth about the sun, so also must it be with those other bodies of the same nature as hers. And such individual parts of those bodies, not principal parts or members, as have by some accident become removed from their proper position will naturally return thereto of their own impulse; precisely as particles of either the dry or the watery matter which, through the action of the sun and of the earth have receded as exhalations or vapours toward members and regions above our world, having resumed their proper form do return to their places. Thus also the particles of those bodies will no more than ours stray beyond a certain limit outside their own containing body, as will be manifest when we shall observe that the matter of which comets are formed doth not appertain to our globe. Similarly the parts of one animal—I speak of the principal and distant parts thereof—will never readily replace even the same parts of another animal, for they belong to separate individuals, just as my hand will never suit thine arm, nor thy head my body. These postulates being accepted, we say that there is indeed likeness between all stars, between all worlds, and that our own and the other earths are similarly organized. Nevertheless it followeth not that where this world is, there too must be all the others; nor that where this earth is situated, there also must be situated all others; but it may well be inferred that even as our earth maintaineth her position, so also do all the others; just as it is not well that our earth should remove from her region of space to that of the other earths, so also is it not well that those others should move into our region; as our earth differeth from those others both as to her matter and in other particular circumstances, so do they differ from her; as particles of our fire tend toward our main fire, and the fiery particles of other worlds tend toward the main fire thereof, and as the [elemental] particles of our earth tend toward our whole earth, so do the particles of another earth tend similarly toward her. So also only by constraint and against their nature could the particles of that earth which we call the moon, with the waters thereof, be brought to move to this earth, or the particles of this earth move toward the moon. For the moon naturally revolveth in her own position in space and attaineth her own region which is there, as our earth appertaineth to her own region here; and as her own particles, whether of water or of fire are in relation to that earth, so are our earth's particles to our earth. The lowest depth of this earth is no point of the ethereal region beyond and outside herself (such as happeneth to parts separated from their own sphere, if this can occur), but is in the centre of her own figure or sphere or weight; just as the lowest depth of that other earth is no place outside herself, but is her own proper middle, indeed her own centre. Similarly the upper portion of this earth is all that lieth on or beyond her circumference. Wherefore the parts either of another earth or of our own are only by constraint diverted beyond their own sphere, but naturally tend toward their own centre. Thus may be understood the veritable similarity between other earths and our own.

ELP. You say most truly that just as it would be inconvenient and indeed impossible that one of these animate beings should move or dwell in the place occupied by another, or should derive her own individual sustenance from other than her own region and circumstances; so also it would be highly inconvenient that the parts of our own should tend or actually move toward the position occupied by the parts of another.

PHIL. You understand that we speak of veritable parts; for concerning those prime indivisible bodies from which the whole universe was originally composed, we must believe that they undergo certain vicissitudes through the immensity of space whereby they ebb and flow, now hither, now thither. And if by divine providence they do not form new bodies nor dissolve from the old, they are at least able to do so. For mundane bodies are in fact dissoluble, though through either intrinsic quality or external influence they may persist to eternity, suffering a certain influx and a similar and equal efflux of atoms; so they remain constant in number though their corporeal substance be, like ours, renewed from day to day, from hour to hour, from moment to moment, by the processes of attraction and digestion of all the parts of the body.

ELP. We will speak of this on other occasions. For the moment, you have given me much satisfaction since you have remarked that just as we should consider any other earth to have suffered constraint if she were to rise toward this region, so also would it be regarded if our earth were to rise in motion toward any of those others; for even as motion from any part of our earth toward the circumference or limiting surface thereof, or toward the hemispherical horizon of the ether, appeareth to be in upward direction, so also doth the direction seem upward from every part of the surface of other earths toward our own, since this earth is circumferential to those as they to her. I agree also that although those earths are of the same nature as ours, it followeth not that they are referred to the same centre; for as the centre of another earth is not the centre of ours, and the circumference of our earth is not theirs, and just as my soul is not yours, similarly my weight and that of my inward parts constituteth not your body nor your weight, even though these bodies, weights and souls, be considered and indeed are of one and the same species.

PHIL. Just so. But I should not therefore have you imagine that if the parts of that earth were to approach our earth, they could not be attracted thereto, even as would happen to the parts of this earth if they were to approach that other: although we do not ordinarily see such events occur among animals or among the diverse individuals of any species of these bodies, except in so far as one deriveth nourishment and increase from another, and one is transmuted into another.

ELP. Very true. But what wouldst thou say if that whole sphere were no further from ours than the distance by which the parts thereof have become removed from her, though they tend to return to their own containing body?

PHIL. I readily concede that if perceptible portions of our earth were beyond the circumference thereof, where is said to be pure and limpid air, they could of their own nature return from that region to their own position. But a whole other sphere would not thus remove, nor would her parts of their own nature descend; rather would they be raised by constraint, just as the particles of our earth would not spontaneously sink to another, but would be raised by constraint. For to every world, the part beyond his own circumference is on high, and his own inward centre below; and the centre to which their parts naturally tend is referred inward rather than to any region beyond them; and this hath not been known to those who, feigning a certain limit and vainly defining [a certain boundary of] the universe, have regarded the centre of our earth and the centre of the world as identical. But the mathematicians of our own time have inferred, published and agreed the contrary view, for they have discovered that the imagined circumference of the world is by no means equidistant from the centre of our earth. Moreover others, yet wiser, having comprehended the motion of our earth, have therefore discovered not only by arguments from their own art, but also by a certain natural reason based on observation of this world and of the universe perceptible to our eyes, that we may more reasonably and without inconvenience formulate a theory more logical and just, which fits the more regular motion of the aforesaid wanderers around the centre, whereby we should understand that earth is as far from the centre of the universe as from the sun. From these same principles, they have easily been enabled to discover gradually the vanity of what hath been alleged concerning the weight of our earth, the difference between our own and other regions, the equidistance from ourselves of the innumerable worlds that we see from here beyond the aforesaid planets, and of the exceedingly rapid motion of all these bodies around us rather than of ourselves around them. And they may become at least doubtful about other grave inconveniences which follow from the suppositions of the current philosophy. To return now to the subject from which we started, I must repeat that neither a whole star nor a part thereof could move spontaneously toward the centre of another, even though the first were so very close to our star that the surface or a point of the circumference thereof were to touch point or surface of the circumference of our own.

ELP. Provident Nature hath provided differently, for otherwise contrary bodies would destroy one another; the cold and moist would annihilate the hot and dry and be annihilated thereby; whereas, placed a certain convenient distance apart, the one liveth and groweth by aid of the other. Moreover, similar bodies, [if placed close together], would hinder one another from convenient intercourse and from the give and take of exchange with the dissimilar, as is occasionally shewn us when our frailty suffereth considerable damage through the interposition between ourselves and the sun of that other earth that we name the moon. What would happen if she were placed yet nearer to the earth and especially if she could thus deprive us for long periods of heat and of vital light?

PHIL. Well said. Continue now the proposition of Aristotle.

ELP. He replieth to an imagined objection [6] that one body cannot spontaneously move toward another, for the further the one is distant from the other, the more diverse will be their natures; against this proposition he maintaineth that greater or less distance doth not cause a difference of nature between one and the other.

PHIL. And this, properly understood, is indeed most true. But we reply to it in another way, and we give another reason why one earth moveth not toward another whether near or distant.

ELP. This I have understood. Yet appeareth to me also true that view attributed to the ancients that the further off a body the less is his aptness (by this name they frequently describe quality or nature) to approach another, because the particles which much air underlieth have less power to pass through the [supporting] medium and to move downward.

PHIL. It is a certain and proved fact that particles of our earth are accustomed to return from certain distant recesses to their own containing body, and that the nearer they reach to it, the more they hasten. But we are now discussing the particles of another earth.

ELP. But since earth resembleth earth, and the parts are also alike, what thinkest thou would occur if they were in close neighbourhood? Would not the parts of any one earth be equally apt to join their own or any other earth, and consequently to rise or to fall?

PHIL. From a postulated inconvenience, if inconvenience it be, what can hinder an inconvenient result? But leaving this aside, I declare that as the parts [of any one earth] are in equal relation to and at equal distance from various other earths, either they will remain in position, or they will tend to a certain region with respect to which they will be said

[6] *De coelo,* I, 8, 276b 11.

to fall, while they will be said to rise with respect to the other, from which they are moving away.

ELP. But indeed who knoweth that the particles of a principal body remove to another principal body even of similar species? For it appeareth that the parts and members of one man do not fit or suit another man.

PHIL. This is true in principle and primarily; in detail and secondarily the contrary occurreth. For we have ourselves seen a nose from a man's flesh become attached to another man in the position previously occupied by his own nose; and we are confident that we could easily implant the ear of a man on to the site of another man's ear.

ELP. This can be no usual surgery.

PHIL. That is it not.[7]

ELP. I return to the point that I wish to elucidate. If a rock were in mid-air, equidistant from two earths, how may we believe that it would remain fixed, and how would it determine to approach one rather than another of the containing bodies?

PHIL. I maintain that since the form of the rock is such that it is no more turned toward the one than to the other, so that each is equally affected thereby, it followeth from the doubtful upshot and the equal cause for motion toward either of the opposite limits that the rock would remain unmoved, being unable to resolve on motion toward the one rather than toward the other, neither one attracting it more than the

---

[7] This is probably a misinterpretation, since such an operation is only possible under modern aseptic conditions. The actual achievement was the grafting of the patient's own skin to form a new organ. The first European to perform this operation is believed to have been the Sicilian Branco in the early fifteenth century. Similar operations were performed at about the same time in Calabria. The earliest and most detailed description of these operations is by Branco's son Antonio. Antonio stated that his father (like the Indians who had long practised the operation) obtained skin for the graft from the patient's mouth and thus caused the face to be deformed. Antonio invented the method of taking skin from the arm, and was thus able to perform extensive operations from nose to ear without disfigurement. The method was made famous by the surgeon Gasparo Tagliacozzi of Bologna (1546-1599) and is constantly mentioned in writings of the period. Cf. B. Fazio, *Storia della litteratura italiana* (Milan, 1824), VI, ii, 732; and A. Corradi, *Dell' antica autoplastica italiana* (Reg. Instituto Lombardo, 1874), p. 226.

other, and it being no more impelled toward the one than toward the other. But if one is more kindred, congenial, or similar, or more calculated to preserve it, the rock will determine to take the shortest and direct way to join that. Since the chief principle of motion is not the desire to gain a body's own sphere and containing region, but the appetite to maintain itself; even as we see flame creep along the ground, bending and turning downward in order to reach the nearest place where it can feed and nourish itself, not troubling to proceed toward the sun to which it could not rise without growing cold on the way.

ELP. What sayest thou to Aristotle's further supposition that kindred particles and bodies, however distant from one another, move always toward their own related main body? [8]

PHIL. Who doth not see that this is contrary to all reason and sense, in view of what we have just said? Certainly a particle outside his own globe will proceed toward a kindred neighbouring globe even though this may not be his original and primary containing body. Sometimes, too, it will approach a body which conserveth and nourisheth it, though of a different species from itself. For the spontaneous impulse proceedeth not from a relation to any one region, point or sphere, but from the natural impulse to seek that position where it may best and most easily find

---

[8] Cf. *De coelo,* I, 8, 276b 22–277a 27. This is part of the argument previously quoted. The point is that if we posit neighbouring worlds containing similar matter (i.e., the four elements), we must believe that the same motion characterizes all kindred particles whether on our earth or elsewhere, and that such motion must be within finite limits. "The particles of earth then in another world move also to our centre and its fire to our circumference. This, however, is impossible. . . . This being so it follows that there cannot be more worlds than one" (*De coelo,* I, 8, 276b 11-21). A similar argument occurs in the same chapter of *De coelo* (276b 30–277a 11). "If the portions in this world behave similarly both to one another and to those in another world, then the portion which is taken hence will not behave differently. . . . The result is that we must either abandon our present assumptions or assert that the centre and the extremity are each numerically one [i.e., that there is only one goal with only one centre and one limit]. . . . The heaven by the same evidence . . . must be only one and no more" (277a 5-11). And again, "Thus, too, fire and earth move not to infinity but to opposite points; and since the opposition in place is between above and below, these must be the limits of their movements. . . . There must, therefore, be some end to locomotion: it cannot continue to infinity" (277a 20-27).

means to maintain itself and to preserve his present state of being, since this, however ignoble, is the natural desire of all things; even as those men most desire life and most fear death who lack the light of true philosophy and can conceive no manner of being other than this life; nor can they believe that there may follow aught other than now appertaineth to them. For they have not arrived at understanding that the vital principle consisteth not in the accidents resulting from material composition, but in that individual and indissoluble substance to which, if indeed there be no perturbation, there beseemeth neither passion for perpetuity nor fear of dissolution; but these appertain to compounds as such, that is according to the law of symmetry and of the accidental, depending on complexion. For neither spiritual substance, which is understood as uniting, nor material substance, which is understood as united, can be subject to any change or passion. Therefore, they seek not perpetuity, nor doth any motion beseem such substance, for it appertaineth to compounds. Such doctrine will be understood when it is known that to be heavy or light appertaineth not to worlds, nor to their parts; for these differences are not absolute in nature but positive and relative. Moreover we have already on other occasions reflected that the universe hath no edge, nor bound, but is immense and infinite. It followeth that the principal bodies cannot determine on action in a straight line with reference either to some centre or bound, for they have the same identical relationship to every point beyond their own circumference; wherefore they know no motion in a straight line except of their own parts; and that not in relation to any centre or mid-point save that of their own complete, containing and perfect body. This, however, we will consider further in the appropriate place. Coming now to the point: I maintain that this philosopher, according to his own principles, cannot demonstrate that a body, though distant, is disposed to return to his own or to a similar containing body. For let him consider the comets, which are composed of terrestrial matter, that hath risen in the form of exhalation to the enkindling region, and the parts thereof are not apt to descend, but, being seized by the power of the *primum mobile,* they circle around the earth. Yet the comets are not composed of *Quintessence,* but are very heavy terrestrial bodies, thick and dense, as may be clearly inferred from the long interval between their appearances and the prolonged resistance which they offer to the fierce, vigorous, burning flame: for sometimes they continue burning more than a month; indeed one hath been seen in our own times to burn continuously for 45 days.[9] If then the argument of weight is not destroyed by distance of the bodies, what is the cause that this body doth not descend nor even remain in place, but on the contrary revolveth around the earth? If thou sayest that it revolveth not of his own impulse but because it is drawn by constraint, I in reply emphasize that according to Aristotle each one of the heavens and stars is similarly drawn around, and these he asserteth to be neither heavy nor light [10] nor of similar [earthy] matter. Moreover the motion of these comets appeareth to be peculiar to themselves, for it never conformeth to day and night nor to the motions of the other stars.

PHIL.[11] This is excellent argument by means of which the Aristotelians can be convinced from their own principles. We will therefore discuss the true nature of comets, giving special consideration thereto. And we shall shew that such burning bodies come not from the fiery sphere, for if so, they would become aflame throughout, since their whole circumference or surface would be enveloped in air attenuated by heat, as those would say, or indeed by the fiery sphere. But we always see them burning on one side, so we shall conclude these comets to be a species of

---

[9] The comet of 1577 played an important part in the overthrow of the Aristotelian cosmology. It was visible from November to January and was closely observed by Tycho Brahe. From the absence of parallax Tycho deduced that this comet must be far more distant than the moon. So here was a fiery substance dwelling beyond the sphere of the four elements. It will be recalled that Tycho was not a Copernican, but he evolved a special cosmology to account for his astronomical observations. While retaining a motionless central earth, he supposed the other planets (*the* planets as he would have said) and comets to revolve around the sun, and the whole system of the sun and its satellites to revolve around the earth. He believed orbits to be of the Aristotelian "perfect" circular form. Cf. p. 343, n. 15. Cf. Clarissa D. Hellman, *The Comet of 1577; Its Place in the History of Astronomy* (New York, 1944).

[10] *De coelo,* I, 3, 269b 30.

[11] The name PHILOTHEO is here repeated as though the speaker were changed, but the speech is all from Philotheo.

star, as the ancients have well said and understood. And such a star, approaching and receding of her own motion toward and from our own, appeareth owing to this advance and retirement first to grow in size as though enkindled, and then to shrink as though dying down; and she moveth not around the earth; her motion is independent of the proper daily motion of the earth which, spinning around herself, giveth the impression that all those luminaries which are beyond her circumference rise and set. Nor is it possible that a terrestrial body of such great size, should be forcibly drawn by so subtle and liquid a body as the air which resisteth naught, or that it should be held suspended thereby contrary to his nature. Moreover if the alleged motion really occurred, it would be solely a motion like to that of the *primum mobile* by which the comet were drawn around, and it would not imitate the motion of the planets; yet, through such imitation, it is believed to be of the nature sometimes of Mercury, sometimes of the Moon, sometimes of Saturn, sometimes of the others. But of this matter also we will discourse in due season. Suffice it now that we have said enough to disprove this fellow's belief that propinquity or distance doth not imply greater or less power of that which he wrongly nameth individual and natural motion. For truth permitteth not that we apply the terms individual and natural to any subject disposed in a fashion that could never be convenient to it. Wherefore since the parts from beyond a certain distance never move toward their containing body, such motion should not be called natural to them.

ELP. Whoever considereth the matter will discern clearly that this fellow [Aristotle] holdeth principles totally contrary to the true principles of nature. He further replieth that if the motion of simple bodies be natural to them, then the simple bodies which exist in many worlds and are of the same kind move either toward the same centre or toward the same extremity.[12]

PHIL. Yet that is what he can never prove, that these bodies must proceed to the same distinct and individual position; for, since the bodies are of the same kind, it may be inferred that the same kind of position is

[12] *De coelo,* I, 8, 276b 29-32.

suitable to them, and a similar centre, which is their own centre; but we may not and cannot infer that they require a numerically identical space.

ELP. He had some presage of this reply, wherefore with all his vain power he thrusteth out [the idea] that a numerical difference causeth not a difference in position.[13]

PHIL. In general we see quite the contrary. But tell us, what is his proof?

ELP. He saith that if a numerical difference in bodies were in fact a cause of difference of position, it would follow that the parts of our earth, being diverse in number and in weight, would have each his own different centre of gravity in a single world, which would be impossible as well as inconvenient, since the number of different centres would be no less than the number of individual parts of the earth.

PHIL. But see what a beggarly persuasion is this. Consider then whether you can thereby be moved a whit from the contrary opinion, or whether it doth not rather confirm you therein. Who doubteth that it would be in no way inconvenient to postulate for the whole mass, for the body and for the entire animal, a single centre to which every part would be related? Each would tend toward it, and thereby they would all be united and have a common basis. And at the same time there can be positively innumerable centres since we may seek, place or suppose a separate centre in each of the innumerable multitude of parts? In man there is but one centre, called the heart; and then there are forsooth many other centres, even as the multitude of parts, so that the heart hath his own centre, the lungs, the liver, the head, the arm, the hand, the foot, this bone, this vein, this joint, each hath his own centre as hath also each of the particles which constitute these members; and they have every one their own distinct and determined situation, both in the primary and general, that is to say in the whole individual, and also in the proximate and particular, that is to say in the special member appertaining to the individual.

ELP. But consider that he may perhaps have meant not that each part

---

[13] *Ibid.,* I, 8, 276b 32–277a 4. This is further expounded to the conclusion, "the heaven must be one and one only" (*ibid.,* 277a 12). See Elpino's next speech.

hath his own centre, but that each hath the centre toward which it tendeth.

PHIL. Ultimately, all tend toward one: for it is not required that all parts of the animal move toward the middle part and centre; this would be impossible and inconvenient; but each is related to the centre by the union of the parts and by the constitution of the whole; for the life and consistence of complex objects is manifested in no other fashion than by the due union of the parts; these must be understood always to have in common that goal which is reckoned for each as their midpoint and centre. Therefore, as regards the constitution of the complete whole, the parts are related to a single centre; while as regards the constitution of each member, the particles thereof are related to the particular centre of that member, in order that the liver may exist through the union of his parts, and similarly the lungs, the head, the ear, the eye, and the other members. Behold then, this is not only not inconvenient, but it is most natural; and there are many centres according to the nature of the many parts and the particles of parts, if he pleaseth; since each one of these parts is constituted, sustained and indeed formed by the constitution, maintenance and the consistency of the others. In truth, the intellect is revolted by the consideration of such idle trifles as are put forward by this philosopher.

ELP. This must be suffered owing to the reputation which he hath gained rather through not being understood than otherwise. But consider a moment, I pray you, how this honest man taketh pleasure in this bad argumentation. You will observe that he addeth these words almost in triumph: "If then, contradiction cannot confute these arguments, there must necessarily be but one centre and one horizon."

PHIL. You speak most truly. Proceed.

ELP. Also he proveth that simple motions are finite and determined, for his assertion that the world is one and that simple motions have each their own proper seat was based on this notion. He argueth thus: Every moving body travelleth from a certain term to a certain term; and, since every change is finite, there is always a specific difference between the *terminus a quo* and the *terminus ad quem*. Such are the changes between disease and health, between smallness and large size, between here and there; for that which recovereth health moveth not at haphazard, but toward health. The motions then of earth and of fire are not in the infinite, but are toward certain terms different from those whence they are moving, for motion toward the summit is not motion downward, and these two regions are the horizons of motion. Behold then, how motion in a straight line is determined. Nor is circular motion less determined, for it, too, is from one definite term to another, from contrary to contrary, as we shall see if we consider the diversity of motion on the circle's diameter. For there is no contrary to the motion of the complete circle, for the circle endeth in no point save that where also it began; yet there is diversity in the parts of the revolution when this is measured from one end of the diameter to the other.[14]

PHIL. As to such argument shewing that motion is determined and finite, none hath denied or doubted this. But it is false to describe it as simply determined upward or determined downward, and this we have proved on several occasions. For everything moveth indifferently hither or thither, wherever may be his place of conservation, and we maintain that, even if we accept the principles of Aristotle and other principles like unto his—nevertheless if there were another body within our earth, the parts of our earth would remain within that body only if held by constraint, for they would naturally rise. Nor would Aristotle deny that if the particles of fire were above the fiery sphere—as for example if they were where these philosophers believe is the cupola or heaven of Mercury [15]—they would then naturally descend. You will see then how far in conformity with nature these people determine upward and downward, heavy and light, when you have considered that all bodies, wherever

---

[14] *De coelo,* I, 8, 277a 14-26.

[15] The cupola or sphere of Mercury was regarded as two beyond that of the sun, the sphere of Venus being between them. Aristotle believed that comets are caused by hot and dry exhalations seeking their "natural" position in the uppermost part of the elemental atmosphere surrounding our earth—and then becoming ignited by the rotating motion of the heavens. (Cf. *Meteorologica,* I, 4, 341b–342a.) Observations by Tycho and others in 1577 and subsequent years had led to the inference that comets were beyond the elemental region. Thus there was involved motion in the ethereal regions. This was an important factor in the downfall of the Aristotelian system. Cf. above, p. 339, n. 9.

they be and whithersoever they move, as far as possible seek and remain in the place of their conservation. Nevertheless, however true it may be that every object moveth through his own centre to and from his own bounds, and that every motion whether circular or in a straight line is determined between two opposite positions, yet it followeth not that the universe is finite in size, nor that there is but one world. Nor is the infinity disproved of the simple motion of any distinct action whereby as we say that spirit which worketh the composition, unity and quickening of our earth may be and will ever be similarly manifested in innumerable other worlds. We may then believe that all motion is finite (speaking of motion in a given present time, not of absolute simple motion comprehending each individual and the whole) and also that there is an infinity of worlds; since even as each of infinitely numerous worlds is itself finite and is in finite space, so there appertain prescribed terms to the motion of each and of their parts.

ELP. You are right. And thereupon, though he can shew no inconvenience against our view, and naught in favour of what he would prove, there is brought forward his final proof that "motion is not infinite; because the nearer either earth or fire approach to their own sphere the more rapid is their motion; wherefore if motion were infinite it would follow that speed, lightness and weight would also be infinite." [16]

PHIL. I wish him much joy of it.

FRAC. Certainly; but this appeareth to me a juggler's game. For if the atoms are endowed with infinite motion by endless change of position from moment to moment, now leaving this body, now entering into that, now joining in this composition, now that, traversing now in this formation, now in that, the immense space of the universe: they will then truly attain infinite positional motion, they will traverse infinite space, and contribute to infinite changes. But it doth not follow that they will be endowed with infinite weight, lightness, or speed.

PHIL. Let us leave aside the motion of the primal particles and elements; and let us consider only the proximate parts pertaining to certain kinds of being, that is of substance, such as those parts of the earth which

---

[16] *De coelo,* I, 8, 277a 27-33.

are indeed earth. Of these it is truly said that in those worlds wherein they exist, in those regions which they traverse, and in that form which they attain, they move only from and toward certain bounds; and from this fact there no more followeth the conclusion that the universe is finite and the world unique than, for example, that therefore monkeys are born tailless, that owls see at night without eyes, that bats make wool. Moreover it is never possible to make concerning these parts an inference such as: the universe is infinite, these are infinite worlds; therefore a single part of the world is endowed with infinite motion, and must be infinitely attracted by an infinitely distant earth, and moreover hath infinite weight. This impossibility ariseth from two reasons. On the one hand, such a transition is impossible; for, since the universe consisteth of opposed bodies and principles, such a single particle could not traverse far through the ethereal region without being overcome by his opposite; so that this part of earth would no longer move, because the substance thereof would no longer be earth, having through the victory of the contrary thereof, changed his complexion and aspect. In the second place, we observe in general that far from there being ever an impulse of weight or lightness from an infinite distance as is alleged, such attraction of the parts cannot take place save within the region of their own containing space; for if they were beyond it, they would no longer move there; for the fluid humours (which within the animal move from the outer to the internal parts, both above and below, rising, falling, moving hither and thither according to all their differences), if placed outside their own proper containing region, even though near to it, would lose their natural force and impulse. For this relation is valid within the measured space of the radius from the centre of a given region to the circumference thereof; for around the circumference is the region of least weight, and around the centre that of most; and in the intervening region, according to the degree of propinquity of centre or of circumference, is more or less weight. This appeareth in the following diagram [Diagram VI], wherein at A, the centre of the region, a stone is, to use common parlance, neither heavy nor light. B denoteth the circumference of the region, where similarly the stone is neither heavy nor light, but remaineth passive, whereby is shown once again the coincidence of maximum and minimum, as is demonstrated at the end of the work *On Origin, Cause and Unity*. The figures 1 2 3 4 5 6 7 8 9 denote the different intermediate spaces.

[*Diagram VI*][17]

B	9	neither heavy nor light.
	8	least heavy, lightest.
	7	considerably less heavy, considerably lighter.
	6	less heavy, lighter.
	5	heavy, light.
	4	heavier, less light.
	3	considerably heavier, considerably less light.
	2	heaviest, least light.
A	1	neither heavy nor light.

Now you see, moreover, that so far from one earth being impelled to approach another, even the parts, if placed beyond their own proper circumference, have no such impulse.

ELP. You regard this circumference as determined?

PHIL. Certainly, in so far as concerneth the greatest weight possible in the greatest part; or, if thou wilt, in the whole earth—since the whole globe is neither heavy nor light. But so far as concerneth the various intervening grades of heavy and light, I say that their diversities must be as numerous as are the diversities of weight of the several parts from the most to the least heavy.

ELP. But this scale must be interpreted with discretion.

PHIL. Every man of wit will be able to interpret for himself. As to the arguments of Aristotle, enough hath been said. We will now see whether he bringeth forward aught further on.

ELP. Pray be content that we speak of this next day. For I am expected by Albertino, who is disposed to join us here to-morrow. From

[17] It will be seen that the left-hand column increases downward from *least heavy* (near the "circumference" B) to *heaviest* (near the "centre" A); while the right-hand column increases upward from *least light* (near the "centre" A) to *lightest* (near the "circumference" B); but at the centre as also on the circumference, the qualities of heaviness and lightness disappear.

him I think you may hear all most weighty arguments which can be brought to support the contrary opinion, for he is very adept in the current philosophy.

PHIL. Be it as you wish.

END OF THE FOURTH DIALOGUE.

FIFTH DIALOGUE

ALBERTINO[1] (*a new speaker*). I should like to know what is this phantasm, this unheard of monster, this human portent, this extraordinary brain, and what is the fresh news brought by him to the world? Or rather what are these ancient and obsolete views thus renewed, what these amputated roots sending forth fresh shoots in this our age?

ELP. They are amputated roots which germinate, ancient things which return yet again, occult truths which are discovered; it is a new light which after the long night riseth over the horizon in the hemisphere of our knowledge and little by little approacheth the meridian of our intelligence.

ALB. If I did not know my Elpino, I know what I should say.

ELP. Say what you please. If you are as intelligent as I believe, you will agree with him as I agree. If you have greater talent, you will agree more rapidly and completely, as indeed I expect. Since those for whom the current philosophy and ordinary knowledge are hard, those who are disciples thereof but little adept (as is often the case though they know it not), such will not easily be converted to our view. For to them universal belief is most potent, and they are dazzled by the fame of those authors placed in their hands, so that they seek the reputation of expounders and commentators. But the others, by whom the received philosophy is clearly understood, have attained a point where they no longer propose to occupy the remainder of their days listening to others; they see by their own light, and with the activity of their mind's eye they penetrate every cranny; and Argus-like, with the eyes of their diverse knowledge they gaze through a thousand doorways on the aforesaid philosophy unveiled. Thus they will be able, on a nearer approach, to distinguish matters of belief accepted as truth on a distant view, by habit and by general consent, from that which truly is and must be accepted as certain, persistent in the very nature and substance of things. Truly, I say, they are ill able to accept our philosophy who have not the good fortune to be dowered with natural wit or are not

[1] Probably Alberico Gentilis. Cf. above, p. 31.

at least tolerably familiar with diverse branches of knowledge; and especially they must have power of intellectual reflexion, whereby they can distinguish belief by faith from belief based on the evidence of true principles. For often an opinion is accepted as a principle that, if well considered, will be found to lead to an impossible conclusion, contrary to nature. I leave aside those sordid and mercenary minds that desire scarcely or not at all to attain truth, being content with what is generally estimated as knowledge, friends not of true wisdom but anxious only for the fame and reputation she bestoweth, seeking the appearance, not the reality [of knowledge]. For I say he is ill equipped for choice between diverse opinions and contradictory statements who is without sound and right judgement on these matters. He will decide with difficulty who hath no capacity to compare them, one with another, and he will experience great difficulty in comparing them when the differences that distinguish them are beyond his understanding. Right hard it is to understand wherein they differ, since the substance and being of each is hidden. And this can never be evident except through a clear understanding of the reasons and principles on which each is based. After you have looked with the mind's eye and considered with well-controlled perception the foundations, principles and reasons on which are based these diverse and opposed philosophies, after you have examined the nature, the substance and the peculiarity of each and weighed one against another on the scales of the intellect, distinguished their differences and compared and judged straightly between them, then without hesitation you will readily choose to consent to the truth.

ALB. Aristotle, our prince of philosophers, affirmeth that it were vain and foolish to exercise ourselves to oppose vain and foolish opinions.

ELP. Well said. But if you examine the matter, this advice and counsel applieth against his own opinions when they are clearly foolish and vain. He who would judge correctly must as I have said be able to renounce the habit of belief. He must regard two opposed views as equally possible and must dismiss all prejudice imbibed since his birth—both that which we encounter in general conversation, and that by which we are (though as dying to the crowd of men) reborn through philosophy among those scholars who are esteemed wise by the majority of men at a certain period. When controversy ariseth between different persons regarded as wise among different peoples and in different ages, I would say that if we would judge aright, we must recall to mind the warning of this same Aristotle that, through concentrating regard upon few facts we may sometimes [too] readily deliver ourselves of opinions; and sometimes an opinion doth command our assent merely by force of custom, whereby that appeareth to us necessary which in fact is impossible; or we perceive and learn that to be impossible which is most true and necessary. And if this occurreth in manifest matters, what must happen in those which are doubtful and depend on well-grounded principles and solid foundations?

ALB. It is the opinion of the commentator Averroes and of many others that what Aristotle hath not known cannot be learned.

ELP. Both he and the multitude of his followers had so low a talent and were in such deep darkness that they could see nothing higher and more brilliant than Aristotle. Wherefore if he and others when they allow themselves to let fall such opinions were to speak with strict accuracy, they would say that Aristotle appeareth to them as a God; thereby they would not so much exalt Aristotle as manifest their own worthlessness. For to them the matter appeareth even as to the ape her own children appear the most beautiful creatures in the world, and her own ape husband the fairest of mates.

ALB. *"The mountains do bring forth."* [2]

ELP. You will see that it is no mouse to which they give birth.

ALB. Many have crossed weapons with Aristotle; but their castles have fallen, their shafts are blunted, their bows have broken.

ELP. What happeneth when one vain thing maketh war with another? One is all-victorious but doth not thereby cease to be vain; and will he not finally be discovered and vanquished by truth?

ALB. I maintain that it is impossible to demonstrate that Aristotle is in error.

ELP. That is too rash a statement.

ALB. I say it only after having examined well and considered yet

---

[2] Cf. Horace, *De arte poetica,* 139.

further that which Aristotle saith. And so far from having detected in him any error, I can discern naught of divinity that he doth not know: and I must believe that no other man can perceive that which is invisible to me.

ELP. You measure then the stomach and brain of others by your own, and believe that to be impossible to others which cannot be achieved by yourself. There are in this world those, so unlucky and unhappy that not only are they deprived of every good, but they have been fated to receive as eternal companion that Erinnys and infernal Fury which forceth them voluntarily to cloak their eyes with a black veil of corrosive jealousy, that they may not perceive their own nakedness, poverty and misery, nor the ornaments, riches and delights of others. They prefer to pine away in filth and proud penury and to remain buried under a dung heap of obstinate ignorance rather than to be discovered turning to a new discipline or seeming to confess that hitherto they had been ignorant, and had been guided by an ignorant man.

ALB. Would you then for example prefer that I should become a disciple of this fellow? What, I who am a doctor, approved by a thousand academies, I who have publicly professed philosophy in the first academies of the world, am I now to deny Aristotle, and crave to be taught philosophy by such fellows [as Theophilo]?

ELP. For my part, I would be taught not as a doctor but as an unlearned man; not in the character that I should, but on account of that which I do not fulfil, I would learn. I would accept as master not only this man, but any others whom the gods have ordained to that office, for they enable me to understand that which I do not now understand.

ALB. Then you would make me a child again?

ELP. Rather that you should discard childishness.

ALB. I give you thanks for your courtesy, that you would so advance and exalt me as to permit me to enter the audience of this miserable wanderer. All know how he is hated in the academies, how he is the adversary of every accepted doctrine, praised by few, approved by none, pursued by all.

ELP. Yea, he is persecuted by all, but by what sort of people? He is praised by few, but those the best and heroes. Adversary of accepted doctrine not as doctrine or as accepted, but because it is false. Hated by the academies because where there is contrast there is no love; distressed because the multitude is opposed to him who separateth himself from them, and he who placeth himself on high maketh himself the target to many. To describe to you his mind as regards speculative matters, I will tell you that he is not so desirous to teach as to understand; he will take it as better news and will be better pleased when he knoweth that you wish to teach him (in so much as he may hope for some result) than if you were to tell him that you wish to be taught by him, for his desire is rather to learn than to teach, and he regardeth himself as apt rather to the former than to the latter. But here he cometh with Fracastoro.

ALB. You are most welcome, Philotheo.

PHIL. And you no less so.

ALB. "If in the forest I chew straw with the ox, the sheep, the goat, the ass and the horse, then, to improve my livelihood, without sin do I come hither to make myself a disciple." [3]

FRAC. Welcome indeed.

ALB. I have up to now esteemed your views unworthy to be heard, still less to be answered.

PHIL. In my early youth and up to a certain term I judged similarly, being entirely occupied with Aristotle.[4] Now that I have seen and meditated more and have a mature experience, I should be able to judge matters: it may be that I have become foolish and have lost my wits. Since this is a sickness which no one perceiveth less than the patient himself, I am the more readily exercised by a suspicion that I

---

[3] Gentile points out that this is from an anonymous sonnet cited also by Luigi Pulci (1431–*circ.* 1487) in the *Morgante Maggiore,* Canto XXV, 13. The first edition of the whole poem was printed in Florence in 1582. The only complete copy known of this edition is in the British Museum and it lacks the title-page. It is stated that the first 25 Cantos of the work were printed surreptitiously by Luca Veneziano in 1481. There were a great number of subsequent editions of the *Morgante Maggiore,* especially in the sixteenth and eighteenth centuries.

[4] Cf. a similar reference to his youthful reverence for Aristotle in *La cena de le ceneri,* Dial. IV, p. 94 (Gentile, *Op. ital.,* I, 103; Lagarde, *Op. ital.,* I, 177); and to similar youthful error in *De vinculis in genere,* Art. XXX (*Op. lat.,* III, 683).

have moved from learning to ignorance, and I am therefore most happy to have come across a physician esteemed by all as able to release me from such a mania.

ALB. Nor Nature nor I can aught do, if the disease hath penetrated through to the bone.[5]

FRAC. Prithee, Sir, feel first his pulse and examine his urine; for afterwards, if we cannot effect a cure, we shall be wary of him.

ALB. The method of feeling the pulse is to see whether you can resolve and find escape from certain arguments which I will now recite to you, which conclusively demonstrate that a plurality of worlds is impossible and an infinity of worlds even less possible.

PHIL. I shall be in no small degree indebted to you when you have taught me this. And should your intention come not to effect, I shall be indebted to you for confirming me in my own opinion. For indeed I deem that from you I shall perceive the full force of the contrary argument; and since you are most expert in the received sciences, you will easily perceive the strength of the foundation and the structure thereof by their differences from our principles. That there may be no interruption in the argument, and that each may have fair opportunity to explain his own views, will it please you to bring forward those arguments which you consider most solid and important and which appear to you most conclusive?

ALB. I will do so. FIRST then, that beyond this world[6] there is believed to be neither time nor space, for there is postulated one primal heaven, a body most distant from us—the *primum mobile;* wherefore we are accustomed to name heaven that which is on the utmost horizon of the world; on it are all the still and motionless, fixed and still bodies which are the intelligences endowing the orbs with motion.[7]

---

[5] This couplet is an echo from Ludovici Ariosto (1474-1533), *Orlando furioso,* XXIV, 3.

[6] The reader may be reminded that for the Aristotelian universe, Bruno as usual uses not the word *universo* but *mondo.* He usually refers to our earth as *questo*—this body. Albertino's confusion is indicated by his applying the same word *mondo* to the Aristotelian universe and to parts of it; and by his using in the same meaning the word *universo* once or twice—in each case indicated in a note to the translation.

[7] *Metaphysica,* 1073a 24 *seqq.*

The world again is divided into a celestial and an elementary body, the latter being bounded and contained, the former the containing limit. And the world [8] is so ordered in rising [scale] from the densest to the most subtile which is above the convex of fire. On this are fixed the sun, moon and other stars, and it doth constitute a fifth essence. The quality thereof is such that it strayeth not forth into the infinite, for it could not be joined to the *primum mobile;* and it encountereth not the other elements, for these would then be around it; and the incorruptible and divine would be contained and comprised by corruptible bodies, which is not seemly. For to the divine there appertaineth a nature conditioned to Form and Action, and therefore to the function of containing, and endowing others with definite form and limit, being itself without limit, form or substance. Having argued thus, we proceed with Aristotle to maintain that [9] if there be a body beyond this heaven, it must be either a simple or a compound body. And however thou mayest reply, I ask thee further, will the body occupy a position impelled by his inner nature, or by the accident of position and by outward constraint? We will shew that no simple body can be there, for it is impossible for a perfect sphere to change position. Since the centre thereof is immutable, the position cannot change, for only by constraint can it attain to any but his own proper position; and a sphere can suffer no constraint, active or passive. Similarly it is impossible that there be outside the heaven a simple body that moveth in a straight line; whether it be heavy or light, it cannot naturally be there, since the natural positions of simple bodies are not those which are called beyond the world: nor can you say that these bodies are there by accident [or constraint by other bodies], for in that case other bodies would be there of their own nature. It is then proved that there are no simple bodies besides those which make up our own world, and these bodies are endowed with three kinds of local motion. Consequently there can exist beyond the world no other simple body, and therefore also no compound body, since the latter is compound of the single, and

---

[8] Albertino adds confusion by using here the word *universo.*

[9] *De coelo,* I, 9, 278b 21–279a 2.

becometh again resolved thereto. It is thus manifest that there exist not many worlds, for the heaven is unique, perfect and complete, and there is and can be no other like it. Wherefore it may be inferred[10] that outside our world[11] there can be neither Space, Plenum, Void nor Time. Space is not there, for if it be a plenum, it will contain either a simple or a compound body; and we have shewn that beyond the heaven is neither simple nor compound body. But if such space be void, then, according to the nature of a void, which is defined as space capable of containing body, a body may reside therein; and we have shewn that beyond the heaven no body can exist. And Time is not there, because Time is the number of Motion, and Motion can only be postulated of body; thus where there is no body, there is no motion and therefore no measurement of motion, and without this there is no Time. Moreover, since we have proved that there existeth no body beyond the world, therefore we have demonstrated that neither Motion nor Time is there, nor aught temporal nor endowed with motion. Wherefore there is but one world.

SECONDLY,[12] the uniqueness of the world may be inferred from the unique motive body [the *primum mobile*]. It is agreed that circular motion is truly unique, uniform, without beginning and without end. If it be unique, it is an effect which can result from only one cause; if then there is one primal heaven beneath which are all the lower heavens, and these conspire to make up a single order, then there can be but one governing and motor power. This being incorporeal, cannot be multiplied by addition of matter. If the motive power is unique, and if a single motive power can give rise only to one motion, and motion whether complex or simple can take place only within a simple or compound mobile body, it followeth that the mobile world[13] is one, wherefore there can be no other worlds.

---

[10] For the following passage cf. *De coelo,* I, 9, 279a 11-18.

[11] *Questo corpo.*

[12] For the Second Argument (somewhat circular!) cf. *De coelo,* III, 2, 300b 32 and *Metaphysica,* XII, 8, 1074a 36-38. Cf. also *Metaphysica,* XII, 8, 1073a 26 *seqq.* for arguments answered on p. 353.

[13] Here again is the word *universo.*

THIRDLY,[14] a unique world may be inferred from the positions occupied by bodies in motion. There are three kinds of moving bodies, those generally heavy, those generally light, and that which is neither. [To the first kind belong] earth and water; [to the second] air and fire; [to the third] the heaven. Similarly there are three different fields for moving bodies. The lowest and central, occupied by a very heavy body; the uppermost region, furthest from this, and the midway region, between the central and the uppermost. Thus the first is heavy and belongeth to the centre; the second neither heavy nor light, belongeth to the outer circumference, while the third is light and belongeth to the space between the other two. There is therefore a lowest region to which tend all heavy objects from any world, and there is an upper region to which tend all light objects from any world; hence there is a region in which the heaven, to whatever world it may belong, doth travel. If then there is but one space, there is also but one world, not many.

FOURTHLY,[15] I declare that [if there were more than one world] there would be various centres toward which move the heavy objects of diverse worlds, and there would be several horizons toward which light objects would move. These positions in diverse worlds differ not in kind but only in number. Thus the centre will be further distant from another centre than from his own horizon. But one centre and another are alike in kind, while centre and horizon are of opposed nature. Wherefore the distance through space will be greater between those of similar kind than between those that are opposed. This is contrary to the nature of such opposites: for when it is said that contrary elements are furthest removed from one another, this should be understood to refer to distance in the same space, which must indeed be between contrary sensible bodies. You see then what would follow from supposing more than one world. It is clear that such a hypothesis is not only false but impossible.

FIFTHLY,[16] if there be more worlds of the same kind, they must be

---

[14] For part of the Third Argument cf. *De coelo,* I, 3, 269b 23-26.

[15] Somewhat on the lines of the Fourth Argument is the passage in *De coelo,* I, 8, 276a 30–276b 24, already cited.

[16] The Fifth is really another presentation of the Fourth Argument. See the final sentence.

equal, or certainly proportional in size[17] which cometh to the same thing as regardeth our proposition. If this be the case, there cannot be more than six worlds adjoining our own: for not more than six spheres can touch a single one without their penetration, just as not more than six equal circles can touch one another without the lines intersecting [Diagram VII]. If this be so, several [i.e., six] horizons will be ranged—at the respective points where the six worlds touch our own world or another—around a single centre. But since the virtue of two opposed elements should be of equal power, and since inequality followeth from this arrangement, you will make the upper elements more potent than the lower, you will make the former victorious over the latter and thus you will dissolve this body.

[*Diagram VII*]

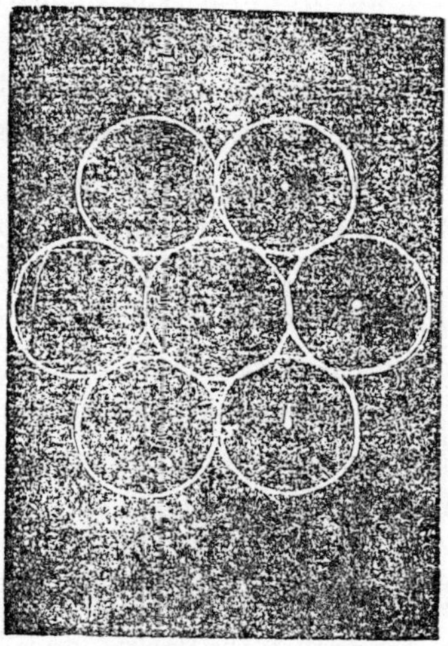

SIXTHLY, since if the circular surfaces of the diverse worlds touch only at a point, there must necessarily remain a certain space between the convex circumference of one sphere and that of another, and either there is something within this space which filleth it, or there is nothing

[17] i.e., either all equal to our universe and to one another, or all of the same proportional size to it and therefore equal to one another.

[Diagram VII]; if there is something, it certainly cannot be of the nature of an element, distant from the convex surface of a sphere, because, as is evident, such a space must be triangular and enclosed within three arcs that form part of the circumferential surface of three worlds: and thus the centre [of a triangle] will be found to be rather distant from the parts nearest to the angles but most distant from the spheres,[18] as may clearly be seen. It will then be necessary to imagine new elements and a new world filling that space, different from our elements and our world. Otherwise it is necessary to suppose a vacuum in the triangular space, and this we postulate to be impossible.

SEVENTHLY, if there are other worlds, they must be either finite or infinite. If they are infinite, the infinite will have issued in determined action.[19] This is for many reasons deemed impossible. But if they are finite, they must be a definite number. And then we shall ask ourselves, why are there exactly so many and neither more nor less? Why is there not one more? What would happen if there were this or that additional world? Whether they be even or uneven in number, why should they be in this rather than in that category? And indeed why is all this matter divided into many worlds instead of being agglomerated in a single globe? Since unity is better than multiplicity, *ceteris paribus,* why is the substance divided among four or six or let us say ten earths, rather than forming a single great and perfect globe? Indeed, just as there ariseth from the possible and the impossible a finite sooner than an infinite number; so, as between the convenient and the inconvenient, unity is more rational and natural than multiplicity or plurality.

SEVENTHLY [*sic*],[20] we see nature in all things close herself in the smallest compass, for as she lacketh not things necessary, so she aboundeth not in superfluities. Since then she can produce her whole effect with those works that are in this world, it were not reasonable to wish to feign that there be more worlds.

---

[18] From *quelli,* i.e., the circumferential surface of the worlds.

[19] *De coelo,* I, 8, 276b 23 and *Metaphysica,* I, 10, 1075a 18.

[20] This is a second heading "SEVENTHLY," but may be regarded as a continuation of the previous Argument. It is, however, answered as Argument Eight.

EIGHTHLY,[21] if there were an infinity of worlds or even more than one, this would be the case chiefly because God could fashion them thus, or rather because they could depend on God. But most true though this may be, it doth not follow that these worlds exist, for besides the active power of God there is needed the passive power of things. For that which can be created in nature dependeth not upon the absolute divine power, since not every active power transformeth itself into passive, but only that which hath subject proportionate to itself; that is, a subject able to receive the efficient act in its completeness. Now naught affected hath such correspondence with Prime Cause. In so far then as concerneth the nature of the world, there cannot be more than one, even though God can make more.

NINTHLY,[22] the plurality of worlds is outside all reason, for there would be in them no civil virtue, which consisteth in civil intercourse. And the gods who had created diverse worlds would have done ill, in that they had not contrived that the citizens thereof should have commerce one with another.

TENTHLY,[23] the plurality of worlds would place obstacles to the labour of every motive force or divinity. For since the spheres must touch one another at certain points [Diagram VII], the one would hinder the movement of the other and the gods could hardly govern the world through motion.

ELEVENTHLY, a plurality of individuals cannot arise from a single one, unless by nature's process of multiplication by division of the substance, which is none other than generation. For it is said by Aristotle and by all Peripatetics that individuals of a single kind multiply only by the act of generation. But those who maintain the existence of a plurality of worlds, of the same matter and kind of form, do not assert that one is transformed into another, or is generated from another.

TWELFTHLY,[24] to perfection nothing can be added. If then this world is perfect, certainly there is no need for another to be added to it. The

---

21 Answered as "your ninth."
22 Answered as "your next."
23 Answered as "your tenth." The correspondence of the numbers is restored.
24 Answered as "your twelfth and last."

world is perfect, firstly as a kind of continuum which is not bounded by another kind of continuum. For an indivisible mathematical point culminateth mathematically in a line which is a kind of continuum; the line culminateth in a surface which is a second kind of continuum; the surface in a solid body which is the third kind of continuum. A body migrateth not, nor removeth into another kind of continuum. But if it be part of the universe,[25] it is bounded by another body; while if it is itself the universe,[25] it is perfect and is bounded only by itself. Thus the world or universe [25] is unique, and should be perfect. These are the twelve [thirteen] arguments which I desire for the moment to put before you. If you satisfy me concerning these, then I am completely satisfied.

PHIL. But, my Albertino, he who proposeth to defend a proposition must first (unless he be indeed a fool) have examined the contrary arguments, just as a soldier would be foolish if he undertook to defend a castle without having considered the circumstances and places from which it may be assailed. The arguments brought forward by you, if indeed they be reasonable, are well known and oft repeated. Most effectual reply may be made to them all by a mere consideration on the one hand of their basis, and on the other of the measure of our own assertion. I will make both clear to you by the course of my reply, which shall be brief. For if you need further speech and explanation, I will leave you to the care of Elpino who shall repeat that which he hath heard from me.

ALB. First, I pray you, make me perceive that this method will not be fruitless nor devoid of satisfaction to one who desireth knowledge, and that I shall certainly not be weary listening first to you and then to him.

PHIL. To the wise and judicious, among whom I count you, it sufficeth to demonstrate in what direction consideration must be given. For they themselves will then proceed deeper in appraising the means by which one or other contrary opinion may be reached. As to your first doubt, we will say that your whole framework crumbleth, since there exist not these differences between various orbs and heavens, and the stars through this vast ethereal space move of their own nature, each

---

[25] *Universo.*

spinning around her own centre and also revolving around another centre. There is, in fact, no *primum mobile* that draweth those many bodies around ourselves as centre. Rather it is our globe which causeth the appearance of this happening, for reasons which Elpino will expound to you.

ALB. Willingly I will hear him.

PHIL. When you have heard and have well marked that such an opinion is contrary to nature, while ours is consonant with all reason, perception and verification in nature, you will no longer say that there is an edge or limit either to the extent or to the motion of the universe; you will esteem the belief in a *primum mobile,* an uppermost and all-containing heaven, to be a vain fantasy. You will conceive rather a general womb in which are situate all worlds alike, even as this terrestrial globe in this our local space is surrounded by our atmosphere and is in no way nailed or attached to any other body, nor hath any base but his own centre. And if it is found that this our globe cannot be proved to be of a constitution different from the surrounding stars, since it manifesteth accidents no different from theirs, then should it no more than any one of them be regarded as occupying the central position of the universe, nor as being more fixed than they, nor will they appear to revolve around it rather than it around them. Whence, since such indifference on the part of nature must be inferred, so also we must infer the vanity of [imagined] deferent orbs; and we must accept the inner impulse toward motion implanted in the souls of these globes, the indifference throughout the vast space of the universe and the irrationality of conceiving any edge or external shape thereto.

ALB. These are things, indeed, which are not repugnant to nature and may be more convenient, but they are hard to prove; and great talent is needed to find an escape from the contrary appearance and arguments.

PHIL. Once the end of the thread is found, the tangle is easily unravelled. For the difficulty proceedeth from the method and from an unfitting hypothesis, namely, the weight and immobility of the earth, the position of the *primum mobile* with the other seven, eight, nine or more [spheres] on which are implanted, impressed, plastered, nailed, knotted, glued, sculptured or painted the stars—and that these reside not in the same space as our own star, named by us earth. But you shall hear that her space, shape and nature are neither more nor less elementary than those of the other stars, nor is she of a nature less apt to motion than each of those other divine living creatures.

ALB. Truly if this thought is once harboured in my mind, all the others proposed by you will in turn easily be accepted. You will have at once cut the roots of one philosophy and implanted those of another.

PHIL. Likewise you will with good reason scorn to accept any longer common opinion based on the impressions of the senses[26] that there existeth a highest horizon, most lofty and noble, the frontier of the divine motionless substances which are the motive powers of these finite orbs. And you will admit that it is at least equally credible that just as this earth is an animal, mobile and travelling by virtue of her own inner nature, such too are all those others. You will regard as mere fantasy, incapable of demonstration, the view that these bodies derive their motion from the motion and transporting power of a body which is without tenacity or resistance, more rare and subtle than the air we breathe; whereas you will consider that our view conformeth to every sane sense-perception and to every well-founded reasoning. You will declare to be no nearer to truth the notion of spheres with concave and convex surfaces moved round and drawing with them the stars; but you will receive as true and in harmony with our intellect and with natural convenience the belief that the stars in conformity with their own inner nature and life follow—as you shall presently hear—their circular courses around and toward one another, without fear either of sinking downward or rising upward; since in the immensity of space there is no distinction of upper, lower, right-hand, left-hand, forward or backward. You will see that beyond the imagined circumference of the heaven, there can be either a simple or a composite body moving in a straight line; for just as the parts of our own globe move in a straight line, so also and no less easily, may the parts of other bodies. For our own globe is composed of no different material to those beyond, nor doth ours appear to revolve around them any less than they around us.

---

[26] *Sensus communis.* The meaning is, the conjoined perception conveyed by all the senses as distinguished from a specialized sense-perception.

ALB. I perceive then more clearly than ever that the smallest error at the start may cause the greatest difference and peril of errors at the finish.[27] A single simple inconvenience will multiply little by little, and ramify into an infinity of others—even as from a little root may grow a vast plant with innumerable branches. On my life, Philotheo, I do greatly desire that thou mayest prove to me this which thou proposest; and since I regard it as worthy and probable, that thou mayest make clear to me also the truth thereof.

PHIL. I will do all for which time and occasion may serve, submitting to your judgement many things which have been hidden from you heretofore not through incapacity but through inadvertence.

ALB. Put the whole before me, in form of article and conclusion, for I know that before you accepted your present opinion you have been able to examine carefully all which pointed to contrary conclusions; for I am sure that the secrets of the accepted philosophy are as clear to you as to myself, wherefore pray proceed.

PHIL. It is then unnecessary to investigate whether there be beyond the heaven Space, Void or Time. For there is a single general space, a single vast immensity which we may freely call VOID; in it are innumerable *(innumerabili et infiniti)* globes like this one on which we live and grow. This space we declare to be infinite, since neither reason, convenience, possibility, sense-perception or nature assign to it a limit. In it are an infinity of worlds *(infiniti mondi)* similar to our own, and of the same kind. For there is no reason nor defect of nature's gifts, I mean either of active or of passive power, that preventeth their existence in all the rest of space, which is identical in natural character with our own, just as they exist in the space around us.

ALB. If that which you first said is true (and so far it appeareth no less likely than the contrary view), then this which you now affirm must necessarily follow.

PHIL. Beyond the imagined convex circumference of the world is Time. For there is the measurement and true nature of motion, since similar moving bodies are there. Let this be partly accepted, partly pro-

[27] Cf. *De coelo,* I, 5, 271b 8-10, reminiscent of *Cratylus,* 436d. Cf. p. 275, n. 14.

posed in regard to what you have already advanced as the FIRST argument for a single world. As for your SECOND argument, I declare to you that there is in truth one prime and principal motive power; but not prime and principal in the sense that there is a second, a third and other motive powers descending down a certain scale to the midmost and last, since such motive powers neither do nor can exist. For where there is infinite number, there can be neither rank nor numerical order, although there is rank and order according to the nature and worth either of diverse species and kinds, or of diverse grades of the same kind and species. There are then an infinity of motive powers [28] as there are an infinity of souls inhabiting the infinite spheres; and because these are form and natural action,[29] there is in relation to all of them a sovereign on whom all depend, a first principle who endoweth with the capacity of motion spirits, souls, gods, heavenly powers and motive forces; and he setteth in motion matter, body, animated being, lower orders of nature, and all which may move. There are then [repeats Philotheo] an infinity of mobile bodies and motive forces, and all of these reduce to a single passive principle and a single active principle, just as every number reduceth to unity, and as infinite number doth coincide with unity; and just as the supreme Agent and supreme active power doth coincide in a single principle with the supreme potentiality, patient of all creation, as hath been shewn at the end of our book *On Cause, Origin and the One.* In number then, and in multitude, there is infinite possibility of motion and infinite motion. But in unity and singularity is infinite motionless motive force, an infinite motionless universe. And the infinite number and magnitude coincide with the infinite unity and simplicity in a single utterly simple and indivisible principle, which is Truth and Being.[30] Thus there is no *primum mobile,* no order from it of second and other mobile bodies either to a last body or yet to infinity. But all mobile bodies are

---

[28] For Aristotle's view, cf. *Metaphysica,* close of Book XII, 1075b 37–1076a 4. Philotheo here opposes also the mediaeval developments of the Aristotelian cosmos.

[29] *Atti intrinsici.*

[30] Cf. Philotheo's final phrase in *De la causa, principio et uno*: "Praised then be the gods and let all living things magnify the infinite, most simple and single highest and most absolute Cause, Origin and One."

equally near to and equally far from the prime and universal motive power, just as (logically speaking) all species are equally related to the same kindred, and all individuals to a single species. Thus from a single infinite and universal motive force in a single infinite space there is but one infinite universal motion on which depend an infinity of mobile bodies and of motor forces, each of which is finite both as to size and power. As for the THIRD argument, I declare that there existeth in ethereal space no determined point toward which heavy objects move as to a centre, and from which light bodies separate themselves as seeking a circumference; for there is in the universe neither centre nor circumference, but, if you will, the whole is central, and every point also may be regarded as part of a circumference in respect to some other central point. As for ourselves, that object is called by us heavy which moveth from the circumference toward the centre of our own globe; and that object is called light which moveth in the opposite direction toward an opposite goal; and we shall see that nothing is heavy which is not also light. For every part of the earth in turn changeth both site, position and also composition, so that through the long course of centuries no central particle faileth to reach the circumference, and no particle on the circumference faileth to become central or to tend toward the centre. We shall see that weight and lightness are no more than the impulse of particles of a body to their own natural containing region, wherever it may be, in which they are best conserved. Wherefore there are no differences of position attracting or repelling different parts. But the desire for self-preservation is an inner force that impelleth every object—provided no obstacle intervene—to flee as far as possible from contrary matter and to join with a convenient neighbour. Thus then, the particles from the circumference of the moon and of other worlds similar to our own in species or kind seek to unite in the centre of their own globe as though impelled by their own weight; while subtilized particles, as though impelled by their own lightness, disport themselves toward the circumference. And this is not because the particles either flee from the circumference or attach themselves to it, for if this were the case, the nearer they approached thereto, the more rapid would be their motion, and the further they retired from it the more forceful would be their advance to a new position; whereas we observe just the contrary, that if they are impelled beyond the terrestrial region, they will remain poised in the air, and will neither mount on high nor sink downward until, either acquiring greater weight by apposition of parts or by increased density through cold, whereby they traverse the air below them and return to their own containing body, or else becoming rarefied and dissolved by heat, they are dispersed into atoms.

ALB. Oh how my mind will be at rest when you have more fully shewn me that the stars are [of a nature] indistinguishable from that of this earthly sphere.

PHIL. Elpino will easily repeat this to you as he hath heard it from me; and he will make you realize more distinctly that no object is heavy or light in respect to the universe, but only in respect to his own region and the body which containeth or maintaineth him. For the tendency to maintain an existing condition impelleth every change of position, as when seas and even drops of water assemble together, or again disperse as happeneth to all liquids exposed to the sun or to other fires. For all natural motion, impelled by the inner principle of a body, is naught but an attempt either to escape an inconvenient and contrary body or to follow a friendly and convenient body. Wherefore nothing changeth position unless driven forth by his contrary; nothing in his natural position is either heavy or light; but the earthy matter, raised up into the air while seeking her natural position, is heavy and is felt to be heavy, just as water if suspended in the air is heavy, though in her own region water is not heavy. Thus to those who are submerged, the whole of the water is by no means heavy, whereas a little vase full of water will become heavy if situated above the air beyond the dry surface. The head on his own body is not heavy; but the head of another laid on top will be heavy, the reason being that the latter is not in his natural position. If then weight and lightness are merely an impulse to a position of safety and escape from a contrary position, it followeth that nothing is by nature either heavy or light, and that nothing is endowed either with weight or lightness if so far distant from his preserving [environment] or so far removed from his contrary as not to be affected by the helpfulness of the one or by the harmfulness of the other. But if, becoming aware of a harmful environment, it groweth desperate and is perplexed and irresolute, it will be vanquished by its contrary.

ALB. Thou hast promised and in great part thou hast performed wondrous things.

PHIL. To avoid repetition a second time, I now commit you to Elpino who will narrate to you the remainder.[31]

ALB. It appeareth to me that I understand all. One doubt raiseth another and one truth demonstrateth another. I begin to understand more than I can explain, and I begin to doubt many things which heretofore I have held as certain. Thus I feel myself little by little prepared to agree with you.

PHIL. When you have heard me in full, you will give me your full assent. For the moment, bear this in mind, or at least be not now as resolutely in favour of the contrary opinion as formerly you shewed yourself before you entered into the controversy. For little by little, as occasion serveth, we shall reach a complete exposition of the subject—which dependeth indeed on several principles and reasonings. For as one error leadeth to another, so is one discovered truth followed by another.

Concerning your FOURTH argument, we declare that albeit there are as many centres as there are individual globes, spheres or worlds, yet it doth not follow that the particles of each are related to any centre but their own, nor that they depart to any circumference but that of their own region. Just as the particles of our earth do not seek any centre but their own, nor do they strive to unite with any but their own globe, so also the humours and parts of an animal ebb and flow in their own subject, nor do they appertain to some other body of a different number. As to your reasoning of the inconvenience that a centre would become further removed from another centre than from the circumference of his own globe, though centres are of the same species while the centre and circumference are of contrary nature and should therefore be furthest removed from one another, I reply as follows: FIRSTLY, that contraries need not be at the furthest distance one from another, inasmuch as one may influence the other or may be patient of influence therefrom; as we

[31] Nevertheless Philotheo proceeds himself to confute Albertino's Fourth Argument.

see that the sun is disposed very close to us among the earths which encircle it, since the order of nature causeth an object to subsist, live and derive nourishment from his contrary, as the other becometh affected, altered, vanquished and transformed by the first. Moreover a short while back we discussed with Elpino the disposition of the four elements which all contribute particles in the composition of each globe, one particle being placed within another, one mixed with another. Nor are they distinguished as a containing and a contained body respectively. For where there is dry earth, there also are water, air and fire, either patent or latent. The distinction made by us among the globes, that some, like the sun, are fiery whilst others, as the moon and the earth, are watery, doth not depend on these bodies consisting solely of a single element, but merely on the predominance of a single element in the mixed substance. Furthermore it is a most false belief that contraries are situated furthest from one another. For in all objects the elements become naturally combined and mixed. And the whole universe, both in the principal and secondary parts, consisteth solely of such conjunction and union, since there is no portion of the earth which is not intimately mixed with water, without which it would have neither density, connection of the atoms withal nor solidity. Moreover what terrestrial body is so dense that it lacketh insensible pores? Without them such bodies would no longer be divisible nor penetrable by fire nor by the heat thereof which is, however, sensibly perceived to issue from the substance of these bodies. Where then in this thy body is a cold and dry portion which is not joined to a moist and warm part, no less appertaining to thy body? This distinction of elements resteth then not on nature but on logic. And if the sun be in a region far removed from that of our earth, yet neither air nor dry land nor water is further from him than from our own globe. For the sun, like our earth, is a composite body, though in him there predominateth a certain one of the above-mentioned four elements, and in our earth, another. Moreover if we would have nature conform to that logic which would impose the greatest distance between contrary bodies, then, between thy fire, which is light, and the heavy earth must be interposed thy heaven, which is neither heavy nor light. Or if indeed thou wouldst limit thy statement by saying that this order is to be understood only of those that are called the four elements,[32] nevertheless thou wouldst be forced to arrange them in different order: I mean that water must then occupy the central position of the heaviest element, if fire is on the circumference of the elemental region in the position of the lightest element; for water which is cold and moist is in both these qualities opposed to fire and must therefore be at the greatest distance from the hot [33] and dry element; while air which you declare to be hot and moist should be furthest from the cold and dry earth. You see then how this Peripatetic proposition remaineth unstable whether examined according to the objective truth of nature or according to his own logical principles and foundations.[34]

ALB. I see it most clearly.

PHIL. You see further that our philosophy is by no means opposed to reason. It reduceth everything to a single origin and relateth everything to a single end, and maketh contraries to coincide, so that there is one primal foundation both of origin and of end. From this coincidence of contraries we deduce that ultimately it is divinely right to say and to hold that contraries are within contraries, wherefore it is not difficult to compass the knowledge that each thing is within every other —which Aristotle and the other Sophists could not comprehend.

ALB. Most willingly I hear you. I know that so many matters and such diverse conclusions cannot be proved all at once, on a single occasion. But since you have revealed to me the inconvenience of those beliefs that I once deemed necessary, I become doubtful of all others which for the same or similar reasons I would deem necessary. Therefore I prepare myself to listen with silent attention to the foundations [of your philosophy], your principles and your reasons.

---

[32] i.e., only when in their elemental purity and not when mixed in corporeal bodies.

[33] Text has *freddo*—but clearly the element is *fire,* hot and dry.

[34] The argument is that if the elements with completely opposed qualities must occupy the positions furthest removed from one another, first it will be claimed that Water must be at the centre and that Fire, its contrary, must be at the circumference; but then, by the same argument, it will be said that Earth and Air, being completely contrary to one another in both their qualities, should occupy the centre and circumference, respectively.

ELP. You will see that Aristotle brought no golden age to philosophy. For the moment, those doubts put forward by you are dispelled.

ALB.[35] I am not so curious concerning those, for I am most anxious to hear the doctrine concerning principles by which these and other doubts will be resolved by your philosophy.

PHIL. These we will consider presently. As for your FIFTH argument, you should know that if we conceive many and an infinity of worlds of nature and composition such as you are accustomed to imagine, it would be almost as though, besides a spherical world containing the four elements ranged in the usual order, and the eight, nine or ten other heavens of a different substance and nature encircling these and revolving rapidly around them, we should then imagine innumerable other worlds also spherical and endowed with motion like our own. Now we should need to produce arguments, and invent how one of these worlds could touch or be continuous with the rest; now we should proceed with fantastic imagination to discuss in how many points the circumference of one world may touch those of the surrounding worlds. You would then see that however numerous were the horizons around a world, they would belong not to one world, but would have each one the same relation to his own centre. For they exercise their influence where they revolve and at the centre around which they spin, just as, if a number of animals were confined together, touching one another, it would not follow that the limbs of one could belong to the limbs of another in such a manner that one or each of them could possess several heads or bodies. But we, thanks to the gods, are free of the embarrassment of craving such explanations. For instead of these numerous heavens, these many swift and stubborn mobile bodies, straight and oblique, to the east and to the west, on the axis of the world, on the axis of the zodiac, in so far and so much, in greater or lesser declination, we have but one single heaven, a single space through which our own star in which we reside, and all other stars perform each their own circuits and courses; these are the infinite worlds, the innumerable stars; this is the infinite space, the heaven comprehending all, traversed by all. Banished is the fantasy that

[35] Turning to Philotheo.

the whole revolveth around ourselves as centre; for we are now well aware that it is our earth which revolveth; and that she, spinning around her own centre, hasteneth during each twenty-four hours to the successive view of the surrounding luminaries. Therefore also the notion is banished of deferent orbs on which the stars are fixed, encircling our own space. To each star we attribute only his own motion, named epicycle, differing from that of each of the other mobile bodies. These orbs, impelled by no other motive force than the spontaneous impulse of the spirit within each, follow, just as doth our own earth, each his course around his own centre and around the fiery element, during long centuries if not indeed to eternity. Here then is the true nature of the worlds and of the heaven. The heaven is such as we see it around our own globe which is, like the other globes, a luminous and excellent star. The worlds are those whose brilliant shining surfaces are distinctly visible to us, and they are placed at certain intervals one from another. But nowhere is one of them nearer to the other than the moon may be to our earth, or our planets to our sun; so that those of contrary nature do not destroy but rather nourish each other, and those of similar nature do not impede but rather give space to each other. Thus from one to another cause, little by little, from season to season, our most frigid globe is heated by the sun, now from this side, now from that, now on this part of her surface, now on that; and through certain vicissitudes she now yieldeth and anon claimeth place from the neighbouring earth which we name the moon, so that now one, now the other body is respectively further from or nearer to the sun: wherefore the moon is named by Timaeus and other Pythagoreans the counter-earth.[36] These then are the worlds inhabited and cultivated each by their own living beings,[37] and themselves the principle and most divine of all living beings[37] in the universe; and each is composed of four elements no less than is this earth on which we find ourselves, though in some there may predominate one active quality, in others, another; so that these are perceptible to us by means of the waters

[36] Cf. *De coelo*, II, 13 293a 20-24; "The Italian philosophers known as Pythagoreans" [believe that a fire and not the earth is at the centre of the universe]. . . . They further construct another earth in opposition to ours which they name counter-earth." Thus the antichthon was not defined as the moon.

[37] *Lit.*, "animals."

thereof, those by their fire. Besides the four elements that compose the heavenly bodies, there is as we have said a vast ethereal region in which they all move, live and grow, the ether which both envelopeth and penetrateth all things. In so far as it entereth into and formeth part of the mixture of the elements, it is commonly named air—the word applying to the vaporous layer around the waters and within the land, shut in among the highest mountains, capable of holding thick clouds and tempestuous winds from South and from North. In so far as it is pure and entereth not into composition, but formeth the site and the enveloping space through which the compound body moveth on its course, we name it properly ether, a name which means its course (*corso*).[38] This ether, though in substance identical with the air which is stirred within the viscera of the earth, is nevertheless differently named. Just as that which is around us is called air, yet when it is in some sort part of us or at least hath a part in our composition—as when it is found in our lungs, our arteries and other cavities and pores of our body—it is called spirit. The same, when around a cold body, becometh condensed into vapour, but around a hot star it is attenuated like flame, which is sensible only if joined to a denser body which becometh ignited by the intense heat thereof. Thus the ether is of his own nature without determined quality, but it receiveth all the qualities offered by neighbouring bodies, and carrieth them with his own motion to the furthest limits of the horizon wherein such active principles have efficacy. Behold then, the nature hath been demonstrated to you of the worlds and of the heaven, so that not only can your present doubt be resolved,[39] but also innumerable

[38] Similar views are put forward by Theophilo in *La Cena de le Ceneri,* Dial. III, p. 73 (Gentile, *Op. ital.,* I, 85; Lagarde, *Op. ital.,* I, 165), and Aristotle's *Meteorologica* (I, 3) is cited as giving the same opinion. In Dial V, p. 105 of the *Cena* (Gentile, *Op. ital.,* I, 111; Lagarde, *Op. ital.,* I, 183), Theophilo recalls "the ancients named *aether* from galleries (*corridori*)" and the point is mentioned in the Argument to the *Cena,* p. 8 (Gentile, *Op. ital.,* I, 10; Lagarde, *Op. ital.,* I, 117). Gentile points out that this may refer to a passage in the *Cratylus* of Plato (410). Cf. above, p. 316, n. 15.

[39] Philotheo has throughout this speech addressed Albertino as "you" (2nd person plural). At this point, he uses "thou" ("potrai essere risoluto"), but reverts to the second person plural, until in the final phrase of the speech he employs the formal address ("vegna a discuoprirla . . . la stimara").

others. And you are now equipped with a foundation for many true physical conclusions. And if some proposition hath hitherto appeared to you propounded but not proved, I shall leave it for the present to your own discretion. And if you are impartial, before you attain to discovering the supreme truth of such a proposition, you will deem it far more probable than the contrary view.

ALB. Speak, O Theophilo, that I may hear thee.

PHIL. Thus we have resolved the SIXTH argument wherein, considering the contact of worlds in a single point, thou askest what object can occupy those triangular spaces so that it be neither of elemental nor of heavenly nature. But we postulate a single heaven in which the worlds have their own spaces, regions and convenient distances. It diffuseth throughout all, penetrateth all and it envelopeth, toucheth and is closely attached to all, leaving nowhere any vacant space; unless, indeed, like many others, thou preferest to give the name of void to this which is the site and position of all motion, the space in which all have their course. Or thou mayest call it the primal subject denoted by that word space, so as to ascribe unto it no limited position, if thou preferest by omission and logically to regard it as something distinct in our mind, but not in nature or in substance derived from being or body; so that nothing be understood to exist which hath not position either finite or infinite, either corporeal or incorporeal, either as a whole or by means of his parts: and this position can finally be no other than space, and the space cannot be other than void. If then we regard this space or void as persistent, we call it the ethereal field which containeth all worlds; if we regard it as a supporting substance, we call it the space, within which is the ethereal field with the worlds; and this space cannot be conceived as existing within another space. Behold then, we are under no necessity to feign new elements and worlds, unlike those who on the lightest provocation begin to name deferent orbs, divine substances, rarer and denser parts of celestial nature, quintessences and other fantasies, names lacking all meaning and truth.

To the SEVENTH argument we reply that the infinite universe is one, a single continuum, compound of ethereal regions and worlds. Innumerable are the worlds, and they should be understood to reside in diverse regions of the single universe, and to exist by the same law of nature as this world inhabited by us is understood and indeed doth reside in her own space and region thereof. This I expounded to Elpino during these last days, approving and confirming that which hath been said by Democritus, Epicurus and many others who contemplated nature with open eyes, nor made themselves deaf to her importunate voices.

Wherefore cease to spew out reason from your mind, struck with terror at mere newness; but rather with eager judgement weigh things, and, if you see them true, lift your hands and yield; or, if it is false, gird yourself to battle. For our minds now seek to reason, since the sum of space is boundless out beyond the walls of this world; what there is far out there, whither the spirit desires always to look forward, and whither the unfettered projection of our mind flies on unchecked. First of all we find that in every direction, everywhere, and on either side, above and below, through all the universe, there is no limit, as I have shown, and indeed the truth cries out for itself and the nature of the deep shines clear.[40]

Lucretius crieth out against your EIGHTH argument [41] which maintaineth that nature should encompass herself. For though we have tested this in worlds both great and small, it can be observed in none of them. For our bodily eye findeth never an end, but is vanquished by the immensity of space presented before it, and confused and overcome by the myriads of stars ever multiplying, so that our perception remaineth uncertain and reason is forced to add space to space, region to region, world to world.

Now in no way must we think it likely, since towards every side is infinite empty space, and seeds in unnumbered numbers in the deep universe fly about in many ways driven on in everlasting motion, that only this one world and heaven was brought to birth. . . . Wherefore, again and again, you must needs confess that elsewhere there are other gatherings of matter, such as this, which the ether holds in its greedy grip.[42]

---

[40] Lucretius, *De rerum natura,* II, 1040-1051. (Bruno quotes in Latin.) In line 1049 Bruno has *infra supraque* instead of the usual version *supra subterque.*

[41] See above, p. 358, n. 20, for divergence in the numeration of these Arguments.

[42] Lucretius, *De rerum natura,* II, 1052-1057; 1064-1066 (quoted in Latin).

He murmureth against the NINTH argument which supposeth, though it cannot prove, that there is not infinite passive power to correspond with infinite active power; [43] and that infinite matter cannot be patient nor infinite space make to itself a field; that consequently act and action cannot become conformable to the agent, and it may happen that though the agent impart the whole act, yet the whole act cannot be imparted. This latter opinion is the clearest possible contradiction to the former remarks. Well then hath it been said:

Moreover, when there is much matter ready to hand, when space is there, and no thing nor cause delays, things must, we may be sure, be carried on and completed. As it is, if there is so great a store of seeds as the whole life of living things could not number, since vigour is the same and nature abideth [44] who can throw together the seeds of things, each into their place, in like manner as they are thrown together here, it must needs be that you confess that there are other worlds in other regions, and diverse races of men and tribes of wild beasts.[45]

To the NEXT argument [46] we reply that there is no need of this courteous exchange of intercourse between the various worlds, any more than that all men should be one man or all animals one animal. And this apart from what we learn by experience, that it is best for the living creatures of this world that nature hath distributed their diverse kinds throughout seas and mountains. And if by human artifice there hath befallen traffic among them, good is thereby not so much added to them as removed, since communication tendeth rather to redouble vices than to augment virtues. Wherefore rightly the Tragic Muse lamenteth:

The lands, well separated before by Nature's laws, the Thessalian ship [47]

---

[43] This in fact was called the Eighth Argument by Elpino, though it becomes the Ninth if his two "Seventh" Arguments are reckoned separately.

[44] Philotheo has a slight variant, *"Visque eadem et natura manet."* The usual version is *"Sique eadem natura manet."*

[45] Lucretius, *De rerum natura,* II, 1067-1076 (quoted in Latin).

[46] Called the Ninth.

[47] This refers to the tradition of the *Argo* built by Argus for Jason who led the Argonauts in this ship on the first considerable voyage undertaken by the Greeks —from Thessaly to Colchis on the Euxine to fetch the golden fleece, which he was enabled to find through the help of Medea, daughter of Peleus, king of Colkos.

made one, bade the deep suffer blows[48] and the sequestered sea become a part of our human fear.[49]

To the TENTH argument[50] the reply is as to the FIFTH. For each world in the ethereal field occupieth his own space, so that one toucheth not nor thrusteth against the other; but they pursue their courses and are situate at such distance that contraries destroy not but rather comfort one another.

The ELEVENTH asserteth that Nature having multiplied by definition and division of matter, entereth on this act only by the method of generation, when the individual as parent produceth another individual. We reply that this is not universally true. For by the act of a single efficient cause there are produced from one mass many and diverse vessels of various forms and innumerable shapes. I leave aside that if there should come to pass the destruction of a world followed by the renewal thereof, then the production therein of animals alike perfect and imperfect would occur without an original act of generation, by the mere force and innate vigour of Nature.

Your TWELFTH and LAST argument maintaineth that because this or another world is perfect, therefore no further worlds are required. I reply that these are certainly not required for the perfection and subsistence of our own world, but that for the subsistence and perfection of the universe itself an infinity of worlds is indeed necessary. It therefore followeth not from the perfection of this or of those that those or this be less perfect; for this world even as those others, and those others even as this, are made up of their parts, and each is a single whole by virtue of his members.

ALB. Thy noble countenance, O Philotheo, shall not be denied me by the voice of the mob, the indignation of the vulgar, the murmuring of fools, nor by the displeasure of satraps, the folly of the crazy, the foolishness of blockheads, the betrayal of liars, the complaints of the

---

[48] i.e., of oars.

[49] Seneca, *Medea,* vv. 335-39 (trans. F. J. Miller, Loeb Classical Library, 1917).

[50] Here the correspondence is restored between the numeration of the Arguments and of their refutation.

malicious nor the backbiting of the envious,[51] nor shall they deprive me of thy divine conversation. Persevere, my Philotheo, persevere. Do not lose heart nor retire, though the great and solemn senate of foolish ignorance threaten thee with many complots and cunning shifts and seek to destroy thy divine enterprise, thine exalted task. For be thou assured that at the last all will see as I now see, and all will acknowledge that it is as easy for everyone to praise thee as it is hard for them all to teach thee. For all (if they be not wholly perverse) will with good understanding deliver favourable verdict concerning thee, just as at last everyone cometh to be taught through the mild mastery of the mind, for only by dint of our own mind may we become possessed of the treasures of mind. And since there is in the minds of all a certain natural holiness enthroned in the tribunal of the intellect and exercising judgement between good and evil, between light and darkness; so it will happen that through the private meditations of each individual, there shall be aroused faithful and just witnesses and defenders in thy cause; and they who make not themselves thy friends, but blockishly seek the defence of gloomy ignorance, and as approved sophists remain thy steadfast and stiffnecked adversaries, these will feel within themselves the hangman and executioner, thine avenger; for the more they conceal him within the depth of thought, the more he will torment them. Just so the infernal Worm based on the bristling hair of the Furies, seeing that his design against thee is frustrated, will furiously turn on the hand or the breast of his impious factor, and will deal unto him that death which he may spread who scattereth the Stygian poison where the sharply pointed teeth of such a reptile have bitten.

Proceed to make known to us what is in truth the heaven, what in truth are the planets and all the stars; how the infinity of worlds are distinguished one from the other, how an infinite Space is not impossible but is necessary; how such an infinite effect beseemeth the infinite Cause. Reveal to us the true substance, matter, act and efficient cause of the whole, and how every sensible and composite object is built up from the same origins and elements. Convince our minds of the infinite

[51] Bruno has *individiosi* (not in Florio) which is surely a misprint for *invidiosi*.

universe. Rend in pieces the concave and convex surfaces which would limit and separate so many elements and heavens. Pour ridicule on deferent orbs and on fixed stars. Break and hurl to earth with the resounding whirlwind of lively reasoning those fantasies of the blind and vulgar herd, the adamantine walls of the *primum mobile* and the ultimate sphere. Dissolve the notion that our earth is unique and central to the whole. Remove the ignoble belief in that fifth essence. Give to us the knowledge that the composition of our own star and world is even as that of as many other stars and worlds as we can see. Each of the infinity of great and vast worlds, each of the infinity of lesser worlds, is equally sustained and nourished afresh through the succession of his ordered phases. Rid us of those external motive forces together with the limiting bounds of heaven. Open wide to us the gate through which we may perceive the likeness[52] of our own and of all other stars. Demonstrate to us that the substance of the other worlds throughout the ether is even as that of our own world. Make us clearly perceive that the motion of all of them proceedeth from [the impulse of] the inward soul: to the end that illumined by such contemplation we may proceed with surer steps toward a knowledge of nature.

PHIL. What meaneth it, O Elpino, that Doctor Burchio hath not so speedily nor indeed ever consented with us?

ELP. It is proper to vigilant wit that by seeing and hearing little he may consider and understand much.

ALB. Although it hath not yet been vouchsafed to me to see the whole body of the shining planet, I can yet perceive by the rays diffused through the narrow slits in the closed windows of my mind, that this is no artificial brightness or sophist lamp, nor proceedeth from the moon or any lesser star. I prepare for a yet greater understanding in the future.

PHIL. Your further friendship will be most acceptable.

ELP. Then let us to supper.

END OF THE FIVE DIALOGUES CONCERNING
THE INFINITE UNIVERSE AND WORLDS.

---

[52] *Indifferenza.*

INDEX

INDEX

INDEX